MICROPROCESSOR BASICS

MICROPROCESSOR BASICS

Selected from

ELECTRONIC DESIGN

Edited by

MICHAEL S. ELPHICK

Managing Editor, *Electronic Design*

HAYDEN BOOK COMPANY, INC.
Rochelle Park, New Jersey

ISBN 0-8104-5763-6
Library of Congress Catalog Card Number 77-71262

2	3	4	5	6	7	8	9	PRINTING
77	78	79	80	81	82	83	84	85	YEAR

Preface

In the few short years microprocessors have been available, they have revolutionized the design of electronic equipment. Using these compact, versatile circuits, an engineer can design computing power into his system wherever he needs it. And, compared with the cost of older circuits that do the same job, the cost is often minuscule.

A microprocessor is a complete central processor unit (CPU) on a single chip of silicon whose dimensions are measured in mere fractions of an inch. With one of these chips, plus a few others of similar size, an engineer can build a microcomputer offering performance equivalent to some early computers that occupied almost an entire room. And some newer chips contain enough support circuitry—memory and peripheral circuits—to form a complete microcomputer without the addition of other chips.

Since their introduction, the prices of microprocessors have tumbled to the point where unit costs of some popular types in large quantities are now under $15.

What makes microprocessors so important, however, is not their small size or low cost. Other integrated circuits offer the same advantages. The truly revolutionary aspect of microprocessors is their versatility, which stems from their programmability. The functions of microprocessors can be changed by modifying the "software" of the same basic system. No longer do different circuits need different basic "hardware." Today, the same microprocessor chip may appear in a laboratory instrument, an automobile, or a video game—programmed in each case to do a vastly different job.

But this ability to substitute software for hardware has proved a mixed blessing for design engineers. The training of most engineers did not equip them with the fluency in assembly language or machine language programming that's needed to design efficiently with microprocessors. Therefore, most engineers have felt compelled to upgrade their software skills and to learn as much as possible about microprocessors.

Magazines such as *ELECTRONIC DESIGN* have played a major role in helping engineers through the traumatic changes wrought by microprocessors. An earlier Hayden book, *Microprocessors: New Directions for Designers,* selected key articles published in *ELECTRONIC DESIGN* from 1973 to 1975. This, the second compilation of articles from the magazine, is built around a popular continuing series called "Microprocessor Basics."

This book emphasizes the in-depth practical information that an engineer needs to evaluate specific microprocessors thoroughly and exploit their capabilities fully. Individual articles provide all the information an engineer needs to start designing with eight of the most popular microprocessors. Additional articles describe specific applications for five widely used microprocessors. Unlike most books which either talk in general terms or assume use of a single type of microprocessor, this book provides detailed coverage of the following important circuits: 8080, 6800, F8, PACE, IMP, 2650, 1802, and 6100.

For each microprocessor, the major advantages are highlighted to speed selection for a specific application. A detailed analysis of hardware and software features, together with listings of support circuits and hardware and software design aids, encourages a more thorough evaluation. (The reader should be cautioned, however, that the prices listed for microprocessors, peripheral circuits, and design aids are largely out of date and are included merely to indicate relative cost.) All major instruction mnemonics are tabulated so that an engineer can easily follow the application examples and move rapidly to writing his own assembly-language programs.

There are nine sections. The first three essentially provide general information that applies to all microprocessors. These sections build a foundation for a better understanding of the rest of the book, which deals with specific types.

Those readers who have already worked with microprocessors may wish to skip the first part of the book and go straight to the section dealing with the device they wish to study. But a reader shouldn't concentrate exclusively on the section that covers his favorite device. Other articles will prove useful to the advanced designer who is able to take application ideas for one microprocessor and apply them to another type. For example, an article on distributed processing appears in Section VI, while an article on interfacing with analog signals is included in Section VIII. Of course, both topics will be of interest to most microprocessor users.

Michael S. Elphick

Contents

SECTION I

Getting Started with Microprocessors

This section provides a broad foundation for the selection and application of microprocessors. It is essential reading for the beginner and forms a useful review course for experienced designers.

The first article explains the terminology that is used to describe the architectural and performance features of microprocessors. The second article discusses the wide range of products available and explores some of the pitfalls of microprocessor selection. The remaining articles highlight three important factors that must be considered in choosing a microprocessor—the hardware and software aids that are available, and the various addressing modes that are possible.

An Introduction to Microprocessors

EDWARD A. TORRERO
Associate Editor,
Electronic Design

Some engineers find all the talk about micro-processors a little like walking into an eight-hour lecture several hours late. This article tries to take some of the mystery out of the subject. It will cover some of the key features common to most µPs.

Microprocessors are a remarkably versatile new tool. They can lower the cost and increase the flexibility of electronic equipment and are ushering in a new era for digital designers.

Together with memory and peripheral circuitry, µP chips form complete microcomputers. In complexity, these micros fall somewhere between conventional minicomputers and small, hand-held calculators.

They're as compact and inexpensive as calculators, but, like minicomputers, can be programmed for a wide range of tasks and work with such peripheral computer devices as printers and magnetic memories.

When many functions must be performed, microprocessors can be used economically to replace or upgrade hardwired, or random-logic, designs involving scores of standard digital ICs (Fig. 1). And in applications emphasizing the random collection and routing of data they use less circuitry than is required with hardwired logic.

Of course, for some applications microprocessors aren't the sole LSI (large-scale integration) alternative. Complex logic decisions can be handled just as well by PLAs (programmable-logic arrays). Numerical computations are performed by ALU (arithmetic-logic unit) or calculator chips—from which a number of microprocessors have evolved. Custom LSI chips form yet another alternative, especially when very high volumes of a system must be produced.

The high chip density needed for microprocessors has generally been obtained by the use of some form of MOS (metal-oxide semiconductor) technology. At first PMOS (p-channel MOS) was employed. Then manufacturers turned to NMOS (n-channel MOS) to obtain increased

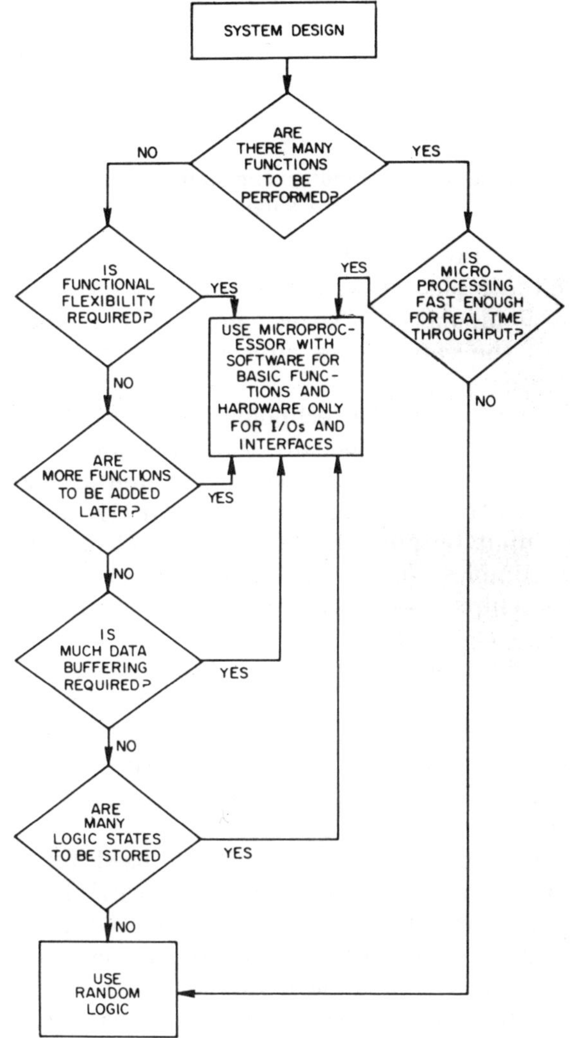

1. The choice between microprocessors and random logic depends on a series of tradeoffs that are illustrated in this flow diagram.

speeds. More recently, power-saving CMOS (complementary-MOS) µPs have appeared. The latter form of MOS combines p and n-channel transistors and features lower dissipation than either PMOS or NMOS.

Microprocessors that use bipolar technology have also been produced, and offer the highest

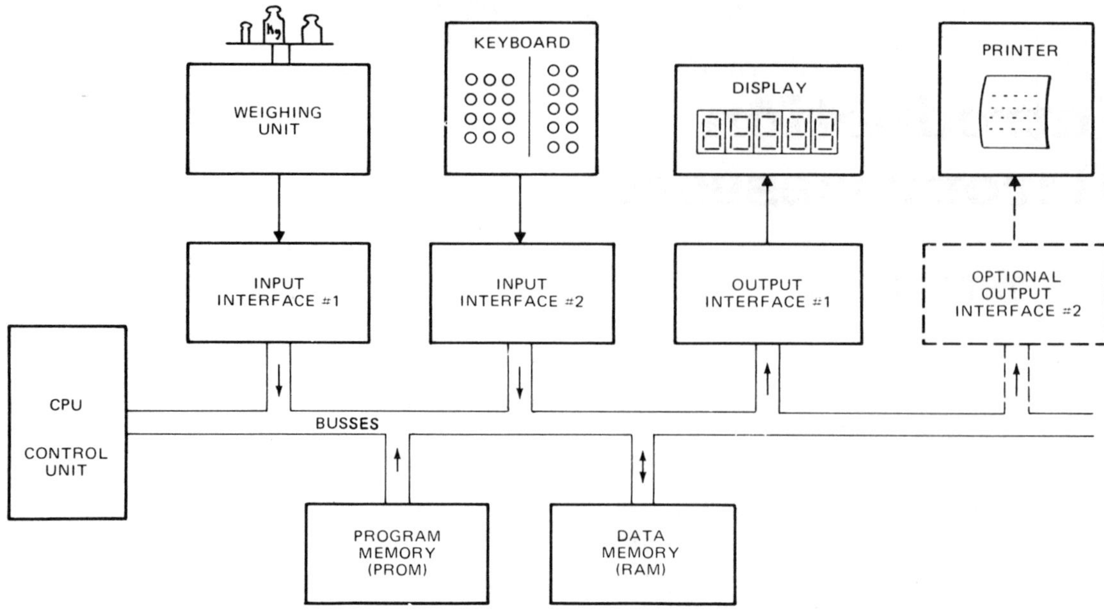

2. **A simple microcomputer application**—an automated scale—can be built with a single μP that communicates with various system components over interconnecting paths known as busses.

speeds. However, the bipolar units generally aren't complete microprocessors. In most cases, several bipolar-μP "slices" must be combined to obtain the capabilities offered by a single MOS μP chip.

Regardless of the technology used, μP systems are organized in basically the same way as conventional computer systems. The major blocks are a central processing unit (or CPU), memory and input/output (I/O) facilities (Fig. 2). In their simplest form, each of these blocks can be a single chip. The μP chip (or chips) contains the CPU.

Within memory there are *instructions*. These are coded pieces of information that direct the activities of the CPU. A group of interrelated instructions stored in memory constitutes a *program*. The memory also holds coded data that are processed by the CPU.

Typically, the kind of memory used for programs is a ROM (read-only memory). From a ROM, information can be obtained, but that information cannot be altered during operation. A PROM (programmable ROM) provides the same function, but internal bit patterns can be set by the user rather than the manufacturer. Data, on the other hand, reside in RAM (random-access memory). This kind of memory allows information to be written and modified as well as read.

In operation, the CPU reads each instruction from memory and uses it to initiate various processing actions. Also, the CPU can rapidly obtain any data stored in memory. Sometimes, though, memory may not be large enough to store all the data needed. This problem can be solved at the *input ports*, where data from external equipment

can be stored. This allows the data to be obtained by the CPU at high rates of speed and in large quantities.

A μP also requires *output ports* through which it communicates its results to the outside world. The output may go to a display or peripheral device, or it may consist of control signals that direct another system.

Throughout the operation, the CPU is very much the system's supervisor. The μP controls the functions performed by other components. It fetches instructions from memory, decodes their binary contents, and executes them. During the execution of instructions the μP references memory and the I/O ports as necessary. It also recognizes and responds to various externally generated signals.

Microprocessor architecture

A μP must incorporate various functional units if it is to properly supervise and manage the operations of a system (Fig. 3). Besides control circuitry, a μP typically has an ALU and a number of registers that provide temporary storage.

The *accumulator* constitutes the one essential general-purpose register. It can serve both as the source and as the destination register for operations involving some other register, the ALU, or memory. Other general-purpose registers often included in a μP can be used to store operands or intermediate data, thereby lessening the possibility of accumulator bottlenecks.

Additional registers have dedicated uses. The *program counter*, for example, keeps track of program instructions by maintaining the *address* of the next instruction in memory. An address is the coded number that differentiates one memory location from another.

Each time the μP fetches an instruction it adds 1 to the program counter, thereby incrementing the counter so that it always "points" to the following instruction. The fetched instruction (in the form of a so-called operation code, or op code) goes to another dedicated register—known as the *instruction register*—and is decoded by internal logic.

The μP tackles each instruction in sequence. It proceeds from numerically lower memory addresses that give the instructions to be executed early, to higher addresses that give later instructions. However, the sequential order can be broken by a "jump" instruction, which directs the μP to a different part of the program.

The order can also be broken by a "call" instruction that gives rise to the execution of a *subroutine*—a program within a program. The subroutine usually consists of a series of instruc-

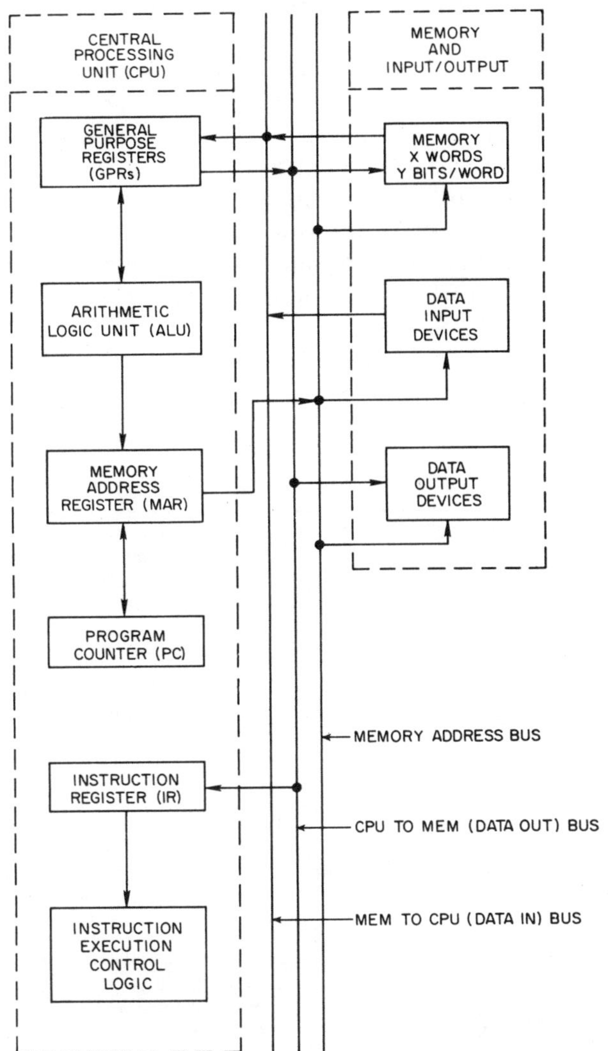

3. **The internal structure of a μP**—its architecture—resembles that of a conventional computer. Three busses are generally needed to provide communication among the μP, memory and I/O devices.

Table 1. Available software tools

Operating software:

    Customer application programs
    Binary loaders
    Relocatable binary loaders
    Operating systems
    Miscellaneous utility programs:
        Math subroutines
        I/O control subroutines
        Paper tape copy and list programs
        Etc.

Program development software:

    Assemblers
    Relocatable assemblers
    Paper tape editors
    Macroassemblers
    Compilers
    General-purpose microassemblers

Diagnostic software:

    CPU diagnostics
    Memory diagnostics
    I/O device diagnostics
    Software diagnostics:
        Debuggers
        Simulators

tions that must be executed repeatedly during the course of a main program.

Prior to its handling of a subroutine, a μP makes use of a storage area known as a *stack*, which may be either on the chip (a hardware stack) or in memory (a software, or *pointer*, stack). The stack is used to save vital μP information, such as the address in the program counter, while the subroutine is being executed. The information saved can then be used to resume operation of the main program once the subroutine has been executed.

Stacks can also be used to *nest* subroutines, in which case one subroutine can call another, and that one can call still another. The extent of this capability is limited by the depth of the stack and its ability to store return addresses following each subroutine.

Interrupt and DMA: μP time savers

Most μPs allow for these kinds of I/O-transfer control techniques: program, program-interrupt and hardware. In the first two cases, used in most simple applications, the μP controls the transfer. In the third case, hardware external to the μP controls it.

When all I/O operations are under program control, all instructions to receive or transmit information are included in the program. Data are transferred whenever the corresponding instruction is executed.

However, considerable μP time can be conserved by the use of either program interrupts or direct-memory access (DMA)—a hardware control. Both allow a computer to devote most of its time to a long program, while simultaneously providing immediate response for shorter, more urgent functions.

The program-interrupt function provides what its name implies: the ability to suspend a running program to perform a higher-priority one. When the latter program is completed, the original one resumes.

One example of the usefulness of an interrupt is in printer buffering. Serial printers are often slow, about 10 characters per second. To print a line of characters without interrupt, the μP transfers a character to the printer, waits 100 ms until that character is printed and then transfers the next character.

This procedure repeats until all the characters in the line are printed. However, only a few microseconds are needed to transfer a character. So the μP spends most of its time waiting for the completion of print operations.

The program-interrupt feature eliminates this waiting time. Now the printer causes a program interrupt when it has completed a character, and the μP then executes a special subroutine. And while the printer is busy, the μP begins or continues the execution of other tasks.

The direct-memory-access feature provides data-transfer rates that are higher than those possible with program-interrupt. DMA allows high-speed transfer of data directly between the memory and an I/O device. Memory cycles are taken from the μP for use by the I/O device that is transferring data.

Typically DMA is used to transfer blocks of words to memory. The I/O device supplies the memory address and data for each word to be transferred. It also contains the logic to increment addresses to succeeding words, count the number of words transferred and determine when the transfer is complete.

With the availability of a host of software tools, a designer seeking to program microcomputer systems need not become enmeshed in the ONEs and ZEROs that make up the micro's inherent *machine language*. Properly used, the software tools can greatly speed development and reduce errors.

Vendors offer three kinds of software: operating, diagnostic and program-development (Table 1).

Operating software is the group of programs that run on the microcomputer under normal use. In a finished system the programs reside in ROMs or PROMs. The user must write his own operating software because it represents the logic design of the system or product being built. A vendor may supply some prepackaged items, such as mathematical subroutines, but the rest must be created to suit the application.

Diagnostic software, on the other hand, is a fixed package of programs supplied by the μP vendor. These test the microcomputer hardware

Table 2. Employ addressing modes to specify data

Addressing mode	Processing required to load address into internal address register	Byte appearance of instruction	Comments
Immediate	Current value of PC indicates the op code and the digital information represented by PC + 1 is the data the op code is to perform its operation on.	op code — K data — K + 1 see comments — K + 2 bit 0.......7	Only one data byte is used except for mnemonic instructions CPX, LDS and LDX which use a second byte.
Direct	The current value of the PC indicates the op code. Increment the PC and then move the data from the location specified by PC + 1 to the address register.	op code — K address — K + 1 0.......7	Two data bytes are used.
Extended	The current value of the PC indicates the op code. Increment the PC by 1 and transfer the data from the location specified by PC + 1 to the address register. Increment the PC again to PC + 2 and transfer the data from the location specified by PC + 2 to the address register.	op code — K address — K + 1 ⎫ 16 bits address — K + 2 ⎭ 0.......7	Two data bytes are used.
Relative	The current value of the PC indicates the op code. Increment the PC by 1 and add the contents of the location specified by PC + 1 to the value of the PC after it is incremented again (PC + 2)	op code — K displacement — K + 1 0.......7	One data byte used..This applies only for branch instructions.
Indexed	The current value of the PC indicates the op code. Increment the PC by 1 and add the contents of the location specified by PC + 1 to the index register.	op code — K data from — K + 1 memory location — K + 1 0.......7	One data byte used.

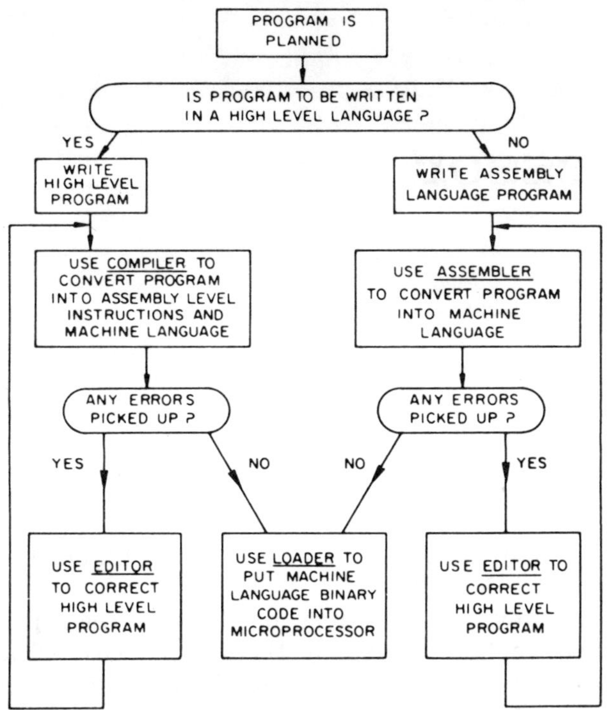

4. The binary code to be placed in a microcomputer's read-only memory can be prepared with the aid of a compiler or assembler, and with an editor and a loader. The compiler permits programming in a high-level language, which is simpler to use than an assembly language.

and verify that the system is operating properly. There are also software diagnostic programs, such as simulators and debuggers, that test for proper program sequencing and functioning.

Program-development software represents the largest investment on the part of the μP supplier. It is this type of software that is usually referred to when one speaks of a vendor's "software support."

For a designer, much of the start-up (development) effort is linked to the coding phase. Coding converts system programs, or algorithms, into instructions that can be loaded directly into memory (Fig. 4). The basic tools, themselves programs, typically require the use of time-sharing services or other computer facilities.

Assemblers—a shorthand way to program

Of all the available software tools, few are more important to designers than the assembler, a program that converts symbolic mnemonic commands into the binary form needed by a microcomputer. The mnemonic commands themselves form an *assembly language* that offers a shorthand way of writing the binary instructions.

Generally, a single assembly statement generates a single storable command. The shorthand statements are grouped into fields designated by the following four names: *label, operator, operand* and *comments*.

The four elements, when combined on a single line, are separated from one another by some form of delimiter, such as one or more blank spaces, a slash or a comma. The comments field is used only to help others understand what the programmer intends; it will not generate any instructions for the microcomputer.

A sample assembler statement might appear as follows:

UPDAT   LDA A   NB   Begin the Loop
label   mnemonic operand   comment

Labels help the programmer use *branch* commands; he can direct the program to go backward or forward to a specific statement in an assembly listing just by giving the statement's label. The mnemonic command LDA A instructs the μP to load the accumulator known as A with the data that will come from the location described by operand NB. The operand tells the μP to fetch data from the location called NB.

How data are addressed affects computing efficiency. Too long an address can slow the micro down. Too short an address can limit the number of words that can be accessed readily.

Common addressing modes appear in Table 2.

Choosing a Microprocessor

EDWARD A. TORRERO
Associate Editor,
Electronic Design

While diversity usually makes a designer's life easier, with microprocessors it can make comparison—not to mention selection—more difficult than ever.

A wide diversity of architectures, support circuits and design aids from available μPs should make it a whole lot easier to pick the right micro. But because microprocessor-based systems must be programmed like conventional computers, you must think of software as well as hardware. Grappling with the intricacies of either could keep you working evenings and weekends, especially since the use of different micros entails different tradeoffs between hardware and software.

Further, the problems of selection may not be helped much by the burgeoning application literature offered with "computers on a chip." You could end up with documentation up to your eyeballs only to discover that key specifications have been inflated or even omitted or that some important characteristics—like operating speed—can't be extrapolated from the mountain of data. Adding to the problems, manufacturers' promotional material may elevate a selling point into an unwarranted selection factor. The prices of microprocessor, or CPU (central processing unit), chips are a case in point.

Manufacturers note that the high-flying 8080 μP, for example, can be purchased now for about $20 in production quantities—quite a drop from its initial price of several hundred dollars. For very high quantities, you can get the price under $10.

But a CPU chip itself is about as useful as a pet rock. For a complete, operating μC (microcomputer), you must add peripheral and interface circuits, as well as memory. A simple μC-based controller could require at least 25 extra chips surrounding the processor. The cost of the additional components exceeds the price of the CPU by a wide margin. Moreover, a package of system components having an attractively priced CPU may have an over-all cost that's higher than one that doesn't.

Whatever the system hardware's cost, it is likely to be dwarfed by the soaring cost of μC software, which can range from hundreds of dollars to thousands for the finished system. For a $30 μP, such software has been known to cost more than $65,000.

Of course, your software development is a "one shot" expense that can be amortized over the life of the product—assuming it is a successful one. But should you decide to switch micros, you won't be able to transfer a design using the first μP's software to the second. The experience gained from one μP can't be applied to another. Different micros come with different software capabilities, hardware requirements and design aids. That first costly system may have to be scrapped completely.

μP products and technologies: a mixed bag

Microprocessors and related circuits can be obtained in a variety of technologies and product forms. Older micros employ p-channel MOS (PMOS) and offer 4, 8 and 16-bit word lengths. The bulk of present MOS micros uses speed-enhancing n-channel MOS (NMOS) for 8-bit units and specifies a basic cycle time of about 2 μs. More recently,. NMOS has been applied to 16-bit μPs and power-saving complementary-MOS (CMOS) has been used to build 8 and 12-bit μPs.

Product forms encompass just about anything you'd care to ask for, from a sack of parts to a μP-based minicomputer. At the simplest level, you can purchase a set of chips that include the CPU, special interface ICs and, generally, special memories. If you don't want to be bothered testing, mounting and interconnecting the chips, you can purchase a logic board instead. The μP-based board comes fully wired and ready to run, although at the very least you generally have to provide system-test equipment and a power supply.

At the high end of the price ladder are complete μP-based development systems, such as Intel's MDS (microcomputer development system), Motorola's Exorciser and National Semiconductor's IMP-16. These units constitute sophisticated hardware/software design aids that offer the conveniences and peripherals associated with minicomputers—at prices to match. A basic system starts at about $5000 and rapidly escalates to about $10,000 if you decide to use such system peripherals as a floppy-disc operating system, video terminal and PROM programmer.

Currently the most popular product form for microprocessors is the do-it-yourself kit. Priced at $500 or less, the μP kit offers designers—especially the growing number of newcomers—an inexpensive and fairly painless way to get a μP system up and running.

However, like the microprocessors they are built around, kits may not live up to all the claims made for them. Ideally a kit should be easy to use and allow some system prototyping. But whether the kit actually does these things often reveals what was left out to keep prices low, even better than it reflects what was put in. The old adage, "you get what you pay for," might well be applied here.

One kit may be priced significantly lower than another, though both use the same microprocessor and offer about the same features. Sometimes the difference in price is due to the use of less expensive ICs in the lower-priced model. These ICs exhibit temperature and voltage limitations that aren't necessarily bad for home experiments, but which could prove disastrous in an industrial environment.

All kits require hand-assembly for program entry. Instructions must be entered one bit at a time, though some units feature hex or octal-code entry, thereby shortening the number of times you have to move a switch or press a button. Manual assembly may not be a problem if your program isn't longer than a few hundred words. But it rapidly becomes unwieldly for a program any longer than that—assuming the kit has sufficient memory to store it.

What you can prototype with a kit depends largely on how much memory comes with it. Capacity ranges from 256 bytes up to 8-k, though most units don't have more than about 1-k of storage. The capacity is sufficient for simple systems.

But storage capacity can easily become a problem for applications that need 1000 or more words of code—like a computer-peripheral controller. Moreover, long programs can't be debugged easily. A hand-assembled program that has errors has to be redone completely, unless spaces (No Op instructions) have been left in the program for corrections.

The most serious problem arises when the set of components doesn't come with adequate monitor and debug programs. A monitor program provides the means to drive a control panel or operate the system through a teletypewriter. A debug program lets you single-step the system one instruction at a time, examine memory, and insert breakpoints. Typically, the monitor and debug programs are combined in ROM and offered as firmware.

Without these essential programs, that μP system does little more than talk to itself. Of course, monitor/debug software can be developed. But presumably you bought a kit because you wanted to learn about microprocessors the easy way.

Chip sets reduce package count

Newer μP-chip sets have overcome one of the most serious shortcomings of early μPs—the need for a host of supporting chips to interface with peripheral devices, data-communication lines and even the μP's own memory. The first 8-bit μP and the only one for about two years—Intel's 8008—required 20 or so additional standard-TTL circuits to make it work.

Constrained primarily by the limitations of an 18-pin package, the 8008 needed the following: registers to address memory, either ROM or RAM; decoders to interface with memories; other ICs to handle μP information and to synchronize the operation of the μP and the support circuits; clock circuits; and a number of interface ICs, depending on the application. For example, in a multichannel data-communications application, each channel requires an asynchronous receiver/transmitter and associated interface ICs.

Now improved μPs like Intel's 8080, Motorola's 6800 and Fairchild's F8 have come along. Special LSI peripheral and memory circuits match and enhance the μPs they support. Together with improvements in the CPU chips, the resulting chip sets constitute minimal-chip configurations that can drastically reduce package count while improving performance.

But even new chip sets may not be all they seem. Some manufacturers stress the fact that their μP systems can run from TTL levels of 5 V and ground. However, more than a single supply may be needed if you decide to use such memories as some of the new 4-k dynamic RAMs, or some PROMs. Also, you'll need another supply if you want to hook up a device that spits out ASCII characters, or more simply, if you try to provide the μP's demanding clock requirements with conventional circuitry.

Expansion can present other problems. Since many chip sets employ nonstandard memories, you're limited in the choice of storage elements, even though the manufacturer claims that any memory works well with the μP—including core, though that admission may have to be pulled out of a semiconductor manufacturer. In some cases, you can use the memory of your choice, but only after you've added special memory-interface ICs to your "minimal" chip system. And if the memory is static, you might use a different interface chip than the one for a refresh-hungry dynamic memory.

Further, several chip sets employ mask-programmable ROMs for program storage. These can be found in such MOS μPs as those that employ bit-slice configurations, as well as those that incorporate the control memory within the CPU circuits. In such cases, your system-development time will have to include the manufacturer's turnaround time for ROM mask programming.

An obvious time-saving solution would be to employ PROMs, especially the erasable kind, as a growing number of designers are now doing. But again, these components can entail additional circuitry and power supplies.

For situations that do entail additional circuits, manufacturers provide an ever expanding line of package-saving MSI (medium-scale-integration) circuits. Unlike key LSI peripherals, though, the MSI units aren't always an economical buy. You do save on, say, a complex data-communications chip or a direct-memory-access controller that replaces 10 or more standard-TTL circuits, but you won't always save with an MSI component that replaces just a few standard packages. The best bet is carefully to select the components you want in a manufacturer's μP family and consider making up the rest with standard TTL.

Shop around, too, for the best price tag on the same component. It wasn't always possible to do so when μPs were virtually sole-source products and typically were offered only as part of complete chip-package orders and only when you purchased the associated memory from the same IC manufacturer. That practice has since died down, mainly because of falling memory prices. But several designers report they still encounter it. If you find this problem, go to an alternate source.

Avoid specification pitfalls

Though microprocessors are far too complex to be characterized by a simple data sheet, specifications for μPs do abound. Ideally one should be able to use the published data to make a selection. However, spec sheets don't always reveal what a μP will do, or how it will react in your application.

A widely omitted spec is noise immunity, even though manufacturers promote their products as ideal for use in industrial equipment. For some μPs, the omission may be intentional. A com-

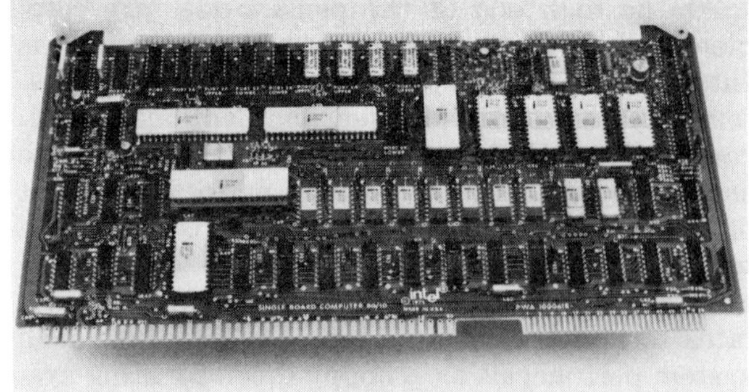

A **single-board microcomputer based on the 8080**— Intel's SBC 80/10—features 48 lines of programmable I/O. The board includes 4-k bytes of ROM and 1-k byte of EPROM.

parison between input levels for peripheral circuits and the address-output levels of the μP may show little or no protection against unwanted transients.

However high noise immunity specs can be expected from newer microprocessors. For example, CMOS μPs from Harris Semiconductor, Intersil and RCA excel in noise immunity—a forte of the low-power technology.

If you don't have the noise immunity needed, you'll quickly discover the fact when you move from a clean, noise-free bench to a production environment. Of course, the problem can be overcome with simple level shifters and pull-up resistors. These components are cheap, but they do take up valuable board space and drive up power dissipation.

Another spec that's hard to find is the length of time the μP will hold data from a memory after Write signals have dropped. Some memories, especially the most inexpensive, can't work with a μP unless they hold data for, say, 100 ns. Too low a hold time results in data loss. Without the hold-time spec, memories added to the system may have to be selected by trial and error.

Speed specs confuse

Of the specs that are generally published, few are more numerous than the ones offered as a measure of a microprocessor's operating speed. A typical data sheet specifies a basic cycle (or microcycle) time, state time, clock rate, execution time, interrupt time, and time to add two decimal numbers, among other "times." Paradoxically, none of these nor any combination gives either a complete measure of a μP's computing speed, or fully tells how much work the μP can do in a unit of time.

Consider cycle time—possibly the most useless measure, though most of the others could lay a strong claim to that distinction. Many microcomputer operations require several cycles to be performed. This is especially true of the more powerful instructions, which take far more time than the basic cycle indicates. Further, it's very possible for one μP with a seemingly high clock rate to perform a fundamental operation—like register-to-register add—more slowly than it is performed in a unit with a slower clock.

In a comparison of different μPs, differences in architecture and chip design tend to minimize the importance of specs like clock rate and cycle time. Moreover, all of these time specs don't measure such critical times as the over-all time needed to perform important routines. Not accounted for are additional delays, particularly those needed to obtain information from memory.

For example, one spec sheet says that a Call instruction for a subroutine takes about 11 states for execution. Since each state takes about 1/2 μs, the Call instruction should be completed in less than 6 μs. However, memory must be referred to five times before the instruction is completed, and each reference typically adds an additional state time since few memories are sufficiently fast. So a Call can easily take significantly longer than expected.

Often the number of instructions is spotlighted as an indication of the μP's prowess. There are several reasons why this emphasis can lead to fallacious comparisons. A number simply doesn't reveal what instructions are available for data movement and manipulation, for decision and control, or for I/O operations.

Nor does a number tell which instructions are single or multibyte in length. Double-byte instructions take twice the memory of single-byte instructions. And missing instructions can always be made up with additional hardware or with software routines, although the latter sacrifices speed. Further, a μP that features a number of addressing modes allows tighter and more efficient coding than a μP with more limited addressing capabilities.

Sometimes the number of available μP instructions depends on which page of the applications manual you're reading—because the manufacturer has multiplied instructions. The multiplying factor may be the number of addressing modes or the number of registers (in, say, a load-to-regis-

ter operation), or the number of conditions (for example, those on which a branch may occur). Other multiplying factors may be used, so that one or more parts of the original instruction set might be multiplied several times.

Improved instruction sets do come with longer-word-length μPs and with advanced versions of older units. For example, 16-bit models can handle multiplication or division with a single instruction. In 8-bit μPs, these functions call for either subroutines or special circuitry.

Further, advanced μPs offer the original instruction set of a predecessor, and more powerful instructions, too. However this "software compatibility" doesn't allow routine upgrading of systems by chip replacement. And a pin-compatible higher-speed version of a μP doesn't produce a faster, more efficient system unless there are some design changes first. In general, expect to redesign if you want to employ the new hardware/software tradeoffs efficiently.

Programming ease: a key selection factor

A microprocessor's instruction set and architecture determine one of the most frequently stressed selection factors—programming ease.

Programming can be very time consuming. Various estimates place the number of lines of "shippable" code that a programmer can write in a day at less than 20 because of the time needed to write the program, run it, and then to debug, check and finally document the code.

However, microprocessor-chip designers are constrained by limitations of technology and packaging; their chips must fit into a package no larger than a 40 or 42-pin DIP. As a result, each μP reflects a very different series of compromises and tradeoffs. Though each manufacturer says his μP is easy to program, the programmer is actually both helped and hindered by each μP. The degree of each depends on the specific application involved.

For example, one μP's instruction set may seem to be quite complete. It has a fine complement of test and branch instructions, all the logic instructions you need and all the memory-reference instructions you could possibly require.

But the μP doesn't allow program-relative addressing, though most other addressing modes are available. If you are writing a large program —as more and more microcomputer designers are —you can't easily relocate a ROM-based program from one memory-address space to another. So design changes may require a redoing of the program.

Another μP may allow the memory-addressing mode as well as indirect and indexed addressing, but at the expense of no direct addressing—the most common type. In this case, you'll be able

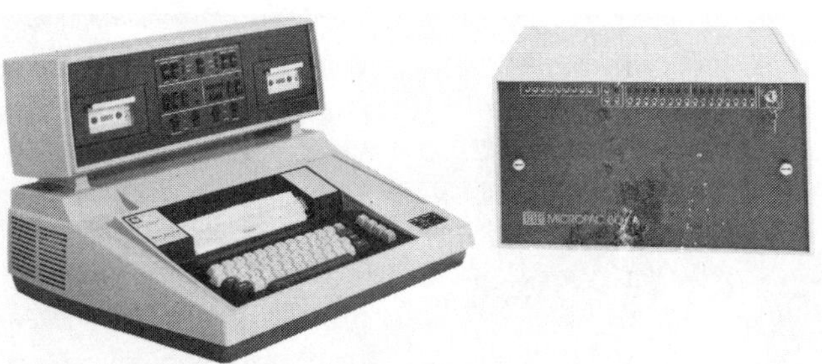

One of the first development systems to use the 8080, Process Computer Systems' Micropac 80/A simplifies the design of controllers for industrial equipment.

to move programs around, but you won't be able to address all of memory without detouring through the index register.

Benchmarks get mixed reviews

One solution to the problem of comparing chaotically different μPs is the use of benchmarks. In theory, these short test routines show how well different μPs perform critical tasks, like moving data from one part of memory to another. These software tests, adherents argue, provide a quick and easy short-cut to the one obvious but unwieldly solution: writing complete, optimized programs for different μPs and comparing results.

In practice, though, different benchmarks from different μP manufacturers show that each has a better product than anyone else. And a benchmark test that puts one μP on top of the heap can be modified ever so slightly so that the pace-setting μP loses out to others. For example, one manufacturer provides a benchmark test that shows its unit is the best mover of data in a μP's memory. But if that pace-setting micro must also deal with an interrupt during data-move operations, it falls far behind the pack.

Benchmarks designed for one particular archi-tecture can be thoroughly ineffective for another. If you're doing a job that requires 16 bits of precision for the job, then a 16-bit μP will out-distance 8-bit versions. When many different operations need to be performed a multiregister μP will outperform one with fewer available registers. For any model, no software test reveals the hardware side of the story—the required support circuits and necessary power supplies, for example.

And for a number of applications, benchmark tests may be just plain meaningless. In a host of μP applications, the micro may spend much of its time waiting for some external event, like the closing of a switch or the pressing of a button, that can take milliseconds just for the contact bounce to die down. A test that merely compares sub-millisecond operating speeds has little relevance to this problem.

Still, benchmarking provides meaningful results when used to compare two slightly different versions of the same system. The difference might be the use of a somewhat altered μP, or a modified I/O scheme. In other cases, design the benchmark to the specific application or task at hand. If you're presented with comparative benchmark tests, be sure they are specified completely.

Design Aids and Evaluation Kits

SAMUEL DERMAN
Associate Editor,
Electronic Design

The explosive proliferation of the microprocessor industry is more than matched now by a rapid increase in the number of μP design aids.

Anyone interested in designing μP-based equipment is immediately confronted with a bewildering variety of teaching aids, learning aids, design aids, development aids, evaluation kits, software and hardware-development aids and kits and on and on.

And because the microprocessor field is both new and growing, exact definitions of these aids simply don't exist.

Aids currently range from tiny devices, whose simple circuitry (less than \$200) is controlled by a few switches and mounted on a single printed circuit (PC) board, to highly sophisticated, computer-based behemoths, bearing a price tag that often runs to tens of thousands of dollars.

Particularly important are the hardware design aids—mainly one or two PC boards—on which the designer can put together a breadboard version of his μP-based system. The price range, approximately \$100 to \$900, is low enough to permit just about anyone to join the μP generation.

Although at first glance it might seem that the cost of a particular design aid should bear a direct relation to its complexity and to the amount of memory it provides, such is not always the case. The amount of memory is certainly a factor, but there are other contributors:

■ Speed. Cheaper units run at a 1-MHz rate rather than at 2 MHz or faster.

■ Documentation. The greater the amount of material provided, the higher the price, in general.

■ The desired market. Equipment aimed mainly for the hobbyist or experimenter usually is made with low-quality components. The result is a low price. Some large semiconductor manufacturers, however, unwilling to compromise their reputation, produce only quality kits—for anybody—that sell for a relatively higher price.

Other semiconductor firms shooting primarily for large-volume sales of their particular μPs may offer design aids at zero profit, or even below cost, to encourage engineers to design with their product.

Consequently, classifying hardware-design aids simply by selling price can be misleading. Categorizing them by the μP they support avoids such a pitfall.

Getting started with the 6800

A simple and inexpensive tool for designing systems based on the 8-bit M6800 μP is the MEK68002 evaluation kit from Motorola, Austin, TX. Except for the power supply, all parts needed to complete the μP-based system and get "on line" are provided.

Consisting of two PC boards, the \$225 kit is configured to allow programs to be entered manually through a 24-key hexadecimal keyboard or via an asynchronous interface adapter for an audio-cassette tape recorder. By avoiding an expensive teletypewriter terminal, the designer can get started at a minimal cost. A 6-digit LED display monitors both the data and address buses. Four other 6800 prototyping kits, all from American Microsystems in Santa Clara, CA, range in price from a low \$152 to a hefty \$950. The EVK 99, 100, 200 and 300 all have the same basic 10-1/2 in. $\times$ 12-in. PC board.

For anyone willing to buy or borrow his own TTL buffers, clock generators and power supply, the EVK 99 can get them off and designing with the 6800. In addition to the 6800 MPU, the EVK 99 comes equipped with four 128 $\times$ 8 RAMs, a peripheral interface adapter (PIA), a 1 k $\times$ 8 ROM and an asynchronous communications-interface adapter (ACIA). The ACIA allows the system to communicate bidirectionally with such serial-data I/O peripherals as a standard teletypewriter.

The EVK 100 (\$295) provides 2 kbytes of ROM, 512 bytes of RAM, and totally buffered MPU lines. Built on a PC card with two edge connectors, one for the MPU bus and one for I/O, the EVK 100 can even be expanded to the EVK 300.

Programming the S6834's 512 $\times$ 8 erasable and electrically programmable memory (EPROM) is available in the higher-priced EVK 200 (\$512). A 1 kbyte random-access memory gives the EVK 200 greater design capability.

The EVK Model 300 (\$950) features 2 kbytes of ROM (with an S 6831), 512 bytes of EPROM, 1 kbyte of RAM, and three PIAs (58 input/output lines). A ROM-subroutine program library and a selectable DMA mode augment the system's versatility.

However, none of the EVK units comes configured with a keyboard. Since external terminals are required to read the program in, their cost must be added to the "get started" expenses.

Although low-cost keyboard entry permits aspiring designers to get started with a small initial investment, a penalty must be paid. The size of the programs that can be entered via a manual keyboard is limited, and the maximum number of program steps is about 150.

Still more μP support

An evaluation kit from RCA in Somerville, NJ, for its 8-bit CDP-1802 COSMAC μP comes with a PC board, byte-input and output ports, a terminal interface, a ROM containing a utility program of commonly required functions, and a RAM for storing the user's program.

With a user-supplied terminal and a single 5-V power supply, the CDP18S020 Evaluation Kit becomes a compact computer system for the evaluation of COSMAC programs and prototyping systems. The kit costs $249. A pocket-sized miniterminal, soon to be available as an add-on for the board, contains both keyboard and digital display and should sell for under $300.

The difference between higher-priced development systems with higher capability and the low-cost hardware designs is clearly illustrated by RCA's more expensive ($3000) CDP18S004 COSMAC Development System. It has 11 plug-in PC cards; fits onto a 19-in. rack; and features editor, assembler and debug programs—and permits complete software development.

An SC/MP kit ($99) from National Semiconductor, Santa Clara, CA, comes supplied with PC board, parts and documentation. However, an external teletypewriter is required for inputting and outputting information.

A recently introduced portable keyboard from National interfaces with the SC/MP kit. The handheld keyboard ($95) avoids the teletypewriter, so the user's initial financial outlay stays low.

Besides a hexadecimal, six-digit display, the keyboard provides keys for inputting commands and hexadecimal data. A 21-wire flat cable connects the keyboard with the PC board.

ABC for the beginner

Two different design aids from Signetics, Sunnyvale, CA, fit into the low-cost category.

For $190, the novice designer can assemble the Adaptable Board Computer (ABC), a flexible prototyping system based on the 8-bit 2650 μP.

ABC includes 512 bytes of read/write memory, two latched I/O ports and three-state buffers on data, address, and control lines. The basic board configuration can be altered by a system of jumper wires and by adding more components to the board.

For those beginners designing with the Signetics 8 × 300 bipolar μP, an evaluation kit, designated the 8 × 300KT 100 SK, is available for $299. The kit's single board includes a 250-ns, 8-bit-μP central processing unit (CPU), four input/output (I/O) ports for interfacing external devices, and 256 bytes of working data storage. The 8 × 300 can be used with any bipolar or TTL-compatible integrated circuits.

A complete single-board system, including CPU, memory, and I/O, is available from Intel, Santa Clara, for designing with the 8-bit 8080 μP. Intel's SDK-80 kit interfaces directly with most terminals (75 to 4800 baud), and boasts 2-μs instruction-cycle time. The board comes with 2 kbytes of ROM (expandable to 4 k) and 256 bytes of RAM (expandable to 1 k).

Although it's a full microcomputer on a single board, the Apple Computer developed by Apple Elec-

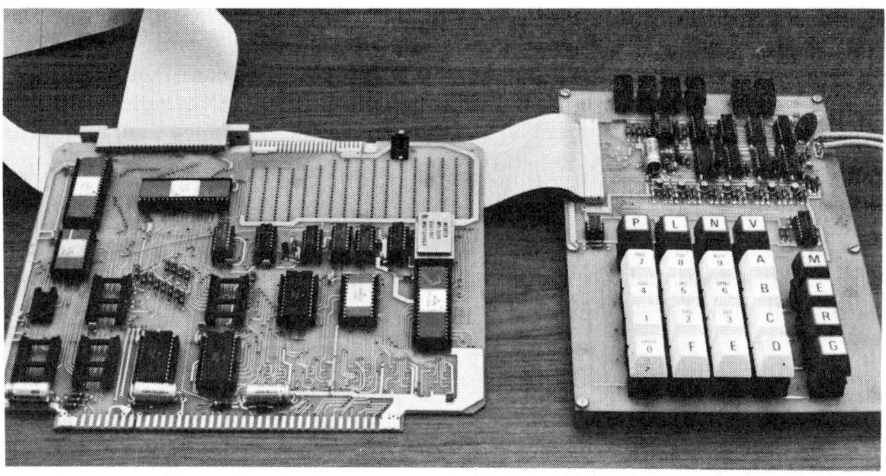

A design aid for the MC 6800 μP is Motorola's MEK6800D2. Programs can be entered through the system's keyboard or via audio cassette interface.

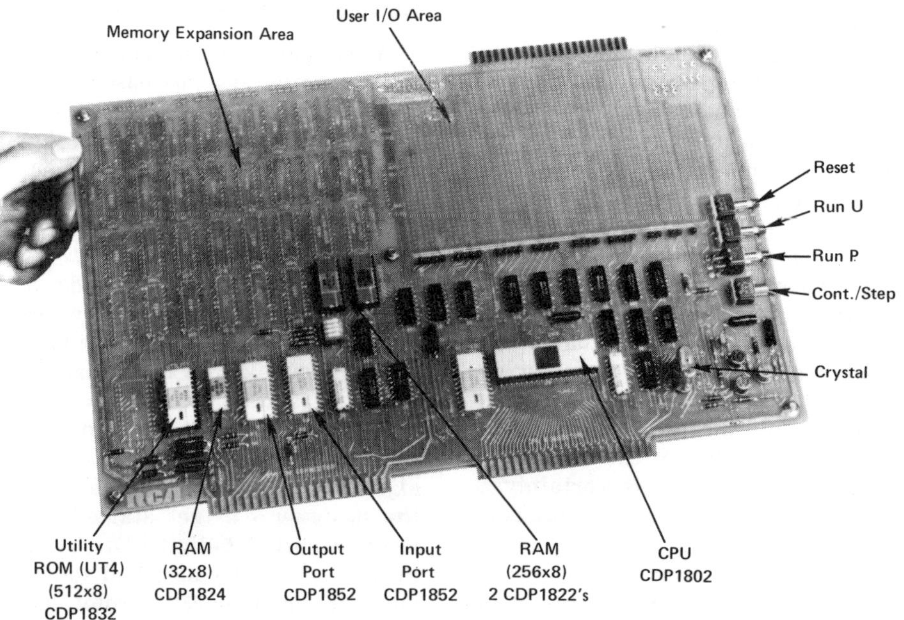

Low-cost design support for RCA's COSMAC is provided by the CDP 18SO20. This unit comes with a 512-byte ROM and a 256-byte program RAM.

tronics in Palo Alto includes a large breadboard area for the engineer to develop his own interface circuitry.

The Apple uses the 8-bit MOS Technology 6502 μP, and comes not only with up to 8 kbytes of RAM, but also with all the electronics needed to interface directly with a video terminal.

A peculiar price of $666.66 may put Apple close to the upper edge of the low-cost spectrum, but it also gives the purchaser a video link that operates six times faster than a standard teletypewriter. The Apple system is formatted to display 960 characters in 24 rows of 40 characters each. Since Apple's video-display section contains its own 1 kbyte of memory, all 8 kbytes of RAM are available to the user for programming.

Two design aids, the SE1 and 2 from Texas Instruments in Houston, allow the 4-bit TMS 1000 μP family's on-chip mask programmable ROM to be replaced with external PROM. Consequently, the designer can develop and modify programs before committing them to final hardware.

Both devices are 64-pin dual inline packages (DIPs). For $43.66 ($26.95 in quantities over 100), the SE1 provides a 64 $\times$ 4 RAM on chip and offers access to 1024 $\times$ 8 bits of external ROM. For $61.12 ($37.33 for 100 or more), the SE2 provides twice the ROM and RAM density of the SE1.

To supply data and control functions, the designer connects a CRT or teletypewriter.

Complete systems

Other systems are complete microcomputers that don't need the breadboarding space. The PC board (or boards) is complete as it stands. To simulate his system, the designer connects his particular I/O devices, including any necessary supplies, or clocks, then programs the μP to accommodate this hardware.

A complete, factory-assembled system for evaluating the IM6100 CMOS μP comes from Intersil, Cupertino, CA. Intercept Jr., which is called a tutorial system by its manufacturer, features one PC board (10 in. $\times$ 11 in.) that mounts all components, including batteries.

Intel's SDK-80 is a complete 8080 microcomputer on a single PC board. Instruction-cycle time is 2 μs.

A single, 12-key keyboard on the unit is used for both operation entries and numerical entries. In fact, each key can enter either a single numerical value or one of three different program operations.

There is no ambiguity. The operator simply keys in his instructions and the numerical data, and a program built into a ROM decides that the entry is to be interpreted either as a numeric or an instruction or a command.

The Intercept Jr. is also the first low-cost ($281) design aid to provide op-coded control functions right on the keyboard, according to Gopal Ramachandran, Intersil's application engineer. The microcomputer comes configured with a 1024 $\times$ 12 CMOS ROM (the IM6312) and a 256 $\times$ 12 CMOS RAM. Memory addresses as well as data are displayed simultaneously in octal language on two, 4-digit LED displays.

Four standard "D" cells supply the required voltage. To compensate for aging batteries the microcomputer is designed to function at supply voltages as low as 4-1/2 V. A receptacle can be added to permit operation from a standard 110-V-ac-to-6-V-dc adapter.

SC/MP, FB and Z80 support

For SC/MP design capability more advanced than the SC/MP kit permits, National Semiconductor supplies a Low Cost Development System (LCDS) with a single chassis. The chassis contains six-digit hex display, PC board, control switches and circuitry—all controlled by a 16-key dual-function keyboard.

For $499, the LCDS includes the following capabilities:

- Displaying the contents of the SC/MP program counter, registers and accumulator.
- Altering the components of the SC/MP program counter, registers and accumulator.
- Displaying the contents of any memory location.
- Interrupting the execution of the user-generated program at any point.

Anyone designing with the 8-bit F8 μP can be helped by the F8 Micro Pro from Fairchild in San Jose, or by the F8 Survival Kit from Mostek, Carrollton, TX. Both aids include a user-operating system for loading, debugging and modifying software, 1 k of RAM, four 8-bit I/O ports, teletypewriter interface, timer and Fortran IV cross assembler. The designer operates the two systems by attaching either a 100 or 300-baud ASCII terminal and a +5 and a +12-V supply. Both Micro Pro and Survival Kit come assembled for $185. (An unassembled version from Mostek is available for $147).

There is a major difference, however. The Survival Kit begins its 1000-byte debug program in memory location zero, which may interfere with the designer's program. On the other hand, the Micro Pro's debug program starts at some high location in memory to avoid such a problem.

A compact, one-board development system with 8 kbytes of memory for the Z80 8-bit μP is available from Zilog in Cupertino, CA. The Z80-MCB comes with the following features:

- A timer chip with four programmable timer-counter circuits for varying the baud rate so that the Z80-MCB-system speed can be matched to that of peripheral, electromechanical devices.
- A programmable, serial I/O port with RS-232 or current loop interface for hooking up to a teletypewriter or cathode ray tube (CRT).
- 4 kbytes of RAM.
- A PC board, smaller than that of most design aids of this type (only 7.7 in. $\times$ 7.5 in.).

The Z80-MCB sells for $475· in quantities of 1 to 9, $435 in quantities of 10 to 24, and $400 for quantities of 25 and over.

Two plug-in accessory boards for mating with the Z80-MCB are also available from Zilog. A floppy-disc controller card, the MCD ($745 in 1 to 9 qty), controls up to four floppy discs, contains 12 kbytes of RAM, two ports for parallel I/O. and a ZDOS operating system.

A RAM memory card containing 16 kbytes of memory, the Z80-MCB ($750), can support up to four such cards for a total of 64 kbytes of RAM.

The 8080 and 6502 revisited

Both the 8080 and the 6502 μPs are also supported by design aids that come complete on a board. Two single-board 8080 μP-based computers from Intel, the SBC 80/10 and the SBC 80/20, provide programmable synchronous/asynchronous interfacing with the RS 232 or a teletypewriter. The 80/10 requires an optional adapter for the teletypewriter. A 1-kbyte memory is provided with the 80/10 and 2k with the 80/20.

The keyboard-controlled, single-card KIM-1 from MOS Technology, Norristown, PA, is a complete microcomputer for designing with the 6502 μP. Besides its 23-key keyboard, the MOS design aid ($245) contains the electronics needed to interface with either an audio-cassette tape recorder or a teletypewriter terminal. With control from the keyboard, KIM-1 can generate hard-copy printout and read or punch paper tapes. A six-digit LED display provides on-board readout.

The memory, which consists of 2048 bytes of ROM and 128 of RAM, can be expanded to 65 k.

Measuring only 7.7 in. × 5 in. Zilog's Z80-MCB provides 4 kbytes of RAM with capacity up to 4 kbytes of ROM. A single 5-V source powers it.

Every extra bit helps

Sixteen-bit μPs provide advantages not offered by the 8-bit devices. For example, more precise calculations can be made at higher speeds. Such a capability requires complex support equipment and, ultimately, more money. Although the high cost of such equipment places them out of the low-cost category they must be included as a necessary adjunct to 16-bit μP design.

For example, the sophisticated, 16-bit "Gimini" from General Instrument Corp., Hicksville, NY, costs $3500. Built around GI's CP-1600 N-channel MOS μP, the Gimini provides a host of capabilities, including:

■ Separate data, address and control buses.

■ Direct addressing up to 65 k words of memory.

■ Nested interrupt system.

Although Gimini comes housed in a cabinet, its ICs and other circuitry are mounted on PC plug-in boards. A card cage behind the front panel holds four PC boards, with space and connectors for nine more.

All control and timing signals as well as data and address buses are fully buffered and available to expand the memory. A cable assembly allows interfacing to a teletypewriter or to a paper tape reader/punch.

Another 16-bit μP, National Semiconductor's PACE, is supported by the PACER, manufactured by Project Support Engineering, Sunnyvale, CA.

For $1195, PACER provides such sophisticated features as the ability to examine and modify the contents of any computer register or memory location, hexadecimal to decimal conversion, and full alphanumeric display.

Software Support for Microprocessors

DAVID C. WYLAND
Microprocessor Design Manager,
Monolithic Memories, Sunnyvale, CA

Software provided by microprocessor vendors is an invaluable tool for the digital system designer. Properly used, it can greatly speed the development and reduce the errors in a program design. For these reasons, logic designers ought to be aware of what software packages are available and how they can be used effectively.

There are three types of computer software: operating, program-development and diagnostic (Fig. 1). This is true for microprocessors as well as for minicomputers and large mainframe computers.

Operating software is the group of programs that runs on the computer under normal use. In a dedicated computer system, the programs are in the read-only memories (ROMs) that come with the machine. For example, in a microprocessor-controlled automatic weighing system, the operating software is the program that calculates and displays the weight. Usually operating software combines user-written and vendor-supplied programs.

Program-development software refers to design tools that help in the creation of operating software. It is a computer-aided-design package, and the tools range from simple assemblers to complex high-level-language compilers.

Diagnostic programs test the computer hardware and verify that the system is operating properly. Typical programs test the central processing unit, memory and selected I/O devices. There are also software diagnostic programs, such as simulators and debuggers. These test for proper program sequencing and functioning.

Who does what in software?

The user must write his own operating software, since this represents the logic design of the system or product being built. The computer vendor can supply some prepackaged items, such as binary loaders and mathematical subroutine packages, but the rest is created by the user for his application. On the other hand, diagnostic software is a fixed package of programs supplied by the μP vendor.

Program-development software represents the largest investment on the part of the computer supplier. It is this type of software that is usually referred to when one speaks of a vendor's software support, and the degree of support can vary markedly from one vendor to another.

If you are a logic designer using microprocessors for the first time, you may ask: "What does all this software do for me?" You have to answer this question to know what you need for your design and how to evaluate what the microprocessor vendor is supplying. The three types of software may be needed even for very simple systems.

A computer system design for, say, an automatic meat scale typically goes through the following steps:

1. State the problem. (Create an automatic meat-weighing scale with digital readout.)

2. Analyze the problem into a sequence of operations that will perform the function.

3. Arrange the sequences in a list or flow chart that will show how they are to be performed.

4. Write the program from the flow chart of operations. If the definition of the operations is detailed enough, this should be a simple conversion. Each operation will be performed typically by a few instructions.

5. Enter the instructions into the computer-system memory. Let us assume that we enter it manually through the computer front panel.

6. Test the program. This will probably be done first by stepping the computer through the program, instruction by instruction, and then at full speed. This corresponds exactly to testing a hard-wired logic system, clock-step by clock-step, and then at full speed. When the program and system have passed these tests, the program design is complete.

Small systems can be designed easily

For a simple program of, say, 20 words, the design is straightforward. Instructions, addresses and data can be generated as binary bit patterns. These bit patterns are entered through the front panel, and the program is then tested. Programs of 100 words or larger, however, create the following problems:

1. Instructions are hard to remember as binary numbers.

2. Addresses are difficult to remember as binary numbers. Also, addresses change when the program changes. It is often hard to remember what the address locations are being used for.

3. It is difficult to follow the program flow with binary addresses and data during debugging.

4. The program must be entered into the computer memory. Programs of over 100 words are impractical to enter manually through the front panel.

5. If you have a system failure during debugging, you need to know what is failing, the program or the hardware.

Program-development software packages attack the first three problems. They make instructions, addresses, and data easier to remember and manipulate by the program designer. Operating software, such as loaders and operating systems, attacks the fourth problem of entering and running the program. Diagnostic software for both hardware and software functions attacks the fifth problem by providing tools that help the designer locate the problem.

Assemblers: Simple, but powerful

Assembler programs represent the lowest level of program-development software. But though an assembler provides but a few basic bookkeeping functions, it allows a programmer to design programs of up to several thousand words.

An assembler provides three functions to the programmer: It allows him to specify instructions by name, to specify addresses by name, and to specify data in several forms other than binary. Instead of writing down a list of binary numbers for instructions, addresses, and data words, the programmer lists shorthand symbols for the instruction words and names for the address words, and he specifies data constants in more

---

Operating software:

 Customer application programs
 Binary loaders
 Relocatable binary loaders
 Operating systems
 Miscellaneous utility programs:
  Math subroutines
  I/O control subroutines
  Paper tape copy and list programs
  Etc.

Program development software:

 Assemblers
 Relocatable assemblers
 Paper tape editors
 Macroassemblers
 Compilers
 General-purpose microassemblers

Diagnostic software:

 CPU diagnostics
 Memory diagnostics
 I/O device diagnostics
 Software diagnostics:
  Debuggers
  Simulators

1. Three types of software—operating, program-development and diagnostic—exist for all computers, from micros to large mainframes.

Source Tape Listing:

     Sample Program

```
       . LOC  2        ; First Word to Location 2
Start: DIA   0, 15     ; Load Reg 0 From Device
                            15, Reg A
       LDA   1, X      ; Load Reg 1 From Location
                            X
       ADD   1, 0      ; Add Reg 1 to Reg 0
       STA   0, Y      ; Save Result In Location Y
       DOB   0, 15     ; Output Result To Device
                            15, Reg B
       JMP   Start     ; Loop Back To Start
X:     30              ; Octal Data
Y:     0               ; Result: Initial Value = 0
       . End
```

Assembler Program Printout:

     Sample Program

```
000002         . LOC  2       ; First Word To Lo-
                                   cation 2

060415  Start: DIA   0, 15    ; Load Reg 0 From
                                   Device 15, Reg A
024010         LDA   1, X     ; Load Reg 1 From
                                   Location X
123000         ADD   1, 0     ; Add Reg 1 To Reg
                                   0
040011         STA   0, Y     ; Save Result In Lo-
                                   cation Y
062015         DOB   0, 15    ; Output Result To
                                   Device 15, Reg B
000002         JMP   Start    ; Loop Back To Start

000030  X:     30             ; Octal Data

000000  Y:     0              ; Result: Initial Val-
                                   ue = 0
               . END
```

Binary Tape Contents:

```
               000002
               060415
               024010
               123000
               040011
               062015
               000002
               000030
               000000
```

2. An assembler generates this sample program. Each line of the source-tape listing contains one or more symbols that define a binary word.

Command	Description
Y	Read in a tape. Tape is terminated by a special end-of-page character.
P	Punch the contents of the buffer with an end-of-page character.
Pn	Punch (n) lines of the buffer with an end-of-page character. Begin at line pointer.
W	Punch the buffer without an end-of-page.
Wn	Punch (n) lines without an end-of-page.
T	Type the contents of the buffer.
Tn	Type (n) lines of the buffer.
I	Insert text following (I) at the line pointer location. Terminate with Escape character.
C	Change line: Find (within the current line) the text string between (C) and the first Escape character. Replace with the text string between the first and second Escape character following (C).
Kn	Erase (n) lines following line pointer.
B	Set line pointer to beginning of buffer.
Ln	Move line pointer down (n) lines. (n) can be negative.

Command Formats: A, A_n
A = alphabetic command character
n = modifier number, as required

A paper-tape editor employs various commands to read alphanumeric characters into a buffer area in memory, modify the buffer's contents and punch a new tape from the modified buffer. Modifications are performed on lines of text, and each line consists of a string of characters terminated by a carriage return.

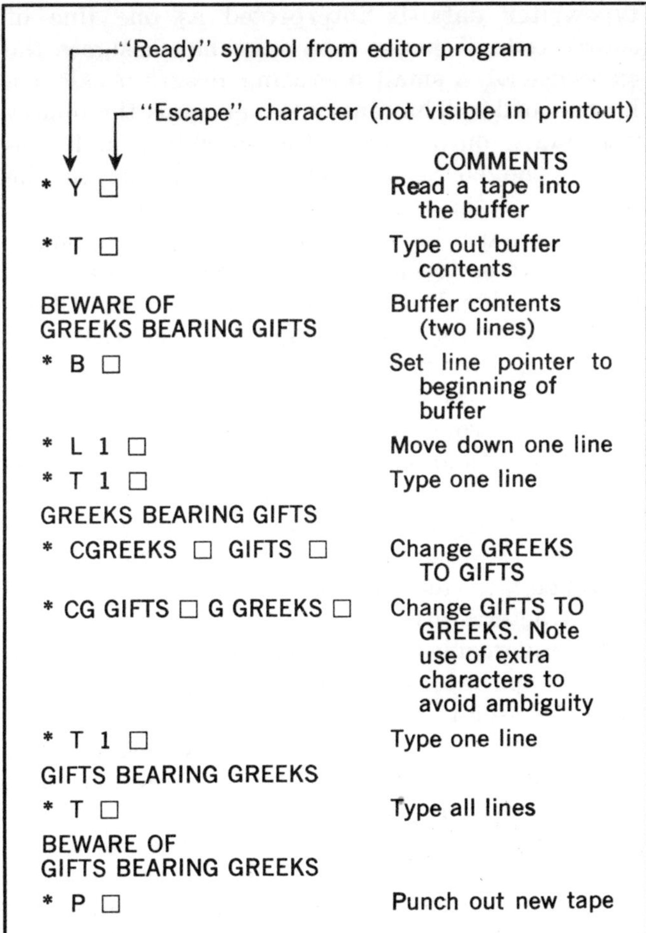

An example of a paper-tape editor's operation employs a Ready symbol and an Escape character.

convenient decimal, octal, or hexadecimal data formats. The assembler program then processes this list to create a corresponding list of binary numbers.

The list of symbols that an assembler processes to create the binary program is called the source program. Each line of the list contains one or several symbols to define one binary word. A line in the source program may also provide information to the assembler program, such as indicating the start and the end of the source program, as well as where the binary program is to be placed in memory. A small assembly-language program illustrates these features (Fig. 2).

Each assembler has its own list of shorthand symbols or mnemonics for instructions. This list may be either fixed or expandable, depending on the design of the assembler. It is possible to write a general-purpose assembler in which all of the instruction mnemonics are defined by the user. These mnemonics are usually three to five characters long.

Memory locations are named by writing the name, followed by a colon, before a line that specifies an instruction, a data constant or another address. The assembler associates the address value for that location with that name. Names are usually restricted to five or fewer characters. There may be other restrictions about numbers and nonalphabetic characters in the names.

Once a location has been named, it can be referred to by that name throughout the rest of the program. This is very convenient, because if the program is changed and the named location becomes a different address, the assembler will automatically use the new number. The programmer does not have to perform any calculations to determine the new address. Likewise he does not have to scan the program to find all of the places where that address may be used and then update them.

The ability to specify data in other than binary form is also a useful feature. It is very time-consuming for a programmer to convert decimal data to binary if he needs to specify a decimal constant. And manual conversion is prone to error.

Microprocessors and small minicomputer systems use paper-tape assemblers. These programs accept the source data on paper tape and also produce the binary program output on paper tape. In the source paper tape, one line of teletypewriter data is interpreted as one line of source code. A paper-tape assembler assumes the existence of a small operating program called a binary loader. The binary loader reads the binary paper-tape output from the assembler and generates the corresponding binary words in the memory of the computer.

The binary loader program, although small, may itself be too long to be loaded into the computer by hand. A second, smaller paper-tape loader program, called a bootstrap loader, is used to load the binary loader into memory. This bootstrap loader is designed for minimum size and easy entry from the front panel.

A paper-tape assembler package usually includes a program called a paper-tape editor whose primary purpose is to overcome a problem that occurs when source tapes are generated. It is difficult to add or delete characters or a line of characters in the middle of a paper tape. The editor overcomes this problem by reading the source tape into a buffer area in memory. It allows the user to add and delete lines and characters to and from this buffer. It punches out the new source tape when additions, deletions and modifications are complete.

Diagnostic programs determine whether a system failure is caused by hardware or software. Hardware diagnostic programs are usually supplied with each machine. Typically one diagnostic program is supplied for the CPU, memory and each I/O device. When a user designs a custom I/O interface, he must also write the corresponding diagnostics. Software diagnostics are called debugger programs. These tend to be loosely classified under the heading of program development software, although, in fact, they are a type of operating software. Obviously, debugger software is considered a marketing tool by the computer vendor in the same category as program development software.

The software debugger program is a collection of useful functions. A simple, teletypewriter-based debugger program will include the ability to load memory from paper tape, dump a section of memory to paper tape, and dump a section of memory to the teletypewriter printer in readable format. It will also include the ability to examine and modify memory locations and to execute a program starting at a specified address.

Debugger permits breakpoints

A debugger has another important feature, called breakpoint. This allows the programmer to stop the program when it reaches a specified point. To use the feature, the programmer inserts a breakpoint at an address in the program. The debugger program then goes to that address, removes and saves the instruction and inserts an instruction that causes the computer to jump back to the debugger program. After returning to the debugger, the original instruction is replaced. Thus the program can be executed up to a point and then stopped. The programmer can then examine the memory to see if failures have occurred.

The debugger program duplicates many of the functions of the computer front panel. But while the computer front panel directly controls computer hardware and is useful for debugging hardware problems, the debugger program focuses on software problems. Its use assumes that the hardware is working well enough for the debugger program itself to run.

More powerful tools

The amount of support software required by the logic system designer depends on the size of the program he intends to write. If the program is less than 200 words, support software may not be required. It may be practical to create the program directly in binary or hexadecimal form, enter it through the front panel and debug it manually through the front panel.

For common programs of approximately 200 to 4000 words, a paper-tape assembler and debug package are sufficient. But for larger programs, systems of programs and programs of a high degree of complexity, more extensive software support packages have been developed. These include (in order of increasing sophistication) relocatable assemblers and loaders, macroassemblers and high-level-language compilers.

A relocatable assembler is the same as a simple assembler, except that it produces its binary tape in a format that is compatible with a relocatable loader. This loader allows the programmer to load several programs at the same time and to stack them automatically in memory. It also provides any necessary communication between programs, such as in a program that calls several common mathematical subroutines. The relocatable loader must modify all addresses used by a given program, since these addresses depend on where the program finally ends up in memory. Thus a relocatable loader is considerably larger and more complex than a simple binary loader.

A macroassembler allows the programmer to create and specify blocks of instructions. Suppose a programmer uses a three-instruction sequence for any call to an I/O device. A macroassembler allows the programmer to define this three-instruction sequence and to assign a special mnemonic to it. When this mnemonic is encountered by the macroassembler during processing of a source program, it will create the corresponding three binary words. These user-defined multiple-word instructions are called macroinstructions.

High-level-language compilers, such as those for Fortran and PL/1, are somewhat like macro-assemblers. A high-level language provides these four features:

1. The ability to specify mathematical operations in algebraic form and have them converted to a series of instructions.

2. A convenient method of handling real numbers in floating-point notation. This is the same as adding a floating-point feature to a fixed-point calculator, since most computers are binary fixed-point machines in operation.

3. The ability to specify data in a matrix or subscript form. Data can be identified by row and column location within a matrix. This is convenient for handling large amounts of data and data arranged in matrix or table form.

4. Indexing macros for a loop sequence. Program loops are very common and typically require several instructions in the beginning and end of each loop.

Programming vs debugging time

These sophisticated software packages have a disadvantage, though. Because of their size and sophistication, they create a distance between the source code and the binary object code. This is inherent in any program-development tool, from a simple assembler up to the most complex compiler, and it's easy to understand why this is so. The more a program does for you automatically, the less aware you are of what it is doing in the resulting binary code. A programmer using the simple paper-tape assembler creates a source program that is very close to the resulting binary code. The symbols used are one-for-one representations of the binary code.

A programmer writing in a high-level language like Fortran may never see the binary code except when he is debugging the program. This distance from the machine code is significant only during program debugging, which requires dealing with the binary instructions being executed by the machine. Debugging a simple assembly-language program is fairly straightforward. Usually the assembler will print a listing of the source-language statement, the resulting binary data and the address where that data will be loaded by the binary loader.

A program written with a relocatable assembler forces you to find out where the relocatable loader put the program in the memory and mentally change all of the addresses on the listing. A program written in Fortran will give you no listing of the binary data that is loaded in the memory, but it will give you the addresses for the data and subroutine packages used. You must

Command	Description
An	Examine/modify accumulator register (n)
En	Examine/modify memory location (n)
Gn	Go to location (n) and execute program
Il,m,n	Initialize: load (n) into all memory locations between (l) and (m)
Dm,n	Dump memory to teletypewriter printer, locations (m) through (n)
R	Read in program from teletypewriter paper tape reader (binary loader function)
Om,n	Punch out memory contents from locations (m) through (n) in binary loader format on teletypewriter paper tape punch
B	Breakpoint examine/set
C	Continue from last breakpoint

Command Formats: A, An; Am,n; Al,m,n
A = Alphabetic command character
l,m,n = modifier number as required by command

Commands for a debugger program allow the isolation of software errors. The debugger has a breakpoint capability that permits the program to be stopped when it reaches a specified point.

then know or learn how the Fortran compiler generates the resulting binary code from its source-statement input.

The use of program-development software tends to result in fewer program errors, because these tools do many things automatically and provide many design-checking features. But if the program doesn't work, sophisticated debugging techniques may be needed.

Special techniques for special problems

Several other program packages commonly available represent solutions to special problems. One of these is the "microassembler," which is actually a misnomer. A microassembler is really a general-purpose assembler that allows the programmer to define the word size of the machine, the instruction mnemonics, and their corresponding binary bit patterns. A microassembler can therefore be used to generate an assembler for a specific machine.

Operating systems are similar to debuggers. They can load and run programs and dump the contents of the memory to a printer or other output device. Often they provide software-diagnostic features. Unlike a debugger, the operating system contains a relocatable loader and can load programs from different sources, such as paper tape, magnetic tape and disc.

An operating system is typically used in conjunction with a disc file or other storage medium and provides a library function as well. This means that the user can specify a program by name, load it, and execute it. The operating system includes facilities for program filing on the storage units. These facilities include program loading, dumping, copying, renaming and deleting.

The operating system also provides a standard set of I/O control subroutines. These allow all programs to use the same method of calling I/O devices. The system can then provide various I/O utility features, such as stopping the program to add paper to the printer.

Simulators are diagnostic tools for the debugging of software. A simulator creates a software model of a hardware computer. Each step of the internal operation of the simulated CPU is visible to the programmer. Complex problems of hardware and software interaction can often be solved with this tool, but it runs 10 to 1000 times slower than the hardware it simulates. This means you cannot use it to solve timing-related problems.

Bibliography:

Wyland, David C., "Design Your Own Microcomputer," *Electronic Design* No. 20, Sept. 27, 1975, pp. 72-78.

Wyland, David C., "Increase Microcomputer Efficiency," *Electronic Design* No. 23, Nov. 8, 1975, pp. 70-75.

Addressing Modes for Microprocessors

LANCE LEVENTHAL
Grossmont College,
El Cajon, CA

Get the most out of your microprocessor-based system by using the optimum addressing mode for each program step. Different addressing techniques—indexed, indirect, relative, paged and others—originally developed for use in large computers, can be used in μP systems.

But beware—even though the technique may have the same name as in larger computers, the internal procedure performed by the μP may be different. The short word lengths used in most μP systems make it difficult to handle addresses. Common processors such as the 8080, 6800, F-8, PPS-8, CDP1802 or 2650 all have word lengths of only 8 bits, though some of these μPs simplify addressing by using 16-bit address busses.

Eight-bit busses are fine for handling 4-bit binary-coded decimal and 8-bit ASCII or EBCDIC characters, but they are not adequate for a viable memory address bus. A typical 8-bit μP, when using direct addressing, needs three memory cycles to get the instruction and address into the processor. Only in the fourth cycle does the μP actually do any useful work (Fig. 1). About 75 percent of all central processor (CPU) time is spent on overhead functions.

Know the different addressing modes

Obviously, a better way than simple direct addressing is needed. With an 8-bit μP, the fewer 16-bit addresses you transfer, the more CPU time and memory space you save. For fixed-program applications, a ROM that holds the operating program would be the simplest solution. However, you cannot store subroutine return addresses in the ROM or modify its program instructions.

Data cannot be stored with the program either; temporary data must be placed in a separate part of memory. That also restricts the movement of the program and data in the memory unless special provisions have been made beforehand.

The limited chip size of μPs keeps the number of registers, busses and other elements minimal. Many signals may have to be generated externally, thus adding to the system cost. Let's take a hard look at the different addressing methods to see how they can increase or decrease the complexity of the system.

Indexing is one of the most commonly used addressing modes. With this technique, the contents of the index register are added to the address supplied with the instruction (Fig. 2). The sum of the two is called the effective address, and is used to fetch the data.

The indexed instruction shown in Fig. 2 is Load Accumulator 300, X. (The , X indicates that indexed addressing is to be used.) If the index register contains the number 15, the indexed instruction has the same effect as a Load Accumulator 315 instruction. The contents of location 315 are fetched and placed in the accumulator. However, we can change the effective address of the indexed Load instruction by altering the contents of the index register. A Load Accumulator 315 instruction, though, is frozen for the life of the program.

Processing of data stored in arrays or tables is the usual application of indexed addressing. An entire array of data can be processed or moved with a simple program, just by starting the index register at a base number and incrementing it each time the program cycles through (Fig. 3a and 3b). Inside the program, indexed addressing is used to get the data. The address supplied with the instruction is the base address of the data stack. Indexing saves program memory space and adds flexibility. When you're only using one element at a time, though, indexing slightly slows down the program since you must add several instructions to increment the index register.

On the other hand, if several elements of an array are used each time the program cycles, indexing can speed things along. All the elements can be accessed just by changing the address that accompanies the instruction. Thus, each time the program cycles, the next six data elements can be accessed with the addresses:

BASE, X

BASE + 1, X

.

.

.

BASE + 5, X.

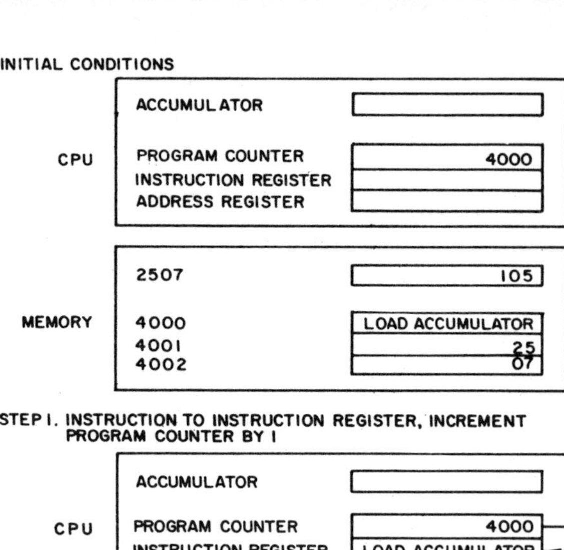

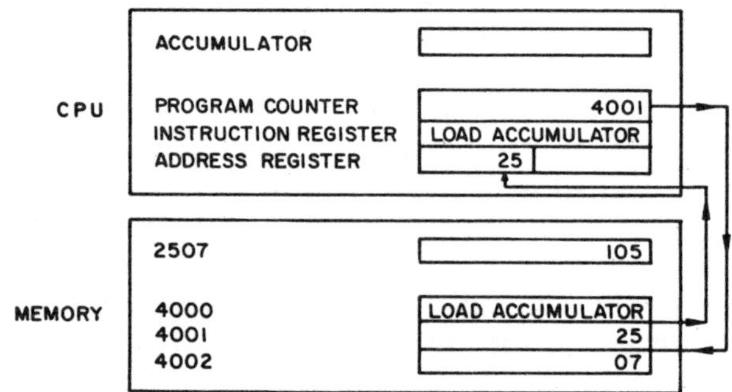

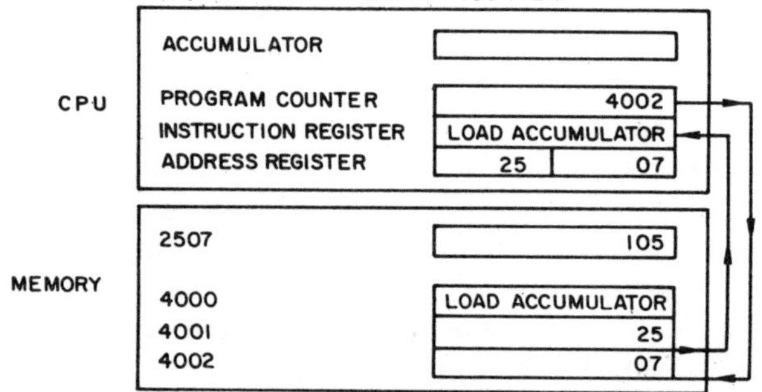

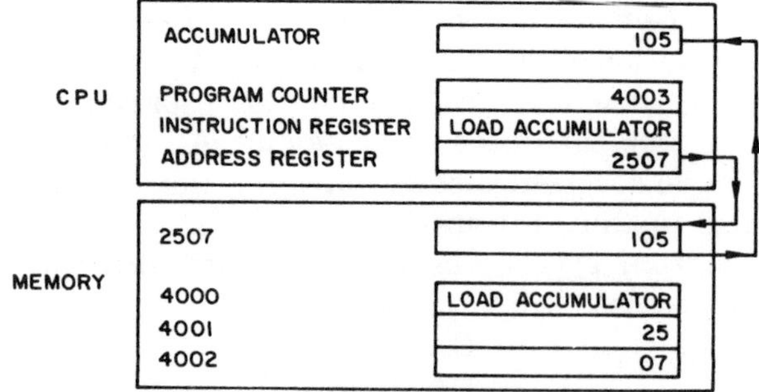

1. **A simple instruction cycle,** performed on an 8-bit μP, requires four memory cycles if data must be fetched from memory. Three cycles are needed to get the instruction and data address and one cycle to actually do any processing.

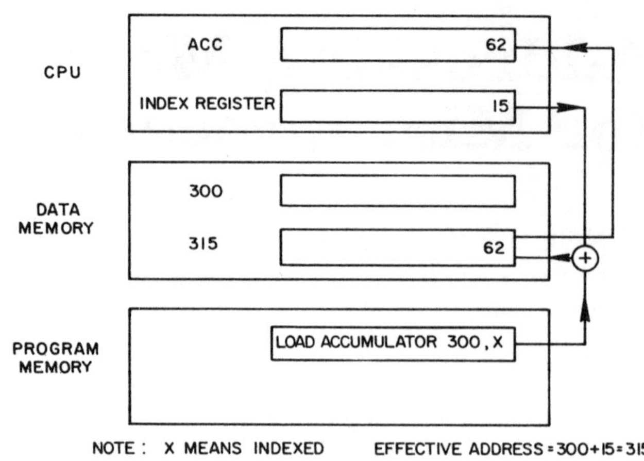

2. **Getting information by indexing** cuts the number of memory cycles needed by the processor, but slows down processing since the contents of the index register are added to the address supplied with the instruction.

For applications that require sorting, searching and editing, this accessing feature is very useful.

Several data arrays can be processed simultaneously if they are similarly structured. For instance, if one array contains names, one contains addresses and another contains Social Security numbers, once you locate a name you also have the location of all of the other data in the accompanying arrays.

Table access is simplified

When indexed addressing is applied to tables, you can simplify any look-up routines considerably. All that has to be done is to put the number of the desired element into the index register, then use the base address of the table as the fixed address.

The table of Fig. 3c shows how you can use a table to convert a number in the index register to a seven-segment code for display. The instruction —Load Accumulator 1000, X—does the conversion. The CPU obtains the seven-segment code from the effective address (1000 plus the decimal digit stored in the index register) and places it in the accumulator.

A microprocessor could do indexing in the same way as larger computers. However, the base address included in the instruction would have to be 16 bits long, and the CPU would have to perform a 16-bit addition of the base address and the index register. In an 8-bit CPU the arithmetic section would have to "double-up" to do the addition, thus slowing down the overall program.

Of course, you can save time and memory by limiting to 8 bits the address that is included with the instruction, and by using a 16-bit index register. The 6800 μP does indexing that way, which is the reverse of normal indexing because the 16-bit base address is placed in the index

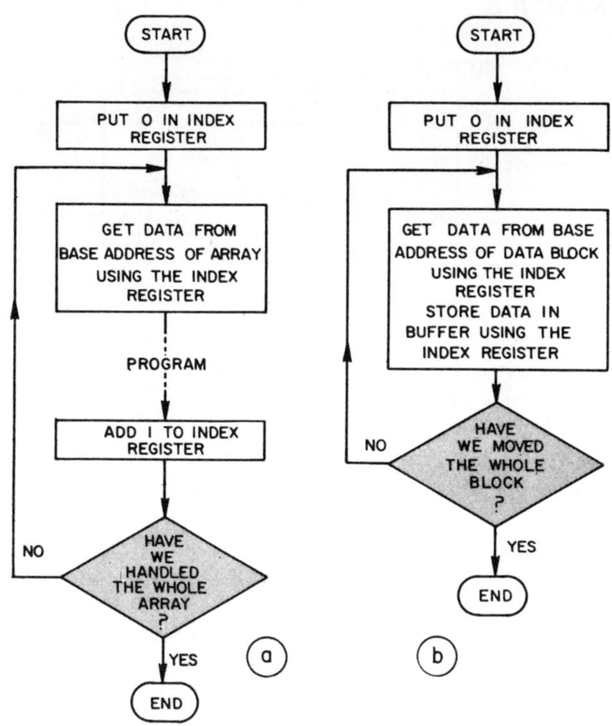

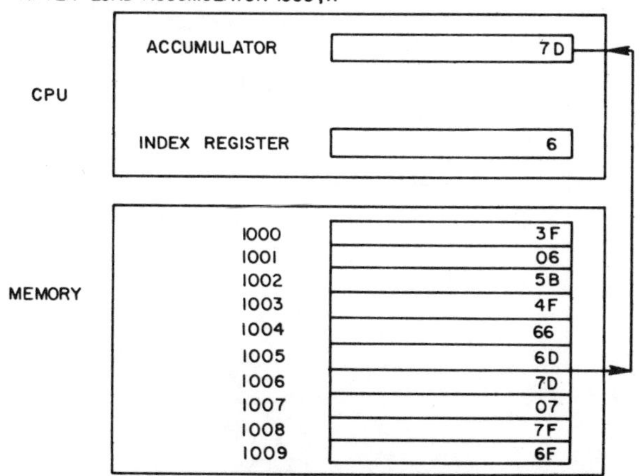

USING INDEXING TO ACCESS A TABLE   c

3. **You can easily use indexed addressing to process** a data array (a), move data blocks from one area in memory to another (b) or to access a table for code conversion look-up (c).

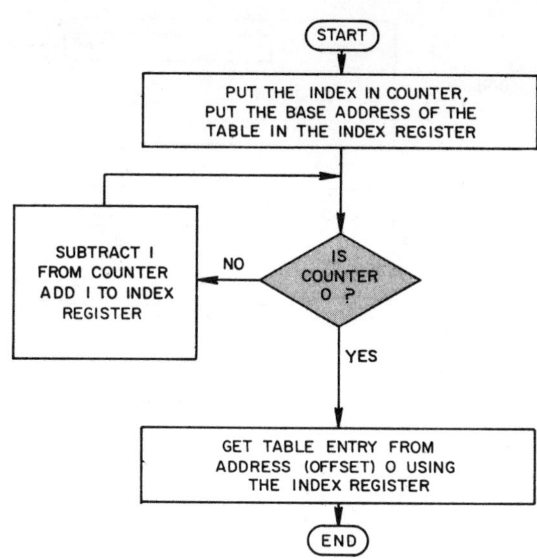

4. **When you access a table using 6800 indexing,** the index register must be used as a counter to keep track of the table entry. When the counter reaches zero the table pointer has reached the desired item.

register instead of in the program memory.

Of course, this addressing mode still requires the CPU to do a 16-bit addition to arrive at the effective address. You must also load, increment and store the contents of the 16-bit index register. However, only rarely will you actually have to load the index register's contents. Often, you can just add one to it in the same way that the program counter gets incremented.

Accessing a table to get an entry can be done in several different ways. One of the simplest uses the index register as a counter to keep track of the table entry and increments the register for each entry (Fig. 4). This procedure is slow and, if used often, can cause major delays in processing the data.

Another way is to perform 16-bit addition in the program. If the 6800 μP is used, the base address is placed in the two 8-bit accumulators and the index added to the eight least-significant bits (LSB). The resulting carry, if any, gets added to the most significant bits (MSB). Unfortunately, the 6800 cannot be instructed to shift the contents of both accumulators into the index register. So, the sum must be temporarily stored in a memory location before you can put it in the index register. This procedure is independent of table size, and requires eight instruction cycles to calculate the effective address and fetch the table entry. A typical program listing might read:

```
LDAA   # UPPER      upper base add to A
LDAB   # LOWER      lower base add to B
ADDB   INDEX        add index
ADCA   # 0          and carry
STAB   SUML         lower entry add.
STAA   SUMU         upper entry add.
```

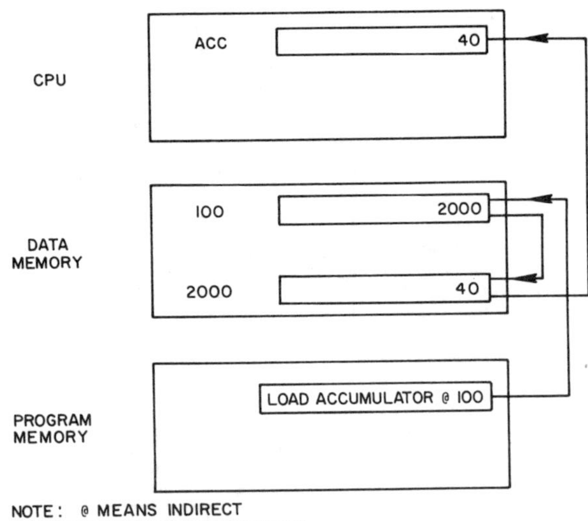

5. You can access the entire memory with indirect addressing but doing so can be confusing because the data byte or bytes fetched are used as the address of the actual data word.

```
LDX    SUMU            get it to index reg.
LDAA   X               get entry
```

Alternatively, you can set up the tables so that their starting addresses are always a multiple of 100 (hexadecimal). Then you can refer to any table by means of an 8-bit address. (An address of 4 means that the table starts at location 400 hex.) To get into the table, place the 8-bit table address in the eight MSBs of the index register and the 8-bit index in the eight LSBs of the index register.

In any of the methods just described, indexing is not really used to full advantage. The CPU does unnecessary 16-bit addition and time is lost for each indexing cycle that adds zero to the contents of the index register.

Get the addresses indirectly

If you can spare a memory cycle, indirect addressing can retrieve the full 64 kilobytes of available memory. When you use indirect addressing, the address supplied with the instruction is used to get the address of the data rather than the data itself (Fig. 5). The effective address is thus part of the data memory. Parentheses are used around an address to indicate that the contents of the location shown are what the CPU is after. Thus: ADDR is an address and (ADDR) represents the contents of that address.

Indirect addressing permits you to store a program in ROM, yet alter the contents of RAM locations called out from the ROM. Thus you can use the same instructions to process data anywhere in memory. All you do is put the starting address of the data into the RAM location specified by the program.

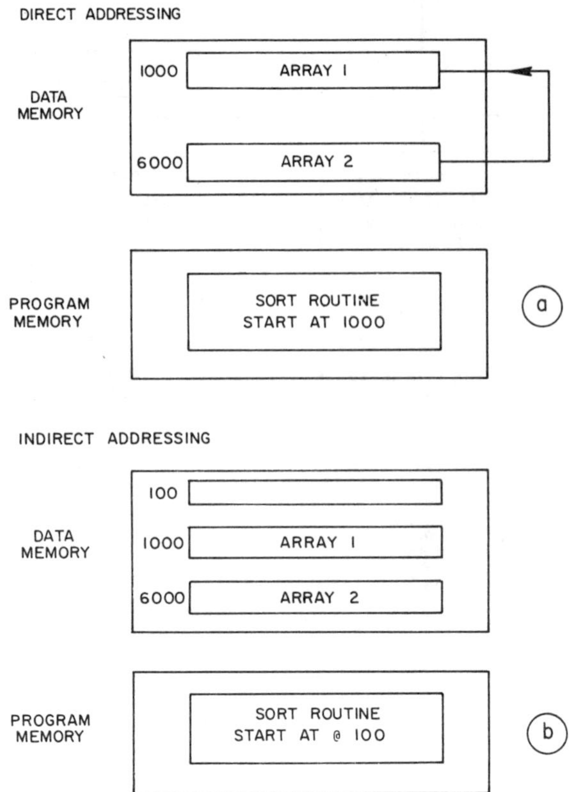

6. To do a sorting routine for an array that starts at an address other than that specified by the program, an extra program that first relocates the array must be included when direct addressing is used (a). Indirect addressing permits you to keep the program simple and start at any location (b).

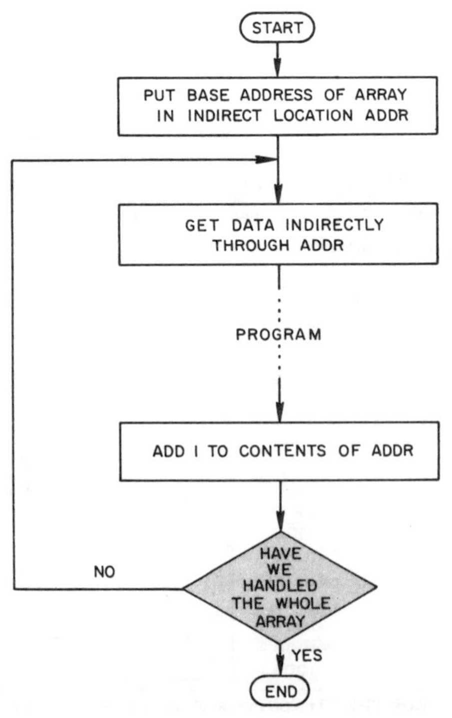

7. To process a data array, indirect addressing can be used, but it won't be the most efficient method because the memory must be accessed twice for each data word.

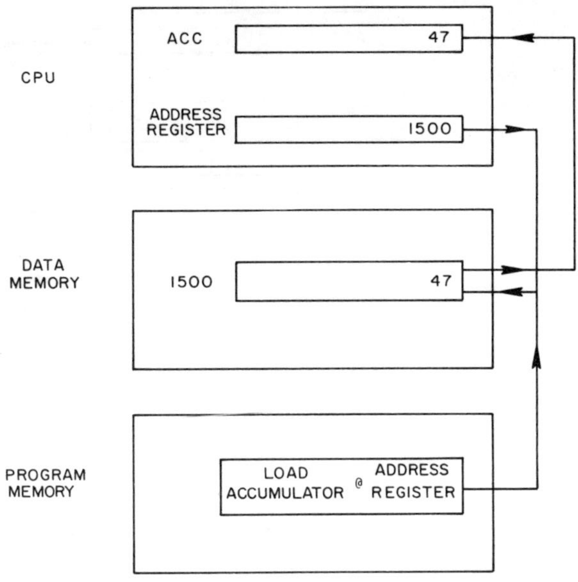

8. Register-indirect addressing can eliminate the delays introduced by memory-indirect addressing. In register addressing, the address of the data is stored in a special register instead of in a memory location.

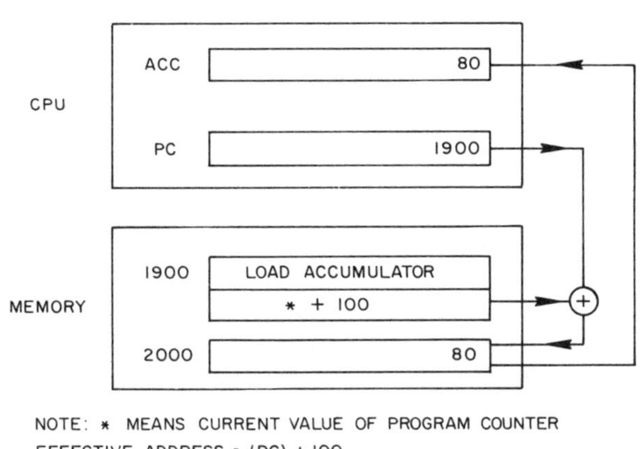

9. Relative addressing techniques require the CPU to add the contents of the program counter to the address that follows the instruction. The sum forms the effective address of the actual data.

Consider a sorting routine that orders an array that starts in memory location 1000 (Fig. 6a) : it cannot be used to sort an array that starts in location 6000. To sort any array but the one that starts in memory location 1000, you first have to move the array. To get around the location problem, indirect addressing can be used in the program to pull the base address of the array from a RAM location (Fig. 6b).

Indirect addressing can simplify array handling, but does add to processing delays, since addresses must be pulled from memory locations. Further, you won't need the index register, and you'll eliminate the additions previously needed

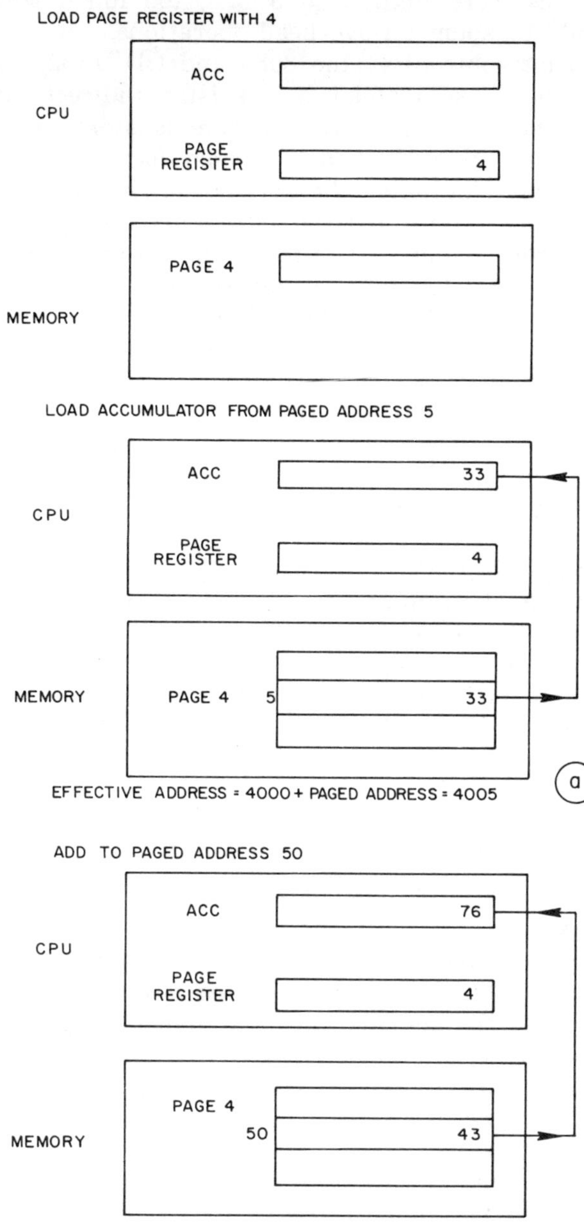

10. When using page addressing, you must first load the system's page register with the hex code for the desired page and refer to a specific address on that page. Then you can get the specific needed data.

to get the effective address.

When you must search a table or array for a particular element, indexing is the simplest method to use. Applications that use all or most of the array elements would probably do better with indirect addressing, though.

Many people find that indirect addressing is difficult to use, because the distinction between data and addresses can be confusing. Most of the popular microprocessors don't have true indirect addressing (as described) available to them, and would need an enormous number of cycles to get a 16-bit address from memory and then use it to get another 16-bit address. Even if some addresses were limited to 8 bits, too much time would be spent on overhead operations.

What some μPs (the 8080 and CDP1802, for example) use instead is "register indirect addressing," in which the address is stored in a register rather than in a memory location (Fig. 8). That eliminates the address fetch cycle. All you have to do to get the data is get the instruction from memory, then place the contents of the address register onto the address bus.

Register indirect addressing does have some advantages over indexing. You do not have to provide an offset as part of the instruction and you can eliminate the 16-bit addition to get the effective address. Thus, you save both program memory and time.

To process a data array, the same procedures used to perform the operations in Fig. 7 can be applied (Fig. 8). However, there is a restriction: you cannot reach any other elements in the array unless the program changes the address stored in the address register. If more than one array element is needed for a program, indexing may prove easier. Indirect addressing is ideal for processing single pieces of data.

Relative addressing keeps addresses short

By using relative addressing you can often keep addresses short and make programs easy to relocate in memory (Fig. 9). To get the effective address, the contents of the program counter are added to the address that is supplied along with the instruction. This procedure is similar to indexing, except that the contents of the program counter are used instead of the contents of the index register.

In Fig. 9, the flowchart shows a procedure that loads the accumulator with data from a memory location that is 100 words away from the instruction. The offset is usually interpreted as a signed two's-complement number so that locations in either direction can be accessed.

Relative addressing is particularly effective if the locations being addressed are very close to the program instruction. And moving programs around in memory won't cause any problems since relative addresses remain the same so you can put a program or subroutine in any unoccupied area of the memory.

Microprocessors can't take full advantage of relative addressing because they have short words and in many cases, read-only program memories. If 16-bit relative addresses are used, they must be stored as two memory words, with two memory cycles needed to recall them. On the other hand, if 8-bit relative addresses are used, you can save space and time but must use locations within ±128 words of the instruction. In most programs, 128 words are not sufficient.

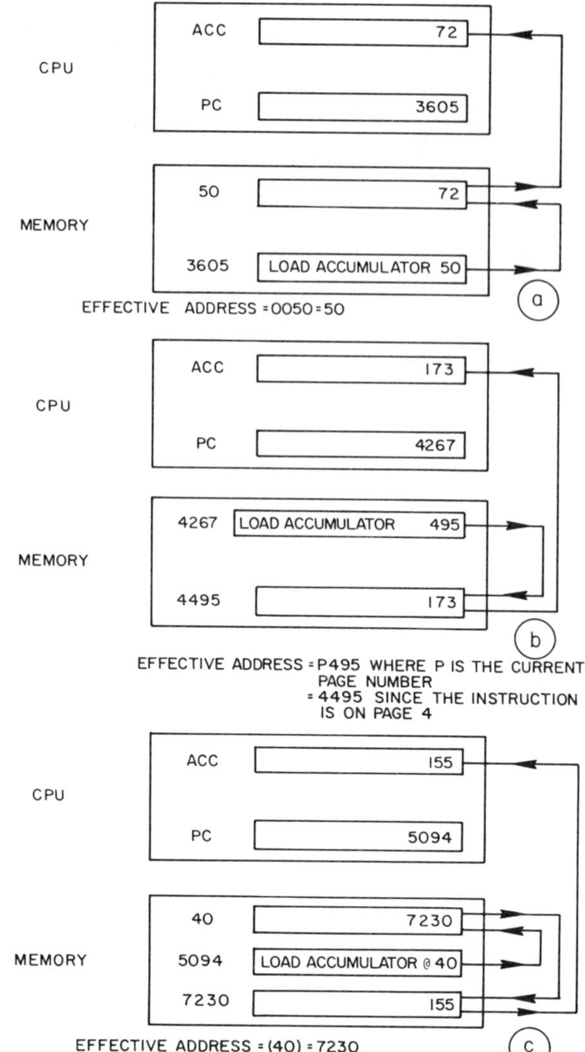

11. **Page-zero addressing permits fast access** of often used data, that are not on the current page, without an extra memory cycle (a). Current-page addressing can rapidly reach locations that are on the same page as the instruction (b). You can also use page-zero addressing indirectly to reach data on other pages (c).

The main advantage of relative addressing in μPs is the use of short offsets as jump addresses. However, just as with indexed addressing, the processor must perform a 16-bit addition to get the effective address each time the relative mode is used. So, slower execution time is traded for memory savings.

Turn the pages carefully

To avoid long addresses in computer programs, paging procedures can be used. Divide the memory into fixed-size sections called pages. You can then refer to a memory location by its page number and its address on that page. Often, the page number is put into a page register and then locations on the same page can be referenced with just the paged address (Fig. 10).

For small programs you can avoid using the

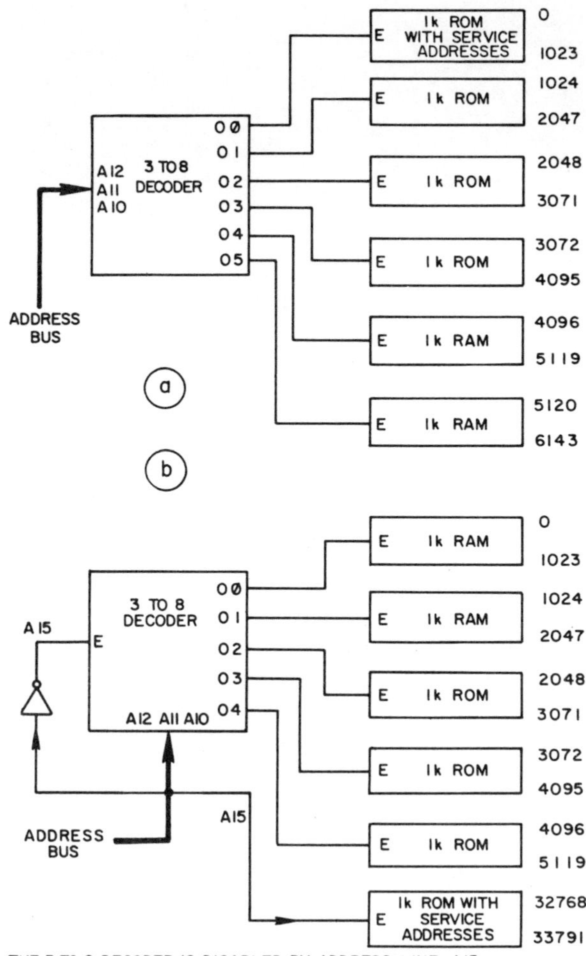

12. **Different memory decoding systems** permit you to store the service routines and addresses in either the lower (a) or upper (b) parts of the memory. With these techniques, you can add extra memory space, if required, up to the addressable maximum. However, memory system design is easier in case (a) since the lower memory configuration is continuous.

page register by limiting the pages that have to be addressed. If only addresses on the first page are used, the technique is called Page-Zero Addressing (Fig. 11a). When you can reach addresses that are on the same page as the current instruction, the technique is called Current-Page Addressing (Fig. 11b). Other pages can be addressed by using an indirect paging method, that is much like the indirect addressing mode (Fig. 11c). Many computers let you select current and zero-page addressing, with just a single bit change in the instruction.

For computers of 16 bits and larger, paging is a great solution to many of the processor limitations. Unfortunately, with μPs, page sizes must be kept to 256 words in order to get paged addresses into 8-bit words. Page zero is, in turn, restricted to 256 words—and there will be many page boundaries that must be handled.

As with relative addressing, you can't use current page addressing for anything except jump instructions because in most cases data are not on the same page as the instructions. Current-page addressing does have the advantages of not requiring a 16-bit addition to get the effective address. The CPU gets the effective address from the eight MSBs of the program counter and the paged address.

If you use page-zero addressing, use a RAM for memory page zero. But remember that you don't want to put your interrupt and startup routines in the RAM, since you'll have to reload them each time the system is turned on. Thus the interrupt and startup service addresses must be stored on a page other than page zero.

However, the addresses on page zero are the easiest to generate since they're only 8 bits long. Additional circuitry, either internal or external, must be used to generate addresses on other pages. Furthermore, decoding is simple if you use a continuous memory that starts at location zero. If the service routines are put at fixed locations, either the memory will have to be divided into sections, or a complex decoding system must be used.

For example, assume you have a system with 6-k words of memory and the lowest 1-k are used to store the service addresses (Fig. 12a). In that case, additional memory can be added without causing any addressing problems. The 3-of-8 decoder can handle up to 8-k words. By using a 4-of-16 decoder you can address up to 16-k words.

A ROM with service addresses at the highest memory addresses can also be used (hexadecimal FF00 and up). The ROM that contains the service addresses must then be placed in a separate area of the memory so that additional memory can be added without moving that ROM (Fig. 12b). System design is made more difficult because the memory space must be divided into two sections.

If service addresses are externally generated to handle large interrupts, systems 8-bit addresses can be generated on page zero by using some encoders. Extra circuitry will be needed to generate 16-bit addresses and place them on the data bus in 8-bit sections.

Bibliography

M6800 Microprocessor Applications Manual, Motorola, Inc., Phoenix, AZ, 1975, pp. 2-45 - 2-46.

Nichols, A.J. and McKenzie, K., "Build a Compact Microcomputer," *Electronic Design*, Vol. 24, No. 10 (May 10, 1975), pp. 84-92.

Torrero, E. A., "Focus on Microprocessors." *Electronic Design*, Vol. 22, No. 18 (September 1, 1974), pp. 52-69.

Torrero, E.A., "An Introduction to Microprocessors," *Electronic Design*, Vol. 24, No. 9 (April 26, 1976), pp. 58-62.

Vacroux, A.G., "Explore Microcomputer I/O Capabilities," *Electronic Design*, Vol. 23, No. 10 (May 10, 1975), pp. 114-119.

SECTION II

Some Alternatives to Microprocessors

Though the versatility of microprocessors makes it possible to use them almost anywhere, this doesn't mean that they always yield an optimum design. Before an engineer commits himself to a microprocessor he should look carefully at the alternatives. For example, a custom integrated circuit may offer higher speed or lower power dissipation. If the equipment is going to be manufactured in huge quantities, the average cost of a custom circuit may be lower than that of a microprocessor system.

For relatively simple logic configurations, the microprocessor may provide overkill capability. Also the microprocessor's iterative procedures may make it much slower than other types of programmable circuits such as the programmable logic array (PLA) or its cousins the programmable gate array (PGA) and the programmable read-only memory (PROM). This section of the book examines the tradeoffs for some of the alternatives.

Microprocessors versus Custom LSI

JIM GOLD
Western Editor,
Electronic Design

Today's design engineer faces a problem: Should he design a new project in-house using a microprocessor, or should he buy a custom LSI circuit from an outside vendor?

Most of the time, the decision isn't easy. The engineer must consider both circuit-development cost and time. These must be balanced against production costs and future design changes.

Sometimes the nature of the product itself may dictate the use of either a custom LSI or a μP. The size of the final product may freeze the choice. It would be nearly impossible to make a μP-based wristwatch and still have it fit on a wrist, and the power consumption would also rule against a watch application. Similarly, most μPs are not fast enough to handle numerous I/O operations on a real-time basis, nor are they structured for a "soft-fail" application such as an automotive controller.

"Engineers are continually forcing μPs into applications where μPs are not suited—high volume applications, where system cost and the limitations of having extra flexibility show up," says John Hall of MicroPower Systems, Santa Clara, CA. "You can mechanize a clock with a μP, but it wouldn't be cost effective."

Ben Anixter of Advanced Micro Devices, Sunnyvale, CA, carries this thought one step further: "Historically, custom circuits always cost more than standard products, although in specific systems standard circuits can represent an overkill or underkill solution."

And that's really the point. How *does* the designer tell which approach is better in his particular situation?

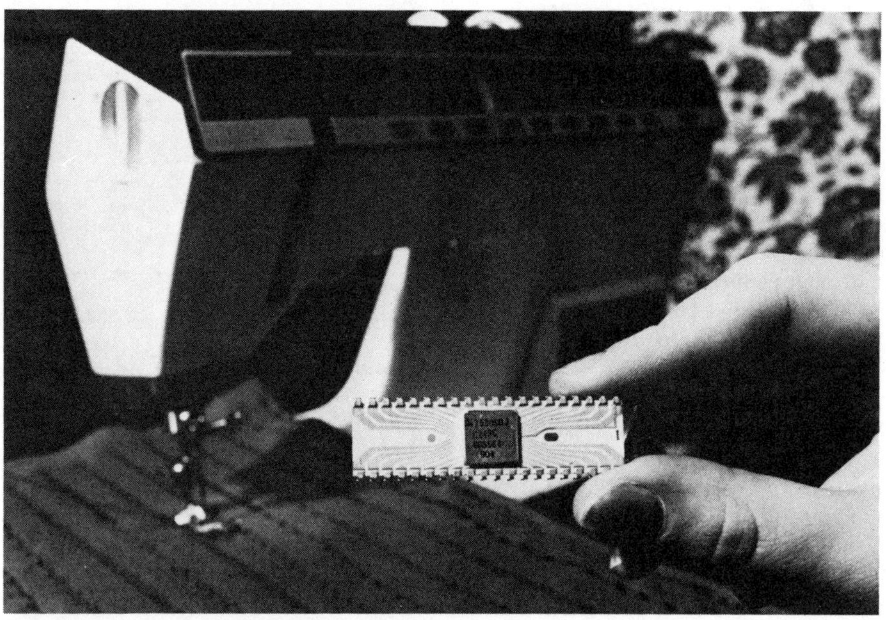

Sewing machine control chip replaces 350 mechanical parts. AMI made the custom LSI circuit to Singer's specifications.

He looks at the number of systems he must build, and he looks at the time it will take to build them . . . and at the manpower and assembly requirements.

He looks at the final product's performance and its required flexibility . . . and at the money required for start-up and at the reliability of custom parts vendors.

Finally, he looks at his crystal ball and projects the project's future. With all this in mind, he sets the project's course and proceeds to implement his decision.

How many systems? When?

"Custom LSI can be attractive to us at the ten thousand pieces per year level," claims Bill Sanderson, custom MOS manager at National Semiconductor, Santa Clara, CA. But most other IC houses require a minimum order committment of 30,000 to 100,000 parts to do business. Generally, the larger the volume of circuits required, the more desirable the custom LSI business becomes for both vendor and customer.

This point is illustrated by the video games market. Home video games sell in large quantities for a low average selling price, and thus are a prime candidate for custom LSI (and, in fact, they are predominantly custom LSI.)

Coin operated arcade-type video games sell in smaller quantities, have more diverse functional requirements, and command a higher selling price. These are generally μP controlled.

Appliance controllers, keyboard encoders, automotive controllers, and electronic organ circuits all are being made today using custom LSI. The television industry is heavily into custom LSI due to the industry's high-volume, very cost-conscious posture.

But there is a practical limit that is reached as the cost of the electronics becomes a smaller and smaller portion of the cost of the finished product, and other factors override volume considerations. Factors such as time.

The time required to produce prototype quantities of custom LSI circuits is an important issue for the designer. Generally six to nine months is a realistic figure, but various manufacturers are developing techniques for reducing it.

American Microsystems, Inc. (AMI) of Santa Clara, CA, is developing a computer-aided layout and artwork generation system, and Signetics has a standard building-block Composite Cell Logic for use on custom circuits. The Signetics approach reduces to about 20 weeks the time needed to prototype quantities at the 300 to 400-gate level of complexity.

"Custom chips in ten weeks for $10,000 are not far off," with improved design and layout aids, according to Jim Meyer of Silicon Systems in Santa Ana, CA.

Time is an important concern in using custom LSI, because in many instances there is a real risk that someone will beat you to the marketplace.

"Future shock is on us in spades," emphasized Bob Lloyd, National Semiconductor's group director for MOS/LSI systems. "The useful manufacturing life of equipment is getting shorter, and sometimes response time in getting to market is more important than manufacturing cost."

Prototype first-generation systems frequently are designed with μPs in them, so they can get into the marketplace quickly, while custom circuits are developed to replace the μPs to lower costs later. "Microprocessor-based systems get to market sooner than hard-wired systems, achieve a greater market share, exhibit longer usage lifetimes, and are more profitable," stated Bill Baker, group director for μPs at National Semiconductor.

The custom LSI vendor is quick to point out that substantial savings can be achieved using their approach in not having to hire hard-

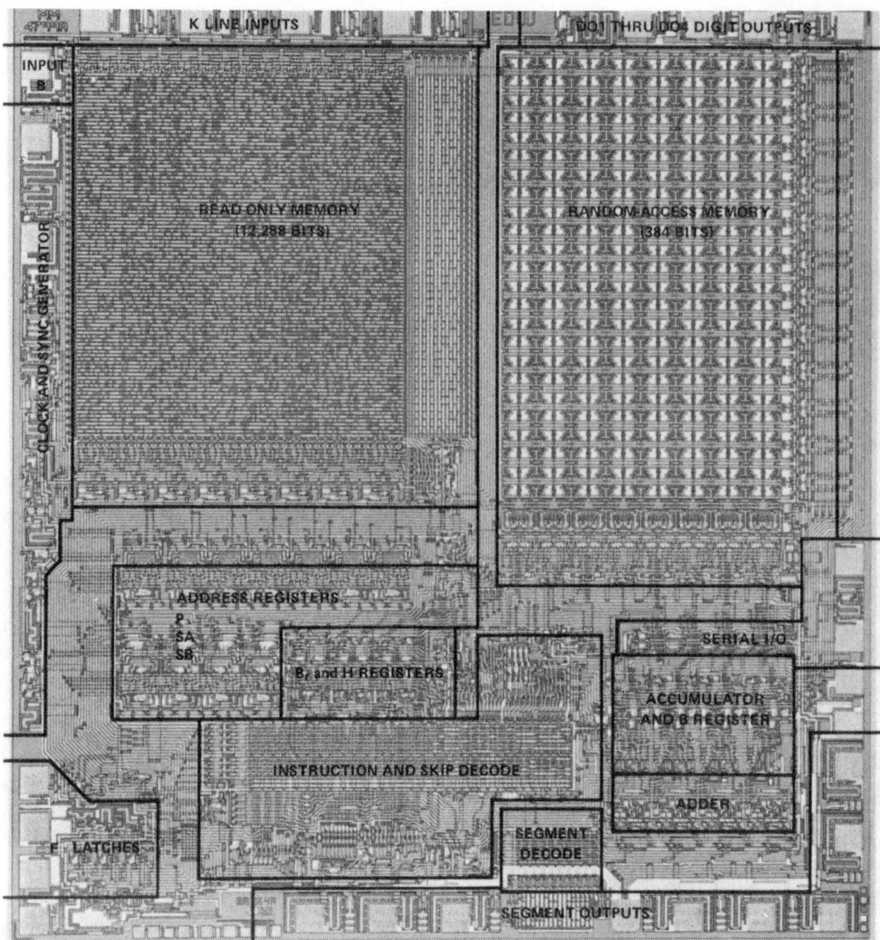

Programmable calculator chip from National Semiconductor processes 4-bit data words and 8-bit instruction words. It contains all system-timing, arithmetic and logic, RAM, and control-ROM functions.

ware, software, and interface engineers to support a μP development project. (This engineers team must also be charged with selecting the correct μP to do the job). In addition, software documentation is not required for the custom LSI part, unless it is programmable.

It is true too, that a number of the standard μP manufacturers have spent significant amounts of money on μP-support hardware and software. Some μPs, such as PACE and SC/MP from National Semiconductor, are grouped into "families" so that understanding of one greatly facilitates learning the other.

Already some μPs are departing from the scene, and the designer who choses the wrong μP for his system may have to redesign if his chosen one is discontinued. Custom circuits, on the other hand, are contracted for on an individual basis and cannot, with impunity, be discontinued.

System assembly costs are also reduced by using custom LSI. There are fewer parts in inventory since one custom chip usually replaces a μP *plus* support chips. There are fewer leads to solder, and thus higher reliability and lower assembly costs.

Smaller, cheaper power supplies can be used with custom LSI designs generally, too.

Performance and flexibility

Microprocessors tend to have only digital inputs and outputs, but custom LSI may have any type of communication with the outside world that the user is willing to pay for. Custom ICs can be designed with specific I/O functions on-chip—for example, triac drivers, or special automotive-sensor interfaces.

Where the particular application is input/output intensive the implementation leans toward a custom chip. But on the other hand, where it is computation intensive, the μP would gain an edge. If the I/O intensive application could be structured into a bus-oriented design, the bus-oriented μP, of course, would be preferred.

Alternatively, applications requiring much floating-point arithmetic might demand either a sophisticated μP or even a minicomputer. The μP is a general-purpose device, and in the absence of other considerations, unless sufficient use is made of its generality, a custom circuit may be a better choice.

A μP is ideally suited for applications in self-diagnostic systems, or systems that can be field-modified to upgrade performance.

In fact, the advent of the μP allows the manufacturer of many similar products to take advantage of the benefits of mass production. He may initially make all of the products identical, and then customize them by providing individual control ROMs for the μPs. For example, one generalized traffic-light controller may be mass-produced, and customized for each street installation by ROM coding.

The μP approach allows simple modification of the circuit operation with software changes, where the custom circuit has only the flexibility it was designed with. This is significant. For example, a recent seatbelt interlock design had to go through over five iterations of functional design before it was acceptable. It used custom-LSI circuitry, for a μP-based design, on the other hand, only the ROM would have had to be changed.

Flexibility may also be needed to respond to competitors' moves in the marketplace.

Start-up costs and risks

"The custom-LSI producer has to get his development money in advance, otherwise there's always the risk that the customer will cancel halfway through the development process," states Clement Lee, LSI product manager for Signetics.

The figures on start-up charges vary from company to company, but they generally range from $25,000 to $60,000, with $35,000 as a good average.

But the dollar-commitment includes more than the initial start-up costs. Custom LSI vendors also generally require a commitment to

158 TTL NAND gates await connections to become a custom circuit. TRW Systems uses this approach to provide six-week turnaround to working parts.

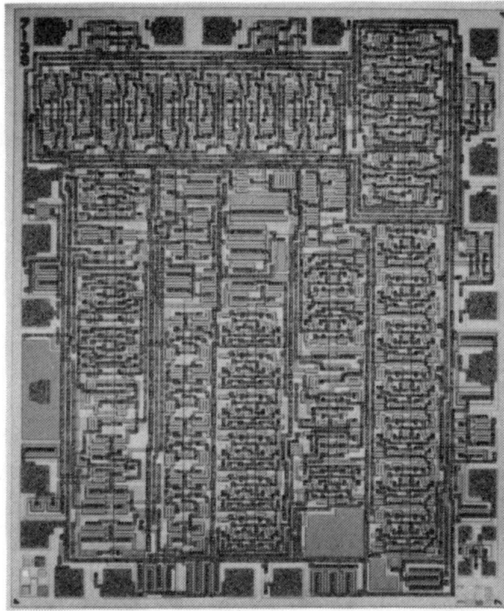

High-density CMOS CB-frequency synthesizer made by MicroPower Systems to Fanon/Courier's design.

buy a certain minimum quantity of parts at preset prices over some period of time.

The larger IC houses frequently require a guarantee of $250,000 to $1-million in profitable sales revenues to institute a custom project. Smaller vendors require correspondingly fewer guaranteed sales.

And there are always some risks in buying custom LSI. One risk is the problem of second-sourcing. It does little good to be able to point to a contract in court when your custom LSI house has trouble delivering parts. Second-sources for custom parts can be as important as for standard ones.

"I don't want to do custom busi-

ness with you if you don't own the mask set, according to Ron Hammer, CMOS product manager for Intersil in Cupertino, CA. "I've never worked for a semiconductor company that didn't have problems occasionally producing products. It's not fair to the customer, nor to the company to sole-source custom products."

But only just recently have custom LSI vendors started cooperating on sharing the process parameters needed to allow use of the same photomasks on two vendors' wafer-fabrication lines. Many processes are still not second-sourced, so the danger of process problems affecting deliveries still exists.

Many IC houses do not like being used merely to process wafers using customers' masks, and Advanced Micro Devices is one.

"Some customers see the vendor as a foundry, remarks Ben Anixter. "Just processing wafers to someone else's masks is not cost effective. The only time to do that is when the industry is in a slump. There just isn't sufficient value-added to make a profit. Capitalism is risk-reward, that's very foreign to the custom circuit guy."

The custom circuit offers the potential user security, in that it is almost impossible for a competitor to copy it exactly in less than a year, according to an LSI feasibility study by MicroPower Systems. Security is particularly important in feature-sensitive consumer industries, such as the television, automotive, and appliance arenas. However, a custom circuit often can be copied functionally by a μP.

Another risk in using custom LSI is that after an IC is designed based upon a breadboard circuit, the IC may not function the same way the breadboard did. Propagation delays on a single integrated circuit are faster than in communicating between chips. Circuit loading is different, and power dissipations change.

Some of these problems can be sidestepped if you use techniques for avoiding race conditions, and employ totally clocked systems. These risks of device nonfunction can be minimized by consultation with custom-LSI vendors.

"The high-volume user is taking us to a more custom product. As a result, we have to take the fat out of our processors," explains Joe Mingione, director of custom products at AMI. "Dedicated processors make a lot of sense—the automotive area comes to mind."

The markets for video games, microwave ovens, whitegoods timers, television, sewing machines, and telecommunications are also fields where custom μPs are now being used.

"If the customer needs the I/O-control-oriented functions of the F-8, there's no way that custom circuits can compete in function. And this holds for the TMS-1000 and 8048, too, claims Don Winstead of Fairchild Micro Systems, San Jose, CA. "We expect to see prices in the \$3 to \$5 range in 100k quantities on these."

These parts and the new PPS-4/1 introduced by Rockwell International in Anaheim, CA, are true μPs, but with customer-specified ROM and RAM on-chip. The F-8 is typical, with a \$1500 charge for masking the ROM and six week delivery on custom-masked parts.

Calculator-oriented μPs

The requirement for families of hand-held calculator products with ever-increasing repertoires of instructions led to small, cheap, simple calculator-oriented processors whose initial hallmarks were keyboard entry and LED-display outputs. These have been expanded in function to BCD output as well, and are well suited to the minimum-system, dumb-controller market. Uses in parking meters and appliance timers, or as computation blocks for μP-based systems, are naturals for this kind of product.

The calculator-oriented processor also, when it does not have all of its ROM and RAM on-chip, may be structured using separate instruction and data busses to simplify programming and optimize memory requirements.

The cost of modifying a calculator-oriented processor (COP) for a custom application is in the \$5000 to \$10,000 range, and about three months are required, according to Bob Lloyd.

"We're seeing a trend toward general-purpose architectures, and general-purpose designs," he explained, "but not a general-purpose chip. We're seeing designs where

Doing it in custom LSI

The first thing the designer must do is define all of the circuit's characteristics as well as possible. That means identifying input and output functions and electrical parameters, and outlining the timing relationships between inputs and outputs. It also means specifying power-supply voltage ranges and operating temperature range.

A schematic or block diagram should be generated to accomplish the required function, and it should be analyzed for freedom from race conditions, and susceptibility to malfunctions due to illegal input state conditions. Breadboard and computer simulation may well be advised in analyzing the schematic before commiting it to silicon.

Then vendors of custom LSI should be contacted to determine the best process and company to manufacture the parts. The complexity of the circuit may play a part in determining the company chosen. While the state of the art in producing commercially feasible LSI is now in the 5000-gate complexity range, many companies are limited to the 500 to 1000-gate custom business.

Having chosen a vendor, the next steps are to negotiate a contract, pay your money, and receive your parts.

Automatic telephone dialer, a custom LSI circuit that uses μP techniques by Synertek, Santa Clara, CA.

we can change either the digit length or PLA terms, for specific applications or to make a specific product."

The easy way out

Finally, for the lucky few designers whose requirements are for small circuits, there is the do-it-yourself approach to custom LSI, in which a standard IC with many unconnected transistors, gates, and other components is produced in large quantities by an IC manufacturer. Then only a customer-specified metal interconnect is required to produce a custom circuit.

In this technique, frequently the designer himself specifies where the metal runs. The only problems are: Does the chip have enough parts, and can they be connected to do the job? But fifty parts delivered in three weeks for \$1800 is an attractive incentive for exploring this route.

Microprocessors versus Programmable Logic Arrays

SAMUEL DERMAN
Associate Editor,
Electronic Design

"The PLA (Programmable Logic Array) may soon be on its way out. It's going the way of the dinosaur and the dodo bird and will eventually be a museum piece. The microprocessor is pushing it out of existence."

"That's not so. The PLA is not only alive and doing well, but in fact a second generation is being spawned. New devices, now on the drawing boards, will be available soon."

These two views are rather extreme. But they do reflect the variety of opinions heard in today's fast-moving IC marketplace. Uncertainty about which of today's PLAs and μPs will still be available in the future is but one of the problems a design engineer must face in choosing between the two devices.

A Pandora's box of other problems exist, and the ultimate choice of whether to go to PLAs or to μPs must be based on careful evaluation of such factors as:

- Speed in getting a product to the market.

- Second sourcing.

- Power-supply requirements.

- Possible obsolescence of essential components.

- Provision for future design changes.

- Speed of handling input/output (I/O) functions.

- Total cost.

- The type of problem to be solved (PLAs and μPs are not equivalent devices).

First come, first sold

Experts agree that a tidal wave of new IC-based consumer equipment is about to engulf the marketplace. They feel that already-existing items such as TV-games, automotive devices and point-of-sale terminals represent only the small, visible crest of an approaching flood.

For many manufacturers about to plunge into these turbulent waters the difference between success and failure may hinge on getting their device to the marketplace fast enough to beat out competitors. And achieving such a

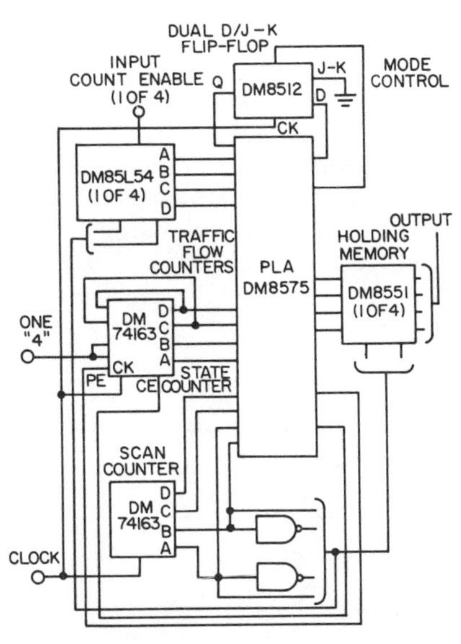

1. **A PLA serves as the control element** to provide the timing interval in this traffic-light controller. Traffic flow in any of four directions is managed by this unit.

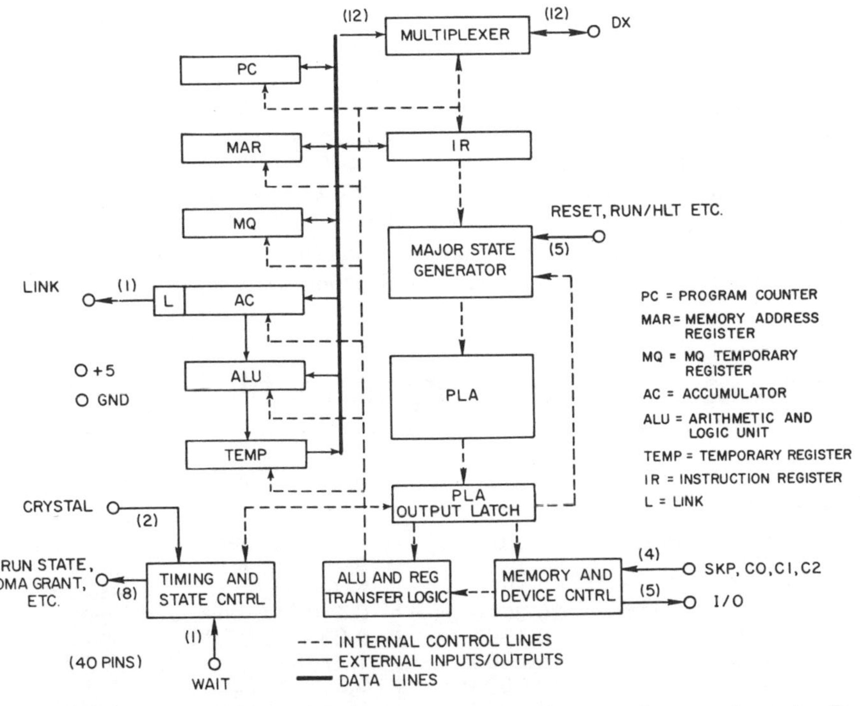

2. **The Intersil IM 6100, 12-bit microprocessor** is one of a number of μPs that use PLAs for sequencing the CPU.

fast design turn-around time may dictate that a Field Programmable Logic Array (FPLA) be used in place of a μP (or any other logic device)—at least at first.

FPLAs, in contrast to earlier mask-programmable units, can be programmed "on the spot" (see box). Any problems that are discovered can be corrected for, simply by programming a new unit and discarding the old one. Later on, as time permits, a mask can be designed so that mask-programmable arrays, which are more amenable to volume production—can be used.

An important point to note is that FPLA prices have been coming down, to the point where it's impossible to state flatly that mask devices are always cheaper for production runs.

Prices as well as ease of programming the FPLA, must be carefully checked against the costs encountered in using a mask. And into the equation must be added the additional expense and anguish that inevitably accompanies the discovery of errors in the logic—after the mask has been delivered.

Applications abound

Like the ubiquitous μP, the PLA can be used to implement or simplify an increasing number of digital logic-based devices.

"A PLA can simplify many traditional ROM applications," says Dale Mrazek of National Semiconductor, Santa Clara, CA. One use he cites is in code conversion. Another is in traffic controllers.

"These controllers usually require a random set of simultaneous input variables to satisfy a particular state. The condition then allows an advance to the next con-

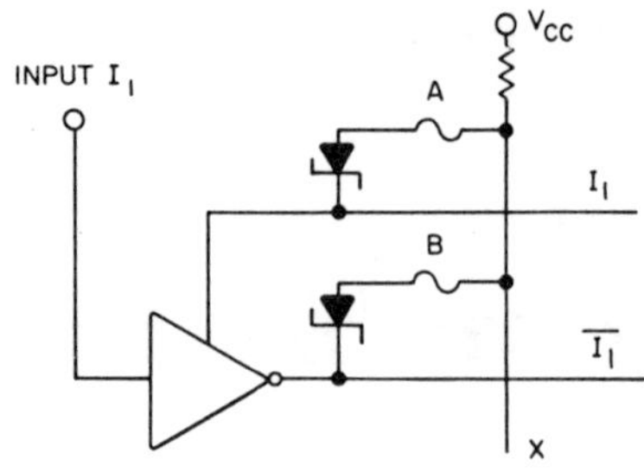

3. **Fusible links in an FPLA** allow the designer to form a wide variety of logic configurations. In this example, one input circuit is connected to an FPLA. The designer can select either the input, I_1, or its complement, $\overline{I_1}$, depending on whether he fuses link B or link A. The resulting signal appears on line X.

troller state of the sequencer," he points out.

In systems such as traffic controllers the PLA is used in an area usually dominated by the μP—applications requiring a time sequence of operations.

For such applications, it may seem that the time and effort required to program the PLA may be less than that needed to develop the necessary μP software. But such a quick judgement may prove erroneous.

In the early stages of μP development, it would have been accurate to state that compared to the PLA, the μP was a more difficult device to program and debug. But today, many engineers are familiar with μPs, and the required software has gone through a "refining" process.

As a result, all one can say nowadays is that ease of programming —whether for a μP or a PLA— depends to a large degree on the

skill and background of the user.

Gopol Ramachandran, senior applications engineer at Intersil, Cupertino, CA, cites an application where the FPLA is currently finding increased use.

Taking advantage of the FPLA's ability to decode a particular address rapidly, engineers are now using these devices to implement the ASCII standard interface bus (IEEE 488-1975).

An FPLA is connected to each piece of equipment on the line, with the FPLA serving as a decoder to determine which items of equipment is being "spoken to" at any particular moment.

Such a decoder can be implemented with random logic as well, or even with μPs, Ramachandran says, but the FPLA does it very simply and economically using only two items, an FPLA and a dual-D flip-flop.

In applications where speed of operation is important, the PLA wins over the μP hands down. The PLA basically senses the logic state of a set of inputs and delivers a particular output in response to these inputs. It's a one-shot operation, and the delay (from input to output) might be on the order of 100 ns or less. For the Signetics 82S100 and 82S101 Bipolar FPLAs for example, the spec sheets list the maximum propagation delay as 50 ns. The Intersil IM5200 FPLA has a maximum delay of 100 ns.

In contrast to the "one shot" action of the PLA, a μP must sequentially step through a series of operations to solve a given logic problem. This, of necessity, takes a longer time. A "logical decode" operation, for example which might take 50 ns using PLAs, would require about 15 to 30 μs

Characteristics of programmable logic

	Speed	Volume Cost/Function	Device Reliabiilty	Programming Method
Random Logic	0.7-200 ns	2 to 50¢/gate	Very High	Wire interconnects
PLA	50 ns	$25	High	Masks
FPLA	50 ns	$30	Medium	Fusible Links
ROMs	20-3000 ns	0.1 to 1¢/bit	High	Masks
PROMs	20-1500 ns	0.25 to 3.0¢/bit	Medium	Fusible Links
EAROMs	450-3000 ns	1-2¢/bit	Medium	Trapped Charges
RAMs	2-3000 ns	0.2 to 5¢/bit	Medium	Writing
CAMs	30-1000 ns	15¢/bit	Medium	Writing
Microprocessors	55-250 ns	$15 to $40/chip	High	Any or all of the above elements

if implemented with a single-chip MOS μP.

It's important, however, to restrict any comparisons of speed only to those (limited) applications that can be implemented by both devices.

Vive la difference

"PLAs and μPs currently do not serve exactly the same function," says Milt Baumwolspiner of Bell Labs, Holmdel, N.J. "It's not like comparing, say LEDs with liquid-crystal displays." PLAs and μPs often can complement each other, as for example when a PLA is used as part of a μP (see Fig. 2).

The non-equivalency of the PLA and μP is further emphasized by John Birkner of Monolithic Memories Inc., Sunnyvale, CA. "In the past, μPs have been used in high-performance applications such as airborne navigational computers or minicomputers. But the direction they're taking today is towards low-performance applications in which the μP is basically the only element needed," he says.

"In large-volume applications the PLA is fitting into the high-performance market, although for certain small applications a PLA and μP can work together."

A simple example, Birkner says is putting a latch at the output of a PLA to generate a sequencer. Such a sequencer can be used for a microcycle timing generator.

Birkner feels that present-generation PLAs find use in two main areas. The first is in micro-instruction decoders in minicomputer-like devices. Macro-instructions may be thought of as operation codes specifying particular subroutines.

The subroutines lead to micro-instruction sequences that directly perform operations such as fetching immediate values, or register or memory contents.

A second popular PLA application is for ROM patches. Suppose a PLA is used to decode an address—in a magnetic tape controller, for example. At some future time the microprogram for the controller may need revisions. Then, rather than throw away all his PROMs and program new ones, the engineer uses a PLA to decode the address locations he wants to change. The PLA can be used either to generate new data or to

All about PLAs

A PLA basically is an array of logic gates (ANDs, ORs, NANDS, NORS, etc.) all formed on a single IC chip. The gates can be joined together to form any combinatorial logic function desired. That is, given a certain digital input, the collection of gates will deliver a particular digital output.

The input signals first pass through a series of AND gates, resulting in a predetermined number of product terms being formed. In present-day PLAs and FPLAs this number runs anywhere from about 40 to 150. The product signals then pass through a set of OR gates to become the final output signals.

A typical FPLA, the Monolithic Memories Model 5780/6780, for example, comes configured with 14 inputs and 8 outputs. Depending on the logic state (one or zero) of each of these 14 inputs, a particular bit pattern will appear at the output. For example, The binary number 00010011000011 at the input might be the signal to cause the number 10010111 to appear at the output.

Figure 4 illustrates two elementary examples of how a PLA can be connected to implement a combinatorial logic function. These examples are based on a PLA with only one output (labelled F_y) instead of eight.

In the first example, the PLA is connected to synthesize the logic function

$$F_y = \overline{CD} + A\overline{B} + A\overline{C} + \overline{A}C$$

Example 2 illustrates the synthesis of $F_y = ABC + \overline{A}\overline{C}D$

PLAs are currently available in two types, depending on the method used for connecting the logic gates.

Mask programmable arrays, as the name suggests, use a pre-designed overlay or mask as the final step in manufacture to form the desired connections.

Field programmable arrays, a more recent development, are manufactured with all their gates initially connected in all possible arrangements. The connections are made through Ni-Cr links, which may be selectively open-circuited (fused) by passing a high current through them. This capability allows the designer to achieve his desired logic synthesis.

Although both the PLA and the FPLA are programmable, they are not erasable. Once programmed, they cannot be changed. In practice, some changes can be made in an already programmed FPLA by blowing out still-intact links, but links, once open circuited, cannot be replaced.

A PLA needs only one power supply, in contrast to present-day μPs, which require anywhere from one to three. Current bipolar PLAs consume about 1/2 W. By contrast, a CMOS μP (RCA's 1802, for example) takes 30 to 40 mW. An MOS μP requires even more power, and a bipolar unit consumes the most.

Current manufacturers of PLAs and FPLAs include National Semiconductor, Monolithic Memories, Intersil, Signetics and Hughes.

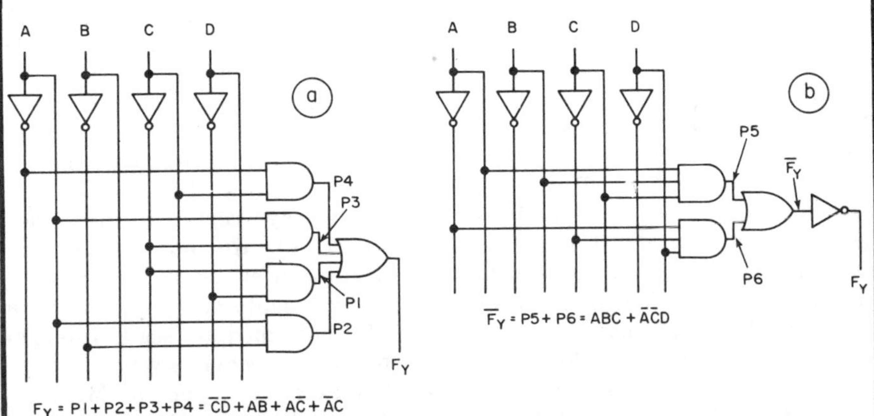

4. A simple PLA with only four inputs and one output can still be configured to provide a large variety of logic functions. Two examples are shown above.

call up another (new) PROM.

For example, if an item of information in location 39 in the PROM msut be changed, then the PLA is programmed to decode that particular location. Then, whenever the PLA senses that location 39 is wanted, it either provides new data or turns on another PROM.

"It's a way of preserving most of your original PROM by adding some patches," Birkner points out. "And if the PLA has terms left over, you can update your old PROM more than once."

Despite the large number of differences that separate the PLA and the μP, there is an area of similarity in the operation of both. Both may be programmed (but in different ways) to allow for design corrections or for future modifications.

The operation of the μP can be changed by changing its software —that is, by reprogramming its ROM. The older, mask-programmable array can be reprogrammed only by designing a new mask. The more recent FPLA is reprogrammed by burning out certain fusable links to form the desired logic pattern.

In designs where it is known that reprogramming will be necessary, it is usually the complexity of the design that will dictate whether a PLA or a μP offers the greater combination of advantages.

Although the PLA is basically a one-chip device, additional elements are often needed to realize a given design. Present-day μPs also generally require the combination of a number of chips of support circuitry to implement a particular application. The minimum number of such elements is two.

But μP designers are not sitting idly by, letting their chips pile up. One direction that μP design is heading, is toward combining the CPU with support circuitry, all on one element.

In the popular F-8 μP family, for example, the one-kilobyte Program Storage Unit (PSU) will be combined with the CPU, reports John Katsaros, marketing engineer at Fairchild Semiconductor, San Jose, CA. "This unit should be out next January," he says.

Reports indicate that Intel is also planning a similar chip, and the Texas Instruments TMS-1000

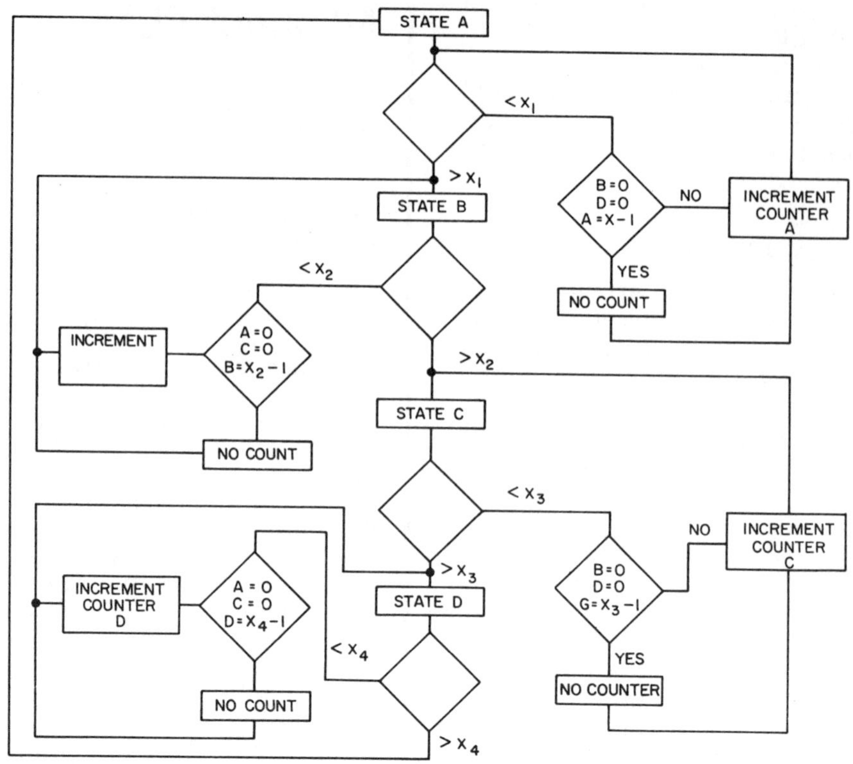

5. **The functions of the traffic controller** are shown in this state diagram. The controller checks all the other states to obtain the correct timing interval for the present state.

unit has been available for some time.

A peek at the crystal ball

What about the future?

Activity in the μP market is well publicized these days, with the latest efforts of manufacturers aimed at squeezing as much capability as possible onto one chip. This trend would remove one of the large drawbacks to wider μP application, namely the need for support chips.

Although the drive to build cheaper, high-voltage (4 and 8-bit) μPs continues unabated, there is still a great amount of effort in the higher-priced 16-bit units.

In the world of PLAs, optimism is not universal throughout the industry. Today's FPLAs (which have largely replaced the older mask-PLAs) are not competitive either in price or in speed with existing small-scale integration (SSI) and medium-scale integration (MSI) technology.

For example, a popular MSI circuit, the Priority Encoder Model 74148 can be synthesized by an FPLA. But when relative cost and speeds are compared, today's FPLA comes out far behind.

The Model 74148 is a 16-pin package, while the larger FPLA comes with 24. Even more important, the PLA sells for $15 to $20, while the MSI unit is now down to about 50 cents. Further, the MSI introduces a delay (input to output) of only about 20 ns as compared to 50 to 100 ns for the FPLA.

Unfavorable comparisons like these are providing incentives for improved designs by at least two FPLA manufacturers.

Easier use and speeds faster than 50 ns are some of the goals planned for tomorrow's FPLAs at Monolithic Memories. Lower prices are in the offing, too.

And at National Semiconductor, although engineers are reluctant to discuss their next-generation FPLAs, it's clear they will contain logic elements even more complex than today's versions.

"Tomorrow's FPLAs will attack the Model 7400 SSI and MSI market," says John Birkner of MMI. When these latest designs go on the market, the attack should become an exciting battle.

SECTION III

Testing and Debugging Microprocessor Systems

Testing large scale integrated (LSI) circuits has always been difficult because of their complexity. But with microprocessors the problems are compounded to the point where there are no easy answers. There are dozens of different microprocessors on the market and, except for de facto standards that result from industry second-sourcing of successful designs, there has been almost no standardization. Furthermore, each microprocessor can be used in so many different ways that it's probably impossible to test for every mode of operation. Even if it were possible, the cost would be prohibitive. Because of its impact on reliability and cost, testing is a crucial topic for everyone involved with microprocessors.

The first article in this section examines the tradeoffs involved for four important approaches: self diagnosis, comparison, pattern generation, and stored-response testing. A second article looks at benchmark testing, in which a microprocessor is timed for some task, such as a short program, that is representative of the actual application. The third article shows how today's advanced logic analyzers can be used to check out microprocessor systems. Readers are also directed to the articles that describe dedicated testers in Sections IV and V.

Test Methods for Microprocessors

EUGENE R. HNATEK
DCA Reliability Laboratory,
Mountain View, California

When it comes to testing LSI microprocessors, about the only thing engineers agree upon is that worst-case and benchmark tests are a must. Which tests to run and what constitutes "worst case" depends on whom you talk to.

Why is microprocessor testing so difficult? Because every microprocessor is different. Variations occur in architecture, chip layout, the random logic of the CPU, the fabrication processes and the instruction languages. Add to these the variations in I/O capabilities and pin count (18 to 48), the various bit sizes (4, 8, 12 and 16 bits) and the different bus organizations, and you can see the problem.

There is no one way to test all units. And, in fact, no one—neither the manufacturer nor the user—knows how to test a microprocessor fully. At best, testing is a trial-and-error situation.

At present four major test categories are available to the engineer: the self-diagnostic method, the comparison method, algorithmic pattern generation and stored-response testing (Table 1).

The economical way to test

In the self-diagnostic method, you use a ROM to load into CPU memory (RAM) a worst-case sequence of instructions. The CPU chip is placed within its intended operating environment, including interrupts from peripherals. The instruction set terminates at some identifiable error location. Error indication, usually identified by an instruction routine, shows if the unit fails or passes.

Most small users of CPU chips test with self-diagnosis, because it can be implemented easily with laboratory equipment or with hardware and assistance from the chip manufacturer. But there are shortcomings to this apparently economical technique, including the following:

■ Multiple errors may negate each other and be undetected.

■ The actual cause of a failure may not be diagnosed.

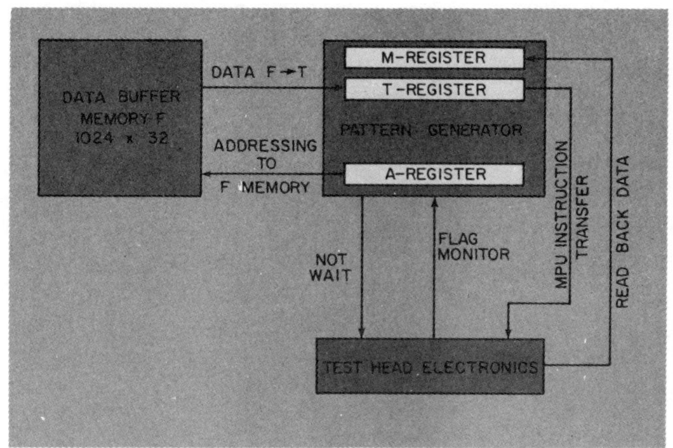

1. Low-cost CPU tester uses algorithmic pattern generation to verify a microprocessor's instruction set. The method can also be used to check memories.

■ Long diagnostics may have to run to completion, even if an early failure occurs. This results in unnecessarily long test times.

■ Without special hardware, external environment conditions, such as interrupts, cannot be tested under worst-case conditions.

The comparison approach

Another widely used test method compares the CPU with a known good device. With both devices mounted close to each other, input data are sent simultaneously to both, but with separate drivers. Output data are monitored from both devices and are considered valid when data coincidence occurs.

The method, which lends itself to production testing, has many inherent benefits. Real-time-cycle response testing is possible. Implementation is not difficult, chiefly because output data need not be stored in a memory for comparison. But, again, there are also drawbacks.

First, dependence on a known good device for comparison imposes the task of defining such a device. Second, dependence on a designer to specify the test pattern tends to limit the flexibility to changes or modifications in the input test pat-

Table 1. Basic microprocessor test methods

Test Method	Application			Devices Tested			Summary of Characteristics	Available Test Equivalent
	*	**	†	Memory	Logic	CPU		
Self-Diagnostic	√					√	Tests •Limited diagnostic (Functional only) Limitations: 1) Error Negation 2) Timing Varies	None Commercially Available
Comparison		√			√	√	Tests: •Functional Only •No Parametric Measurements Limitations: 1) Dependence on Known Good Device 2) Identical Faults Between Known & Unknown Device Undetected 3) Inflexibility to Change Input Test Pattern 4) Synchronization Between Good CPU & DUT	None Commercially Available
Algorithmic Pattern Generation	√				√	√	Tests: •Functional Only •Flexible programming Limitations: 1) Partial Outputs 2) Personality Board 3) Requires That Test Engr Understand CPU Architecture & Application	Macrodata MD-104 Micro Control M-10 Data Test DT-400
Stored Response	√	√	√	√	√	√	Tests: •Functional Parametric & Dynamic •Extensive Engrg & Evaluation Modes •Multiplexed Operation •Emulation 1) Easy To Implement 2) Uses Reference Device •Simulation 1) Harder To Implement 2) Minimal Programming Effort 3) Flexibility To Change Program 4) High Hardware Cost For Super Buffer & Added PROMs & Pattern Generator 5) Depends On Known Good Device	Fairchild Systems Technology S-610 Macrodata MD-154 MD-501 Tektronix S-3260

* Incoming Inspection   **Production   † Engineering Evaluation/QC

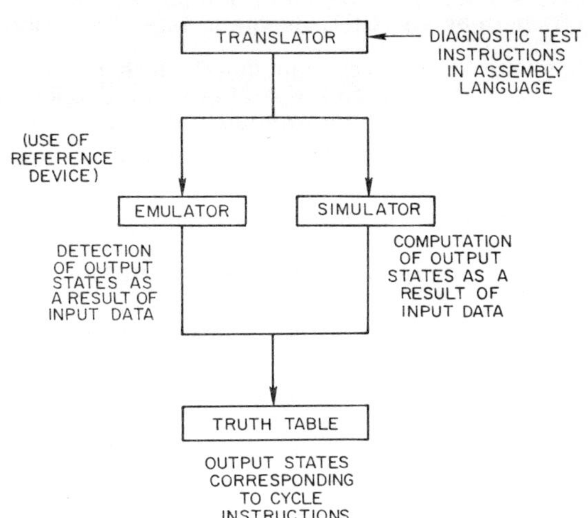

2. Steps in emulation and simulation testing: Both methods store user-written diagnostics in bulk memory.

tern, making the degree of test completeness somewhat questionable. Another problem can be encountered when you attempt to synchronize the known good CPU and the one under test. Finally, limitations in functional testing under dynamic conditions and lack of parametric measurements are severe drawbacks.

Algorithmic pattern generation

Still another test method—one that keeps cost down and can be used to test memories as well— is algorithmic pattern generation (Fig. 1). A CPU usually contains an instruction set that specifies an operation in conjunction with an operand. Each instruction is well-defined, in the sense that an exact result can be expected after execution of an instruction over its existing operand. However, it is not always feasible to monitor the executed output of a single instruction. Instead, it may be necessary to execute a series of instructions before you can monitor the output.

Since you are especially interested in your own set of instructions, user-oriented testing of any CPU can be reduced to verification of all instructions. But because you may have your own instruction-verification sequence, the ability to readily change the instruction sequence becomes a most desirable feature.

With the pattern-generation technique, you store all instructions (op codes) in a high-speed, local-buffer memory. Depending on the complexity of the expected output, some instructions will go into the local buffer, while the rest are generated by the high-speed pattern generator. All instructions—when addressed in local buffer memory and sent to the CPU—are verified in the

proper sequence. By proper sequence is meant the order of execution of each instruction—arranged at your discretion. This gives you complete control over the device program and permits you, in principle, to attain any needed information about the CPU.

Note that this method is limited to partial functional testing and excludes parametric or dynamic tests. Cost is low, since you need only an optimized data buffer memory. And the method provides flexibility: You can generate your own instruction verification program to take full control of the test program or to change or modify the existing program. Also, the technique lets you diagnose multiple faults.

One note of caution: Because you take control of the test problem, you must be thoroughly familiar with the CPU—from the device architecture to the function of each instruction, arrangement of instruction execution order, and the allocation of local-data buffer memory and expected result generation.

Stored-response testing

The final test category—stored-response testing—encompasses two test development methods and two pattern-generation techniques. Each method stores and executes user-written diagnostics quite differently. With stored-response, you keep an emulation or a simulation program in bulk memory (usually a disc) and then apply the program to the CPU under test to generate output data response.

The emulation process consists of the following steps (Fig. 2): (1) The diagnostic program (in assembly language) is loaded into the test system, translated to machine language (1's and 0's) and then applied to a reference device; (2) During a learning mode, the reference device is tested on a cycle basis with a comprehensive set of diagnostic instructions; (3) The output states of the reference device are recorded in memory; (4) The entire truth table of the device is developed into user language, as well as machine language invisible to the user; (5) The test sequence so derived is then used to test the CPU.

You can simulate the sequence of operation of a CPU in conjunction with all peripheral devices, such as RAMs and ROMs. To do this requires a large RAM or PROM to store a predefined sequence of instructions associated with the appropriate data set. Simulated outputs can be sampled and their logic states identified at a defined sampling period.

In this way, an output pattern can be identified with its corresponding input pattern. This information can be stored in an appropriate buffer memory and, finally, transferred to disc or magnetic tape for permanent storage. To execute

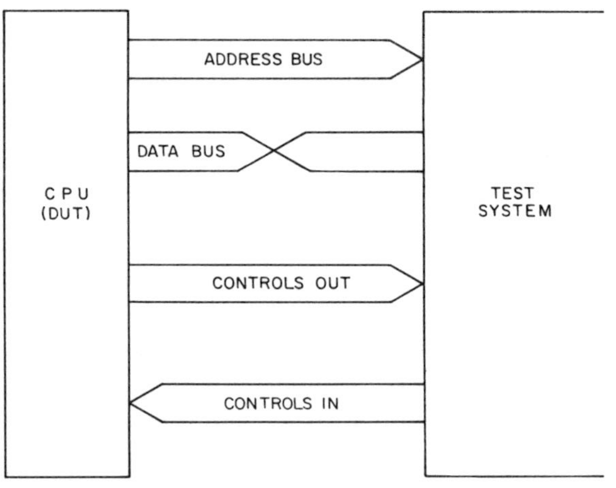

3. The test system provides all necessary stimuli and then senses the microprocessor's response. In most cases the data bus is a two-way street.

Table 2. CPU test system requirements

Computer with 16 to 64K bytes of memory.
Disc storage: Approximately 1 million words.
I/O peripherals: CRT, magnetic tape, line printer.

Software: High-level language, foreground and background operations, production and engineering evaluation modes.

Functional tests: 10-MHz data rate——MOS and bipolar levels.

Parametric tests: Several digitally programmable sources, voltage, current, stress, continuity power dissipation and MOS and bipolar levels.

Dynamic tests: Digitally programmable timing channels.

Pin electronics: Flexible pin electronic modules, 60-to-64-pin capability, separate drivers and detectors per pin with force, compare, inhibit and mask modes at data rates.

Local memory: Each DUT pin has local memory capable of 10-MHz data rates. Chaining or nesting capabilities exist.

the test, the stored pattern is transferred from disc or magnetic tape back to the buffer memory and then to the device under test.

Two independent steps are involved in the technique: pattern identification and test execution. The first step is a one-time operation. Unless program modification is necessary, the generated pattern will be stored permanently on the disc. The second step is a typical procedure that executes the test in a burst mode.

Advantages offered by simulation include easy programming of the test system and flexibility to change the program so that device characterization is easily implemented. But there are tradeoffs. Hardware cost is significantly increased by the need for a "super" buffer; additional PROMs are required for each modification of the program, since the simulator is usually generated by the PROM; and the cost of the pattern simulator and its maintenance—which may require substantial support—must be added to the cost of the test system. In addition simulation depends on a known good device.

Diagnostic emulation, which tests the CPU with its operating instructions, points to the fact that microprocessors are instruction-sensitive. One such problem is related to the jump, interrupt and scratch-pad memory instructions. In MOS LSI, these effects certainly seem to be a way of life. However, simple instructions apparently cause no problem.

Both emulation and simulation have advantages and drawbacks. The emulation method is easier to implement but uses a reference device. The simulation process is more difficult to achieve without extensive knowledge of intrinsic device characteristics, and it requires a high-level language. Some engineers find that their test system computer or software is limited and resort to offline simulation. Note that most CPU suppliers use a variation of the stored-response method to verify the integrity of their devices.

What about test equipment? Of necessity, that required for microprocessor testing is complex and costly. Fig. 3 shows the interface between a microprocessor and its test system. The system must supply stimuli on the clock, control and data-input lines and must sense responses on control, address and data-output lines. Since most microprocessors use a bidirectional data bus, the tester must enable and disable the drivers at high speeds.

For characterization testing, you need a system that can gather and manipulate vast amounts of data, then reduce the information to a meaningful display. One example: The Tektronix S3260 test system. For larger CPUs (12 and 16-bit), you need very large bus and data-handling capabilities that can operate at high speeds (20 MHz) and handle variable instruction sets.

The test system should be able to modify the test program rapidly through an iterative CRT. However, test systems of this caliber are very expensive ($250,000 and up) and not justifiable, unless large quantities of CPUs are to be tested or continuous characterization programs will be performed on a regular basis. For incoming inspection tests, low-cost ($10,000 to $30,000) dedicated testers will provide the desired confidence level (Table 2).

Bibliography:

Christos Chrones, "Testing Microprocessor Chips: A Large Scale Challenge," *Electronic Packaging and Production*, April, 1975.

Benchmark Testing of Microprocessors

SAMUEL DERMAN
Associate Editor,
Electronic Design

The past few years have seen a proliferation in the variety and the complexity of microprocessors. This has been matched by a corresponding increase in the intensity and frequency of headaches afflicting engineers planning to use these devices. The reasons are not hard to find.

In contrast to the less complicated transistor or integrated circuit, a μP's characteristics cannot be fully described by merely presenting data on a specification sheet. For example, a transistor spec sheet might list the gain-bandwidth product. This figure can then be used in design calculations, no matter what the application.

The characteristics of the μP, however, depend strongly on the application, and even on the skill of the user. In the hands of an experienced programmer a μP might perform a given task in a shorter time than under a less-skilled operator.

Benchmarks enter the picture

In an effort to try to evaluate and select from among the increasing variety of μPs, engineers seized upon a tool that was already in use in the computer industry: the benchmark test, a short program or group of routines designed to evaluate the computer's data-handling abilities. The test measures the μP's execution speed and the amount of memory required to perform a given task.

The number of bytes of memory required is directly related to the number of instructions. Execution time is obtained by summing the individual μP steps and multiplying each step by the manufacturer-supplied operation time.

Since the earliest μPs were used for data calculations, such tests seemed valid. But within a short time it became apparent that applications for μPs had spread beyond the confines of mere data handling. New fields opened up for dedicated control in such areas as traffic control, intelligent computer terminals, and electronic test equipment.

Benchmarks called into question

When such applications were considered, the usefulness of the benchmark as a valid μP comparison test began to come into question. One of the reasons cited was that standard benchmark programs are often useless where the μP will be used as a dedicated controller.

In data-manipulation applications, the characteristic speeds are usually measured in microseconds. In contrast, for simple control applications (switches, relays, lights, etc.) the important times are on the order of tenths of a second, so benchmark programs that test only computational speed are irrelevant.

Other disadvantages have emerged. Some of these are:

- It is difficult to establish a general benchmark test useful for all the μPs on the market.
- It is difficult to define a BM test that is not weighted in favor of a particular type of μP architecture.
- For a benchmark to be valid, it must be closely related to the specific μP application. To write such a program takes time, skill, and money.

These problems have not yet been resolved. In fact, the benchmark test has fallen into distinct disfavor over the past year, according to Don Carley, μP-applications engineering manager at RCA, Somerville, NJ. There are even those who question the validity of using the benchmark test altogether.

Those opposed to benchmarking point out yet another problem. They feel that the benchmark test, with its emphasis on speed of processing, may tend to push the μP industry in the wrong direction. Their reasoning is as follows:

One of the big advantages of the μP is that it permits development of a whole class of new, low-cost products. The lower the μP cost, the greater the potential variety of products, and the wider the expected market. In an effort to come up with better benchmark test results, μP manufacturers may tend to pack more performance into their devices than is really required for most applications. The result is an excellent product, but one of limited use and increased cost.

Despite this seemingly formidable array of difficulties, μP benchmarks are still in current use.

Designs of microprocessor software and hardware are discussed by Larry Solomon, Don Carley, and Alexander Young of RCA's Solid-State Division.

There are a number of compelling reasons.

First, and most important, a simple substitute for the benchmark test has yet to be found. Despite its faults, the benchmark does provide a measure of a μP's execution time and memory capability. Based on this data, some preliminary selection can be made from among competing μPs.

Deene Ogden, manager of systems engineering at Texas Instruments, Houston, TX, emphasizes another reason: an important indicator of the cost of programming a μP is the number of instructions, and the clarity and ease of preparation of the code.

"The benchmark test helps determine the cost of the software-development effort. One μP may require many fewer instructions than another, even though both μPs use the same amount of memory. The μP requiring the fewest instructions will usually be easier to program and will contain fewer errors."

Phil Roybal, director of μP marketing at National Semiconductor Corp., Santa Clara, CA, stresses the fact that the benchmarking can provide a fair idea of the end costs of the basic system, such as the memory, or the interfaces.

"You will be in a good position to make trade-offs within the manufacturer's line or among manufacturers. For instance, you can decide to put in an intelligent I/O device to take some of the load off the μP, thus cutting memory and processor costs—but also spending more money on I/O devices."

Use benchmarks carefully

Experts agree that no matter how simple or complex the benchmark, it must be used with care.

"Your test has to be applications oriented," stresses Alex Goldberger of Signetics, Sunnyvale, CA. "What you should do is take a typical part of your program, or a critical part, and try that on several competing μPs and see how they perform."

Some frequently used μP routines that can be benchmarked are:

■ Service an interrupt (ability of the μP to stop what it's doing and do something else).

■ Move a block of data from one part of memory to another. The block can be anywhere from about 50 to 100 bytes.

■ Send data to the outside world; for example, to a teletypewriter.

■ Call a subroutine.

■ Multiply or divide two numbers.

■ Convert D/A or A/D (using appropriate software).

One method of applying benchmark tests that is currently receiving increased attention is to assemble a mix of programs for use as the test. In order for this test to be valid, the mix must span those types of calculations that are ultimately to be performed by the μP. That is, it must have some relation to the intended application.

"If no application is being considered, and a general evaluation is sought, a mix of programs is the only method which can be used for benchmarking," notes Paul Rosenfeld, software prod-

Programming a simple process

The steps needed to benchmark a microprocessor are illustrated by this sample program, designed to input two bytes of data from two different devices. The signals might be the outputs of two analog-to-digital converters, or they might come from mechanical position resolvers.

The program does the following:

The two digital inputs are compared, and if they are numerically equal, the Q flag is set to "1." If they are unequal, the Q flag is set to "0" and the larger signal is sent on to a third device. The first diagram, an elementary flowchart, gives an overview of the process. The second figure flowcharts the steps in detail.

Once the flowchart is prepared, the next task of the benchmark programmer is to write the actual program, which is shown in the table.

Such a program lists each step executed by the μP in performing its task.

Next, from information supplied by the manufacturer (by means of a spec sheet or otherwise), the μP evaluator obtains the amount of time required for each step, and the number of bytes of memory required. The total memory bytes needed, together with the total time—taking into account any looping (repetitive) operations—represents the benchmark results for this particular program.

Using the RCA COSMAC μP, each instruction takes 16 clock periods. The μP clock runs at a 6.4 MHz rate (for a 10-V supply voltage). The time for each instruction, therefore, is 2.5 μs.

The program flowcharts were supplied by RCA's Solid State Division, Somerville, NJ.

Assembly listing for two-byte processing program

Program counter (Hexadecimal)	Instructions and data (Machine language)	Line number	Assembly language (Mnemonic)	Comments
0000	7A;	0001	REQ	Reset Q to "0"
0001	F800;	0002	LDI A.1 (STORE)	Set storage pointer R(2)
0003	B2;	0003	PHI R2	to point at a free location
0004	F81C;	0004 GO:	LDI A.0 (STORE)	in RAM M(STORE)
0006	A2;	0005	PLO R2	" "
0007	E2;	0006	SEX R2	
0008	69;	0007	INP 1	Read 1st input byte into D
0009	A3;	0008	PLO R3	Save the first input
000A	6A;	0009	INP 2	Read 2nd input byte into
000B	;	0010		memory
000B	83;	0011	GLO R3	Load the 1st input into D
000C	F7;	0012	SM	1st input minus 2nd input
000D	38 18;	0013	BNF RES2	Branch to RES2 if 2nd input
000F	;	0014		is greater than 1st input;
000F	;	0015		otherwise:
000F	83;	0016	GLO R3	Load the 1st input into D
0010	F3;	0017	XOR	M(R(2)) XOR D, to check if the
0011	;	0018		two inputs are equal
0011	3A 16;	0019	BNZ RES1	Branch to RES1 if not equal
0013	;	0020		(1st input is greater than
0013	;	0021		2nd input); Otherwise:
0013	7B;	0022	SEQ	Equal; set Q flag
0014	3004;	0023	BR GO	Go back to beginning
0016	;	0024		
0016	83;	0025 RES1:	GLO R3	Load 1st input into D
0017	52;	0026	STR R2	Store it at M(STORE)
0018	;	0027		
0018	61;	0028 RES2:	OUT 1	Output larger value
0019	7A;	0029	REQ	Reset Q flag
001A	3004;	0030	BR GO	Go back to beginning
001C	;	0031		
001C	;	0032 Store:	ORG *	Storage area
001C	;	0033		
001C	;	0034		
001C	;	0035		
001C	;	0036		
001C	;	0037	END	End of program source
0000				

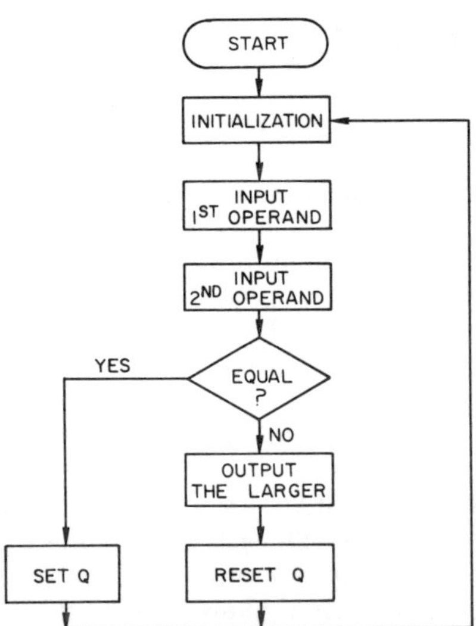

A Basic program flowchart for processing two input bytes, is shown. The program inputs the two bytes, compares them, and outputs the larger. If the bytes are equal, the Q flag is set to "1."

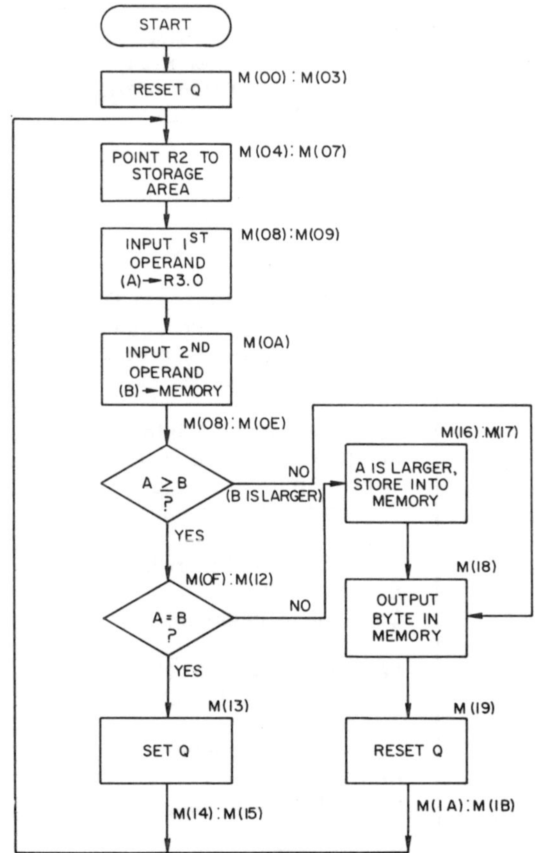

The detailed flowchart for processing two input bytes is used as the basis for writing the microprocessor program.

ucts manager at Intel, Santa Clara, CA.

If there is one area of strong agreement in the industry, it is the fact that the benchmark test should be only one of a number of μP-selection criteria. Some of the others are:

■ The number and cost of the power supplies necessary.

■ The noise immunity.

■ Second sourcing.

■ The number of clocks required.

■ Compatibility with rest of system.

■ Type of vendor support (for example, whether assemblers are available).

■ Documentation (for example, are there sufficient application notes).

One important aspect sometimes overlooked in benchmarking, is consideration of the skill of the individual who actually writes the benchmark program. "Programmers of unequal ability are often given the job, with the result that the better programmer generates a more efficient code," notes TI's Ogden.

"If possible, a single programmer, or programmers of equal ability, should prepare benchmark tests. Also, since the bulk of the applications program will be written by programmers of average ability, to ensure validity the benchmark test should also be written by an average programmer rather than by one of unusual skill."

There are a number of sources where potential users of μPs can obtain benchmarks. Standard benchmark routines are available from data processing consultants. AH Systems, Chatsworth, CA, for example, currently offers five standard benchmark tests, with more in preparation.

A ploy sometimes resorted to by a μP user on the lookout to save money is to ask the vendor to write a benchmark program for his (the user's) intended application. The vendor often complies because he wants to make a sale. In addition, the vendor's program writer gets a chance to emphasize the product's advantages to the potential purchaser.

Such free help often has some disadvantages, however. By having someone e'se do his benchmarking, or by resorting to "canned" standard routines, the user will never learn how difficult (or how easy) it is to program different μPs.

"Learning about the processor by actually working on it, is at least as important as those other two 'classic' μP-selection criteria, program length and program time," says RCA's Carley. He says the importance of benchmarks today lies in their ability to show how easy it is to deal with a particular μP.

"The old-time definitions of how long a program is, or how fast it is, are losing ground. In most applications the time doesn't matter, and the cost of the additional memory is so low, that it's not a significant factor."

System Testing with a Logic-State Analyzer

W. A. FARNBACH
Engineering Section Manager,
Hewlett-Packard, Colorado Springs

Unless you enjoy spending weeks or months in unraveling complex puzzles, take a systematic approach when you develop μP-based systems.

Two basic procedures underpin the approach: turn the system on one piece at a time, and debug software and hardware together. The tool that allows all this is the logic-state analyzer.

With the analyzer, you can develop a μP system with the same technique you usually use to develop a cascaded amplifier. That is, you usually turn on and check out the amplifier one section at a time by injecting a signal into the input and measuring the output of each section with a voltmeter, spectrum analyzer or oscilloscope. In turning on μP systems, analyzers offer a similar approach, and so ease the development process.

In operation, analyzers measure information transfer—program addresses, program instructions or any data that appear on any of the busses or ports within the μP system.

One analyzer can display sixteen 16-bit data words at one time, or sixteen 32-bit words with a companion analyzer. These words are displayed as ONEs and ZEROs and are selected with a pattern trigger and digital delay (Fig. 1).

The pattern, or data word, is selected by setting the 32 pattern-trigger switches to high, low, or off. The delay can be such that the display starts anywhere from 15 words before the pattern trigger, to 99,999 words after the trigger. Since the analyzer has a digital memory, data can be captured single-shot and displayed indefinitely.

Another useful analyzer feature is an output that can trigger a scope at any byte in a digital process. With the trigger, you can examine waveforms in detail.

Sequential operations cause problems

In developing a systematic process for turning on a μP system, remember that it's the data transactions on the various busses that determine a system's function. Consider the μP system of Fig. 2. If all of the elements in this system are

1. **A functional display of ONEs and ZEROs** gives designers an overview of the operation of a digital system. Words are captured in the analyzer's memory.

wired up, plugged in and turned on, chaos will almost surely result. Any small wiring mistake or logic error can cause the system to run amok.

Such alarming behavior results because the entire system is one giant digital-feedback loop. The next value of the program counter depends on the current instruction, but the latter depends on the current value of the program counter.

Interchanging two address lines causes the instructions to be executed in an entirely random sequence. A small logic error, which allows two ROMs to respond simultaneously to an address, will cause the outputs of the ROMs to be wire-ANDed, again putting entirely random instructions on the data bus.

Similarly, data stored in memory—to be read back later for conditional branches—are determined by instructions executed long ago, and the instructions to be executed in the future depend upon those stored values. Current or post values of the I/O ports also participate in decisions that affect future operation.

The only reasonable approach to turning on such a system is to break the feedback network

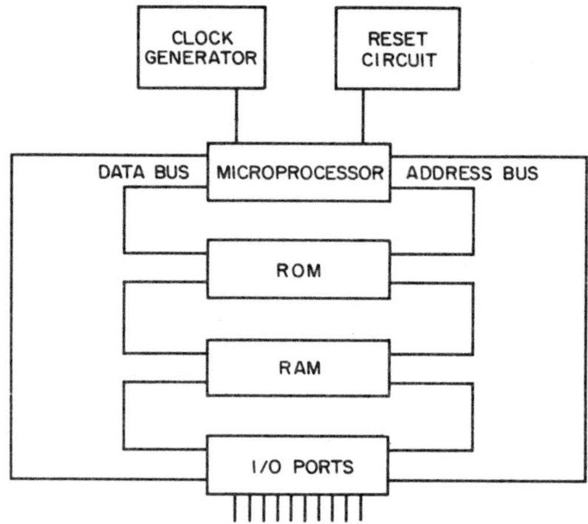

2. Generalized microprocessor system contains fixed programs in ROMs and data in RAMs. Interaction between the memory and μP appears like a feedback loop.

into pieces, so that each piece can be turned on independently.

The first candidates for turn on are the clock generator and reset circuits. These relatively simple timing circuits are best tested with a scope for proper timing and waveshape. Once these circuits are within specs, the next step is to check the interaction between the μP and the ROM.

A crucial path: μP to ROM

The linkage between the ROM (or RAM) and the μP is the first to be established because with this link, the processor can be programmed to serve as a signal generator for testing the remaining blocks. The linkage is tested in three steps:

First, you must establish that the NOP (no operation) instruction is being transmitted correctly to the processor. Second, establish that the program addresses are transmitted correctly to the ROM. Finally, determine that the ROM interprets the program addresses correctly.

To perform the first step, plug in only the μP and put the NOP code on the data bus (Fig. 3a). In forcing the data bus to NOP, realize that many μPs will try to put data onto the bus during an operating cycle. If the data bus is simply wired to the NOP state, then the data-output buffers in the μP can be destroyed. You can avoid this problem in two ways.

Since the μP data inputs are usually high impedance, the data bus can be forced safely to NOP with large resistors. Or, it can be forced to NOP through a set of three-state gates. Connect the three-state control to the processor read/write line so that the gates are active only when the processor reads data.

This set-up will cause the program counter in the processor to increment. That is, the processor will execute a NOP, increment the program counter, execute the next NOP, and so on. You can easily measure the counting sequence on the address bus with the analyzer. Simply connect the 16 data inputs to the address bus at the ROM socket, and connect the clock input to the data-transfer processor clock.

The count sequence also can be easily verified. Just trigger the analyzer on 0000_{16}, increment the delay generator through several values, and compare the count displayed on the state analyzer with the delay setting. Obviously, the count (in decimal) and the delay value will be equal if the ROM receives correct addresses.

In this way, you verify that the processor is executing NOPs and that the addresses are correctly transmitted to the ROM. If the addresses do not form a counting sequence, then an examination of the address pattern should quickly reveal if address lines are interchanged or are inactive, or the processor is executing an unexpected branch instruction.

If you suspect that the processor is not executing NOPs during the instruction read phase, then connect the state analyzer to the data bus directly at the processor.

Check waveforms at each change

At this point, it is also important to examine the waveforms on the busses and the control lines. Any incorrect timing, marginal voltage levels, noise or crosstalk should be eliminated before proceeding. In fact, you must do this every time you add a new block to the system. Any input or output hung onto a common line can cause a problem.

The analyzer's scope-trigger output is very useful, especially as more blocks are added. For example, to examine the waveforms on the data bus when the bus is driven by the RAM outputs, you need only trigger the analyzer on the RAM read address or on the address of the RAM read instruction, then trigger the scope with the analyzer's pattern-trigger output.

Although such testing may seem needlessly repetitive, it takes very little time if there is no problem, and saves a great deal of time, if there is one by pinpointing the troublesome block.

Next, plug in some ROMs with known stored information and connect only the address lines and chip-select logic (Fig. 3b). Since the instructions returning to the processor are still NOPs, the program counter will continue a simple count. This time, however, the ROMs will cycle through all possible addresses so that you can measure the ROM outputs with eight data inputs to the analyzer.

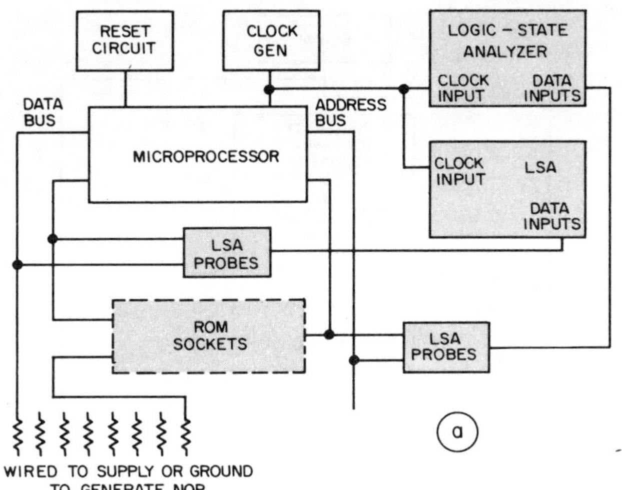

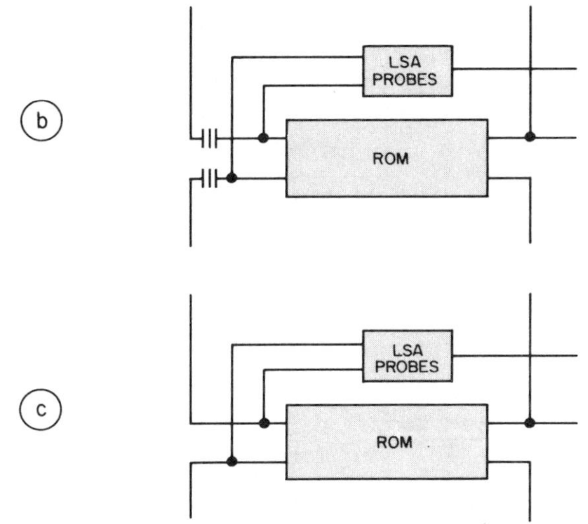

3. **To check transactions between** the μP and ROM requires three steps. The first step verifies NOP transmission (a), the second checks ROM addressing (b) and the last step tests the completed link (c).

Keep 16 data inputs connected to the address bus, if possible. It isn't necessary to measure all possible values of ROM output, but you should check sufficiently to verify that the correct ROM is selected and that every ROM is addressed correctly.

Since not all 65-k addresses are ordinarily allocated to ROM, it might be necessary to connect temporarily some pull-ups to the ROM outputs. With pull-ups, an address outside the allocated ROM addresses will generate a known data word (all highs).

You should also check some addresses outside those of the ROM to verify that the ROMs are off when they are not addressed. Remember to check the waveforms on the address bus and central lines, particularly on the control lines of the ROMs.

Finally, complete the processor-to-ROM link by removing any circuitry required to force the NOPs onto the μP and connecting the ROM outputs onto the data bus (Fig. 3c). A ROM contain-

ing a simple program, with several unconditional jumps, should be installed (Fig. 4). Verify operation of this program by monitoring the address bus with the analyzer.

The program includes RAM access and I/O instructions so that the RAM and I/O control cycles can be checked before the RAM and I/O devices are installed. The timing of these cycles is easily checked. Just use the analyzer to trigger a scope at the beginning of each RAM or I/O instruction.

It isn't necessary to monitor the data bus—unless there is a problem—because the sequence of program addresses is ample to verify proper execution of the program. Although only a very simple program is required to test the μP-to-ROM data link and the RAM and I/O control cycles, a more elaborate program can be used if desired.

Debugging RAM and I/O

In no case, however, should any branches on RAM or I/O instructions be used at this point, as the RAM and I/O blocks have not yet been turned on and debugged. If enough ROMs are available, the test ROM, and any others used in the turn-on procedure, should be saved for future units.

The checkout of the μP-to-ROM data link is by far the most tedious. The reason is that this link must always be a feedback process. That is, each instruction depends on the address, and each address depends on the previous instruction.

The RAM and I/O blocks can be turned on much more directly, and in any order. If you choose the RAM first, you can connect it to the system in one operation.

With the RAM connected, run the ROM test program briefly to verify operation. Pay particular attention to the timing of the RAM control signals during the RAM read and write instructions. The usual cause of failure at this point is a shorted address or data line, two lines shorted together, or an unwanted RAM response.

Again, the analyzer will reveal quickly the location of the problem, and a scope triggered from the analyzer will show the nature of the problem. With the ROM program verified, now run a RAM test.

A RAM test program should write to every location in memory, then read each location back and verify the data. With an eight-bit-wide memory, watch out for a pitfall:

The eight bits of memory represent only 256 states. Conventional memories are usually much longer. This means that each possible data pattern must be written several times to fill the memory. If the same data are written into each block of 256 words, an error in any of the higher order addresses can be masked.

An extreme example of such masking is the case where all address lines (A8 to A15) are disconnected. Any simple perturbation of the 256-word pattern—such as shifting the pattern one word location in each block—will reveal the problem (Fig. 5).

For example, if you count from 0 to 255 in the first block, you should count from 1 to 255, then go back to ZERO in the next block; next, count 2 to 255, and go back to ZERO and ONE in the next block, and so on. The flowchart of an effective RAM-module test program is shown in Fig. 6. Remember, this test verifies that the

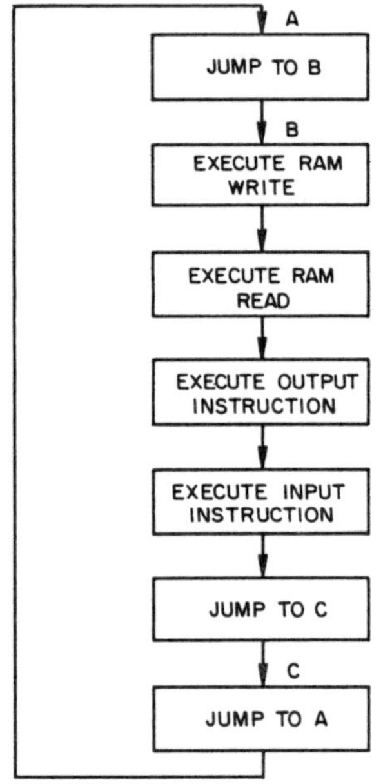

4. **Verification program** checks out the ROM-to-processor data link. Also checked are I/O control cycles.

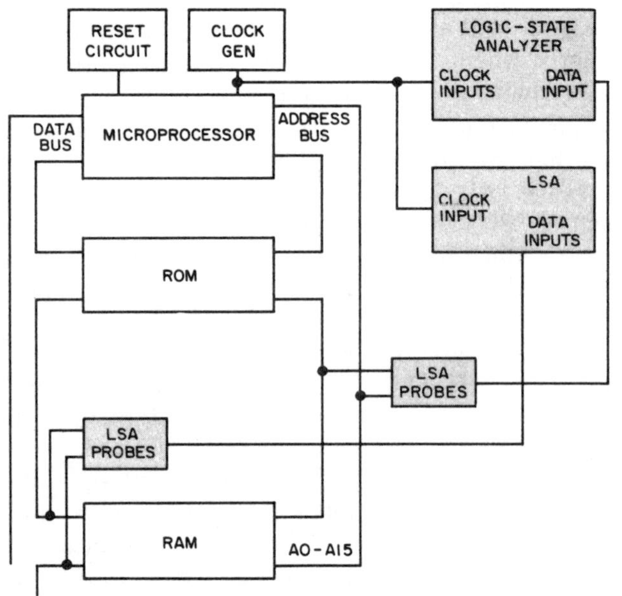

5. **Test set-up to turn on the system RAM** verifies the writing and reading of each location in memory.

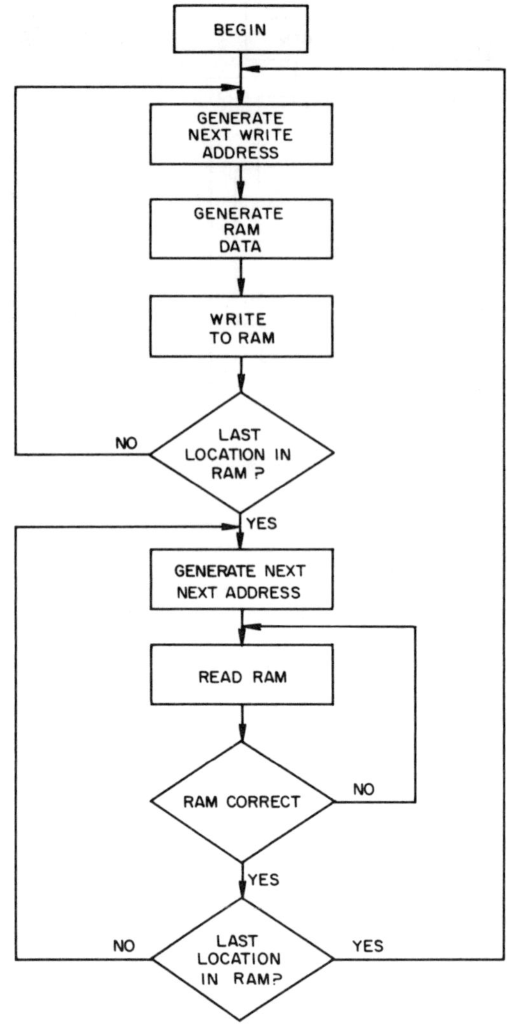

6. **RAM-module test program** wrings out memory system operation, as monitored by the logic analyzer.

memory system is working correctly—it does not check each cell of each memory location.

Again, if you design the program so that all locations are written and then read back, the analyzer quickly shows whether the data are correct. An oscilloscope triggered by an analyzer shows whether the waveforms are correct.

Although the I/O block is relatively easy to turn on, the discussion here is somewhat general since I/O structures vary more than other blocks from one μP system to another. The main point is to test the I/O ports before connection to peripheral devices, such as keyboards, displays, or circuits to be controlled. The first step is to put the ROM test program back in, and verify that the control timing is correct with the ports connected during the I/O instructions.

You can check the output ports easily with a simple program that first sets all the ports to ZERO, then sets each port in turn to ONE, and finally sets each port back to ZERO one at a time. When testing the output ports, connect the analyzer to one block at a time.

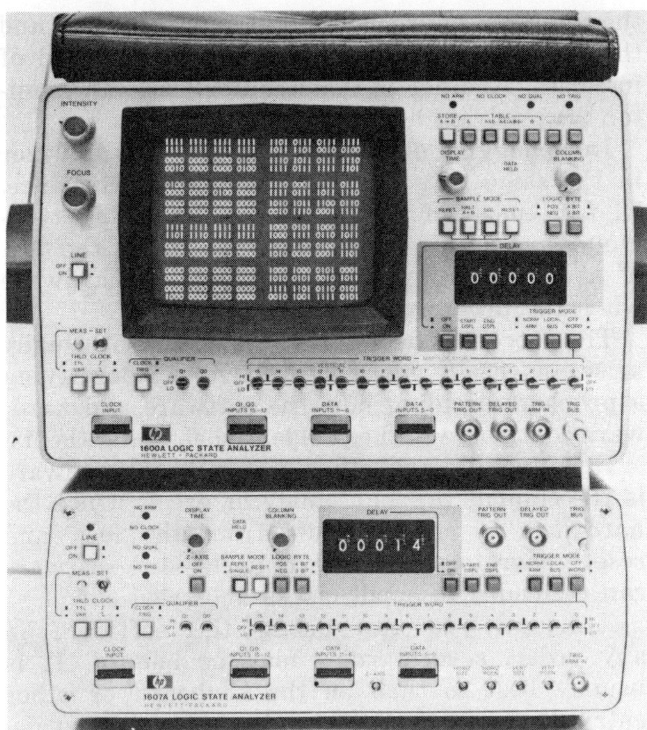

Logic state analyzer shows up to sixteen 32-bit words at a time. Data are put into memory when the instrument recognizes a selected word or are captured after a set delay.

If sufficient data channels are available on the analyzer, connect these to the address bus as well (Fig. 7). The object of this exercise is to see if the output ports are connected in the proper order and can be set both high and low.

The input ports are similarly tested. The program should check for each input high, then for each input low.

The test, of course, is performed by a program that loops until the input under test is forced to the desired state, then jumps to another loop (Fig. 8). A simple approach is to pull all of the inputs either high or low, whichever is easier, through a resistor.

Assuming you selected the "high" approach, write a program that has two loops: the first to test for a specific input low and the second for that input high. While the analyzer monitors the address bus and at least the one input under test, force the input low with a grounded wire. The analyzer will show which loop the processor is in, exactly when the input went low and—usually in a second pass—when the input went high.

Although this process may seem tedious, the time required to write the test programs must be spent only once. The programs will be invaluable at every phase of system development.

The process of developing the software is quite a bit like turning on the hardware. The major idea is to develop the software in pieces. This idea isn't new. Nobody in his right mind sits down, writes six-thousand words of code, plugs

it in, and expects the whole thing to work right off. You must develop and test the coding in manageable bytes. Three alternatives are available: simulators, breakpoint registers and logic analyzers.

A simulator—either a development system or a large computer—can be a valuable aid in testing such complex algorithms as sorting routines or mathematical functions. But it is difficult to adequately simulate the software that performs the bulk of I/O operations—and it's at the I/O ports that major trouble usually develops.

Breakpoint registers and a single-step button are another way to follow the operation of a program. Such registers, or control panels, suffer from several drawbacks:

First, to build the control panel requires a fair amount of time and effort. Second—and far more serious—the operation of the processor must be slowed down by a factor of several million to observe the process at human speeds.

Not only does this great reduction in speed cause major changes in the operation of the whole system, it can make even a simple algorithm take a long time to complete.

In the third technique, using the logic-state analyzer, it doesn't really matter whether the software has been simulated beforehand or not. (Although, as mentioned before, if a simulator is available, it can be a help in developing some parts of the software.) One clear advantage of

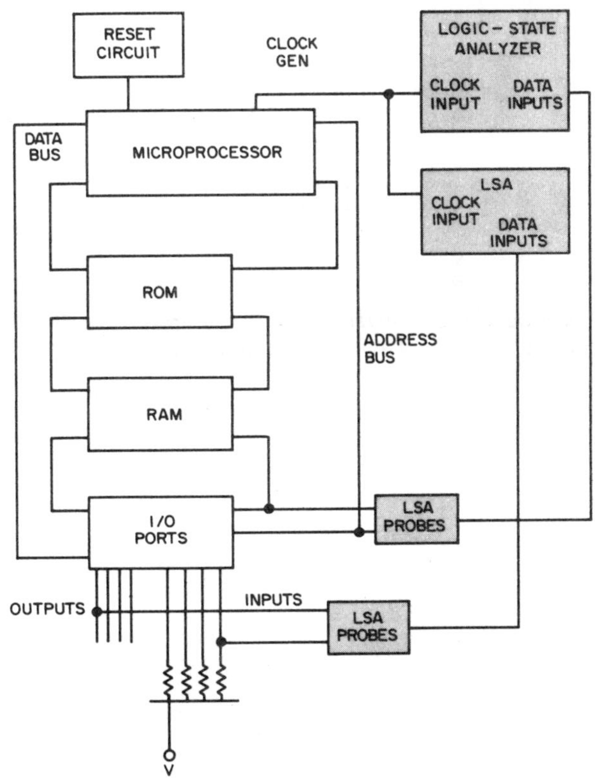

7. **Test the I/O ports** before you connect the system's peripherals. First, verify control timing.

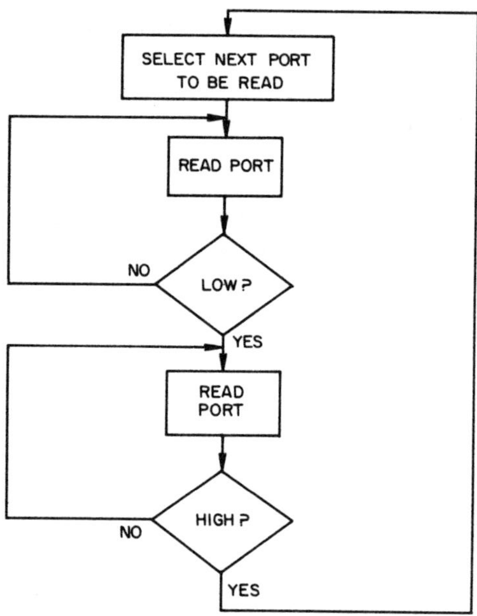

8. Input-port test program loops around to force the desired state, then jumps to another loop.

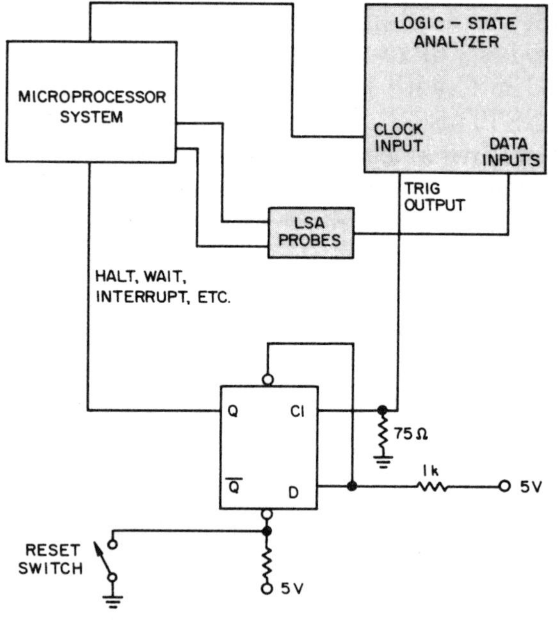

9. Connect the analyzer's trigger output to a flip-flop, and the instrument can halt or interrupt μP action.

the analyzer approach is that the hardware and the software are debugged in parallel instead of in series. Another is that the analyzer can monitor the program flow in real time.

In debugging software, you use the analyzer in the same way as when debugging hardware. In fact, most of the hardware debugging techniques are simply a matter of monitoring the flow of a simple program, then fixing the hardware when the program does not work.

The process of debugging software, as it usually arises, is really more a problem of identifying a problem, deciding how the software and hardware contribute to the problem, then doing the fix.

In pinpointing whether software or hardware is the culprit, the logic analyzer excels. Once the hardware is checked out—from the lock and reset generators, to the I/O ports—the software can be loaded in small blocks and tried out.

Although you can debug the software in any order, several rules may be helpful. It is usually best to turn on the keyboard or other entry device first, then any display or output device. Next, turn on the hardware and software together.

Note that the logic-state analyzer can serve as a breakpoint register. Connect its trigger output to a flip-flop and use the flip-flop output as the break signal (Fig. 9).

Bibliography

Farnbach, W. A., "Logic State Analyzers—a New Instrument for Analyzing Sequential Digital Processes," *IEEE Transactions on Instrumentation and Measurement*, Vol. IM 24, No. 4, December, 1975, pp. 353-356.

Farnbach, W. A., "Troubleshooting in the Data Domain Is Simplified by Logic Analyzers," *Electronics*, May 15, 1975, pp. 103-105.

House, C. H. "Engineering in the Data Domain Calls for a New Kind of Digital Instrument," *Electronics*, May 1, 1975, pp. 75-81.

Small, C. T. and Morrill, J. S. Jr., "The Logic State Analyzer, A Viewing Port for the Data Domain," *Hewlett-Packard Journal*, August, 1975, pp. 2-10.

SECTION IV
Designing with the 8080

The Intel 8080, together with its higher performance successor the 8080A, is generally recognized as the most widely used microprocessor. It owes its popularity to the relatively small number of components needed to assemble a complete system. Yet this compactness is achieved without sacrificing versatility. The eight-bit NMOS microprocessor chip is supported by a line of programmable LSI peripheral circuits that simplifies microcomputer design and provides a flexible interface bus. The 8080's bus organization has become so popular that it is now widely accepted as a standard for microcomputer-based data acquisition.

Though Intel has not formally licensed any alternate sources, parts similar to the 8080A are now available from several other companies. These include Advanced Micro Devices, Hitachi, National Semiconductor, NEC Microcomputers, Siemens, and Texas Instruments.

A new one-chip version, the 8085, includes the clock and controller circuits within the basic CPU chip. Also it offers higher speed and more interrupt levels. At present this version is available only from Intel.

The first article gives a comprehensive description of the 8080 and other components in the MCS-80 system. It describes the architecture and the performance tradeoffs. Also it lists the complete instruction set and gives programming guidelines. A couple of other articles show how to enhance the microprocessor's performance; one author adds logic circuits to improve bit manipulation, while another uses the "Ready" line to speed data access. The remaining articles look at debugging and testing techniques.

Build a Compact Microcomputer with the 8080

A. J. NICHOLS
Manager, Microcomputer Applications,
Intel, Santa Clara

KENNETH McKENZIE
Manager, MCS-80 Microcomputer System,
Intel, Santa Clara

Systems based on the single-chip 8080 μP can be built with far fewer components than has been possible until now. What makes the parts reduction possible is the availability of programmable LSI interface circuits.

These programmable I/O and peripheral devices provide the means to standardize hardware designs for system interfaces. They can be used to upgrade or replace specialized logic assemblies involving scores of conventional digital circuits.

An additional benefit of these peripheral LSI circuits: they simplify microcomputer design. Since the bus standardizes the internal interface structure, a system designer's main task reduces to that of organizing external interface and interrupt structures. The complete 8080 system can be used as an interrupt-driven system in on-line computation and control applications.

Basic system components

The 8080 microcomputer system (MCS-80) consists of a family of n-channel MOS and Schottky-bipolar devices, and development support products (Tables 1 and 2). It is based on the 8080A CPU group, which consists of an 8080A 8-bit central processing unit, an 8224 clock generator and an 8228 system controller. The CPU can directly address up to 65,536 bytes of memory and 512 I/O ports (256 input, 256 output ports).

Bipolar timing, bus control and drive functions normally required to support the CPU are integrated into the 8224 and 8228. Major I/O and peripheral units are programmable: they are both configured and controlled by software. The I/O units provide serial data and parallel I/O;

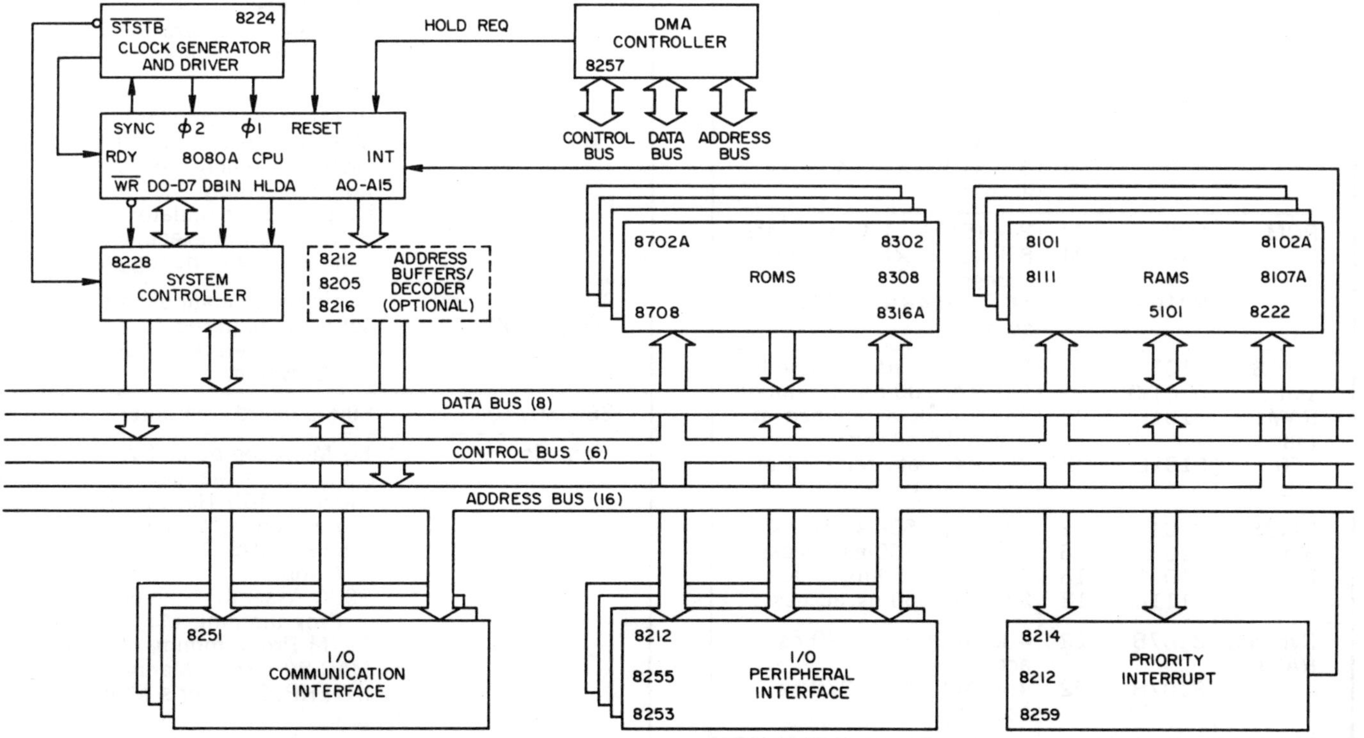

1. **The 8080 microcomputer system** features a modular organization, based on a bus standardized by the 8080 CPU group—the 8224 clock generator and driver, 8228 system controller and 8080A.

the peripheral units augment the CPU group's control capability by managing multilevel interrupts, peripheral-service timings, and direct-memory access (DMA). Memory components have industry-standard configurations.

The CPU options provide typical instruction cycle times as low as 1.35 μs in the commercial temperature range and 2 μs in the military range (M8080A). Introduced in 1974 as the first NMOS CPU, the 8080 has become an industry standard. It now accounts for more than half of

Table 1. MCS-80 system components

Function	Type	Pins	Name/specification
CPU Group	8080A	40	8-bit CPU, 2-μs cycle
	8224	16	Clock generator
	8228/38	28	System controller
CPU Options	8080A-1	40	1.3-μs instruction cycle
	8080A-2	40	1.5-μs instruction cycle
	M8080A	40	2 μs, −55 to 125 C
Input/ Output	8212	24	8-bit I/O port
	8251	28	Programmable communication interface
	8255	40	Programmable peripheral interface
Peripherals	8205	16	1-of-8 binary decoder
	8214	24	Priority interrupt-control unit
	8216	16	4-bit bidirectional bus driver (50 mA), non-inverting
	8226	16	4-bit bidirectional bus driver (50 mA), inverting
	8222	22	Dynamic RAM refresh controller (for 8107B)
	8253	24	Programmable interval timer
	8257	40	Programmable DMA controller
	8259	28	Programmable interrupt controller
EPROMs	8702A	24	2 k (512×8), 1.3-μs access
	8708	24	8 k (1024×8), 450-ns access
ROMs	8302	24	2 k (512×8) 1-μs access
	8308	24	8 k (1024×8), 450-ns access
	8316A	24	16 k (2048×8), 850-ns access
CMOS static RAMs (all 650-ns access)	5101	22	256×4, 15 nA/bit standby
	5101-3	22	256×4, 200 nA/bit standby
	5101L	22	256×4, data retained at 2 V_{CC}, 15 nA/bit
	5101L-3	22	256×4, data retained at 2 V_{CC}, 200 nA/bit
NMOS Static RAMs	8101-2	22	256×4, 850-ns access
	8102A-4	16	1024×1, 450-ns access
	8102A-6	16	1024×1, 650-ns access
	8111-2	18	256×4, 850-ns access
Dynamic RAMs	8107B	22	4 k (4096×1), 420-ns access
	8107B-4	22	4 k (4096×1), 270-ns access

Note: All access times are maximum values

Table 2. Microcomputer-system support products

Microcomputer Development System (MDS) and peripherals	8080 system with interrupt and DMA control, expandable memory and I/O Diskette system ROM simulator Universal PROM programmer CRT console Line printer High-speed paper-tape punch High-speed paper-tape reader Teletypewriter
ICE-80 In-Circuit Emulator	Used with MDS for in-circuit hardware/software debugging in product's own environment
MDS Resident Software Packages	System monitor supports diagnostic aids and real-time checkout; controls system and drives peripherals Macro assembler translates symbolic assembly language to machine code, provides full macro and conditional assembly Text editor supports program entry and correction; includes string search, substitution, insertion and deletion commands DOS (Diskette Operating System) supports symbolic file management for development of programs and filing of data such as diagnostic information ICE-80 supports debugging with English-language type commands ROM-SIM supports the ROM simulator (a high-speed RAM memory)
Cross-product software packages	PL/M cross compiler MAC-80 cross compiler provides full macro and conditional assembly INTERP/80 simulator supports program-execution simulation and debugging
SDK-80 System Design Kit	Contains all components and software required to assemble and operate a basic 8080 system
SBC-80/10	Single-board computer
Manuals	80 Microcomputer Systems User's Manual Intellec MDS Hardware Reference Manual Intellec MDS Operator's Manual 8080 Assembly Language Programming Manual PL/M Programming Manual MAC-80 User's Manual INTERP/80 User's Manual

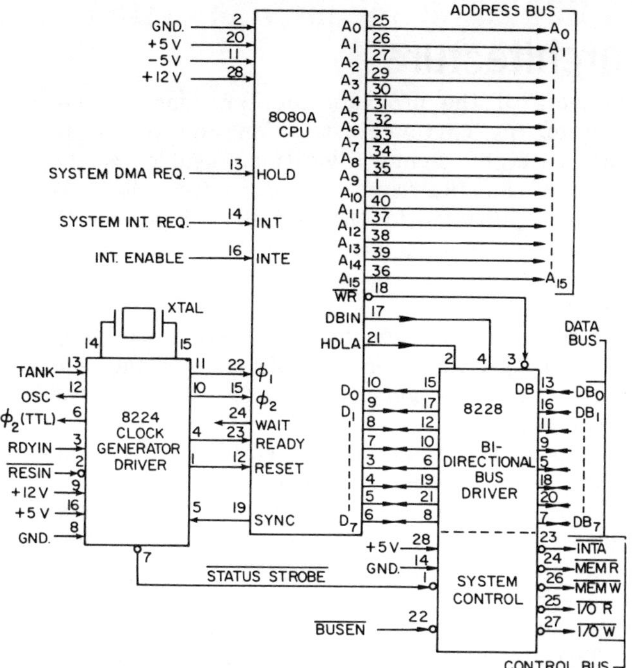

2. **The CPU group connects** to the address, data and control busses—the three elements of the system bus. The Interrupt Acknowledge output of the 8228 may be tied to 12 V through a 1-kΩ resistor and used as a vectored single-level interrupt control.

all microcomputer applications, and components are being widely second-sourced.

Microcomputer architecture

The 8080-based microcomputer features a modular architecture (Fig. 1). The CPU group represents the only dedicated components in the μC (Fig. 2). The remaining subsystems—memory, I/O and peripheral control—are modular. They are constructed by use of other components in building-block fashion on the bus.

The CPU group standardizes system-bus control logic and ac timing and dc electrical characteristics. Other components interface directly with the group via the bus. Thus, the over-all design is comparable to that of a computer with standardized "mainframe" logic and modular peripherals that plug into the bus.

The system bus consists of three groups of interconnections: A_0 to A_{15}, a three-state bus used by the CPU to address memory locations and to select ports; DB_0 to DB_7, a bidirectional, three-state bus driven by the 8228 and used for all information transfers; and the control bus. The latter includes control lines operated by the 8228, which gates selected devices on and off the data bus.

The bus is TTL compatible and is driven by the CPU group at or above TTL drive levels (1.9 mA on all 8080A outputs and typically 10 mA for the 8228). In general, bus buffers—or bidirectional driver and decoder units—are required only in large systems.

The CPU group performs the following:

■ Makes all CPU inputs essentially asynchronous. Selected device operations align with CPU operations regardless of the device's operating times.

■ Stabilizes the data bus to ensure the validity of transferred data.

■ Sinks and sources the currents required to maintain direct component-to-bus interfacing as the system expands outward from the CPU group.

Programmable peripherals

The key I/O and peripheral devices are these:

■ 8255 programmable peripheral interface, which provides three ports (24 lines) for parallel I/O and control.

■ 8251 programmable communications interface, a universal synchronous/asynchronous receiver/transmitter (USART) for serial data I/O.

■ 8259 programmable interrupt controller, which allows eight levels of priority-interrupt control, expandable to 64 levels.

■ 8253 programmable interval timer, which consists of three 16-bit BCD/binary counters. The circuit may be used to set system-timing delays, replacing software-timing loops.

■ 8257 programmable DMA controller, which offers four channels of direct-memory-access control for bulk-data transfers between peripheral equipment and RAM.

A designer seeking to use these devices chooses control words and algorithms from sets supplied for each device. He then adds them to the intialization or service routines of the system-application program. Initialization control words, for example, define communication and control configurations of the 8255's 24 I/O lines. Algorithms govern the priorities of the interrupt levels controlled by the 8259.

Of course, since software defines the devices' functions, it can also be used to change them. One method is to use control words as replaceable software modules. One set of basic hardware can then be used with various peripheral equipment in different end-products.

Furthermore, operating modes can be changed "on the fly" during system operation. This feature permits dynamic changes in priority levels, thereby enhancing a system's real-time response. When the CPU determines that particular types of services become more critical than others, it can rearrange the priorities.

All units contain internal control logic and "housekeeping" functions. These reduce CPU overhead software. They enable the CPU to manage the I/O structure with acknowledgements and operating commands after receiving requests for service (interrupt and DMA). Thus they help

Microprocessor architecture

The nucleus of an 8080-based system is, of course, the CPU, a single-chip, 8-bit parallel processor.

In turn, an important part of the CPU is its register section, a static RAM array organized into six 16-bit registers. The array's six 8-bit general-purpose registers (they may be addressed individually or in pairs) provide single or double-precision (16-bit) operators.

Up to 64-kilobytes of memory may be directly addressed. The stack pointer allows any portion of RAM memory to be used as an external stack, so that subroutine nesting is bounded only by memory size. The stack can be used to store the contents of the program counter, flags, accumulator and all six general-purpose registers.

The arithmetic logic unit (ALU) performs arithmetic, logic and shift/rotate operations. Associated with it are an 8-bit accumulator, and 8-bit temporary accumulator, and a 5-bit flag register (zero, carry, sign, parity, auxiliary carry). Testing the auxiliary carry for decimal correction allows decimal arithmetic to be performed.

Accumulator-group instructions include arithmetic and logic operators with direct, register-indirect and immediate-addressing modes. Move, load and store-instruction groups can be used to move either 8 or 16-bits of data between memory, the six general-purpose working registers and the accumulator. In each of these cases, the same addressing mode can be used. Jump, jump conditional and computed jumps provide program branching.

Calls to and returns from subroutines can be made conditionally and unconditionally. RST (restart) provides a single-byte Call instruction for interrupt operation. This Call saves the contents of the program counter upon completion of the current instruction and points to any of eight memory locations usable as the start of an interrupt-service routine. RST is normally initiated by the peripheral logic, which can also generate additional Call instruction bytes for vectoring to more than eight interrupt levels.

A basic instruction cycle is four states long (T_1 through T_4). For example, adding the contents of an 8-bit general-purpose register to the accumulator (ADD r) requires three states for the instruction fetch and one state for execution. Some instructions take two execution states.

A machine cycle is required for each fetch and for each memory or I/O access. Each instruction cycle must begin with a fetch, but other machine cycles may be used in succession, between the fetch and the execution state or states.

The first machine cycle of an interrupt operation resembles a fetch but does not increment the program counter. Thus, when the peripheral logic generates the Call, the program-counter contents are automatically saved. Other system-status information can also be saved in the RAM stack. The stack pointer automatically provides for retrieval of the interrupted program address upon completion of the interrupt.

A Hold input causes the CPU to complete an instruction's execution, then come to rest. Hold is generally used during DMA operations. In this case, the CPU doesn't use the bus during the last two states (T_4 and T_5), so DMA operations can overlap instruction cycles.

A Ready input inserts a Wait state (or states) after T_2. The Halt instruction stops the CPU in the next machine cycle after T_2. A Reset, Hold or Interrupt brings the CPU out of Halt.

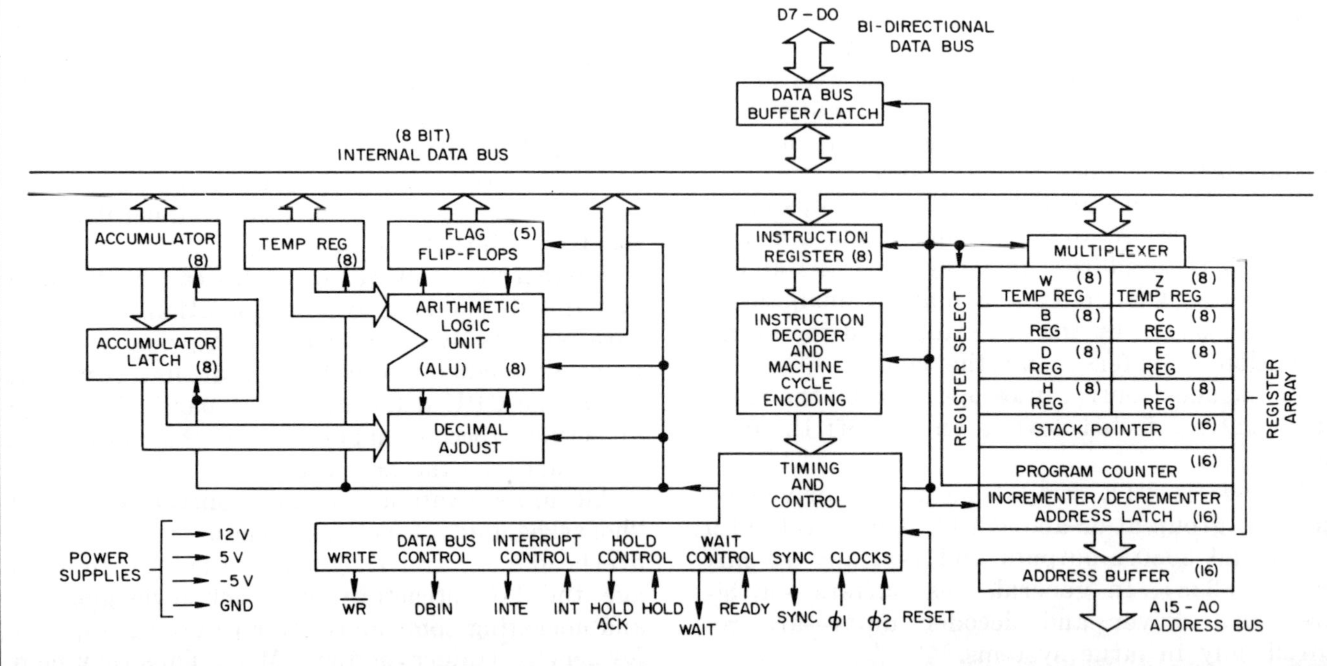

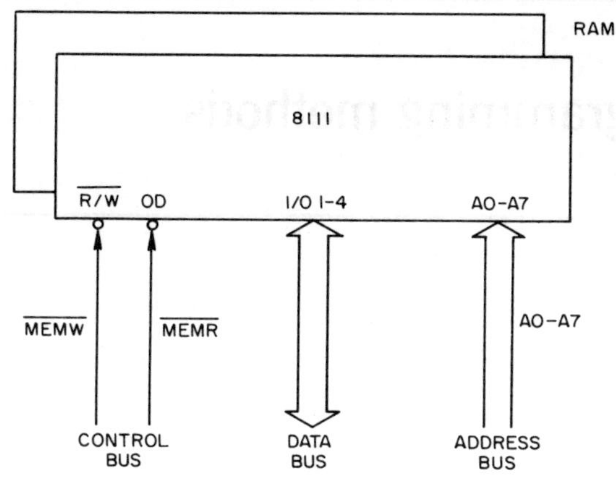

3. **In a typical memory interface** to the system bus, two 8111, 256 × 4-bit, static RAMs are operated in parallel to provide byte-wide data.

the CPU perform an increased number of real-time tasks.

Two ways to handle interrupts

All I/O devices, including the 8253 timer, can generate interrupt requests. The 8080 handles interrupts in one of two ways: vectored interrupts and Call structures. In the first case, a vector instruction (RST) "points" the program counter to the specific memory locations to be used as the starting points of service routines. RST acts as a program Call. The vector instruction is generated by an interrupt-control device, and up to eight branches can occur.

In the second case, the CPU's regular Call structure may still be used. Thus, any location in memory can be the start of a service routine and the number of interrupt levels is bounded only by memory size. Again, the interrupt-control device generates the Call instruction.

Implementing the interrupt-handling techniques are these circuits:

- 8228 system controller, which generates one vector (RST 7). This provides a single-level interrupt control built into the CPU group.
- 8259 programmable interrupt controller, which generates eight Call vectors and can be cascaded for up to 64 service levels.
- 8214 priority-interrupt control unit, which is similar to the 8259, but has fixed priorities, and can be expanded from 8 to 40 levels.

The interface structure may be isolated from memory or may share the memory-address space. This gives the programmer the option of using either I/O or memory-reference instructions (that read, write or operate on data in memory) for I/O operations. Memory-reference instructions can significantly increase throughput in applications requiring frequent I/O data manipulations. Also, they allow more ports to be ad-

dressed without decoding, thereby reducing component count.

When a DMA Request is acknowledged, the 8257 takes control of the system bus. It uses the CPU Hold function to suspend CPU operation and transfer blocks of data. Hold Acknowledge tells the DMA controller to take control of the bus.

Operations of the system bus

During each machine cycle, the CPU first addresses the device to be used in the data transfer. Then it sends to the 8228 system controller a status word defining the operation to be performed, and uses the data bus to make the transfer.

The control lines operated by the 8228 handle device input and output gating. The 8228 controls data-bus flow through its bidirectional driver. The status words are translated into specific gating signals: "write" signals MEMW and I/OW, and "read" signals MEMR, I/OR and INTA (interrupt acknowledge).

Bus timing requires that a specific peripheral device should respond to or be prepared to receive valid data within a specific "window" in the CPU cycle. The window is obtained by giving the device time to settle between addressing and gating. Adjustments for devices that have a relatively long cycle time are made with a function called Wait Request (or Ready).

The function, a special feature of the 8080, allows timing signals to be extended without seriously sacrificing CPU speed. For example, a designer can choose an inexpensive memory, one that has an access time of twice the CPU state time. However, typical instruction-cycle time increases only 25 percent. The Ready function inserts a synchronized Wait state into the cycle between addressing and gating, and increases the cycle from four states to five. Using other methods, the clock period would be doubled, resulting in a 100% increase in cycle time.

The Ready control can be used to insert one or more Wait states into every machine cycle, or it can be used selectively to accommodate different devices. Ready control also simplifies single-step operations.

During each cycle the CPU also sends to the 8228 various gating commands (Data Bus In, Write, and Hold Acknowledge). Other commands include Interrupt Enable, which is used to permit or inhibit interrupts, and Wait, which signifies that an idling state is in progress.

Memories needn't slow the system

Typical memory organizations and memory-to-bus connections are indicated in Fig. 3. In large

Instruction set and programming methods

The basic instruction set of the 8080 can be divided, for convenience, into data-transfer, arithmetic, logic and branch groups. The final division is stack, I/O and machine control (see instruction table).

The first byte of an instruction is an operation code. The op code is supplemented in many cases by one or two address or data bytes. Data stored in memory or registers may be addressed in one of four modes:

- Direct—a memory address of the data is contained in bytes 2 and 3 of the instruction;
- Register—the register or register pair containing the data is specified by the instruction;
- Register indirect—a register pair containing the data's memory address is specified by the instruction;
- Immediate—the instruction contains the data, rather than the data address.

Branch instructions specify the next instruction by containing the next instruction address (direct) or by indicating a register pair containing the next instruction address (register indirect).

Two complete sets of software packages are available to the programmer: those resident in the Intellec MDS system, and cross products (available on both computer tape and time-shared computer networks) written in ANSI-standard Fortran IV.

The cross products and resident software generate completely compatible code. Routines written with either method can be linked, emulated and debugged in the microcomputer environment with the Intellec MDS system, which can also be used to combine the debugging of pro-

```
                        /*   BUBBLE SORT DECLARATION   */
SORT  PROCEDURE (N) ADDRESS.
     /*      N    LENGTH OF A
            COUNT    NR. OF SWITCHES PERFORMED TO-DATE
            SWITCHED    (BOOLEAN) HAVE WE DONE ANY SWITCHING YET ON THIS SCAN   */
     DECLARE (N, I, SWITCHED) BYTE.
            (TEMP. COUNT) ADDRESS.

     SWITCHED  1.                /*   SWITCHED   TRUE MEANS NOT DONE YET   */
     COUNT  0.
     DO WHILE SWITCHED.

          SWITCHED   0.          /*   BEGIN NEXT SCAN OF A   */
          DO I   0 TO N-2.
               IF A(I)  A(I+1) THEN
                    DO.                    /*   FOUND A PAIR OUT OF ORDER   */
                    COUNT = COUNT + 1.
                    SWITCHED = 1.          /*   SET SWITCHED   TRUE   */
                    TEMP   A(I).           /*   SWITCH THEM INTO ORDER   */
                    A(I)   A(I+1).
                    A(I+1)   TEMP.
                    END.
          END.
          /*   HAVE NOW COMPLETED A SCAN   */
     END   /*   WHILE   */.
     /*   HAVE NOW COMPLETED A SCAN WITH NO SWITCHING   */
     RETURN COUNT.
END SORT.
```

A. **"Bubble sort"** routine written in **PL/M** arranges data pertaining to events according to the frequency with which individual events occur. Events occurring most frequently move to the top.

gram and hardware design.

Programs can be written with a macro assembler or PL/M compiler (PL/M is Intel's high-level programming language). The macro assemblers translate mnemonics into machine code. PL/M allows programs to be written in a natural algorithmic language and eliminates the need to allocate memory or manage register usage.

An example of a sorting routine written with PL/M appears in Fig. A. The free-form input shown is translated into 8080 object code by the compiler; the programmer can concentrate on the software design structure and system-logic requirements. Fig. B illustrates a macro-assembly approach to programming one of the peripheral components.

Data transfer group

MOV r1, r2	Move register to register
MOV M, r	Move register to memory
MOV r, M	Move memory to register
MVI r, data	Move immediate (to register)
MVI M, data	Move immediate (to memory)
LXI rp, data 16	Load immediate (to register pair or to stack pointer)
STA addr	Store direct (accumulator to memory)
LDA addr	Load direct (memory to accumulator)
XCHG	Exchange H&L with D&E registers
STAX rp	Store accumulator indirect (with address in registers B&C or D&E)
LDAX rp	Load accumulator indirect (with address in registers B&C or D&E)
SHLD addr	Store H&L direct
LHLD addr	Load H&L direct

Arithmetic group

INR r	Increment register
DCR r	Decrement register
INR M	Increment memory
DCR M	Decrement memory
ADD r	Add register to A
ADC r	Add register to A with carry
SUB r	Subtract register from A
SBB r	Subtract register from A with borrow
ADD M	Add memory to A
ADC M	Add memory to A with carry
SUB M	Subtract memory from A
SBB M	Subtract memory from A with borrow
ADI data	Add immediate to A
ACI data	Add immediate to A with carry
SUI data	Subtract immediate from A
SBI data	Subtract immediate from A with borrow
INX rp	Increment register pair (or stack pointer)
DCX rp	Decrement register pair (or stack pointer)
DAA	Decimal adjust A (gives two BCD digits)
DAD rp	Add B&C, D&E or H&L to H&L

```
                 ;      MODE INSTRUCTION
                 ;      ==== ===========
                 ;
                 ;      2 STOP BITS
                 ;      PARITY DISABLED
                 ;      8 BIT CHARACTERS
                 ;      BAUD RATE FACTOR OF 64
                 ;
                 ;      COMMAND INSTRUCTION
                 ;      ======= ===========
                 ;
                 ;      NO HUNT MODE
                 ;      NOT(RTS) FORCED TO 0
                 ;      RECEIVE ENABLED
                 ;      DATA TERMINAL READY
                 ;      TRANSMIT ENABLED
                 ;                        '
      0000  3ECF       MVI   A,MODE
      0002  D3FB       OUT   CNCTL   ; OUTPUT MODE SET TO USART
      0004  3E27       MVI   A,CMD
      0006  D3FB       OUT   CNCTL   ; OUTPUT COMMAND WORD TO USART
```

(a)

```
      ; FUNCTION: CI
      ; INPUTS: NONE
      ; OUTPUTS: A - CHARACTER FROM CONSOLE
      ; CALLS: NOTHING
      ; DESTROYS: A,F/F´S
      ; DESCRIPTION: CI WAITS UNTIL A CHARACTER HAS BEEN ENTERED AT THE
      ;              CONSOLE AND THEN RETURNS THE CHARACTER, VIA THE A
      ;              REGISTER,  TO THE CALLING ROUTINE.  THIS ROUTINE
      ;              IS CALLED BY THE USER VIA A JUMP TABLE IN RAM.
      ;
01D0          CI:

01D0.  DBFB       IN    CONST   ; GET STATUS OF CONSOLE
01D2   E602       ANI   RBR     ; CHECK FOR RECEIVER BUFFER READY
01D4   CAD001     JZ    CI      ; NOT YET - WAIT
01D7   DBFA       IN    CNIN    ; READY SO GET CHARACTER
01D9   C9         RET
```

(b)

B. Typical routines for the 8251 programmable communications interface are written with the 8080's macro assembler. The first routine (a) initializes the circuit. The second (b) specifies the input character, C1. Another program, similar to (b), specifies the output character.

Logic group

ANA r	AND register with A
XRA r	EXCLUSIVE-OR register with A
ORA r	OR register with A
CMP r	Compare register with A
ANA M	AND memory with A
XRA M	EXCLUSIVE-OR memory with A
ORA M	OR memory with A
CMP M	Compare memory with A
ANI data	AND immediate with A
XRI data	EXCLUSIVE-OR immediate with A
ORI data	OR immediate with A
CPI data	Compare immediate with A
RLC	Rotate A left
RRC	Rotate A right
RAL	Rotate A left through carry
RAR	Rotate A right through carry
CMA	Complement A
STC	Set carry
CMC	Complement carry

Branch group

JMP addr	Jump unconditional
Jcond addr	Jump on condition specified (carry, no carry, zero, no zero, positive, minus, even or odd parity)
CALL addr	Call unconditional
Ccond addr	Call on condition specified (see above)
RET	Return
Rcond	Return on condition specified (see above)
RST	Restart
PCHL	H&L to program counter

Stack, I/O and machine control group

HLT	Halt
IN port	Input (from port to A)
OUT port	Output (from A to port)
PUSH rp	Push register pair on stack (in memory)
PUSH PSW	Push A and flags on stack
POP rp	Pop register pair off stack
POP PSW	Pop A and flags off stack
XTHL	Exchange top of stack with H&L
SPHL	Move H&L to stack pointer
EI	Enable interrupts
DI	Disable interrupts
NOP	No op

memory arrays, drivers and 8205 one-of-eight decoders may be added as bus interfaces.

Access times have no effect on component-to-bus interfaces. The 8111 256 × 4-bit static RAM and 8316A 2048 × 8-bit ROM, for example, have maximum access times of 850 ns while the CPU can operate at a state time of 480 ns or less. A Wait state is simply inserted into the cycle time. If the designer decides to change to faster memory, the logic element used to activate the 8224's Ready Input is simply removed.

Available EPROMS (erasable and electrically reprogrammable PROMS) are interchangeable with the 8316A, mask-programmed ROMs. The EPROMS are 24-pin static devices with three-state, byte-wide outputs. The 8316A 16-kilobits ROM is generally used to double storage density after program development with an 8708 8-k EPROM.

The 8107B 4-k dynamic RAM may be used for large memories. An available 16-kilobyte dynamic-RAM board (Model in-481) matches CPU speed and synchronizes memory-to-CPU operations. Also, Schottky-bipolar PROMs and ROMs are available for very fast program storage.

Organizing the system interface

The organization of I/O and peripheral devices can proceed in one of three ways: isolated or memory-mapped, or a combinatian of each (Fig. 4). When memory and I/O are controlled separately, up to 65,536 memory bytes and 512 input and output ports can be directly addressed.

With memory mapping, the I/O is controlled by memory-control lines and operated with memory-reference instructions. I/O shares the memory-address space, and a memory-address bit is typically used as a flag to denote that an I/O operation is occurring. A combination of the two techniques is exemplified by a memory-mapped scheme for I/O devices, and isolated I/O for peripheral units.

The memory-mapped approach is often advantageous for complex structures, because memory-reference instructions offer numerous shortcuts in I/O data manipulation. Further, substantial I/O structures can be operated without address decoders.

In either case, two port-selection (or port-addressing) methods apply—linear or decoded select. With linear select, a single address bit forms an exclusive enable for a specific device, and no decoders are used. In decoded select, the address bus is decoded into exclusive enables to maximize the number of directly accessible ports.

Memory-mapped I/O with linear select makes up to 39 ports (up to 312 I/O lines) available without decoders. If this technique is used for

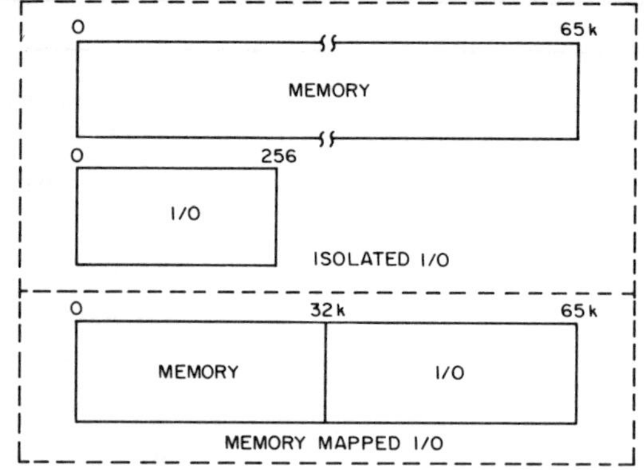

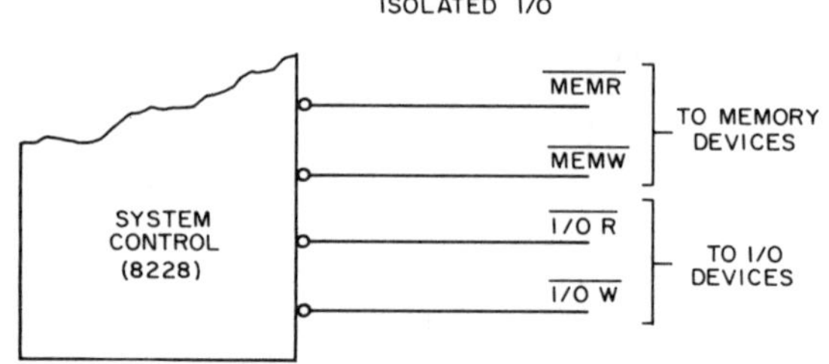

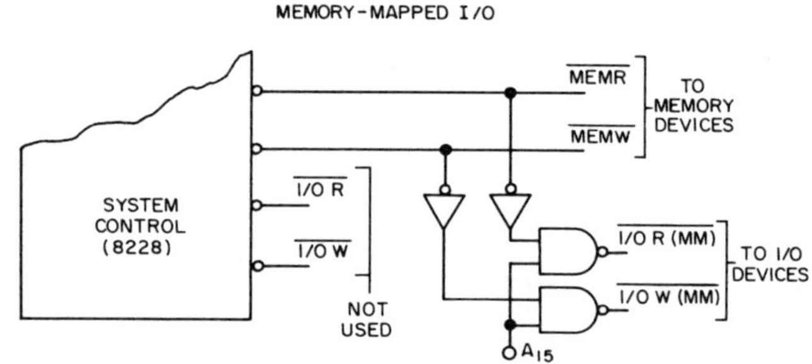

4. **I/O can be organized** by either an isolated or a memory-mapped method. The latter allows the use of memory-reference instructions, and employs memory-read and write control lines for I/O devices. An address bit acts as an I/O flag.

I/O devices, an isolated I/O and linear-select method can still be used for peripheral devices. With decoded select, either method provides a structure of practically unlimited size.

Design and development aids

For design prototyping, Intel supplies the SDK-80 system design kit, which contains the following:

■ A basic 8080 system—8080A CPU group, two 8111 static RAMs, two 8708 EPROMs, plus the 8251 and 8255 peripheral circuits. One of the EPROMs is pre-programmed with a system monitor;

■ PC board, discrete components, sockets and other hardware. The board is pre-drilled for expansion and has an area for adding wrapped-wire interconnections;

■ Design and operating manuals.

Software and hardware development are supported by the Intellec MDS (microcomputer development system) and the ICE-80 in-circuit emulator subsystem. The basic MDS contains an 8080 system, with optional peripherals, and resident software.

The MDS can be used for program generation, assembly, emulation, and debugging. It can also be used as a system prototyping tool. Software includes a monitor and a disc-operating system as well as programming packages.

The ICE-80 module and its supporting software offer two unique development features:

(1) Debugging in the actual operating environment. Since ICE-80 plugs into the 8080A CPU socket on the microcomputer board, all operations of the system bus can be controlled and analyzed through the MDS console. An auxiliary connector can be used to observe the operations of external devices;

(2) Debugging can be done through the console, with readily understandable commands. Also, symbols can be used to refer to critical program labels and parameters, rather than to absolute memory locations.

An example of a system based on the 8080 is the SBC-80/10 Single Board Computer. It contains a general-purpose 8-bit microcomputer designed to be used as a plug-in component.

Boosting Bit-Manipulation Capability

WILLIAM H. SEIPP
Project Engineer,
Eagle Signal Industrial Controls Division,
Davenport, Iowa

Inadequate bit-manipulation capabilities for microprocessors can be overcome either by using microprogrammable chips or by the addition of simple logic external to the CPU chip. The latter approach offers the advantages of standardized instruction sets, high logic speed, much simpler software requirements and use of established assemblers.

Typical industrial processes require hundreds of single-bit calculations to determine the state of individual outputs in response to the state of individual inputs. Also, arithmetic capability is needed for the implementation of decimal arithmetic, timing, counting, data-sequencing and process-control functions.

The lack of efficient bit-manipulation capabilities in available μP chips can discourage their use in industrial controllers. Bit-mode calculations may require as many as 20 software steps to perform a single-bit operation—with correspondingly large execution-time and memory requirements (Fig. 1).

Handling single-bit data

The processing of single-bit information in a μP designed for parallel-data processing involves masking techniques and the shifting of data to match bit positions. Bit information can be found in industrial real-time applications in the form of limit switches and pushbutton inputs, and in solenoid and motor-control outputs. The individual control circuits are usually arranged in 8-bit-input and output words for best use of μP addressing capabilities.

Prior to performing logic operations, the I/O words containing the desired control-circuit bits must be masked and the data shifted so that bits share a common bit position (as indicated in Fig. 1). After the logic operation is performed, the output word must be updated. This requires further masking and possibly further shifting before the logic output is updated.

Addition of bit-mode hardware to the 8080

INPUT	WORD A	1LS IS BIT 7
ANA	0200	MASK OUT ALL BIT 1LS
MOV	B, A	SAVE IT
INPUT	WORD B	2LS IS BIT 4
ANA	020	MASK OUT ALL BUT 2LS
RLC		
RLC		SHIFT TO MATCH BIT POSITIONS
RLC		
ANA	B	1LS AND 2LS
RLC		SHIFT TO MATCH OUTPUT
RLC		BIT POSITIONS
LBA		SAVE RESULT TEMPORARILY
INPUT	OUTA	SOLA IS BIT 2
ANA	0375	MASK OUT ONLY BIT 2
ORA	B	INSERT NEW BIT 2 VALUE
OUT	OUTA	RESTORE OUTPUT WORD

1. **The software implementation of a bit mode** for the 8080 microprocessor takes 97 μs and requires 23 bytes of program memory. The program reads the state of normally open contacts, 1LS and 2LS. When both are closed, relay coil SOLA is energized.

microprocessor reduces the program of Fig. 1 to the one shown in Fig. 2. Typical logic for input and output circuits appears in Figs. 3 and 4. Similar logic is used in Eagle Signal's EPTAK Microprocessor System.

Input-bit data are pre-selected and directed to the D_0 data bit of the microprocessor data bus (Fig. 3). Pre-selection eliminates the software-shifting requirement and standardizes the bit position in the central-processing-unit (CPU) accumulator for all bit operations. Masking is performed by zeroing all other data bits.

The processing of Boolean-logic equations often requires the use of inverted data from some input circuits. (Inverted data close the normally open contacts in Fig. 1.) The AND-OR-Invert gate selects the True, or inverted, representation

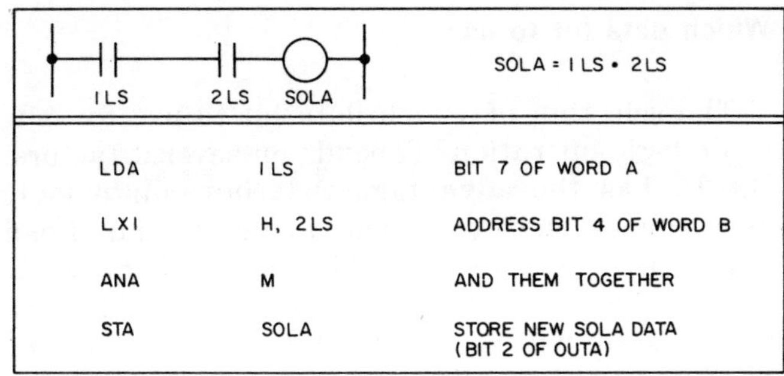

2. **With hardware bit mode, the 8080 program takes** only 43 μs and needs just 10 bytes of memory.

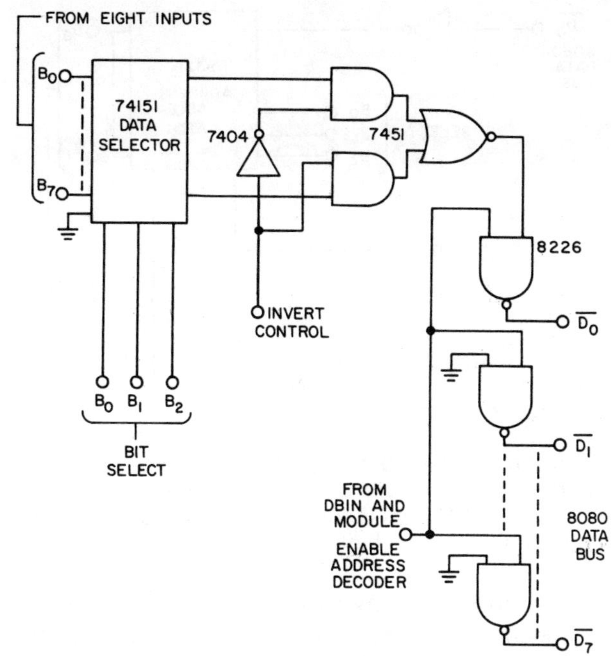

3. **The bit-mode input logic employs a data selector** to pre-select the D_0 data bit, and to direct it to the 8080 data bus. Pre-selection eliminates the need for software shifting. Only one input circuit need be used with the CPU, since it can select the bit or byte required.

of the pre-selected input before it transfers to the CPU data bus.

Simple circuitry stores output data

Because of the standardized bit position in the CPU accumulator, only simple circuitry is required to store output data (Fig. 4). The use of an addressable latch circuit (the 9334) assures storage of output data corresponding to the appropriate bit, and does not affect the other data bits in the 8-bit word. The addressable latch simulates the software masking and shift operations. Generally, inverted data aren't stored in the output circuits, although that would be possible with circuitry similar to that shown in Fig. 4.

The basic concept of bit-mode logic can be expanded to include byte-mode read and write operations and to obtain a combination input/output circuit. Instead of duplicating the mask and shift logic for each input module, you can use a single circuit in the CPU module, but the CPU must be able to select the bit or byte-mode circuits as required. A mode-control signal can be provided for this purpose.

Bit-mode logic must still be duplicated on each output module to keep over-all logic costs low. The output circuit may also be modified to include the input function. Output data can then be retrieved for later processing of other logic operations or logic equations.

The CPU must provide new control signals for proper operation of the input and output circuitry. These signal lines include those for bit-addressing, true/invert data control and bit/byte control. In systems with small numbers of I/O circuits these control lines may be derived from the standard input or output instructions of the μP chip.

The 8080A, for example, allows an 8-bit address in its input and output instructions. The use of three of those bits for bit selection and one bit for the invert control limits system capacity to 128-bit inputs and 128-bit outputs. The inclusion of a bit/byte mode-control signal as one

of the I/O address lines would further reduce the number of input and output circuits to 64.

Memory mapping boosts I/O

A greater number of circuits can be obtained through use of memory mapping. In this method, input and output circuits are assigned memory addresses. The EPTAK system, for instance, assigns input and output circuits to the upper addresses of the μP's total memory-addressing capacity. In a microprocessor with 64-k memory capacity (16 address lines), the upper 16-k might be reserved for I/O circuits. This does not pose a severe limitation on software capability; there are still 48-k memory addresses available for program storage.

In the memory map, upper address bits A_{14} and A_{15} (both logic ONE) select the input/output circuits as opposed to memory circuits. Control bits are assigned to other address lines. A_{13} is assigned the function of invert control, and A_{12} to the bit/byte mode select. The EPTAK controller uses two types of input/output circuits. One is denoted "chassis I/O" and the other is called "track I/O." These are selected by the A_{11} address line.

Chassis I/O modules include pushbutton, display, digital and analog I/O. Track I/O consists of individual input and output blocks for interface to 120 V ac machine-control devices. Lines A_8, A_9, and A_{10} select the desired bit or byte, depending on the selected mode. If the I/O module is designed to have more than one byte of data, the

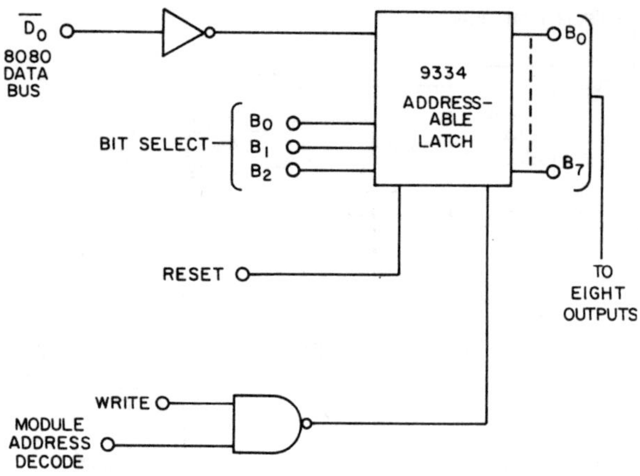

4. **The bit-mode output logic reserves** lines B_0 to B_7 for system inputs or data-bus inputs (when the circuit is used on the CPU module). The circuit can be enabled by any I/O address that calls for bit mode.

module cannot be operated in the bit mode without special circuitry. The eight low-order address bits are used to select one of 16 modules in a chassis (A_0 to A_3) and one of 16 chassis in a system (A_4 to A_7).

The trade-off of memory for I/O circuits does more than increase the I/O capacity of a μP controller. It also decreases I/O access time because memory references require shorter cycle times than typical input and output instructions do. Also, direct memory addressing is provided for logic operations, such as AND and OR. These logic operations are not provided with the standard input and output instructions in the 8080.

The mere transition from I/O instructions to memory mapping provides increased software flexibility in its own right. It is, therefore, advantageous even in small systems to use a memory-mapping technique for input/output operations to gain the increased I/O speed and flexibility. But since smaller systems do not require a great amount of memory and because memory cost is low, simplified external bit-mode logic using I/O instruction can be emphasized over more complicated logic for memory mapping.

Which data bit to use

The selection of which data bit to use for bit-mode logic operations depends on several factors. Bit D_0 has the advantage that immediate logic operations—such as Load Logic 1 and Load Logic 0—result in an 8-bit binary 1 or 8-bit binary 0 loading into the accumulator. And the logic results will be either a binary 0 or a binary 1. This provides a simple, one-to-one correspondence between the single-bit binary code and the 8-bit binary number. Tests for conditional jumps use the accumulator zero flag.

The problem with the D_0 bit position occurs with instructions such as Invert, which involve the entire 8-bit byte and not just the bit in the D_0 position. In fact, all logic operations affect the entire 8-bit byte. This in itself is not a problem because the hardware masks out all bits but the one desired in a store operation. The proper setting of the zero flag for conditional jumps requires operations such as Invert to be followed by a mask operation—like ANA 1. An alternative bit-invert instruction is XRA 1, which doesn't need a mask operation.

Selection of the D_7 bit position also has advantages and disadvantages. In an 8-bit microprocessor chip, the D_7-bit position is the sign bit. The sign flag can be tested directly regardless of the data in the other positions of the accumulator without the need for a mask operation. However, the binary data corresponding to bit-logic ZERO and bit-logic ONE are 0 and -128 (octal 200), respectively.

Thus the selection of the standardized data bit boils down to a matter of notational convenience and the number of times that will be required to test the logic bit. Most relay-logic and Boolean-logic expressions entail Load, And, Or and Store operations. These require no bit testing and therefore the bit position is fairly arbitrary. The selection of D_7 over D_0, though, gives an average 3% decrease in execution time and in memory requirements, for a typical application.

Speeding Microprocessor Responses

EUGENE FISHER
*Design Engineer, Lawrence Livermore Laboratory,
Livermore, California*

Microcomputer designs don't require techniques based on minicomputer hardware to achieve high speeds. Though designers often employ speed-enhancing interrupt or direct-memory-access (DMA) techniques borrowed from the mini world, the same improvements can be obtained far more simply. All that's needed is a microprocessor whose operations can be suspended readily during data transfers. Microprocessors like Intel's 8080 permit just this kind of solution.

When applied to an 8080-based floppy-disc controller, the simple approach requires only about 20 ICs. By comparison, an interrupt structure uses 40 to 80 ICs, and a DMA approach needs 80 to 100. Moreover the 8080 exercises full format and timing control over floppy-disc functions, with all of the algorithms contained in less than 512 words of ROM.

The alternatives

Interrupt structures often require hardware that is external to the microprocessor, as well as special programming (Fig. 1). Further, high-speed applications can easily require all of the microprocessor's real-time capability. For this reason, other interrupt sources usually must be disabled during the execution of the high-speed routine. Also, it may be necessary to save—in advance—sensitive registers to increase the speed of the interrupt service routine.

After an interrupt in the application program, a series of vectors (either hardware or software) transfer program control to the interrupt-service routine. This routine is the actual program that performs the synchronized I/O transfer. After the servicing of the interrupt, control returns to the application program to prepare again for the next high-speed interrupt service. As many as 100 bytes of code may be needed to handle the high-speed interrupt. This doesn't include the code for standard I/O that would be required without interrupt synchronization.

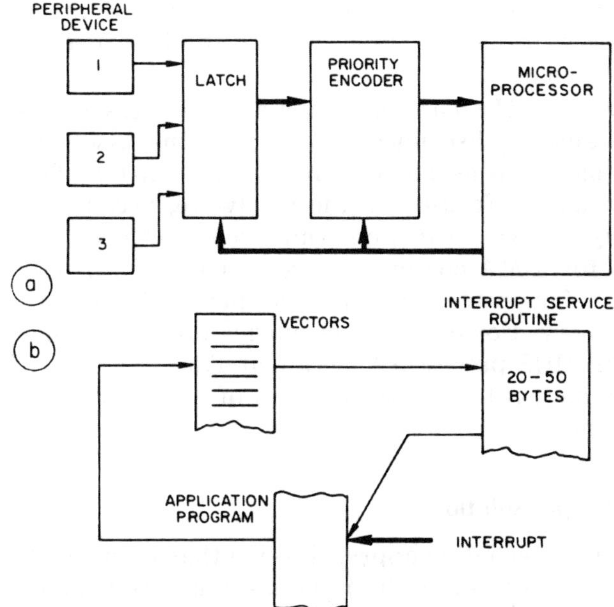

1. **Interrupt techniques may entail the addition** of such external circuits as storage latches and priority encoders (a). Typical response time is 32 μs. However, the major portion of an interrupt structure resides in software (b). Interrupt techniques can achieve typical data rates of about 31-k bytes per second.

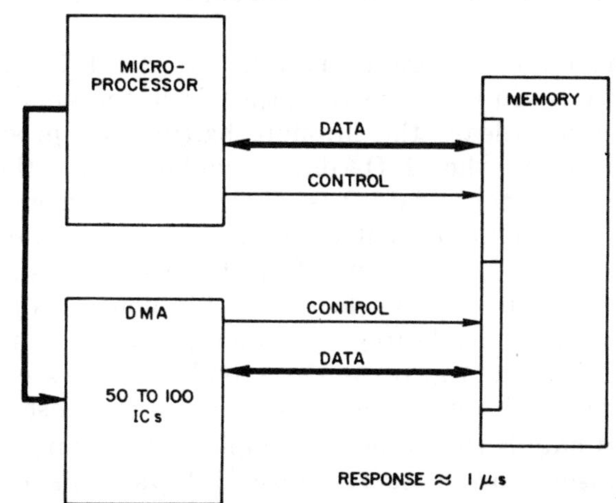

2. **Direct-memory access, or DMA, requires a separate,** external controller that communicates directly with memory. When built with standard ICs, the controller can use up to 100 circuits.

Debugging of this interrupt service is extremely difficult, since it cannot be effectively simulated on a separate computer. In fact, debugging is a very time-consuming effort, requiring the use of all of the system's hardware or a trial-and-error method using oscilloscopes and other external hardware. This difficulty alone has discouraged designers. The typical speed for an interrupt interface is approximately 31,000 bytes per second.

Unlike the interface for a high-speed interrupt, the direct-memory-access interface isn't really part of a microprocessor or microcomputer system. It actually is a separate hardware controller that communicates directly with the computer memory (Fig. 2). The only function a microprocessor has in these cases is to initialize the data channel.

Once DMA has begun, the microprocessor must be able to disconnect itself from the associated memory, so as not to inhibit the transfer. Thus debugging focuses on the hardware, because the only software functions employed are those needed for DMA-channel controls. The typical data-transfer rates are limited primarily by the memory. For example, memories for most single-chip MOS processors operate at 415 ns to 1 μs. So the data rate can be in excess of 100-k bytes per second.

A simple solution

An alternative approach—one that requires the μP to halt for each transfer—takes full advantage of the processor. The technique can be applied to any microprocessor that has Ready-line synchronization or otherwise allows the stopping of the processor for data transfers. The hardware to implement this synchronization appears in Fig. 3. The block diagram shows that a simple, external flip-flop can synchronize the microprocessor.

The circuit operates as follows: An I/O instruction—in this case an output from the microprocessor—clears the flip-flop, halting the processor with the I/O data available on the microprocessor's data bus. The external device takes the data presented by the microprocessor and then returns a signal. Called DONE, the signal is used by the synchronizing flip-flop to raise the Ready line, letting the microprocessor continue. The microprocessor responds to an external input within one cycle—500 ns in our case.

Not only is this interface simple, but the microprocessor worst-case response is 1 μs. This response time is comparable to a DMA transfer, but with none of the associated hardware complexity. And the software is extremely simple; no difficult timing loops are required.

The output instruction actually stops the proc-

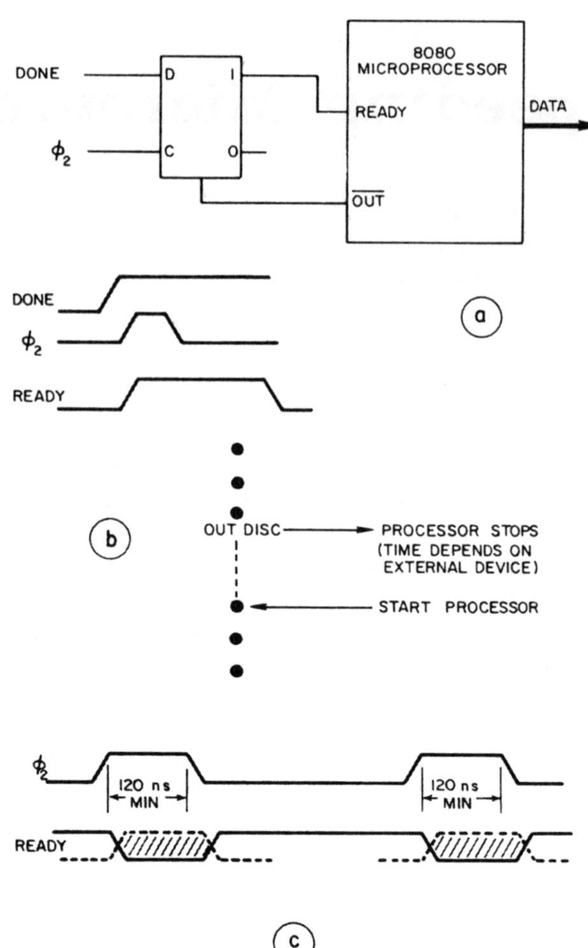

3. **The alternative to DMA and interrupt techniques** employs a microprocessor's Ready line (a) to suspend the processor's operation during data transfers (b). The Ready line is sensed by the microprocessor during phase two of state T_2 or T_W, the Wait state (c). This straightforward approach has a response time of 1 μs, and it yields data rates of 62-k bytes per second.

essor for a time that depends on the external device. If the microprocessor is already running at 100% utilization, there isn't time for other operations anyway. Thus the time lost by halting the processor is of no real consequence. And now software for the output or input is merely a standard I/O operation, with synchronization and data timing taken care of automatically. The data rate is 62-k bytes per second—a program-execution limitation.

Employing the Ready line

The Ready line on the 8080 processor was designed primarily to interface the processor to a slow memory or a slow I/O operation. But while the processor is stopped, the data bus is present on the processor's data lines. On an input instruction, the processor takes the data within 500 ns after starting or after the assertion of the Ready Signal. After the Ready line is raised,

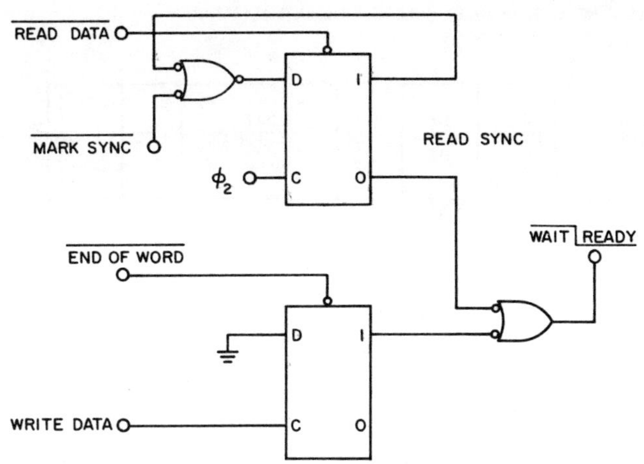

4. **The synchronizing circuit for the Ready line** employs two flip-flops, one for the output and one for the input.

the microprocessor responds within the next clock cycle. Thus over-all response is about 1 μs when a 500-ns clock is used with the 8080.

A typical Ready-line synchronization circuit appears in Fig. 4. Two synchronizing flip-flops are used, one for input and one for output from the peripheral. In both cases all synchronization is handled by an external flip-flop. Even the requirement for an external D-type flip-flop has been eliminated by a new clock driver recently announced by Intel. The synchronizing of the Ready line can be taken care of by the new IC.

Programming constraints

The program must be able, of course, to accept synchronization by the external hardware. In the sample program (Fig. 5) the timing of each instruction in a critical loop has been calculated. This is necessary to ensure that the next I/O instruction is asserted in time. The routine allows the maximum data-transfer rate for the 8080 by employing the processor's stack pointer.

By adding the two halves of the loop, we see

that the maximum time between instructions is 16 μs. Also the response to an external stimulus is 1 μs. And the data rate for this interface is twice that possible in any equivalent interrupt-driven interface.

Specifying the interface

Our floppy-disc application employs the IBM format (Fig. 6). Note the different types of sector information. Each has a unique indicator —a Mark—for Index, Data, Deleted Data and Address. A Mark doesn't contain a full set of clock pulses, and the missing clocks and Mark words, form synchronizing elements. Another critical item is the cycle redundancy check (CRC) character. This appears at the end of each data sector. It must be read to determine if there has been an error in reading or writing.

The data rate in this format is 4 μs per data bit, with the clock pulses coming between each data pulse (Fig. 7). The data rate of the standard floppy disc is 4 $\times$ 8 bits/byte, or 32 μs per 8-bit byte. However, to eliminate any possibility of timing problems, the interface is designed for twice that rate, or 16 μs per 8-bit byte—an effective transfer rate of 62-k bytes per second. And to eliminate the need for double buffering, the previously collected data word is read before the next clock pulse occurs. This results in the 2-μs interval at our double speed.

Solving interface problems

The "missing"—but implied—clock signal is detected by a retriggerable, monostable multivibrator. With the aid of a separate clock signal from the floppy disc (Fig. 7b), the detected signal is then used to synchronize an 8-bit register and to generate an end-of-word signal.

A 4-bit counter (Fig. 8) regenerates the missing pulses. The microprocessor's crystal clock

```
005161    333 011      ROVR:     IN DATAR     :READ ONE WORD—5.5
005163    157                    MOV L - A    :SAVE −2.5
005164    015            .       DCR  C       :BUMP CNTR −2.5
005165    345                    PUSH  H      :STORE TWO WORDS −5.5
005166    333 011      DATCOL:   IN DATAR      :NEXT—AND CRC WORD 1 −5.5
005170    147                    MOV H - A    :SET UP WORD—2.5
005171    302 161 012            JNZ ROVR     :AGAIN—5
005174    333 011                IN DATAR      :CRC WORD 2
005176    333 011                IN DATAR      :CRC DELAY WORD
005200    333 007                IN STAT      :CHECK STATUS
005202    027                    RAL         :SET UP FLAG
005203    052 301 014            LHLD TEMP    :GET THE STACK POINTER
005206    371                    SPHL         :RESTORE SP
005207    332 217 012            JC CRER      :CRC ERROR
005212    311                    RET          :WE MADE IT
```

5. **The time of each instruction in a critical loop** must be calculated to ensure that I/O instructions are asserted soon enough. A portion of the read routine lists these times in microseconds.

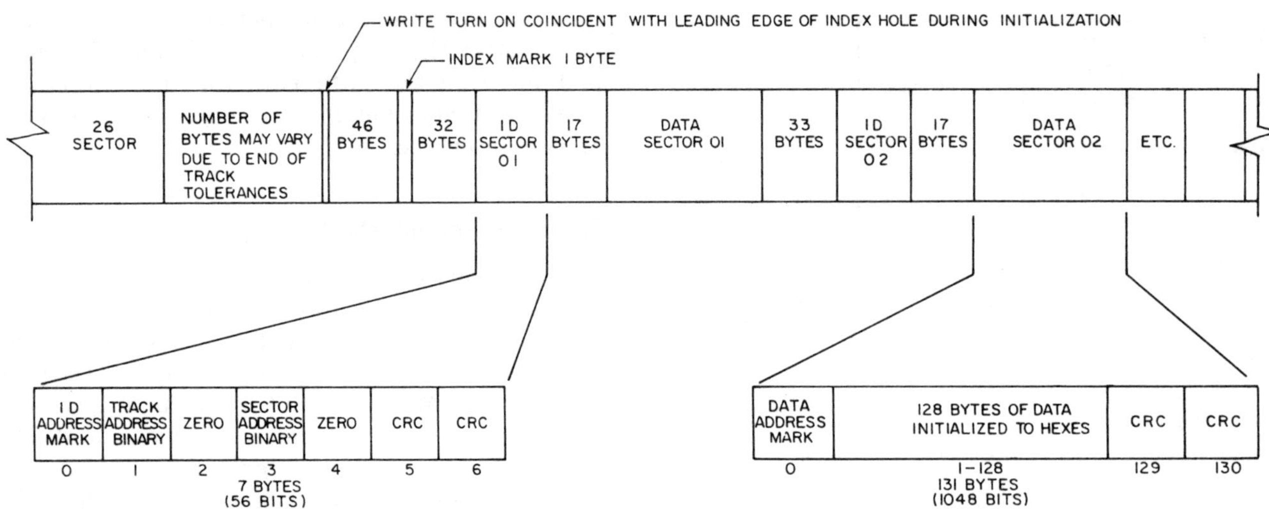

6. **An IBM data format applies to our floppy-disc** example. Different sectors of information use an indicator

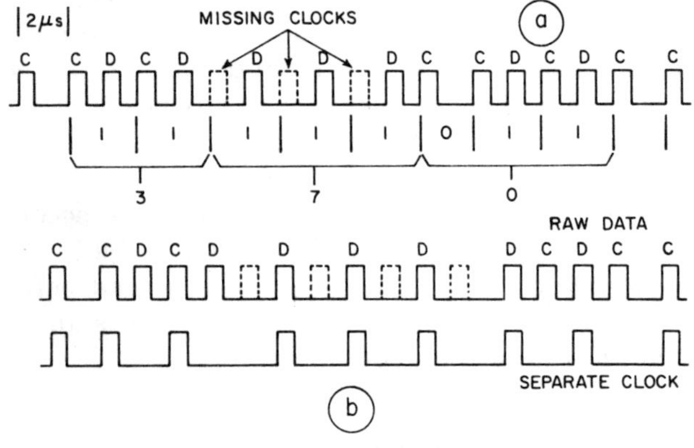

7. **The Data Mark has a transfer rate of 2 μs** per bit (a), or twice that of the usual format. This eliminates possible errors and the need for double buffering. The missing clock pulses are generated with the aid of a separate clock signal (b) from the floppy disc.

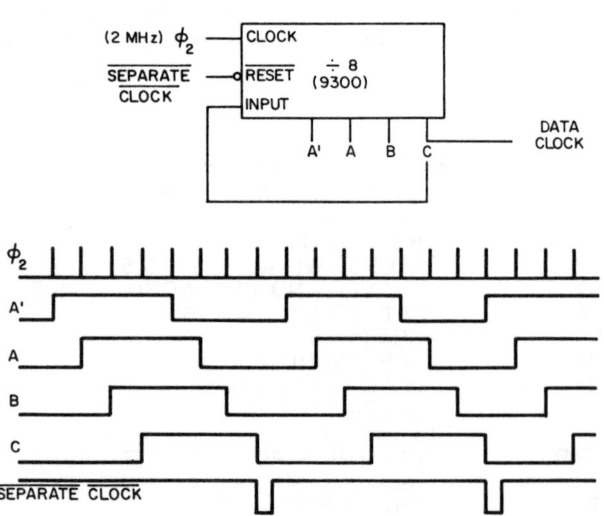

8. **A simple 4-bit counter,** synchronized to each separate-clock pulse from the floppy disc, regenerates the missing clocks.

known as a Mark. It relies on a series of implied—but not present—clock pulses for synchronization.

provides the time base for the counter and thus, the floppy disc.

The counter is synchronized with the data received from the floppy disc, thereby providing a clock signal that doesn't have missing pulses. This counter and the crystal clock also generate the accurate timing pulses required for the Write operation to the floppy disc.

A single IC—the 8-bit register—handles both the serialization and deserialization of the signal from the floppy disc to the microcomputer (Fig. 9). This register has a common I/O; the same eight pins are used for parallel data input and output. Three-state data lines are compatible with the 8080 microprocessor data bus.

The Ready-line synchronizer for our application appears in Fig. 10. To detect a Mark word, the microprocessor sends the input signal called $\overline{\text{READ MARK}}$. This signal sets the flip-flop called Mark Sync, which suspends microprocessor operation until a "missing" clock signal occurs. When missing pulses are detected, the synchronizing flip-flop resets, allowing the processor to read the Mark word collected.

At this time the microprocessor verifies that the correct Mark word has been read. If it is not the correct word, the microprocessor loops back, sending out the $\overline{\text{READ MARK}}$ signal. Again, the processor stops until the next Mark word is received. The timing diagram shows an input Mark signal being sent two times. The first time it detects the address sector and the second time a data sector.

After the Mark word has been read, the succeeding data words must be read to verify the data format, the data transfer or the address sector. Therefore a second input signal called $\overline{\text{READ DATA}}$ is sent in a manner similar to that of the Mark operation just described. However, the input-data synchronizer resets at the end of

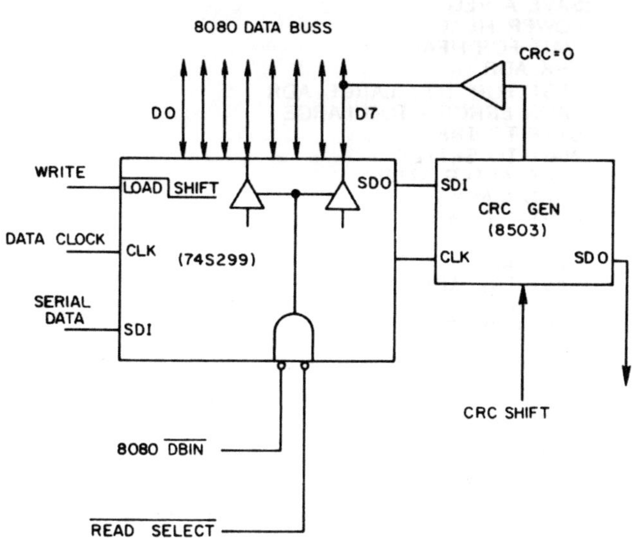

9. An 8-bit shift register, synchronized by the "missing" clocks, provides the parallel-to-serial conversion of the signal from the floppy disc. The second IC generates the cycle-redundancy-check character.

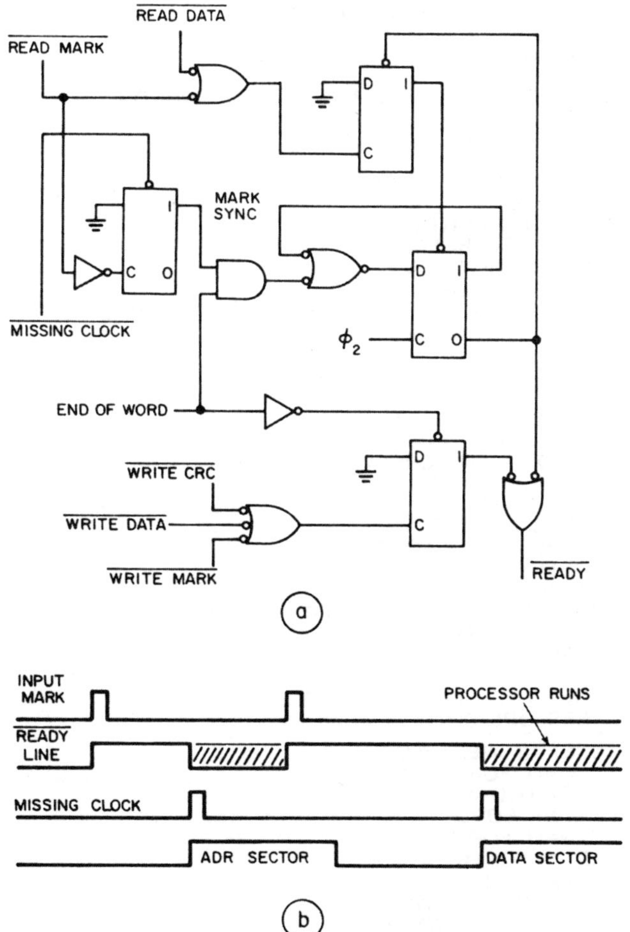

10. The Ready-line synchronizer for the floppy-disc application employs only four flip-flops and a few gates (a). The input Mark signal is sent twice (b) to detect address and data sectors.

each data word rather than at the end of a Mark word. The processor reads the data word at the end of each serial string in less than 1 μs, giving a 100% safety factor even for a floppy disc having twice the usual storage capacity.

The lower portion of the synchronizer controls Write operations for the Ready line. Three types of Write signals require synchronization: Write Mark, Write Data and Write CRC. Write Data simply writes the next 8-bit data word from the microprocessor into the shift register at the appropriate time. The Write Mark signal loads an 8-bit shift register (not shown), and this generates the missing clock lines for the writing of a Mark word.

Also on this shift register, Data Bit 6 is provided for one of the inputs, thereby allowing the software to create any of the three missing clock words required. The Write CRC command converts the CRC generator from a coded mode to a 16-bit serial shift register. The latter shifts out the collected CRC data word.

The control of the floppy disc functions—such as Head Load, Head Step In and Head Step Out —are handled in the usual I/O fashion, with flip-flops set to perform the required functions.

Key portions of the software for the floppy-disc application appear in Fig. 11. The first routine verifies that the floppy-disc head is actually on the correct track. The sequence is as follows: Wait for an address Mark; read the rest of the address sector; save the critical words of interest, the track and sector addresses; verify that there are no errors; then drop into a routine that steps the head to the desired track. Note that no critical timing loops are required. The only requirement is that the program return within 16 μs, so it can read the next data block.

Fig. 11b shows the code used to read a data block from the floppy disc and to store it in memory at the maximum transfer rate. This routine uses the processor's stack pointer to store 16 bits or two bytes per operation (thereby transferring data at 16 μs per byte). Note that this code lists timing intervals in the comment, so the programmer can actually count the instruction times that will result.

Fig. 11c shows the code that writes a data file on the floppy disc. This routine is similar to the previous one. However, a preamble of zero words must be written before the actual data file. Also, the last CRC character must be followed with a zero word.

(On overleaf.)

11. Excerpts from the program, compiled by an 8080 macroassembler, illustrate the three major routines. The first, a search routine, checks to see that the disc head is properly positioned (a). The next routine reads a block of data in the disc and stores it in memory (b). The third routine writes data into the floppy disc (c).

Address	Code	Label	Instruction	Comment
004403	365	STRT:	PUSH PSW	;SAVE A REG
004404	323 012		OUT HDDN	;LOWER HEAD
004406	315 222 011		CALL LDDLY	;WAIT FOR HEAD
004411	176		MOV A - M	;TRK ADR
004412	376 112		CPI 112Q	;TEST FOR TOO LARGE ADR
004414	322 147 011		JNC NOADER	;ADR ERROR—TOO LARGE
004417	315 242 011		CALL SEEK	;STEP TO TRK
004422	315 222 011		CALL LDDLY	;WAIT TO SETTLE
004425	333 010		IN RDMRK	;SYNC AFTER STEP
004427	333 010	TSTRD:	IN RDMRK	;READ MARKS
004431	376 376		CPI 376Q	;WAIT FOR ADR
004433	302 027 011		JNZ TSTRD	;LOOP
004436	333 011		IN DATAR	;TRK ADR
004440	107		MOV B - A	;SAVE TRK ADR
004441	333 011		IN DATAR	;ZEROS
004443	333 011		IN DATAR	;SECTOR ADR
004445	333 011		IN DATAR	;ZEROS
004447	333 011		IN DATAR	;CRC
004451	333 011		IN DATAR	;CRC
004453	333 011		IN DATAR	;CRC DELAY WORD
004455	333 007		IN STAT	;CHECK CRC
004457	027		RAL	;SET UP FLAG
004460	332 165 011		JC ERROR	;CRC ERROR
004463	072 300 014		LDA ADR	;GET EXISTING ADR

(a)

Address	Code	Label	Instruction	Comment
				;ROUTINE TO READ A DATA SECTOR
005064	333 010	READ:	IN RDMRK	;ENTER SECTOR ADR IN B
005066	376 376		CPI 376Q	;LOOK FOR ADR MARK
005070	302 064 012		JNZ READ	;LOOP BACK
005073	333 011		IN DATAR	;SKIP TRK ADR
005075	333 011		IN DATAR	;SKIP ZERO WORD
005077	333 011		IN DATAR	;READ SECTOR ADR
005101	270		CMP B	;TEST SECTOR
005102	302 064 012		JNZ READ	;WRONG SECTOR—LOOP
005105	333 011		IN DATAR	;ZEROS
005107	333 011		IN DATAR	;CRC
005111	333 011		IN DATAR	;CRC
005113	016 013		MVI C . 13Q	;SET UP JUNK-IN-GAP COUNTER
005115	333 011		IN DATAR	;CRC DONE GAP WORD #1
005117	333 007		IN STAT	;CHECK CRC
005121	027		RAL	;SET UP FLAG
005122	332 217 012		JC CRER	;CRC ERROR
005125	333 011	CRAPLP:	IN DATAR	;SKIP THE JUNK-IN-THE-GAP —13 WORDS
005127	015		DCR C	;DONE? —2.5
005130	302 125 012		JNZ CRAPLP	;NOPE LOOP BACK —5
005133	041 000 000		LXI H - 0	;CLR H AND L
005136	071		DAD SP	;ADD STACK POINTER
005137	042 301 014		SHLD TEMP	;SAVE SP
005142	016 100		MVI C - 1000	;SET DATA CNTR
005144	061 000 014		LXI SP - BUFF	;POINT TO BUFFER
005147	333 010		IN RDMRK	;WAIT FOR DATA
005151	376 373		CPI 373Q	;TEST FOR DATA MARK —3.5
005153	302 213 012		JNZ CRERX	;NOT A CRC ERROR BUT GET OUT FOR NOW —5
005156	333 011		IN DATAR	;FIRST WORD —5.5
005160	147		MOV H - A	;SET UP —2.5
005161	333 011	ROVR:	IN DATAR	;READ ONE WORD—5.5
005163	157		MOV L - A	;SAVE —2.5
005164	015		DCR C	;BUMP CNTR —2.5
005165	345		PUSH H	;STORE TWO WORDS —5.5
005166	333 011	DATCOL:	IN DATAR	;NEXT—AND CRC WORD 1 —5.5
005170	147		MOV H - A	;SET UP WORD—2.5
005171	302 161 012		JNZ ROVR	;AGAIN—5
005174	333 011		IN DATAR	;CRC WORD 2
005176	333 011		IN DATAR	;CRC DELAY WORD
005200	333 007		IN STAT	;CHECK STATUS
005202	027		RAL	;SET UP FLAG
005203	052 301 014		LHLD TEMP	;GET THE STACK POINTER
005206	371		SPHL	;RESTORE SP
005207	332 217 012		JC CRER	;CRC ERROR
005212	311		RET	;WE MADE IT
005213	052 301 014	CRERX:	LHLD TEMP	;GET THE STACK POINTER
005216	371		SPHL	;RESTORE SP

(b)

Address	Code	Label	Instruction	Comment
005024	174	OVR:	MOV A - H	;SET UP NEXT WORD —2.5
005025	323 014		OUT DATAW	;WAIT FOR DISC—5.5
005027	341	DATWT:	POP H	;GET TWO WORDS —5
005030	175		MOV A - L	;NEXT WORD —2.5
005031	323 014		OUT DATAW	;WAIT FOR DISC—5.5
005033	015		DCR C	;BUMP CNTR—2.5
005034	302 024 012		JNZ OVR	;OVERS—5
005037	174		MOV A - H	;SET UP LAST WORD
005040	323 014		OUT DATAW	;OUT LAST WORD
005042	323 016		OUT CRC	;SHIFT OUT CRC
005044	323 016		OUT CRC	;IBID
005046	257		XRA A	;CLEAR THE A
005047	323 014		OUT DATAW	;WRITE OFF —LAST WORD IS ZEROS
005051	052 301 014		LHLD TEMP	;GET SP
005054	371		SPHL	;RESTORE SP
005055	311		RET	;FAREWELL

(c)

Running Microprocessor Software

JONATHAN A. TITUS
President, Tychon, Inc.,
Blacksburg, Virginia

You've put your microcomputer together and checked it out. You're ready to run programs. Or are you? Do you first have to build a front panel, backed by extensive starting hardware? You'd like to avoid that, of course.

You'd like to develop schemes to start the microcomputer without fuss. But you don't want to sacrifice flexibility, especially where software is frequently changed or where starting schemes must handle dedicated systems that also need flexibility.

In the 8080—the μP that's finding widest use —the first page of memory, or the first 256 locations, contains some special locations that need defining (Table 1). In the following examples, assume the high address is always 000 (octal), unless otherwise noted.

One of the easiest ways to start software is to use read/write (R/W) memory, starting at location 0. A front panel is used to load a starting address and a Jump instruction. When the 8080 is reset, control then jumps to the start of any program, anywhere in the available memory. This method is flexible since you can use the vectors at locations 10 to 70 if you wish. The use of R/W memory doesn't dedicate these points to a particular application.

It can be a bother, however, to use a front panel. And you can't assume that users will immediately understand how to get information into the computer with the switches and controls.

If you use a read-only-memory (ROM) or programmable-read-only-memory (PROM) for the first page of memory, the Jump instruction at locations 0, 1 and 2 will always point to the same place—a very useful feature if a Monitor, Bootstrap or Debug software routine is always resident in the computer.

Using ROM or PROM also means that before you program, you must decide upon some use for the vector addresses 10 to 70. Those addresses then become committed, and you can't help but lose some flexibility.

A useful variation of the ROM method permits the starting address to exist in PROM and the vector addresses to exist in R/W memory. How can this be possible? Just as you program the Start PROM to jump to the starting address of the Bootstrap, you also program the vector addresses to jump to free locations in R/W memory (Fig. 1).

Now whenever you reset the 8080, the system will immediately execute the Jump to the Boot-

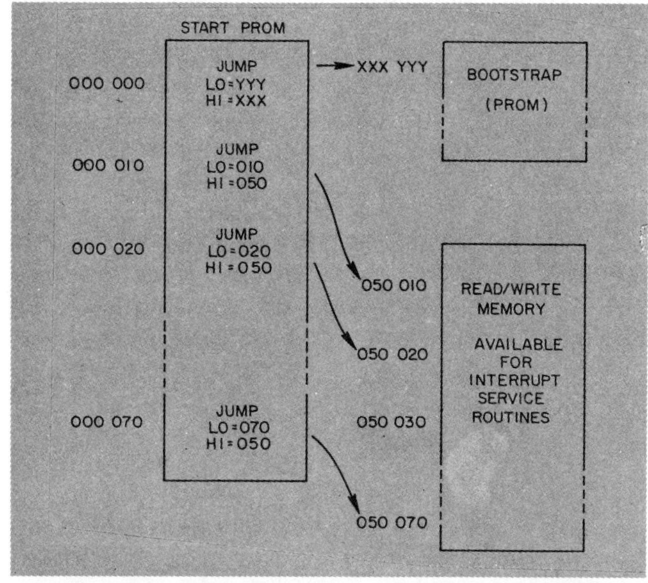

1. **By using a PROM,** you can jump to a Bootstrap routine or relocate the 8080's interrupt-service routine. The pre-empted position can hold a "start" program.

Table 1. 8080 locations available for start-up

Locations	Use
0	This is the RESET, or starting address. When the 8080 chip is reset, it executes the program that starts at location 000 000.
10, 20, 30 40, 50, 60 and 70	These are the RESTART instructions' vector points. They are the starting addresses of interrupt service routines. If interrupts or restart instructions aren't used, you can use these locations in any way you wish.

strap. If a vector or a restart instruction is to be used, the servicing software must be put at a high address of 050 and a low address corresponding to the low address of the vector point. This means than an interrupt—which will point the computer to 000 010—will be "jumped" to 050 010, where the necessary software resides in R/W memory. The jump is very useful when you use a Debug package to test a system before production.

Although the Jump scheme preserves the flexibility of the vector points in R/W memory, you can have only one starting address at locations 0, 1 and 2 for each Start PROM. Of course, you can always work with a collection of PROMs with various starting addresses for various programs. But this is a waste, and switching the PROMs takes time.

Another method can be used to specify any starting address and still give the use of the vector points, but without a front panel. You still use a PROM to move the vector points to R/W memory with jumps. Instead of jumping from address 0 to the Bootstrap, you jump to a routine that delivers and uses the starting address in a

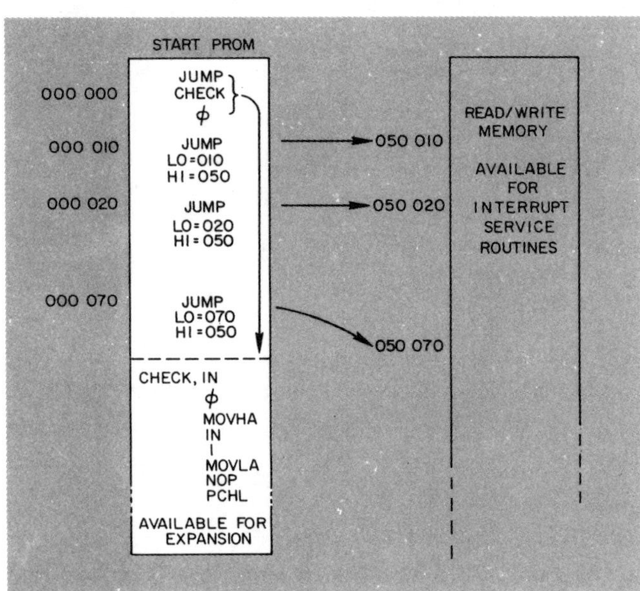

2. **Starting addresses can be specified** without a front panel. A Check routine placed in PROM uses input data as an address to which to jump.

Table 2. Routine to use input data to generate JUMP address

CHECK	IN	INPUT HI ADDRESS BYTE FROM
	∅0∅	PORT 0
	MOV H,A	MOVE IT TO REGISTER H
	IN	INPUT LO ADDRESS BYTE FROM
	∅01	PORT 1
	MOV L,A	MOVE IT TO REGISTER L
	NOP	NO OPERATION
	PCHL	MOVE H&L TO PROGRAM COUNTER & START EXECUTING FROM THAT ADDRESS

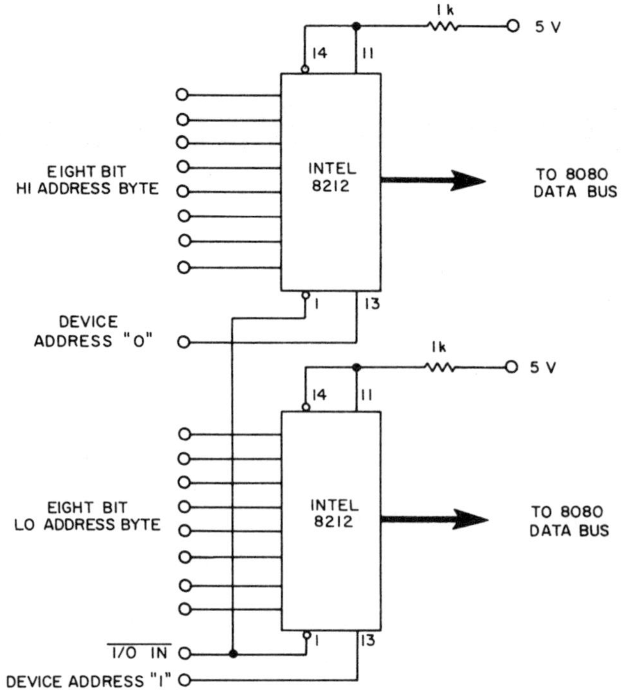

3. **Software-controlled address input:** Three-state devices are used at the input.

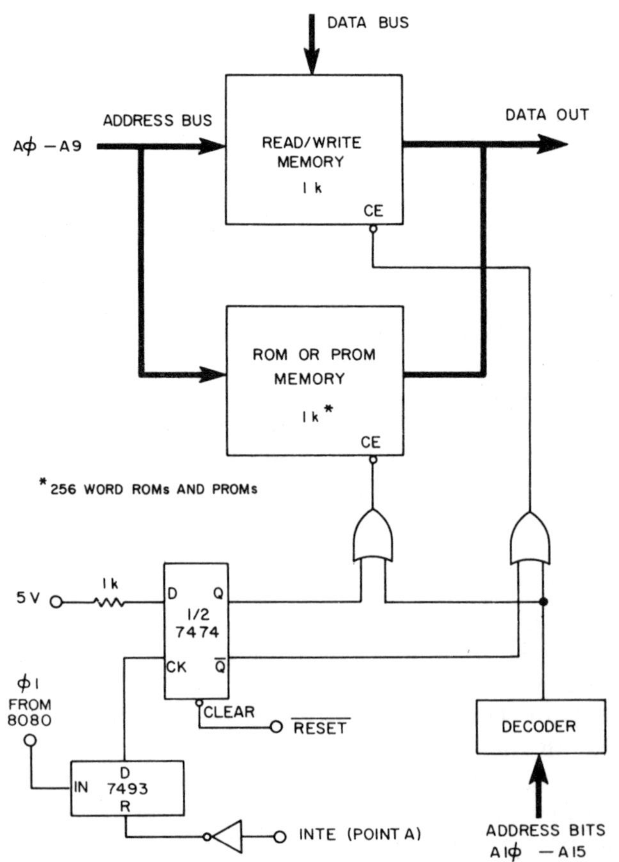

4. **Software-switched memory** can be used when all 256 initial locations are already committed. A flip-flop switches the chip enables.

jump instruction. Here, you simulate the front panel with thumbwheel or DIP switches (Fig. 2).

The Check routine is simple: it takes the data from two 8-bit input ports and uses the data as the address to which to jump (Table 2). The hardware for this method is also simple, as shown in Fig. 3. Besides the I/O decoding, only two 8212 I/O chips (Intel) are needed. This is a neat solution since you don't need a front panel, vectors are preserved in R/W memory, and any starting address can be specified.

Existing software may need modification since the actual locations of the interrupt or restart service software have been changed, in this case from 000 0X0 to 050 0X0. The Check routine could fit between locations 0 and 10, but remember, you have moved it elsewhere in PROM to leave room for expansion.

Flip-flop selects the right chip

In some systems, the first 256 memory loca-tions are already committed. But you still would like a flexible starting method without having to change software. You can use software to "switch" back and forth between ROM and R/W memory. Set up a bank of ROM and R/W memory (1 kwords) with the same address, but use a flip-flop to switch the chip enables (Fig. 4).

The PROM in Fig. 4 contains the Check routine, and you add an enable interrupt (EI) in place of the NOP instruction. Use the interrupt enabled signal (INTE) to switch the flip-flop and the chip enable signals, but only after eight $\phi1$ TTL clock pulses occur. The pulses are accumulated by a 7493 binary counter, which clocks one half of a 7474 flip-flop.

The time delay of eight clock pulses occurring after the interrupt is enabled allows you to operate on the PCHL instruction before switching memory banks. This example uses the interrupt-enable output from the 8080 chip but sometimes you may not want the interrupt enabled when starting execution of software.

Designing a Microprocessor Analyzer

LARRY BRUNI
Senior Associate Engineer,
Kimball Systems, Belleville, N.J.

For a few hundred dollars, you can put together an analyzer that traces the operation of a completed microprocessor-based product.

Although the analyzer is designed to monitor 8080 systems, its concept can be applied to other μPs—the PPS4, for example, a μP as different from the 8080 as you can get.

If you'd like, you can call the analyzer a snapshot test box (STB) since the unit captures, or takes pictures, of the information on the system's address, data, and status busses.

With the STB, you can avoid the use of prototyping equipment for testing. Although widespread, that approach is self defeating because the development equipment performs the CPU and memory functions—the very things that need monitoring in the final product.

Packaging of the STB can range from a bench-console to a portable unit for field-service.

The STB captures information without affecting the operation of the 8080, except for an additional 20-μA/0.8-mA (sink/source) load on each of the bus lines. Displaying the snapshot on the front panel are 140 LEDs arranged in five rows, M_1 to M_5, corresponding to the five-machine-cycle maximum of the 8080's instructions (Fig. 1).

Each row is divided into address-bus, data-bus and status LEDs. Status signals monitored include: hold acknowledge (HLDA), interrupt acknowledge (INTA), memory read (MR), memory write (MW), stack read (SR), stack write (SW), input read (IR) and output write (OW). Because not all 8080 status modes can occur for a given machine cycle, there is no SR LED in rows M_4 and M_5.

Loading the 'camera'

To take a snapshot of any given instruction address, first you set 16 front-panel switches to the address binary number. Another control—called the address-direction switch—provides a snapshot of the instruction executed just before that set on the address switches.

With the direction switch, you can trace backwards through a program and determine the

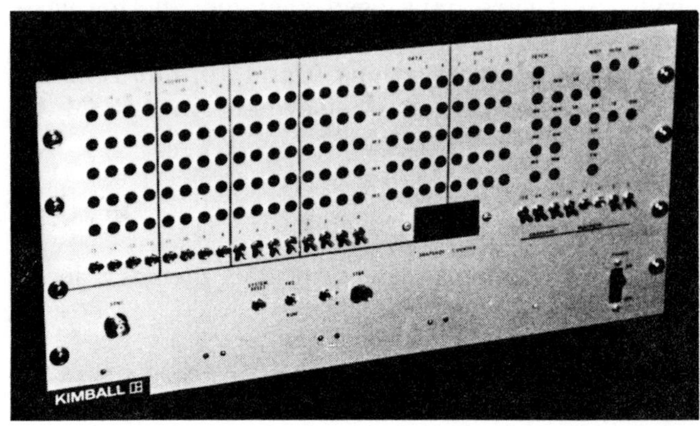

1. **Rows of LEDs display transactions** that occur on a μP's address, data and status busses. The counter shows how many times a given address is executed.

point from which a subroutine was called in the main program loop. Such capability is especially useful when calls are numerous and spread out.

The P setting of the address-direction switch results in a snapshot of the present instruction, and still another position (F) snapshots the following instruction for forward program tracing.

A three-digit decimal counter displays the number of times a snapshot occurs at a given address, up to a number set by the eight binary multiplier switches on the front panel. With the multiplier at zero, each pass through a set instruction is captured and counted. Other multiplier settings determine the number of instruction passes before a snapshot is taken.

When the counter reaches maximum, all decimal points light up, and the counter remains at .9.9.9 until it is zeroed by the STB reset switch.

Note that even though the counter stops incrementing at maximum count, a snapshot still occurs for each pass through the selected address. The reset switch also lights all front-panel indicators as a self test. When you want to capture a previous instruction, the multipliers must be set for a count greater than zero.

What if you don't know where a program is? Another feature of the STB allows random shots of executed instructions. Set the address direction for "present," the multiplier for "one" and place the freeze/run switch in FRZ position.

The next instruction executed by the µP will be snapped, regardless of the setting of the address switches. Now push the reset button, and you can take random pictures. Set the multiplier to zero, and a snapshot occurs for every instruction fetch.

The resulting display on the LEDs is a blur as every instruction runs through. With the "blur," you can spot shorts on bus lines, check if the program range is within limits and immediately know if the µP system is "on the air."

Another useful feature of the STB is a sync pulse that you can use to externally trigger an oscilloscope at the instant a snapshot occurs. You'll find the pulse most helpful when checking I/O operations, especially when you use the multiplier to isolate certain operations in a continuous program loop.

Fig. 2 shows a block diagram of the STB. Note that the system reset signal is the only output

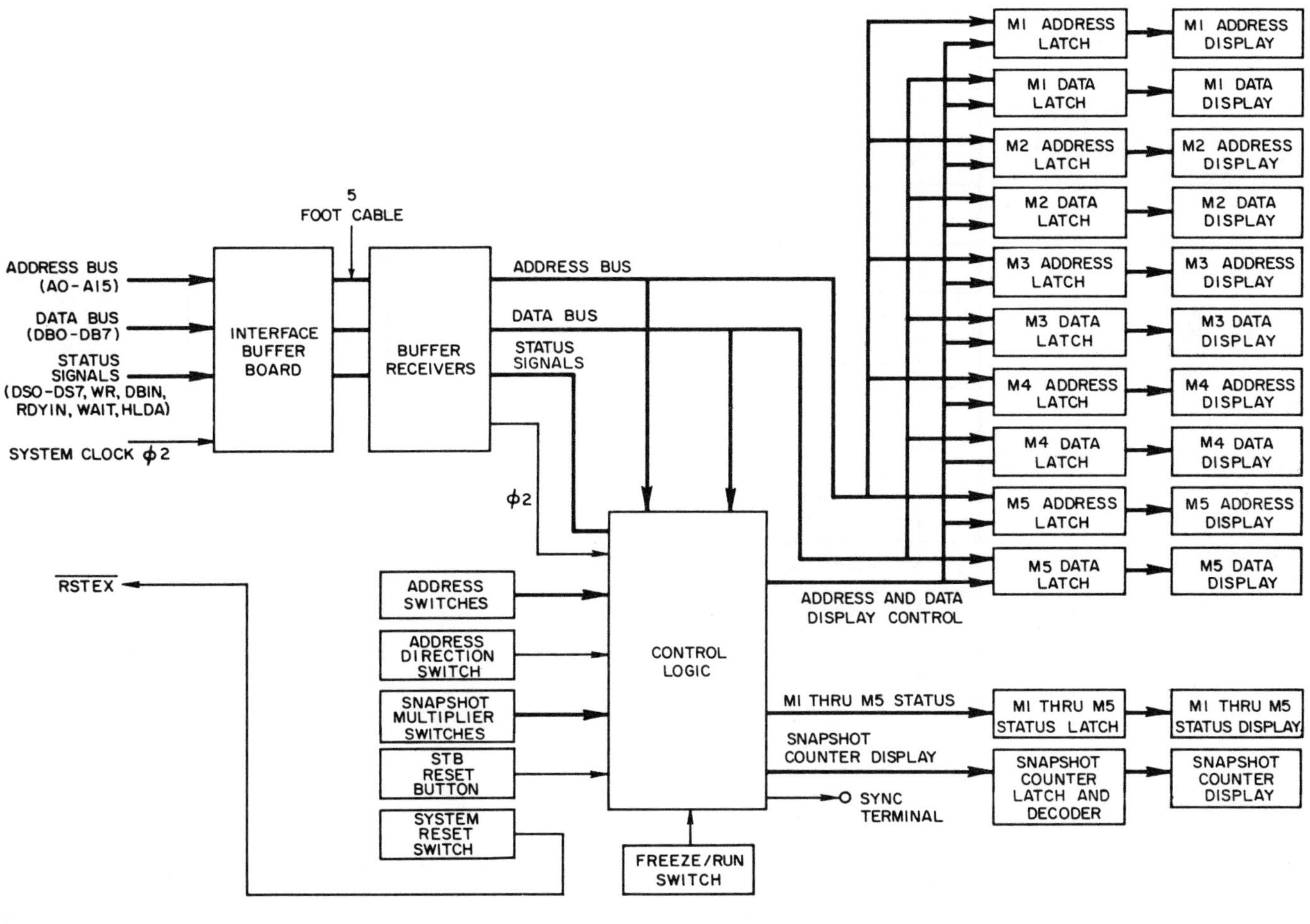

2. **How the test box works:** Routing and logical processing of input signals is the job of the control-logic block, which is built around a state counter. Low-power Schottky is used throughout.

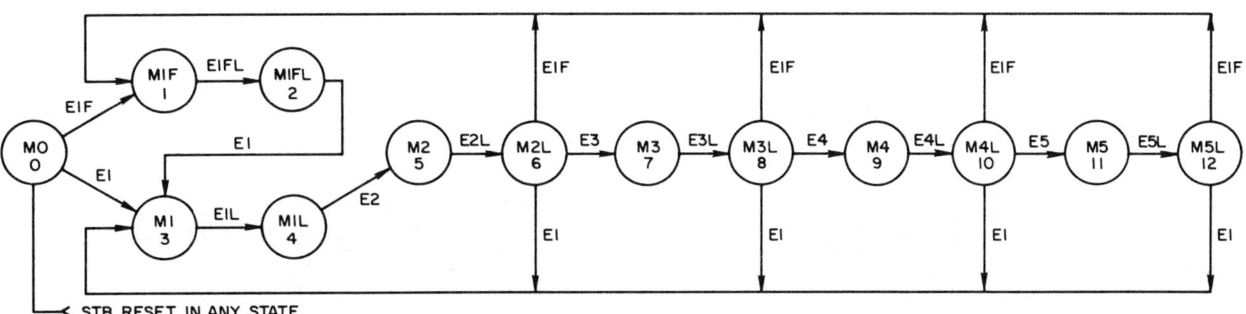

3. **A state counter keeps track** of µP machine cycles. The M numbers shown correspond to internal cycles of the 8080 µP. To isolate the various states, transition states are added between machine cycles.

to the μP system under test. Except for the control logic, the electronics of each block are straightforward. Wherever possible, low-power Schottky logic is used (the 74LS prefix is omitted on the schematics).

Watching over machine cycles

Heart of the control logic is a state counter, with the M numbers of each state corresponding to 8080 machine-cycle numbers (Fig. 3). A transition state (suffix L), added between each machine cycle, isolates one state from the next.

With the address-direction switch in position, P, and the snapshot multiplier set for a count of one or zero, the control logic waits in state M_0 and compares the 8080 address bus with the STB address switches. When the two addresses are identical, a "hit," the counter advances to M_1.

Each subsequent machine cycle taken by the 8080 instruction advances the counter to its next state. If the instruction contains three cycles, the counter traverses M_0-M_1-M_{1L}-M_2-M_{2L}-M_3-M_{3L}-M_0. At counts M_1, M_2, and M_3, the information on the

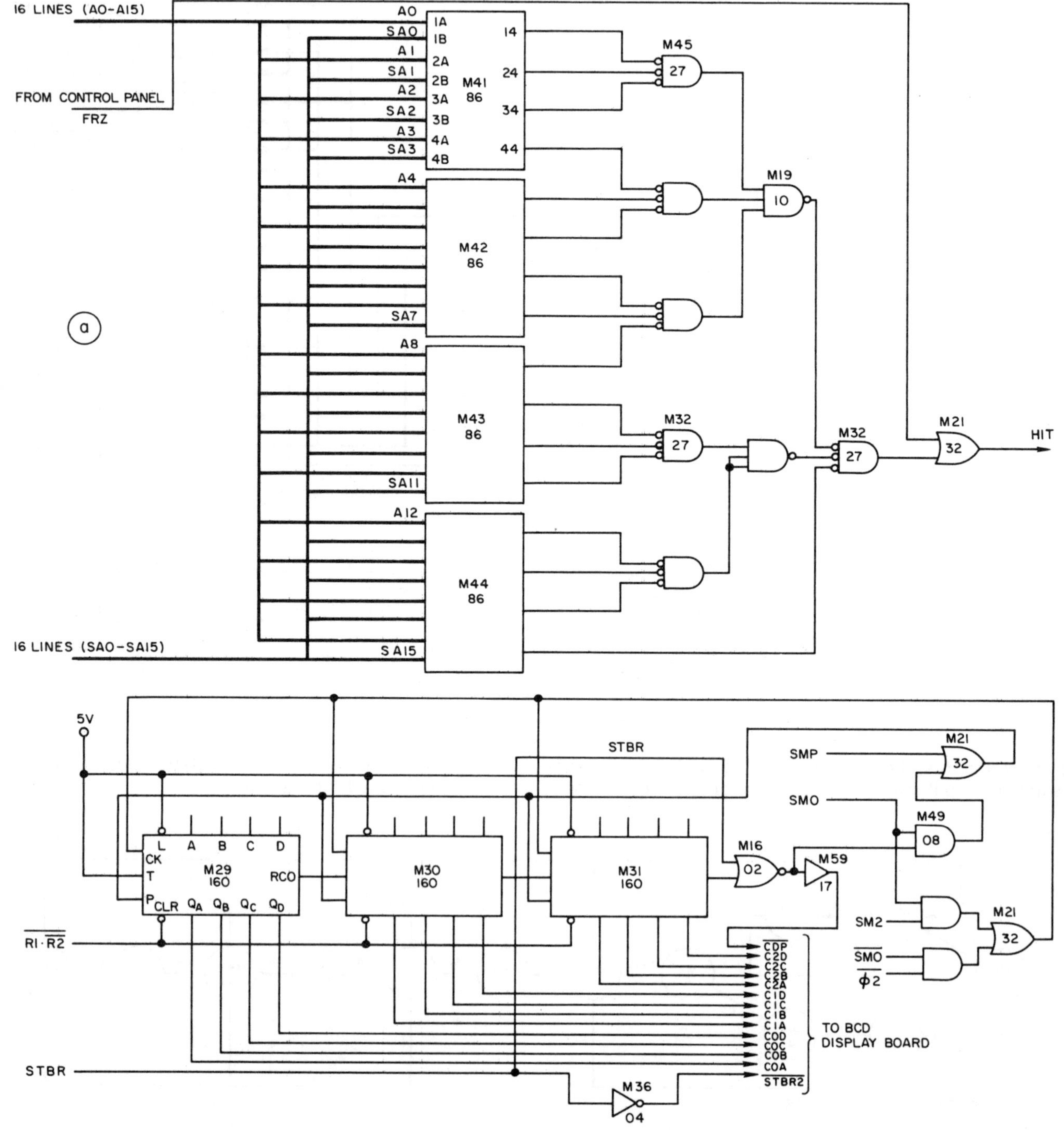

4. Control logic forms the various functional signals of the test box. The "hit" signal indicates an address match (a); and the Snap and Go signals are used to activate and cycle the state counter ("b" on facing page).

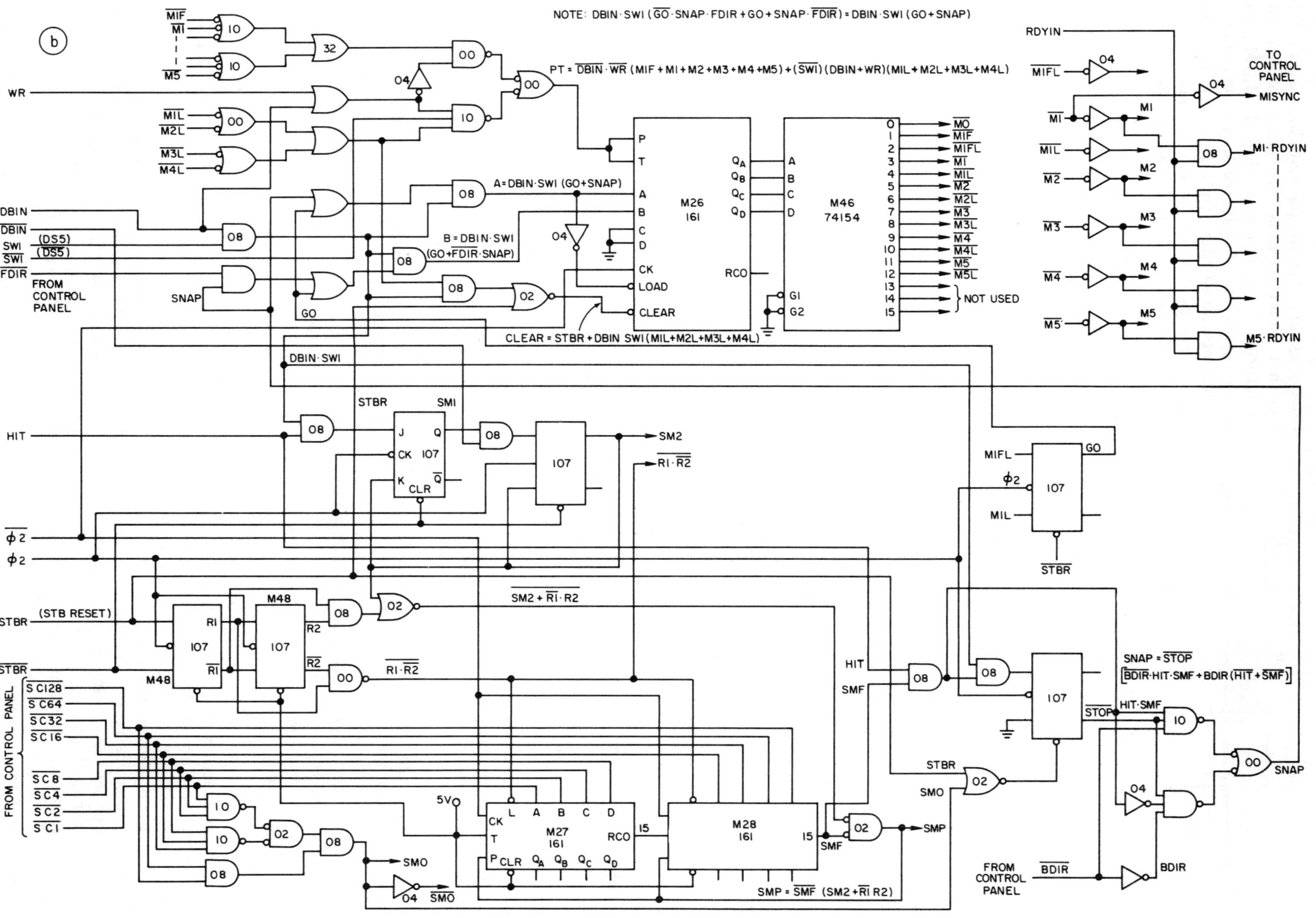
b
NOTE: DBIN·SWI (GO·SNAP·FDIR + GO + SNAP·FDIR) = DBIN·SWI (GO + SNAP)
PT = DBIN·WR (MIF + MI + M2 + M3 + M4 + M5) + (SWI)(DBIN + WR)(MIL + M2L + M3L + M4L)
A = DBIN·SWI (GO + SNAP)
B = DBIN·SWI (GO + FDIR·SNAP)
CLEAR = STBR + DBIN SWI (MIL + M2L + M3L + M4L)
SNAP = STOP
[BDIR·HIT·SMF + BDIR (HIT + SMF)]
SMP = SMF (SM2 + RI·R2)
MICROPROCESSOR BASICS
83

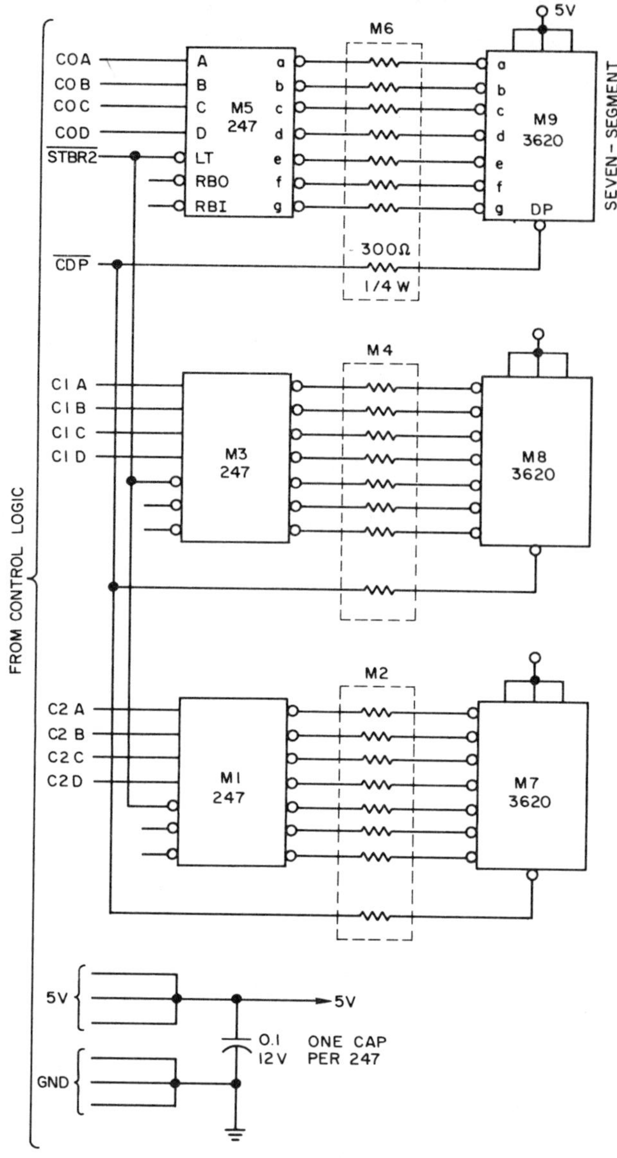

5. **The snapshot counter** is composed of three 7-segment LED digits. All decimal points light on overflow.

address, data, and status buses latches for display on the appropriate row of LEDs.

With the multiplier set to a count of zero, the state counter activates at every hit. A multiplier setting greater than zero delays activation of the state counter until the number of hits is one less than the multiplier reading.

When you set the address-direction switch for backwards tracing (B), the state counter cycles at every instruction executed by the 8080. Just before cycling through M_1, the STB checks for an address hit. On hit occurrence, the counter does not cycle, leaving the display latched with the last executed instruction. The snap-shot multiplier must be set for a count of one or more.

In the forward tracing mode (F), the state counter again waits for a hit. When a hit occurs, the counter cycles M_0-M_{1F}-M_{1FL} and back to M_0 regardless of the number of instruction cycles.

During cycling, the unique state M_{1FL} sets a flip-flop that then "prompts" the state counter into an information-capturing cycle—M_1-M_{1L}-M_2, and so on—when the next instruction is executed.

The interface-buffer contains seven 74LS04s, which serve as drivers for the various 8080 bus signals. Each of the signals coming into the STB is terminated by a Schmitt-trigger hex inverter (74LS14). All necessary logic inversions are performed, and the processed signals then go to the control logic (Fig. 4 and 5).

How the control logic works

Besides receiving the interface signals, the control logic receives all of the lines coming from the front-panel switches. The signals on the lines vary between 5 V dc and ground.

Flip-flops SM_1 and SM_2 in Fig. 4 shape the hit signal into an enable level for the snapshot multiplier counter, composed of M_{27} and M_{28}. The multiplier number decrements in the binary counter by two's-complement addition. When enough hits have decremented the multiplier to zero, a carry-out occurs at M_{28}, pin 15.

The carry-out, signal SMF, allows the next hit to activate the STB state counter by means of the "Snap" signal. Notice that a multiplier switch setting of zero decodes into signal SMO, which resets the "Stop" flip-flop. The arrangement allows the first and each subsequent hit to take a snapshot without pushing the STB reset button.

Flip-flops M_{48} in Fig. 4 define the leading and trailing edges of the pulse produced when you momentarily push the reset button. The leading edge defined by the logic operation, $R_1 \cdot \overline{R_2}$, parallel loads M_{27} and M_{28} with the inverse of the multiplier number.

Release of the button generates $\overline{R_1} \cdot R_2$, which adds one to the count and completes the conversion of the multiplier number into two's-complement form. Bouncing of the reset switch has no adverse effect on M_{27}, M_{28}.

The STB state counter is composed of M_{26} and M_{46}. The clear line of M_{26} zeros the state counter. Depending upon the setting of the address-direction switch, the state counter is parallel loaded to state M_{1F} or M_1 when a Snap pulse occurs.

The counter advances through its remaining states when the P and T inputs of M_{26} are enabled under control of signals DB1N and WR from the 8080. Signal SW1 is status bit DS5 of the 8080 and defines an instruction fetch.

Unless the address-direction switch is set to forward (FD1R signal), once the state counter completes its cycle it is prevented from any other action by the setting of the Stop flip-flop. With the switch on forward, the GO signal cycles the state counter on the next instruction.

A separate decimal counter, composed of M_{29},

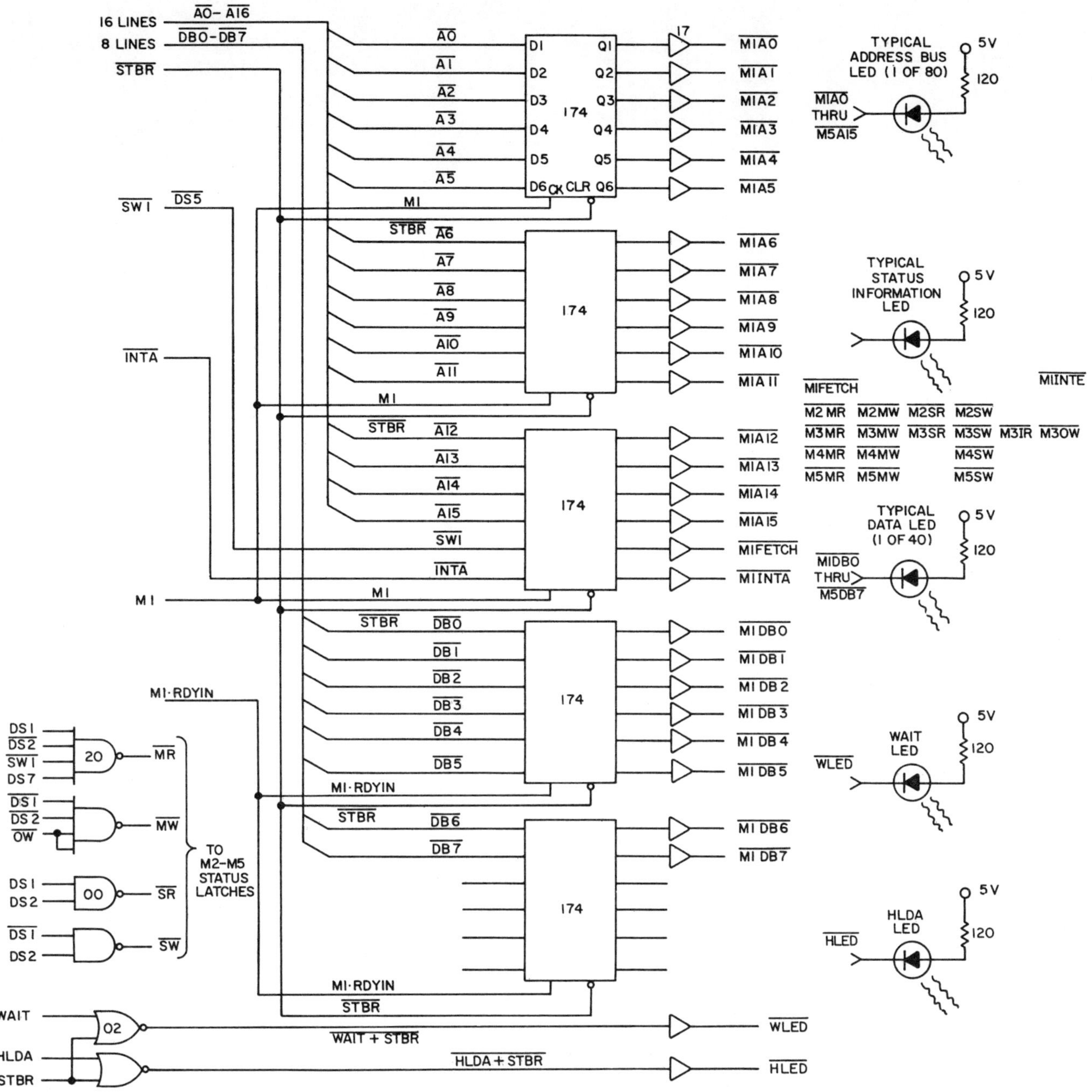

6. Latches and drivers for the display are activated by the state-counter, with a delay to account for system-memory access time. All segments and decimals are lighted to test operation.

M_{30} and M_{31} in Fig. 5, forms the front-panel snapshot-counter display. Two modes of counter operation are possible, depending on the state of signal SMO. When SMO is true (snapshot multiplier set at zero) the counter increments on every SM2 pulse until it overflows.

Overflow disables the counter, keeping the front-panel display at .9.9.9. When you set the snapshot multiplier to a number greater than zero (SMO false), signal SMP increments the counter, and that limits the display to the number at which the single snapshot occurs.

Fig. 5 also shows the address-comparison logic used to produce the hit signal. Notice that the freeze signal, FRZ, from the control panel forces the hit signal to true. This causes an immediate snapshot of the next instruction.

As a test, the STBR signal lights all segments and decimal points on the snapshot counter, a seven-segment, binary-coded decimal display (Fig. 6). In normal operation, the decimal points are lit when the counter overflows.

Latches for the LEDs and drivers are strobed by the appropriate machine-cycle signal from the state counter (Fig. 7). The Ready signal (RDYIN) of the 8080 delays data-bus capture to compensate for the access time of the memory in the system under test.

SECTION V
Designing with the 6800

As evidenced by the number of application articles submitted to ELECTRONIC DESIGN magazine, the Motorola 6800 rivals the popularity of the 8080. One factor contributing to the eight-bit NMOS microprocessor's widespread use is the broad range of compatible peripheral circuits available from Motorola. The software programmability of key interface elements enhances system flexibility. Among the popular features of the 6800 are five-volt operation and a dual bus structure for data and address lines.

Licensed alternate sources for the 6800 include American Microsystems Inc., Fairchild, Hitachi, and Thompson-CSF.

The first article in this section provides a comprehensive description of the 6800 and shows how to assemble and program complete systems. The next article on assembly language programming, uses the 6800 as an example, but the information is sufficiently general to be useful to engineers using other microprocessors. Other articles describe a debugging system for the 6800 and applications in data acquisition and instrument control.

Assemble a Complete Microcomputer with the 6800

TOM MAZUR
Supervisor, Technical Communications,
Motorola Semiconductor Products, Inc., Phoenix

When the single-chip MC6800 microprocessor was introduced in 1974 by Motorola, it offered designers three advantages over competing 8-bit units. It offered a dual bus structure for data and address lines and software-controllable interface elements. Further, it could operate from a single, 5-V supply. Several other companies have since introduced μPs with similar features, but so far few have equalled the flexibility of the interface circuits and the wide range of circuits available.

The software-programmable input/output elements—the peripheral interface adapter (PIA), the asynchronous-communications interface adapter (ACIA) and the synchronous serial data adapter (SSDA)—provide standard hardware interfaces, but can be switched under software control to act as either an input or output port. The single-supply operation of the μP, its associated I/O circuits and its memory circuits, permit full compatibility with TTL-level signals and power supplies.

Systems go together simply

Only five circuits are needed to form a minimum microcomputer system: an MC6800 μP, an MC6820 PIA or 6850 ACIA, a RAM or ROM for program storage, an MC6870 system clock, and, of course, a power supply (Fig. 1). The components are linked together by an 8-bit data bus and a 16-bit address bus.

The current family of M6800 circuits is listed in Table 1. The newest device in the family is the XC6852—a synchronous serial-data adapter (SSDA). This circuit is used to synchronously transfer blocks of data to and from the system data bus. The 6800 can address up to 65,535 memory bytes. Since each I/O device is treated as a location in memory, the system can theoretically handle as many I/O ports as there are memory locations.

All the timing functions are controlled by the two-phase system clock, which can be set for any frequency from 100 kHz to 1 MHz. The clock modules are thick-film hybrid circuits that con-

tain a crystal oscillator and waveshapers, as well as TTL and NMOS level drivers.

The other support circuits listed in Table 1 are NMOS, except for the bus transceiver, extender and buffers, and clock buffer, which are bipolar. And all circuits operate from a 5-V source—with the exception of the MCM6832, 68708, 6604 and 6605 memories. The four excep-

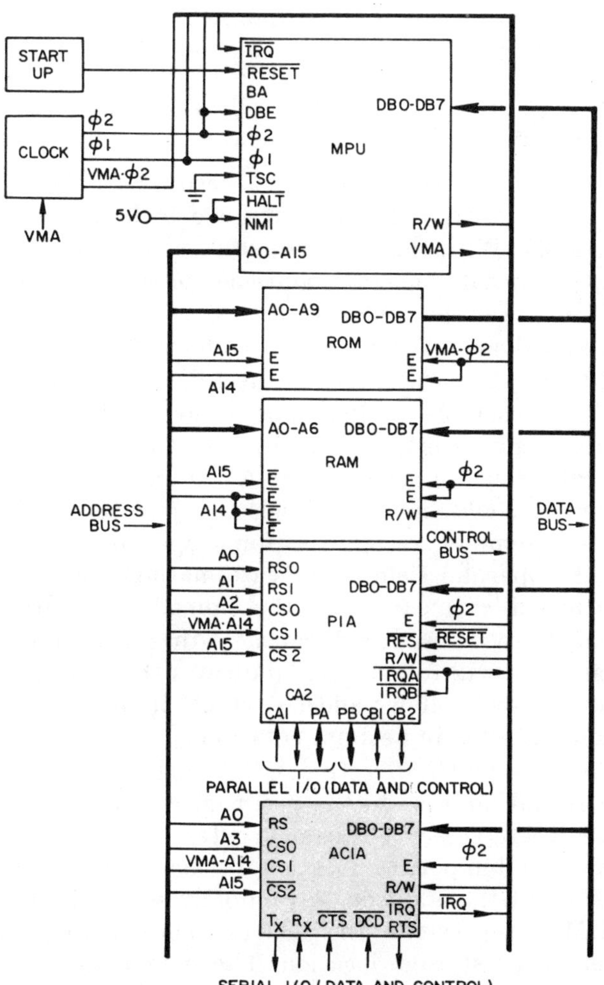

1. **The simplest microprocessor-based computer** can be built with only three or four chips, a clock and a power supply. All communication takes place over an 8-bit data bus and a 16-bit address bus.

tions require additional +12 and −5 V sources. On the 6800, address and data-bus lines are buffered by three-state drivers for added interfacing ease.

The PIA permits a data interface to instruments and other sources of parallel digital data (Fig. 2a). It has two 8-bit bidirectional busses and four interrupt/control lines. One of the output busses is CMOS compatible and the other is TTL-compatible.

For serial-data interfaces, the ACIA can provide serial-to-parallel data conversion (Fig. 2b). It can simplify the interface requirements between the μP and such serial devices as modems, typewriter terminals and printers. The SSDA performs a similar function as the ACIA, but for synchronous serial data (Fig. 2c). This unit is useful for transferring large blocks of data, as found in disc or tape memory systems.

Also available is a low-speed modem that can serially transmit data at rates of up to 600 bits/s over voice-grade telephone lines (Fig. 2d). It translates TTL-level data to and from FSK (frequency-shift keyed) signals. Available memory circuits are in industry-standard pinouts to simplify interconnections and component selection.

Using the MC6800

To control the 6800 μP, there are only six registers within the IC that have to be accessed (Fig. 3). With these six registers you can control the external memory and peripheral devices. Memory can be added in any sized block, up to 64-k. All peripheral circuits connect to the data and address busses, and to the μP's control lines.

The assembly listing of a program that adds four numbers is shown in Fig. 4. Addition is set to take place in accumulator A, although accumulator B could have been selected just as easily. The assembler recognizes some special symbols in the operand field to indicate mathematical notation: a # means that the immediate address mode is to be used; a $ indicates that a hexadecimal value will follow; a % indicates that a binary number will follow; and no symbol indicates that the number is in decimal notation.

An assembler directive, ORG (origin) assigns an initial address to the program counter (PC). The RMB (reserve memory bytes) directive reserves a temporary location in memory for the results of the addition. A randomly selected label, TEMP, represents the address chosen for the temporary storage location. The mnemonic operators LDA (load accumulator) and ADD (add) represent two-byte, two-cycle instructions that will be executed in the immediate address mode. The operator STA (store accumulator) is a 2-byte, 4-cycle instruction that will be executed in

the direct address mode if the address of the operand is within the lowest 256 bytes of memory space. Finally, the directive MON (return to console) indicates that the end of the source file has been reached.

Let's step through this program to see how the μP actually carries out the commands. Lines 00100 and 00110 just identify the program and tell the μP to set the PC to 000A. The next line sets up a temporary storage location called TEMP. When phase 1 of the clock goes low the PC is incremented to 000B. The next time phase 1 goes high, 000B is gated onto the address bus, and when phase 1 goes low again the PC increments to 000C.

When phase 2 goes high the contents of location 000B are put onto the data bus and when the phase 2 clock goes low the data on the data bus are gated into the instruction register where the internal ROM can decode the instruction. The contents of 000B are 86 (hex)—the op code for an LDA A (load accumulator A in the immediate mode) instruction.

Phase 1 again goes high and the contents of the PC are gated onto the address bus. When phase 1 goes low, the PC increases to 000D. When phase 2 goes high the contents of 000C, which are 19 (hex), are put on the data bus and after phase 2 goes low, the contents of location 000C

Table 1. 6800 System components

Model	Description	Price
MC6800	Microprocessing Unit (MPU)	$29.95 (50-99)
MC6820	Peripheral Interface Adapter (PIA)	$12.00 (100-999)
MC6850	Asynchronous Communications Interface Adapter (ACIA)	$12.00 (100-999)
XC6852	Synchronous Serial Data Adapter (SSDA)	$15.00 (100-999)
MC6860	0-600 bps Digital Modem	$14.00 (100-999)
MC6862	2400 bps Modulator	$21.00 (100-999)
MC6870A MC6871A MC6871B	Two-Phase Microprocessor Clocks	$18.40 $20.00 (50-99) $20.00
MC6880/ MC8T26L	Quad Three-State Bus Transceiver	$ 3.95 (100-999)
XC6881/ MC3449P	Bi-Directional Bus Extender/ Switch	$ 3.50 (100-999)
XC6885-88/P XC8T95-98P	Hex Three-State Buffers/Inverters	$ 1.65 (100-999)
MCM6810L	128 × 8-Bit Static RAM	$ 7.00 (100-999)
MCM6830L	1024 × 8-Bit Read-Only Memory	$13.80 (100-999)
MCM6832L	2048 × 8-Bit Read-Only Memory	$18.40 (100-999)
MCM68308 MCM68317 MCM68708	1024 × 8-Bit Read-Only Memory 2048 × 8-Bit Read-Only Memory 1024 × 8 Bit Alterable ROM	Consult Factory
MCM6604L	4096-Bit Dynamic RAM	$13.95 (100-999)
MCM6605L	4096-Bit Dynamic RAM	$20.50 (100-999)
MPQ6842	MPU Clock Buffer	$ 2.75 (100-999)

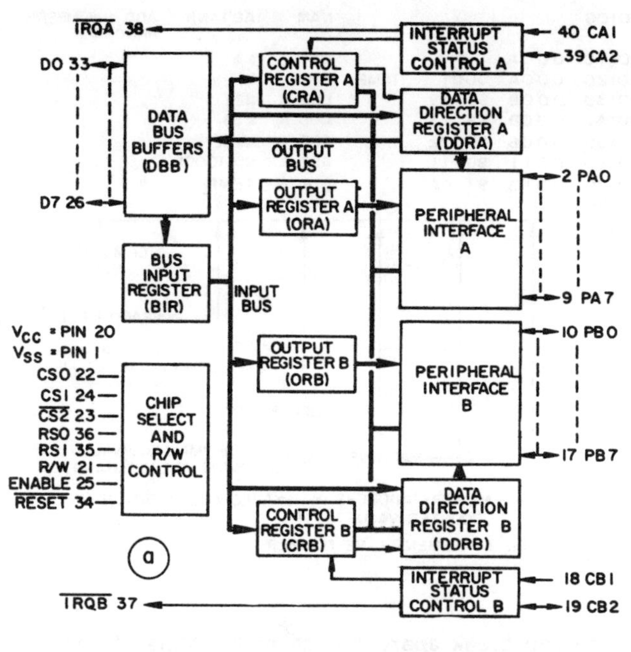

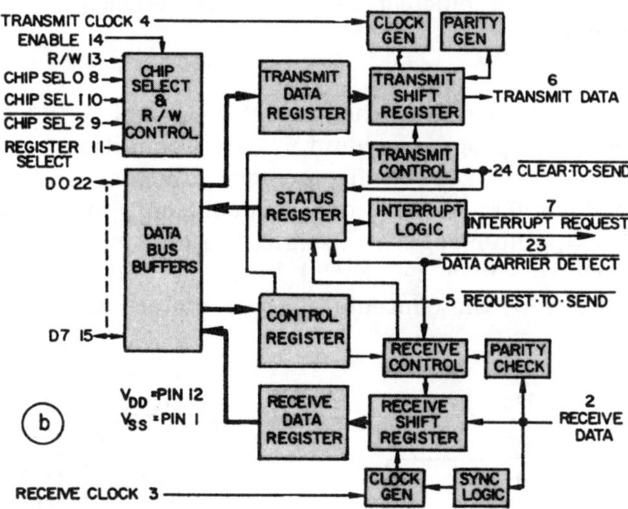

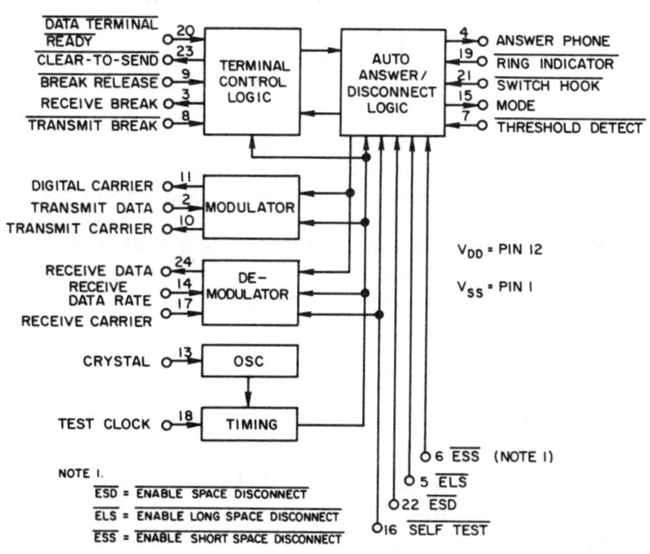

are loaded into accumulator A. At this point the decimal number 25 is in the accumulator.

The next three instructions follow the same routine, adding the numbers 35 (decimal), 32 (hexadecimal) and 10001 (binary) to the accumulator. The PC has now been increased to 0013, and that value appears on the address bus.

The byte from location 0013 is fetched and interpreted to be an STA A, direct instruction.

2. **The four most often used peripheral devices,** the peripheral interface adapter (a), the asynchronous communications interface adapter (b), the synchronous serial interface adapter (c) and the modem (d), help the 6800 communicate with the outside world. All units operate from a single supply and are TTL compatible.

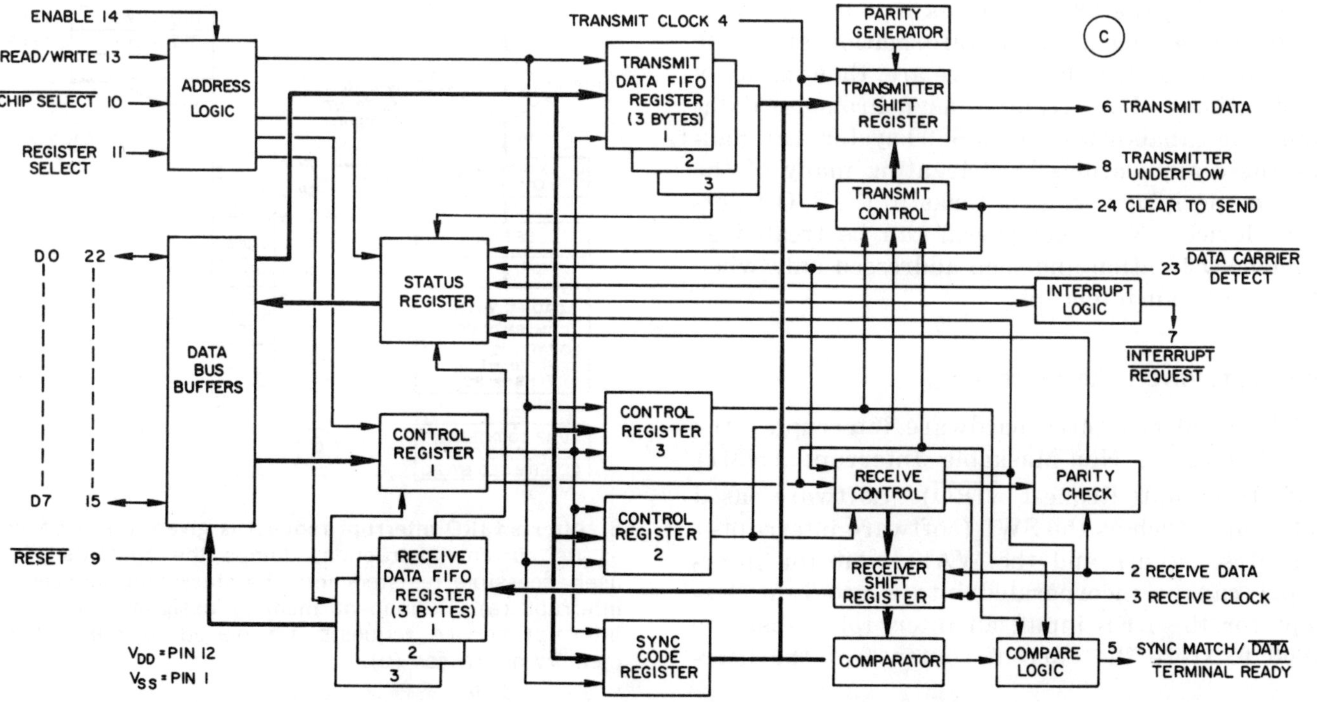

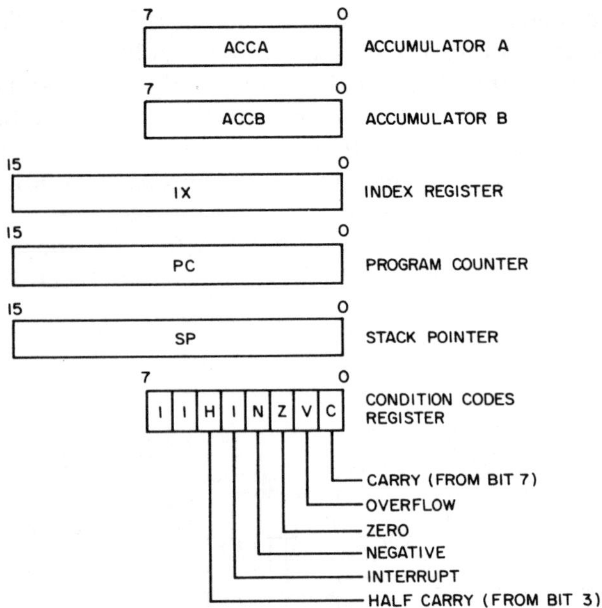

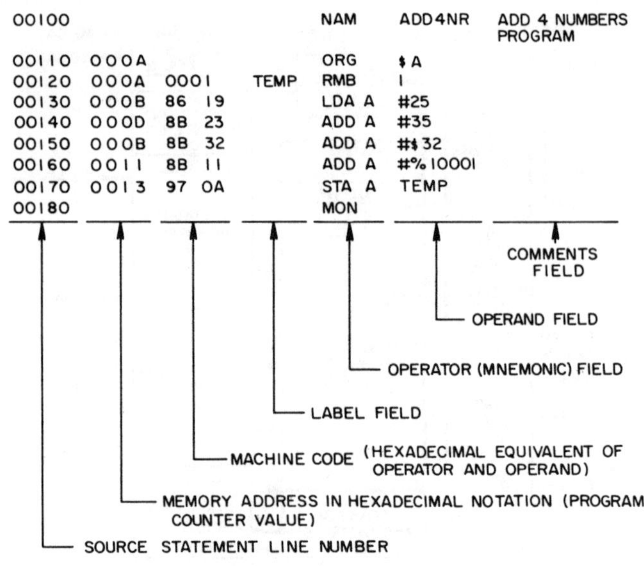

3. When you program the 6800, you will find there are only six user-accessible registers that must be controlled to get the microprocessor to function.

4. You can break apart the assembly listing of any program into its different fields for easy deciphering and debugging.

When phase 1 goes low the PC is incremented to 0014 and then when phase 2 goes high 0014 is loaded onto the address bus. After phase 2 goes low, the contents of location 0014 are transferred to the address bus. The next clock cycle gates the contents of the accumulator into the location specified by the address bus.

Many of the instructions, such as the ones used in this example, affect the status of the Condition-Code-Register (CCR) bits. Each bit may be set or cleared as a result of an instruction. For diagnostic purposes, the status of the six active bits of the CCR may be displayed after each instruction execution.

Internally, the 6800 operates in a synchronous mode, processing data-bus information at a rate determined by the clock. There are, though, many applications that require asynchronous data-handling capabilities. The M6800 system can handle these applications by delegating many of the routine peripheral-control tasks to the I/O interface devices. Each peripheral can be treated as a memory location and then addressed only when it requests an interrupt.

Interrupts divert the processor

The 6800 has three hardware interrupts—the Reset ($\overline{\text{RES}}$), Non-Maskable Interrupt ($\overline{\text{NMI}}$) and Interrupt Request ($\overline{\text{IRQ}}$). Software-based interrupts such as the SWI (software interrupt—initiates action) and the WAI (wait for interrupt) can be incorporated into a program. Except for the $\overline{\text{RES}}$ input, all interrupts cause the 6800 to store the current contents of the user-

accessible registers (accumulators A and B, index register, program counter, and condition-code register) in read/write memory locations known as the stack—a last-in first-out memory space. A stack-pointer register assigns the contents of the stack to seven sequential locations and is used to retrieve the contents of the registers after the

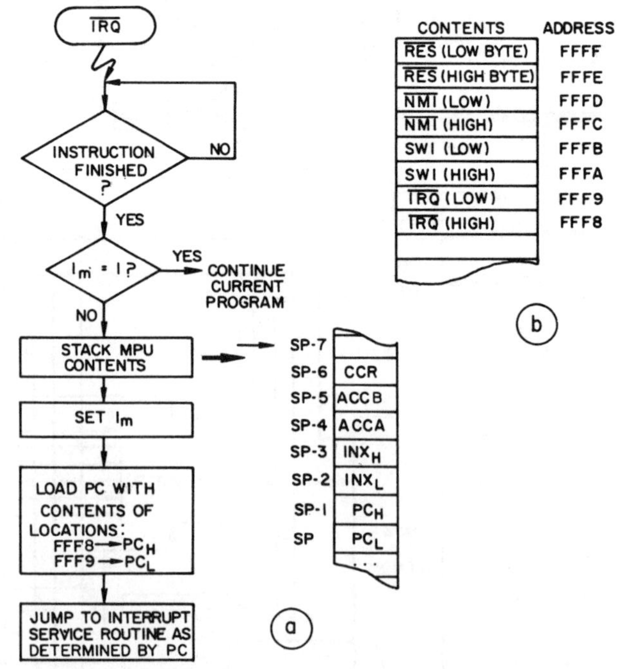

5. After an $\overline{\text{IRQ}}$ interrupt request is given, the μP finishes its current instruction, dumps the contents of its user-accessible registers into the stack and services the interrupt (a). Permanent memory assignments for the interrupt service requests are placed in the last few memory addresses (b).

interrupt is serviced.

A typical $\overline{\text{IRQ}}$ service-flow chart is shown in Fig. 5a. After the μP registers are put into a stack, the Interrupt Mask (IM) bit of the Condition Code Register is set high to lock out any other interrupts until the current interrupt is serviced. If system interrupts must be handled on a priority basis, a Clear Interrupt Mask (CLI) instruction can be added to the beginning of the current interrupt-service routine. Then any number of additional interrupts can be nested in the stack awaiting their turn for service. The only limitation is the size of the read/write memory.

After IM is set, the program counter is loaded

Microprocessor architecture

The MC6800 microprocessor is a single-chip, 8-bit parallel processor housed in a 40-pin dual in-line package. The μP has a variable-length stack, maskable interrupt vectoring, direct memory addressing capability and six internal registers, as well as 72 variable-length instructions and seven addressing modes.

Inside the μP are three 16-bit registers, which form the Stack Pointer, Program Counter and Index Register. There are also three 8-bit registers that are known as the condition-code register and accumulators A and B. Since the address register is 16 bits wide, up to 64-k words can be directly addressed.

The stack pointer contains a 2-byte register that holds the address of the next available location in an external push-down/pop-up stack (usually part of the external RAM). The stack is usually used to store the contents of the program counter, accumulators, index register, and other information necessary for the μP to resume operation after an interrupt is serviced.

The arithmetic and logic section of the μP (the ALU) does all the bit manipulation under instruction-set control. In conjunction with the ALU, the two accumulators hold the data that go into and come out of the logic array.

The instruction register, along with the on-chip decoder and control-logic array, manage the internal operations of the μP. Combinations of commands and addressing modes produce a total of 197 executable instructions that are assembled in one, two or three bytes of machine code.

A two-phase clock controls all the timing of the μP. On the first phase the contents of the program counter are transferred to the address bus. The Valid-Memory-Address line then goes high to indicate a valid address is on the bus. On the negative transition of the clock, the program counter gets incremented.

When phase 2 of the clock goes HIGH, data are put on the data bus. (The direction of data flow—to or from the μP—is determined by the Read/Write control line.) Then, when phase 2 goes LOW, data are latched into either the μP or the memory. This sequence occurs every time the μP addresses a location and transfers a data word.

Incoming commands go into the instruction register and are then decoded by the Instruction

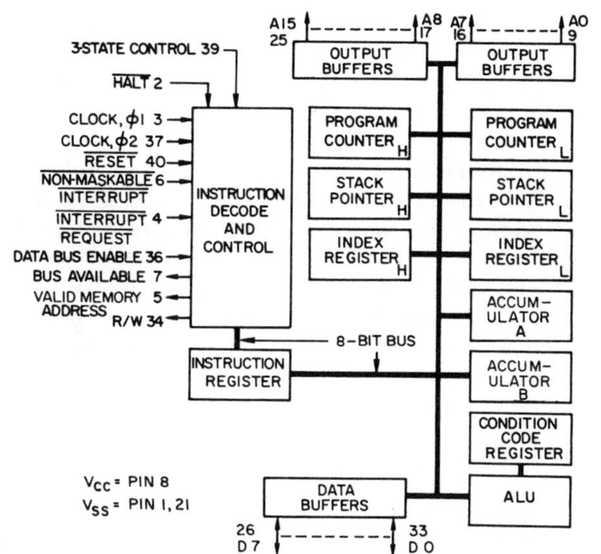

Decode and Control array, which in turn controls the ALU. All the registers and input and output buffers are interconnected on an 8-bit-wide data bus.

The nine control lines available on the MC-6800 package permit various machine operations or provide special control functions. The Go/Halt line permits you to stop all μP operation when put into the Halt position (LOW). The Three-State Control line permits you to cause the Read/Write line and all the address lines to go into the OFF (high impedance) state. You can then use the address bus for DMA applications.

The Read/Write line tells the peripheral devices whether the μP is in the read (HIGH) or write (LOW) state. When the Three-State Control line goes HIGH, it forces the R/W line OFF (high impedance). A Valid Memory Address line tells the memory and peripheral devices that the information on the address bus is a valid address.

For control of the data bus, two lines are available—the Data Bus Enable, which enables the bus drivers when it is placed in the HIGH state, and the Bus Available which, when brought HIGH, indicates that the μP has stopped and that the address bus is available.

MC6800 programming methods and mnemonic definitions

To get a good look at the basic instruction set of the MC6800, you can divide it into accumulator and memory, index register and stack, jump-and-branch and condition-code instructions (see table). Each instruction requires one byte and is followed by either one or two additional bytes—of an address location, data or even another instruction.

The MC6800 offers seven different ways to address data:

(1.) Inherent. This mode lets you use the operand as the address for the data to be manipulated. The operand may be either one or two bytes long.

(2.) Accumulator. Although similar to inherent addressing, in this mode the operator defines the location being addressed.

(3.) Immediate. In this mode, the byte following the instruction is used as the operand of the instruction. No reference to the memory need be made.

(4.) Direct. For direct addressing, the μP can only reach locations 0 to 255 because only a single-byte operand is used. After an instruction is encountered in this mode, the μP looks at the program counter's contents, adds one and uses that number as the location of the data word.

(5.) Extended. This mode is similar to the Direct mode except that a 2-byte operand is used, thus permitting the μP to reach the remaining memory locations, 256 to 65,535. After an instruction is encountered, the μP looks at the contents of the program counter, adds one and uses that number as the first half of the memory address. This repeats and the original value of the program counter plus two becomes the second half of the memory address.

(6.) Relative. You can specify a memory location whose address, relative to the value in the program counter, can be up to 125 locations below that value or up to 129 locations above the value. To go further than the 129 locations requires an unconditional jump, jump to subroutine or return from subroutine.

(7.) Indexed. The numerical address is not fixed, but depends on the contents of the index register.

Addressing-mode selection is made when the

Nomenclature		
ACCA	Accumulator A	
ACCB	Accumulator B	
ACCX	Accumulator ACCA or ACCB	
CC	Condition code register	
C	Carry bit of CC	
V	Two's complement overflow indicator bit of CC	
Z	Zero indicator bit of CC	
N	Negative indicator bit of CC	
I	Interrupt mask bit of CC	
H	Half carry bit of CC	
IX	Index register, 16 bits	
IXH	IX, higher order 8 bits	
IXL	IX, lower order 8 bits	
PC	Program counter, 16 bits	
PCH	PC, higher order 8 bits	
PCL	PC, lower order 8 bits	
SP	Stack pointer, 16 bits	
SPH	SP, higher order 8 bits	
SPL	SP, lower order, 8 bits	
M	A memory location (one byte)	
M + 1	The byte of memory at location 0001 plus the address of the location indicated by M	
REL	Relative address	

Accumulator and memory instructions		
Operation	Mnemonic	Description
Add	ADDA ADDB	Adds contents of ACCX and contents of M; places results in ACCX.
Add accumulators	ABA	Adds contents of ACCB to contents of ACCA; places results in ACCA.
Add with carry	ADCA ADCB	Adds contents of C bit to the sum of the contents of ACCX and M; places results in ACCX.
Logical AND	ANDA ANDB	Performs logical AND between the contents of ACCX and contents of M; places results in ACCX.
Bit test	BITA BITB	Performs logical AND comparison of contents of ACCX and M and modifies N, Z and V bits of CC. Contents of ACCX and M are not changed.
Clear	CLR CLRA CLRB	The contents of M or the contents of ACCX are replaced with zeros.
Compare	CMPA CMPB	Compares the contents of ACCX and M and modifies the N, Z, V and C bits of CC. Contents of ACCX and M are not changed.
Complement, 1s	COM COMA COMB	Replaces each bit of the contents of ACCX or M with its one's complement.

programs are written. If you manually translate the program into machine code, the addressing mode is inherent in the operation code.

Several different methods of generating the machine-level codes are available to the programmer. For in-house development you can use an assembly program available either from time-sharing services or from the EXORciser development system. Time-sharing services also offer a high-level language called MPL (a subset of PL/1) that is especially handy for applications that involve mathematical computations of data.

The compiler program of MPL translates source statements into M6800 assembly-level programs. Already written assembly-level instructions can be embedded in the compiled program to permit optimization when programs are already available. An assembler program then takes the assembly-level program and makes two passes in the first, it assigns numerical values to source-statement labels, then checks syntax and lists errors. On the second pass, undefined symbols from pass one are defined and an assembled listing is provided. The assembler has

12 directives, which can be used to assign data values, allocate memory and control the sequencing and formatting of programs.

Also available are an interactive simulator program that duplicates, on a host computer, the exact execution of the assembled machine-language program. Another useful program is the Build Virtual Machine, which permits you to reorganize the software you have under development. This program helps to determine and minimize memory requirements.

For development systems such as the EXORciser, a macroassembler is available. Macroinstructions represent a sequence of assembly-level instructions. The macros simplify program development, when instruction sequences must be repeated, by providing the programmer with a shorthand notation of the sequences.

In the EXORciser, the Evaluation Module II and in the Design Evaluation Kit, available firmware includes EXbug, MINIbug and MIKbug, respectively. These programs contain routines for loading user programs, for debugging them and for providing interactive control of the prototype system.

Complement, 2s (negate)	NEG NEGA NEGB	Replaces each bit of the contents of ACCX or M with its two's complement.
Decimal adjust, A	DAA	Adjusts contents of ACCA and C bit to represent correct BCD sum and carry after an ABA, ADD or ADC operation on a BCD operand.
Decrement	DEC DECA DECB	Subtracts one from the contents of M or ACCX.
Exclusive OR	EORA EORB	Performs logical Exclusive OR between contents of ACCX and M; places results in ACCX.
Increment	INC INCA INCB	Adds one to the contents of M or ACCX.
Load Accumulator	LDAA LDAB	Loads contents of M into ACCX.
OR, Inclusive	ORAA ORAB	Performs logical OR between contents of ACCX and M; places results in ACCX.
Push data	PSHA PSHB	Contents of ACCX stored on stack at the address contained in SP; SP then decremented by one.
Pull data	PULA PULB	SP incremented by one; ACCX loaded from stack, from the address contained in SP.
Rotate left	ROL ROLA ROLB	All bits of ACCX or M shifted left by one bit. Bit 0 of the byte loaded with the initial C bit. C bit loaded with the initial MSB of ACCX or M.
Rotate right	ROR RORA RORB	All bits of ACCX or M shifted right by one bit. Bit 7 of the byte loaded with the initial C bit. C bit loaded with the initial LSB of ACCX or M.
Shift left, arithmetic	ASL ASLA ASLB	All bits of ACCX or M shifted left by one bit. Bit 0 of the byte loaded with zero. C bit loaded with the initial MSB of ACCX or M.
Shift right, arithmetic	ASR ASRA ASRB	All bits of ACCX or M shifted right by one bit. Bit 7 of the byte loaded with a zero. C bit loaded with the initial LSB of ACCX or M.

Operation	Mnemonic	Description.
Shift right, logic	LSR LSRA LSRB	All bits of ACCX or M shifted right by one bit. Bit 7 of the byte held constant. C bit loaded with the initial LSB or ACCX or M.
Store accumulator	STAA STAB	Store the contents of ACCX at M; the contents of ACCX remains unchanged.
Subtract	SUBA SUBB	Subtract the contents of M from ACCX; place the results in ACCX.
Subtract accumulators	SBA	Subtracts the contents of ACCB from ACCA; places results in ACCA. Contents of ACCB not affected.
Subtract with carry	SBCA SBCB	Subtracts the contents of M and C from ACCX; places results in ACCX.
Transfer accumulators	TAB TBA	Moves contents of ACCA to ACCB (TAB) or vice versa (TBA). The contents of the transferred accumulator are not changed; the contents of the receiving accumulator are changed.
Test, zero or minus	TST TSTA TSTB	If MSB of ACCX or M is one, then the N bit of CC is set to one. If the contents of ACCX or M are all zeroes, then the Z bit is set to one.
Index register and stack manipulation instructions		
Compare index register	CPX	The contents of IXH and IXL are compared to M and M+1, respectively. The N,Z and V bits of CC are affected.
Decrement index register	DEX	Subtracts one from the index register. Z bit of CC is affected.
Decrement stack pointer	DES	Subtracts one from the stack pointer. CC not affected.
Increment index register	INX	Adds one to the index register. Z bit of CC is affected.
Increment stack pointer	INS	Adds one to the stack pointer. CC not affected.
Load index register	LDX	Loads IXH and IXL with contents of M and M+1, respectively. The N,Z and V bits of CC are affected.
Load stack pointer	LDS	Loads SPH and SPL with the contents of M and M+1, respectively. The N,Z and V bits of CC are affected.
Store index register	STX	Stores IXH and IXL at locations M and M+1, respectively. The N,Z and V bits of CC are affected.
Store stack pointer	STS	Stores SPH and SPL at locations M and M+1, respectively. The N,Z and V bits of CC are affected.
Transfer from IX to SP	TXS	Loads SP with contents of IX minus one. Contents of IX unchanged.
Transfer from SP to IX	TSX	Loads IX with contents of SP, plus one. Contents of SP unchanged.
Jump and brand instructions		
Branch always	BRA	Branch to the address equal to PC+0002+REL.
Branch if carry clear	BCC	Branch to the address equal to PC+0002+REL, if the C bit = 0.
Branch if carry set	BCS	Branch to the address equal to PC+0002+REL, if the C bit = 1.
Branch if equal to zero	BEQ	Branch to the address equal to PC+0002+REL, if the Z bit = 1.
Branch if $\geq$ zero	BGE	Branch to the address equal to PC+0002+REL, if the logical Exclusive OR of N and V bits = 0.
Branch if $>$ zero	BGT	Branch to the address equal to PC+0002+REL, if the contents of Z+ [N + V] = 0.
Branch if higher	BHI	Branch to the address equal to PC+0002+REL, if the logical AND of C and Z bits = 0.
Branch if $\leq$ zero	BLE	Branch to the address equal to PC+0002+REL, if the contents of Z+ N + V = 1.
Branch if lower or same	BLS	Branch to the address equal to PC+0002+REL, if the contents of C+Z = 1.

Branch if < zero	BLT		Branch to the address equal to PC+0002+REL, if the contents of N + V = 1.
Branch if minus	BMI		Branch to the address equal to PC+0002+REL, if the contents of N = 1.
Branch if ≠ zero	BNE		Branch to the address equal to PC+0002+REL, if the contents of Z = 0.
Branch if overflow clear	BVC		Branch to the address equal to PC+0002+REL, if the contents of V = 0.
Branch if overflow set	BVS		Branch to the address equal to PC+0002+REL, if the contents of V = 1.
Branch if plus	BPL		Branch to the address equal to PC+0002+REL, if the contents of N = 0.
Branch to subroutine	BSR		Branch to the address equal to PC+0002+REL. PC+0002 stored in the stack.
Jump	JMP		PC loaded with a numerical address; a jump to that location occurs.
Jump to subroutine	JSR		PC incremented by 0002 (indexed address mode) or 0003 (extended address mode), then stored in the stack. PC loaded with a numerical address; a jump to that location then occurs.
No operation	NOP		Advances PC; no other registers affected.
Return from interrupt	RTI		CC, ACCX, IX and PC restored in the states that were saved in the stack.
Return from subroutine	RTS		SP incremented by one; PCH loaded with the contents of the location specified by SP. Again, SP is incremented by one; PCL loaded with the contents of the location specified by SP.
Software interrupt	SWI		PC incremented by one; then PC, IX, ACCX and CC stored in the stack. SP decremented by one after each byte is stored. I bit then set and PC then loaded with the address specified by the software.
Wait for interrupt	WAI		Registers operated on and saved as in SWI instruction, except I bit is not set. Program execution suspended until interrupt occurs on IRQ line. When IRQ goes low, and provided that the I bit is clear, program execution proceeds as in SWI.
Condition code register manipulation instructions			
Clear carry	CLC		Carry bit reset to zero.
Clear interrupt mask	CLI		Interrupt bit reset to zero.
Clear overflow	CLV		Overflow bit reset to zero
Set carry	SEC		Carry bit set to one.
Set interrupt mask	SEI		Interrupt bit set to one.
Set overflow	SEV		Overflow bit set to one.
Transfer from ACCA to CC	TAP		Transfers the contents of bit 0 through 5 of ACCA to the corresponding bit positions of CC. Contents of ACCA not changed.
Transfer from CC to ACCA	TPA		Transfers the contents of bit 0 through 5 of CC to the corresponding bit positions of ACCA. Bits 6 and 7 of ACCA are set to one. Contents of CC not changed.

with the contents of two memory locations that are permanently assigned to the $\overline{\text{IRQ}}$ interrupt (Fig. 5b). The addresses, listed in hexadecimal, are the uppermost locations of the available address space. These locations should contain the addresses of the first instruction of each interrupt routine. Once the interrupt is serviced, a Return from Interrupt instruction (RTI), placed at the end of the routine restores IM and the μP returns to whatever it was doing prior to the interrupt.

The $\overline{\text{NMI}}$ interrupt is similar, except that it only waits until the current instruction is finished before storing the registers in the stack, instead of waiting until the $\overline{\text{IRQ}}$ line is reset by the current program. In effect, the $\overline{\text{NMI}}$ request has a higher priority than $\overline{\text{IRQ}}$, and is often used with a power-failure sensing circuit or with a peripheral unit that must be immediately serviced.

The $\overline{\text{RES}}$ interrupt differs from the other two in that it immediately sets IM, loads the program counter with the contents of the location assigned to $\overline{\text{RES}}$ and jumps to a service routine. This interrupt is normally used following power-on to begin a program that sets the initial conditions of the μP and the bus.

Hardware interrupts usually occur at random intervals, but software interrupts are usually planned and occur at predetermined points on a program to aid in debugging.

Interfacing to the system bus

Various peripheral circuits used to interface to the outside world can be controlled by software. Each of the units must be connected to both the data, address and control busses.

The PIA provides two 8-bit bidirectional data busses through pins PA0 to PA7 and PB0 to PB7 and four interrupt/control lines—CA1, CA2, CB1 and CB2 (Fig. 6a). The peripherals on side A are 5 V, CMOS compatible. The ones on side B are TTL compatible. The data flow occurs between the PIA and μP over eight bidirectional lines, DB0 to DB7. Five additional lines connect to the system's address bus.

A peripheral can signal the μP for service via the $\overline{\text{IRQA}}$ and/or $\overline{\text{IRQB}}$ lines. If necessary, the μP can acknowledge the request via the CA2 and CB2 lines. Since data transfers on the 6800 data bus usually take place on the phase-2 portion of the clock cycle, the phase-2 signal is used by the PIA as a timing reference. It is connected to the enable pulse input of the PIA. Direction of data flow is controlled by the μP R/W line, which is connected to the matching line on the PIA.

The ACIA serial-to-parallel interface circuit can be configured under software control to handle any of eight preset serial codes (Fig. 7a). It connects to the data, control and address busses in the same way the PIA does (Fig. 7b).

Separate inputs are available on the ACIA to permit clocking of transmitted or received data, at frequencies of 1, 16 or 64 times the data rates. Counters in the ACIA can be programmed by the μP to divide external clock signals by 1, 16 or 64. Received-data synchronization is accomplished internally in the $\div16$ and 64 modes. There are also three control lines that permit limited control of a peripheral such as a modem.

There is also an extra safety feature on the ACIA. As power is applied to the adapter, an internal circuit detects the power-line transition and holds the registers in a reset condition to prevent spurious outputs from affecting a peripheral that might already be operating.

The SSDA interface circuit appears as two

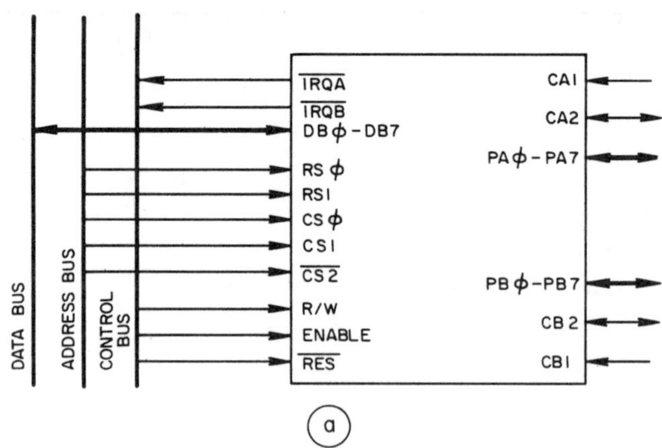

		Control register bit		Location selected
RS1	RS0	CRA-2	CRB-2	Location selected
0	0	1	×	Peripheral register A
0	0	0	×	Data direction register A
0	1	×	×	Control register A
1	0	×	1	Peripheral register B
1	0	×	0	Data direction register B
1	1	×	×	Control register B

× = Don't care   (b)

	7	6	5 4 3	2	1	0
CRA	IRQA1	IRQA2	CA2 control	DDRA access	CA1	control
	7	6	5 4 3	2	1	0
CRB	IRQB1	IRQB2	CB2 control	DDRB access	CB1	control

(c)

6. **The PIA connects into the 6800 system** with eight bidirectional data lines, five address lines and another five control lines (a). Register selection for the output port and for the flow direction can easily be done under software control (b and c).

memory locations to the μP. Internally there are actually seven registers. Data transferred to and from a peripheral must be accompanied by clock signals that are synchronized to the data. Transfer rates of up to 600 kilobits/second are possible. A power-on protect feature, similar to one in the ACIA, is also included.

To speed data flow over a telephone line, the low-speed modem circuit can operate in full-duplex, half-duplex or simplex modes. It can also be used in the answer or originate mode and can respond to a hang-up request. When the circuit is used to originate a call, the output will be a 1070-Hz signal for a space (ZERO) and a 1270-Hz signal for a mark (ONE). When the modem answers a call its modulator output will be 2025 Hz for a space and 2225 Hz for a mark.

A wide range of memory types and sizes is

Table 2. Support software and hardware

Support software	Available versions for:		
	Time-sharing systems	In-house computer systems	Design instrumentation
MPL compiler	GE International System; UCS	Sigma 9, Honeywell 6000, IBM 360/370 CDC6000	
Assembler	GE; UCS: Dentsu; Honeywell-Bull	Sigma 9, HP2100 IBM 360/370, NOVA, Honeywell 6000, CDC6000, PDP11	Resident editor/assembler versions for EXORciser and evaluation modules
Simulator	Same as assembler	Same as assembler	
Build virtual machine	Same as assembler		
HELP	Same as assembler		
Macro assembler			Resident version
EXBUG			EXORciser firmware
MINIBUG II			Evaluation Module II firmware
MIKBUG			Design evaluation kit firmware

Support hardware	Description
EXORciser	Basic EXORciser consists of an MPU module, debug module, baud rate module, power supply and chassis.
EXORciser optional modules	input/output, ACIA, PROM programmer, wrapped wire and extender modules. 2k × 8 static RAM, 8k × 8 dynamic RAM, 16k × 8 dynamic RAM, EROM/RAM,
System analyzer	Used to monitor and modify programs; contains 4k-bytes of RAM plus hex display and I/O control logic. The SA can be installed in the EXORciser or used as an independent, portable test instrument.
User system evaluator	For prototypes developed or transferred outside of the EXORciser chassis, and for production level testing, USE can be employed for test and debugging purposes. Operating with a single, shared-processor, the USE/prototype interface can be changed at will, allowing elements of the prototype to be tested and debugged in real time.
Component tester	Functionally tests the M6800 MPU, PIA, ACIA, ROM and RAM. Up to eight test heads can be connected to a single EXORciser for volume testing.
EXORdisk	A twin-drive floppy disk peripheral for the EXORciser that provides a low-cost-per-bit storage medium. Included with the EXORdisk is a disk operating system called EDOS.
EXORtape	A high speed papertape reader for the EXORciser. Data can be loaded at rates of up to 250 characters per second.
Evaluation Module II	A microcomputer on a single board; contains an MPU, 3 RAMs, 2 ACIAS, a PIA, an MC6871A clock oscillator, an MC14411 bit rate gen., data, address and control bus and peripheral interface buffers. A ROM contains the MINIBUG II loader/diagnostic program. Two of the RAMs provide 256 bytes of storage for users' programs. A 24-pin socket on the board will accommodate 2704 or 2708 type PROMs that contain user-generated firmware. The module interfaces with a TTY or RS232C data terminal.
Design evaluation kit	A low-cost microcomputer kit; contains an MPU, 2 PIAs, an ACIA, 2 RAMs, and a ROM that holds the MIKBUG loader/diagnostic program. One of the RAMs provides 128 bytes of storage for users' programs. The kit interfaces with a TTY or RC232C data terminal.

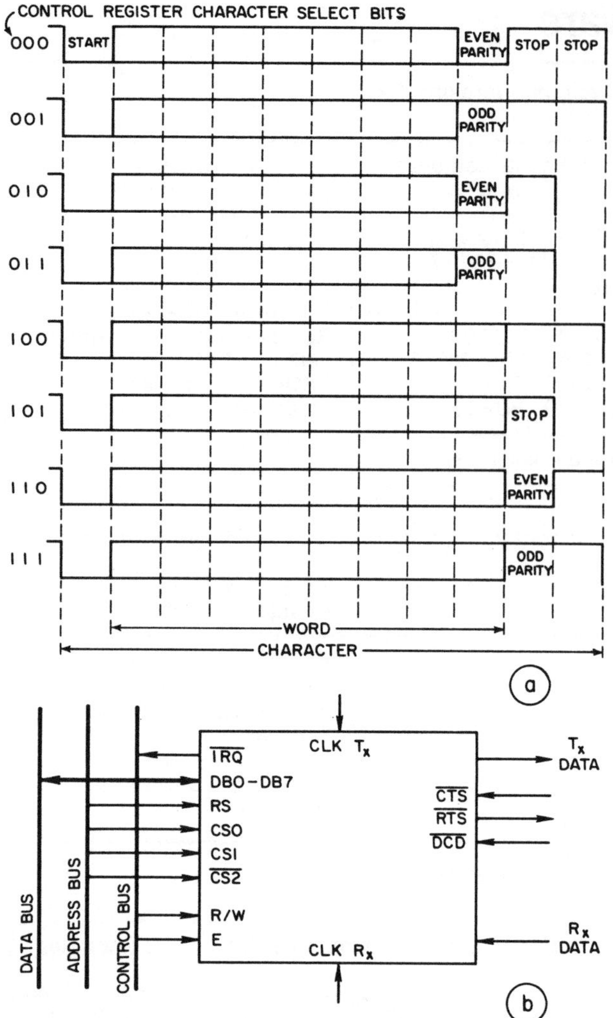

7. A three-bit input to the control register of the ACIA can set any of eight serial word formats (a). The ACIA connects easily to the general system bus (b). The eight bidirectional data lines are still needed. Only four address lines and three control lines are necessary.

available for use with the 6800 μP. Some typical sizes include the 128 $\times$ 8, byte-oriented RAM and the 1024 $\times$ 8, byte-oriented ROM. The RAM is a static unit and requires no refresh. It has TTL-compatible inputs, a bidirectional, three-state I/O bus and four negative and two positive chip-enable lines.

The 8-k ROM is mask programmable and has four enable lines. The enable lines are defined by the customer, when the mask is designed, to be either positive or negative. Input lines are TTL-compatible and there are three-state outputs.

Access time of the RAM can be as short as 350 ns to as long as 1 μs for the read function, depending upon the model selected. The ROM has an access time of 500 ns.

Other sizes of RAMs and ROMs are also available, along with clock buffers, alterable ROMs, dynamic RAMs, bus extenders and three-state buffers.

When the M6800 system runs at full speed (that is, at a clock rate of 1 MHz) memory components must have access times of 575 ns or less. Of course for cost tradeoffs slower memories can be used if the clock rate is decreased, or if you switch to dynamic memories that can be accessed faster but which require extra refresh circuitry.

The MC6800 uses two nonoverlapping clocks that time the execution of a program. Dynamic RAMs place an additional constraint on the clock: the output phases can be held in one state no longer than 5 μs without affecting the contents of the dynamic RAM.

Development aids fill most needs

A comprehensive array of support software and system-development tools is available from Motorola and other companies. The most powerful of these tools is the EXORciser. It contains a complete M6800 operating system, and built-in firmware to help design and debug prototype systems. The basic EXORciser consists of three plug-in boards, a power supply and a chassis. The three modules are the μP card, the debug card and a baud-rate module. The μP and debug cards each require one of the 14 card slots in the EXORciser chassis. The other 12 slots are available for custom-designed interfaces and circuits.

On the μP card is the μP, a clock, bus control logic, and clock-control circuit and three-state buffers.

The debug module contains ROMs, RAMs, a PIA, an ACIA, a PROM and an assortment of logic, buffers and opto-isolators for bus control and for data-terminal interfaces. Firmware on the board consists of the EXbug loader/diagnostic program.

On the baud-rate module is a crystal-controlled bit-rate generator that permits data rates of 110 to 9600 baud. The chassis power supply provides 5 V at 15 A, 12 V at 2.5 A and −12 V at 1.5 A to handle almost any circuit requirements.

For smaller design applications, the MEK-6800D1 Design Evaluation Kit or the M6800B Evaluation Module II are available. The MEK kit consists of a printed-circuit board and M6800 family ICs. Also included is a ROM that contains MIKbug, a debugging routine.

The Evaluation Module II is a self-contained microcomputer on a single board, similar to the Design Evaluation Kit, except that it comes completely assembled. It contains a μP, three RAMs, two ACIAs, a PIA, a ROM, a clock oscillator and a bit-rate generator. Also included are the data, address and control-bus buffers.

Assembly Language for Microprocessors

SEYMOUR T. LEVINE
Software Engineer, Timeplex, Inc.,
Hackensack, N.J.

Learning assembly language programming isn't hard. All an assembly language program consists of is a list of mnemonic commands that tell the microprocessor what to shift, pull from memory, which registers to clear, where to store data, etc. To do any work with microprocessor systems, programming is a necessity.

All μP manufacturers use a form of mnemonics, but unfortunately they are different from one vendor to the next. Therefore, to learn the basics of assembly-language programming, we will use the Motorola M6800 μP and its software as an example, since its structure is fairly generic and since it is now available from more than one source.

A μP can be viewed as a group of registers that, upon command, extract data from a memory bank, perform the programmed operations and then return the data to the memory or to an output device. To do all these operations, the μP-based system must contain these main sections (Fig. 1):

■ MPU—the main processing unit. This houses the registers, control gating and counters needed to manipulate and keep track of the data.

■ ROM—the read-only memory. It usually contains the binary equivalent of the assembly-language program that gives the MPU all of its instructions.

■ RAM—the random-access memory. This can be used to hold the active part of the program and any other data that are being inputted or generated. It usually is very volatile and is only for temporary storage.

■ PIA—the peripheral interface adapter. This lets the MPU and memories talk to external devices, such as terminals, printers and tape drives in parallel data words.

Communication between the various sections of the μP system is done over a multi-line communications bus. One part of this bus is unidirectional—from the ROM to the MPU and contains mainly instructions and perhaps key constants. The rest of the bus is bidirectional— the MPU can communicate with the RAM and

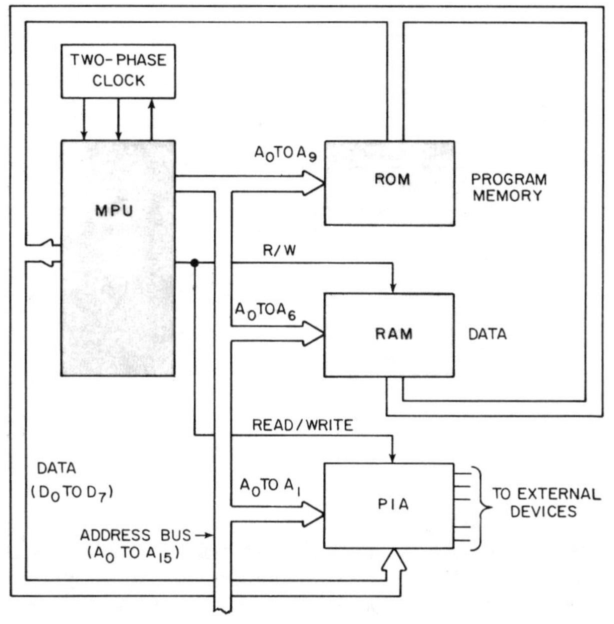

1. **All major functional blocks are connected** by a 16-bit address bus and an 8-bit data bus in the M6800 μP-based system.

PIA, and the PIA can talk to the RAM directly as if all of these were simply read/write memory.

In large systems the computer words are usually long enough to obtain the entire data word or instruction at once. In the smaller μP systems the words are only about half the size, and in some cases two or more words (of 8 bits each) must be used to supply data or give instructions. One prime example of this is when the data needed for the MPU to complete an instruction is external to the MPU.

When this happens, the MPU must reach out to successive locations where the data are stored and bring them to the registers within the MPU. To do this, address words must be issued to direct the data into the register.

Since all the MPU consists of is a bunch of registers connected by a complex gating arrangement and a controlling set of counters, let's examine these sections a little closer. The MPU

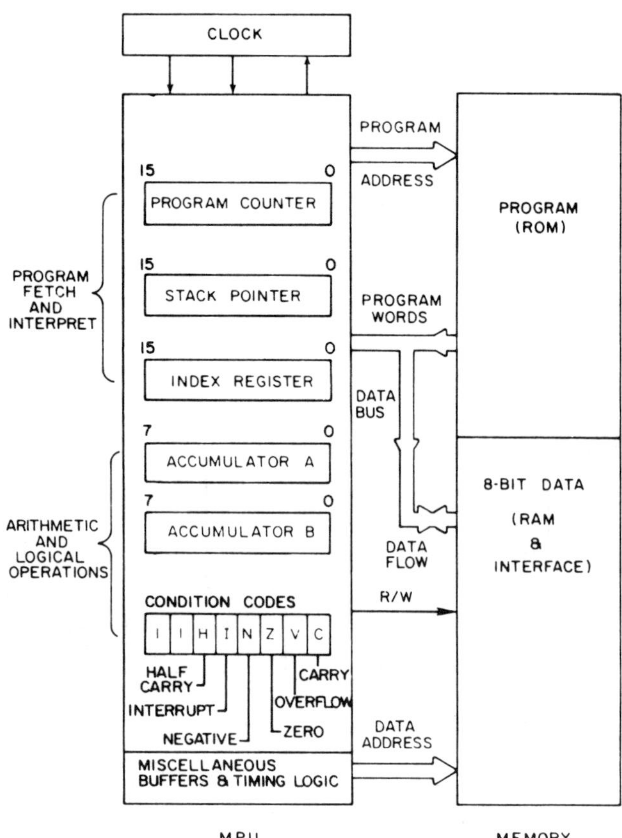

2. **Inside the MPU** are the different counters and registers that let you separately keep track of both the program and data. And, correspondingly, the programmer treats memory as if it were composed of two parts—a data or variable section and a command or instruction section. Also included are the logic circuits and control gates needed to do all the arithmetic operations.

can be divided into two main blocks (Fig. 2): (1) Program fetch and decode, and (2) The arithmetic/logical processor.

Separate the commands and data

The first steps of the processing cycle depend on the data within the program counter of the MPU. These data determine which operation the computer is to perform. Subsequent cycles may generate read or write commands to the data or variable section of the memory in order for the processor to manipulate the data.

As a rule, the clocked program counter (PC) generates sequentially increasing addresses to pull control words from the ROM or other control block. The PC controls the entire operation of the processor, unless commands are encountered in the program flow that cause the counter to depart from sequential operation. The next value of the PC may then depend upon commands for conditional branching (similar to Fortran IF

statements) or direct branching (like GO TO in Fortran). The PC value may also be forced to a specific location by the presence of an external interrupt.

Data addresses depend on the type of command and can be modified by the value stored in the index register. The read/write control line of the MPU tells it whether it should fetch or store data.

Although the MPU operates under binary control, the chance for an error, should the program or data be entered manually, is enormous.

Assembly language is a shorthand way of writing the binary instructions that can be converted into binary form by an assembler. And, as a rule, a single statement generates a single storable command. These shorthand statements are grouped into fields and are designated by the following four names: Label, Operator, Operand, Comments.

The four elements when combined on a single line are separated from one another by some form of delimiter, such as one or more blank spaces, a slash or a comma. The Comments field is used only to help others understand what the programmer intends; it will not generate any instructions for the computer.

A sample working instruction for the M6800 might appear as follows:

UPDAT LDA A   NB   BEGIN THE LOOP
Label   Mnemonic Operand   Comment

Labels help the programmer use branching commands, since he can then write the equivalent of a GO TO statement just by associating it with the label. The mnemonic command LDA A instructs the μP to load the accumulator known as A with the data that will come from the location described by the operand. The operand, NB, instructs the μP to fetch data from the location called NB. This pseudo English tells the MPU that the binary data in the byte following the LDA instruction names or points to the address from which the MPU is to fetch the desired data (Fig. 3).

Assign values to the symbols

Once an assembly language program is written, you must systematically determine the locations in which the program is stored in ROM or RAM. First, concentrate on the commands and store each command in sequentially ascending order of memory locations.

Whenever a label is noted, write the address of the memory location presently associated with that label. Since the mnemonic operation codes have unique binary descriptions assigned by the manufacturer, there is no difficulty in storing them. This process is usually done in most larger systems by the assembler, which converts the

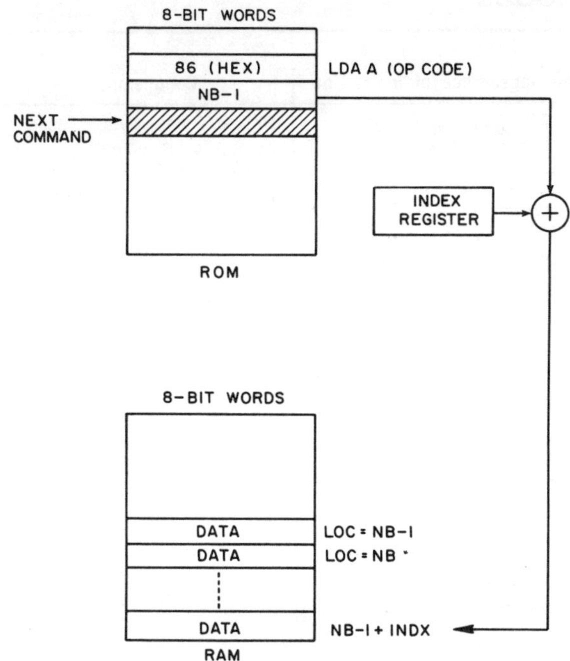

3. When the op code LDA A is given, the byte of binary data following the instruction is added to the index register information to supply the address of the data needed by the op-code instruction.

mnemonic into binary and assigns numbers to all labels.

After the commands are all located, you must provide unique locations for storing the operands or data. These locations don't have to be in any particular sequence, except that arrays usually receive consecutive assignments. Once fixed, these addresses provide the data to fill in some of the missing command words when the assembler assigns location and sequence numbers.

Returning to the sample instruction given earlier, we could have chosen the location FFF (hexadecimal notation) for NB. Assemblers let the user specify the origin or starting address for his commands and the locations for his data.

These addresses are referred to as directives (to the assembler), and while they influence the final values selected for the numerical data other than operation codes, they do not result in any extra instructions. But they can be confusing, since the format of the directives often resembles the actual assembly code. Similarly directives to insert constant values at certain locations in ROM resemble MPU commands. Fortunately most assemblers sort them out and arrange them in columns.

Address the data properly

When you specify the address of data, use the most direct way—too long an address and the computer slows down, too short and you have a

limited amount of memory available. This can break a system if you're not careful.

The M6800 provides a wide variety of different addressing modes (see Table 1):

- Inherent—Operations are performed on or between registers within the MPU chip.
- Accumulator—Operations affect only the data in the accumulator such as clear, complement, shift, etc.
- Relative—The memory address to which the MPU refers depends on the value of the program counter.
- Immediate—The instruction contains the value of the operand to be used in the computation.
- Direct—The instruction provides the necessary address (up to 8 bits for the M6800).
- Extended—This form of direct mode can address 64 k words of memory (16-bit address).
- Indexed—Memory reference depends upon the data stored in the command word plus the contents of the index register.

Another form of addressing used on almost all minicomputers and large machines is called indirect. This is a two-step process: First, the CPU fetches data from an address. Then it uses the data word as the address of the operand.

The M6800 uses commands that range from one to three bytes long: Inherent and accumulator modes use one byte; relative, immediate, direct and indexed modes use two; and extended uses three.

Motorola has developed a program that accepts symbols and mnemonics to assemble a program. The symbols that indicate the address mode include the asterisk, period, pound and single alphabetic characters. These are used in the operand field.

The asterisk indicates that the relative address mode is to be used, and it has been accepted as the de facto standard for this mode by many companies. Another way of looking at this symbol is to think of it as the present value of the program counter.

The pound character, #, designates the use of the immediate addressing mode. An alphabetic character (X for Motorola) indicates that indexed addressing is to be used. Each of the symbols is, of course, mutually exclusive—only one addressing mode can be used at a time. The Motorola assembler will select either extended or direct addressing by default if the other modes are not specified. If the numerical address lies within the range 0 to 255, default is to direct addressing, while if the address specifies a location out of that range, extended addressing is used.

The relative addressing mode, though, is restricted to branching instructions, such as BSR (branch to subroutine).

Table 1. Explanation of various addressing modes

Addressing mode	Processing required to load address into internal address register	Byte appearance of instruction	Comments
Immediate	Current value of PC indicates the op code and the digital information represented by PC + 1 is the data the op code is to perform its operation on.	op code — K data — K + 1 see comments — K + 2 bit 0 7	Only one data byte is used except for mnemonic instructions CPX, LDS and LDX which use a second byte.
Direct	The current value of the PC indicates the op code. Increment the PC and then move the data from the location specified by PC + 1 to the address register.	op code — K address — K + 1 0 7	Two data bytes are used.
Extended	The current value of the PC indicates the op code. Increment the PC by 1 and transfer the data from the location specified by PC + 1 to the address register. Increment the PC again to PC + 2 and transfer the data from the location specified by PC + 2 to the address register.	op code — K address — K + 1 ⎫ address — K + 2 ⎭ 16 bits 0 7	Two data bytes are used.
Relative	The current value of the PC indicates the op code. Increment the PC by 1 and add the contents of the location specified by PC + 1 to the value of the PC after it is incremented again (PC + 2)	op code — K displacement — K + 1 0 7	One data byte used. This applies only for branch instructions.
Indexed	The current value of the PC indicates the op code. Increment the PC by 1 and add the contents of the location specified by PC + 1 to the index register.	op code — K data from — K + 1 memory location — K + 1 0 7	One data byte used.

When you write programs for the M6800, they can be done in modular form and then strung together. To do this, though, you must make use of the stack pointer (SP) within the μP chip. The SP register provides an address that is used for subroutine jumps, or if the program is interrupted, it holds data from some of the other registers.

The stack is a set of memory locations that are addressed and sometimes modified when interrupts or subroutine jumps are invoked. A jump-to-subroutine (JSR) command orders the μP to increment and store the program counter value in the next empty stack location and then jump to the new (subroutine) location. The stack pointer is also set to the next empty location, just in case another subroutine or interrupt command is given.

The return-from-subroutine (RTS) instruction decrements the stack pointer and places the contents of the register specified by the pointer back into the program counter. Two additional instructions—mnemonics PSH (push data) and PUL (pull data) allow transfer of accumulator data to and from the stack.

An interrupt command causes the μP to react as if indirect addressing is in effect. After the MPU completes its current instruction, it initiates the following sequence of operations:

■ Stores the contents of the program counter, accumulators and condition code registers into the interrupt stack registers.

■ Generates a 16-bit address that points to locations n-2 and n-3.

■ Follows instructions starting at a location prestored by the user in locations n-2 and n-3.

The last eight memory locations of the stack should be reserved for interrupt vectoring (another name for such indirect addressing). This allows for four 16-bit words to redirect the MPU. For instance, beginning with location FFF8 (hex), you could have:

FFF8	MS ⎫	
FFF9	LS ⎭	Hardware interrupt
FFFA	MS ⎫	
FFFB	LS ⎭	Software interrupt
FFFC	MS ⎫	
FFFD	LS ⎭	Nonmaskable interrupt
FFFE	MS ⎫	
FFFF	LS ⎭	Restart

The software interrupt lets you develop an over-all systems executive or monitor. Thus if a program module has some data to send through the asynchronous communications interface adapter (serial data port)—ACIA—it could execute a software interrupt and vector the MPU to the appropriate input/output routine.

Let's look at a sample program

To write a program without the aid of an assembler, start with a list of the commands you

Table 2. Program to clear 10 registers

ROM Location (decimal)	ROM Content		
	(hex)		comment
000	7F		op code
001	8 bits⎰		address of
002	8 bits⎱		buffer (1)
			in binary
003	7F		
004	8 bits⎰		address of
005	8 bits⎱		buffer (2)
.	.		
.	.		
.	.		
027	7F		
028	.⎱		address of
029	.⎰		buffer (10)

Table 3. Rewritten clearing program

Label	Op code	Operand or location
	LDX	#BUFFR*
	LDA A	# 1
BEGIN	CMP	A # 11
	BEQ	PROC
	CLR	O, X
	INC	A
	INX	
	BRA	BEGIN
PROC	. . .⎱	
	. . .⎱	New program
	. . .⎰	section

*The pound sign shows that immediate addressing is to be used for the first three commands.

Table 4. Assembled clearing program

Label	ROM location (decimal)	Op-code (hexadecimal)	Description or name of op code
	000	FE	LDX
	001 ⎱	two binary	extended address to
			first location of
	002 ⎰	bytes	data-symbol BUFFR
	003	86	LDA A
	004	01	with literal 1
BEGIN	005	81	CMP A
	006	0B	with literal 11
	007	27	BEQ
	008	06	relative address to location 015
	009	6F	CLR (see note 2)
	010	00	indexed by 0
	011	4C	INC A
	012	08	INX
	013	20	BRA
	014	see note 1	
PROC	015	XX	Any op code
	.		Subsequent instructions
	.		and literals
	.		

Notes:
1. Use hex equivalent of —10 in location 14 to get a relative branch back to location 005 which continues the loop.
2. This is an indexed address command with 0 shift that refers to one of the locations in the array BUFFR.

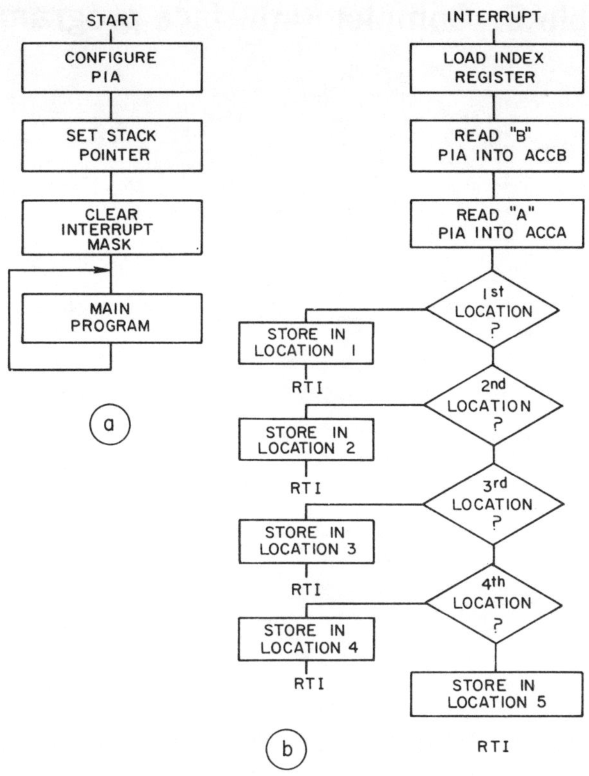

4. **The interface program** has an executive portion (a) with only a few steps and an interrupt subroutine (b) with many steps.

will use to process the data. Remember, the program will reside in the ROM until needed, and the RAM will be used to hold the active part of the program.

Let's start with a simple program that will clear a set of data locations named BUFFR. We will assume that BUFFR consists of 10 consecutive locations and exists in the RAM data space. The program could then consist of the clear command (CLR) given 10 times, with the location in the operand field:

```
CLR       BUFFR(1)
CLR       BUFFR(2)
   •
   •
   •
CLR       BUFFR(10)
```

The location of BUFFR was chosen so that extended addressing is used. The resulting hex characters appear in ROM as shown in Table 2. The contents of the op-code byte—in this case, 7F—informs the MPU that extended addressing is to be used. Use of an index register, though, can replace the repetition of the same command with a short program loop. The same program to clear 10 locations can be rewritten as shown in Table 3.

The program operates as follows: Before the main program loop begins, the program loads the

Table 5. Complete interface program

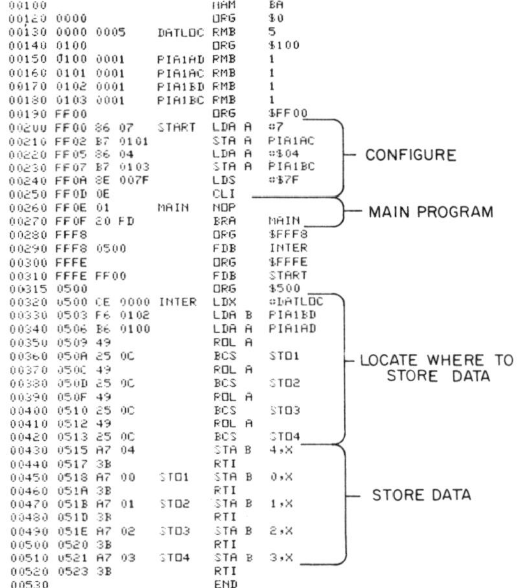

```
00100                        NAM   BA
00120 0000                   ORG   $0
00130 0000 0005   DATLOC RMB      5
00140 0100                   ORG   $100
00150 0100 0001   PIA1AD RMB      1
00160 0101 0001   PIA1AC RMB      1
00170 0102 0001   PIA1BD RMB      1
00180 0103 0001   PIA1BC RMB      1
00190 FF00                   ORG   $FF00
00200 FF00 86 07  START  LDA A   #7
00210 FF02 B7 0101         STA A   PIA1AC
00220 FF05 86 04           LDA A   #$04
00230 FF07 B7 0103         STA A   PIA1BC
00240 FF0A 8E 007F         LDS     #$7F
00250 FF0D 0E              CLI
00260 FF0E 01     MAIN   NOP
00270 FF0F 20 FD           BRA     MAIN
00280 FFF8                 ORG     $FFF8
00290 FFF8 0500            FDB     INTER
00300 FFFE                 ORG     $FFFE
00310 FFFE FF00            FDB     START
00315 0500                 ORG     $500
00320 0500 CE 0000 INTER  LDX     #DATLOC
00330 0503 F6 0102         LDA B   PIA1BD
00340 0506 B6 0100         LDA A   PIA1AD
00350 0509 49              ROL A
00360 050A 25 0C           BCS     STO1
00370 050C 49              ROL A
00380 050D 25 0C           BCS     STO2
00390 050F 49              ROL A
00400 0510 25 0C           BCS     STO3
00410 0512 49              ROL A
00420 0513 25 0C           BCS     STO4
00430 0515 A7 04           STA B   4,X
00440 0517 3B              RTI
00450 0518 A7 00  STO1   STA B   0,X
00460 051A 3B              RTI
00470 051B A7 01  STO2   STA B   1,X
00480 051D 3B              RTI
00490 051E A7 02  STO3   STA B   2,X
00500 0520 3B              RTI
00510 0521 A7 03  STO4   STA B   3,X
00520 0523 3B              RTI
00530                      END
```


address of BUFFR(1) into the index register and sets location A to 1. At the command labeled BEGIN, the program compares A to 11 (decimal notation) and if A $\neq$ 11, the program performs the next instruction, CLR. As the program continues in the loop, A will increase to 11, and when the program reaches the BEQ command it breaks out of the loop into the next program.

The entire program that must either be put on paper tape or into ROM is shown in Table 4. This type of programming is fine for small programs where you can keep track of variable locations, but for larger programs some sort of assembler is needed. Assemblers can refer to unnamed locations as a numeric expression that involves a label name. Thus BRA = BEGIN + 1 would refer to location 5—that of the next instruction.

Commercial assemblers let you locate the origin of programs anywhere in ROM through the ORG directive. For example, ORG 100 states that the given program segment is to start at ROM location 100. The EQU directive equates a symbol with a numerical value, another symbol or an expression. The RMB command reserves memory bytes. These and other directives assign values and addresses in data memory.

Interface instruments with software

To interface anything to the μP, you must make connections through a form of PIA or ACIA. The PIA handles parallel data, while the ACIA handles serial. Let's look at the complex problem of interfacing an instrument to the μP.

As a starting point, assume the instrument delivers a parallel digital data word. The PIA would then be used to interface the instrument. Inside the PIA are enough interface circuits to handle two peripherals. The PIA is internally divided into two symmetrical (noted as A and B), but independent, circuits that consist of three registers each. Each half contains a data direction register, a control register and an output register.

The registers are eight bits wide and are externally controllable. To define the operation of the PIA A or B side, an 8-bit word is loaded into the control register, and to define the data lines as inputs or outputs, an 8-bit word is loaded into the data direction register. Finally the actual data to be transferred goes into the output register.

The instrument we want to interface has data and a data ready line that can be used to signal an interrupt of the processor. Both halves of the PIA must be used to move the data from the instrument to the memory. The B side of the PIA holds the data word, and the A side identifies that word.

Basically the PIA and μP operate together as follows: When the interrupt occurs, the B side of the PIA is read into the B accumulator of the μP. Then the A side of the PIA is read to define the memory location of where the data stored in accumulator B should be placed. Next the data are transferred from the accumulator to the memory location, and then the μP goes back to waiting for another interrupt.

The MSB of the A side data word specifies the first location, the next bit the next location, and so on. If a ONE is not present in any of the four MSBs, the data are to be stored in the fifth location. These data locations are contiguous, with the first at an address we'll call DATLOC and all others in increasing sequence. When any of these locations receives a data word, the new data wipe out the old.

The CA1 terminal of the PIA can accept the interrupt signal generated by the rising edge of a waveform. This configures all the data ports as inputs, while the other interrupt lines CA2, CB1 and CB2 are not used. The flow charts for the system program to pull in data are shown in Fig. 4.

When started, the program configures the PIA, sets the stack pointer and clears the interrupt line and can proceed to do any program it has in memory. When an interrupt comes, present values of the last instruction and program counter and registers are stored in the stack, and the interrupt program is set in the program counter. When the interrupt routine is finished, the μP registers are reset to their values just before the interrupt and the main program continues along.

Table 5 shows the complete instrument interface program developed by Motorola Semiconductor Products to do the job.

A Universal Test System

JIM BARNES
*Senior Project Engineer, Motorola Semiconductor
Products, Inc., Phoenix*

BERT BERGQUIST
*Design Engineer, Motorola Semiconductor
Products, Inc., Phoenix*

When you near the end of a μP-based design and face the problem of joining the nearly completed hardware to the almost finished software, let a universal test system officiate at the final coupling.

Such a test system can be very useful. First, it allows you to communicate with the μP system through a keyboard. Second, the program can be loaded into a RAM memory from tape generated by either time-sharing or a proprietary development system like Motorola's Exorcisor. Then the μP system can be operated from the program as stored in the RAM. Third, selected portions of the program can be exercised, and the program modified to perform special tests or system-hardware adjustments. The RAM memory can be tested to ensure that it is operating properly.

A particular advantage in programs with a short turn-around time is that system development and software debugging can proceed on hardware in the breadboard or prototype stage.

Finally, as the system nears completion, it can be operated entirely on its own, but with the test option available in case problems develop.

The test system can still be used for production units even after the μP product is finished. And when the products are out in the field the test system can serve as a troubleshooting aid, for both hardware and software.

No need to change standard procedure

In developing a μP system you usually follow a standard sequence of steps: 1. The system requirements are written down in statement form. 2. Algorithms are developed from these statements. 3. Rough code is written and assembled to implement the algorithms. 4. The code is simulated and refined on either a time-sharing system or on a proprietary development system like the Exorcisor or Intellec.

Eventually, you must fit the refined program into the hardware system. This ultimate marriage may not occur until after the system is prototyped. What makes the test system so ef-

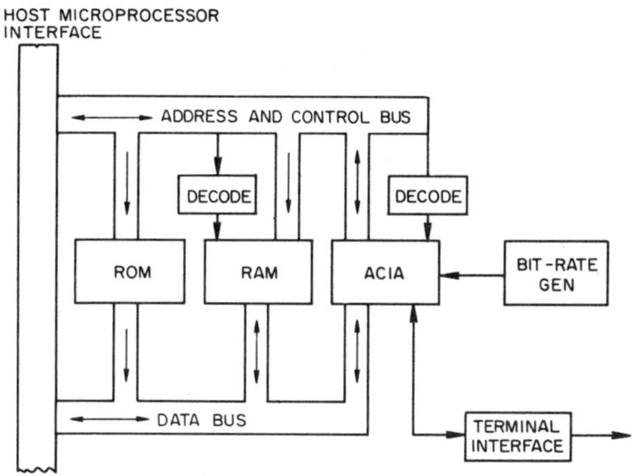

1. **A universal test system consists** of a number of LSI and MSI packages. The ROM holds the test program, the RAM acts as a scratchpad, and the ACIA interfaces the terminal with the test system.

fective with small μP systems is that it interfaces with existing hardware without significant modification to that hardware.

Hardware for the test system consists of three LSI packages, four conventional IC packages, an interface connector to the terminal and additional interface connections to the data, address and control buses of the host μP (Fig. 1).

The LSI packages—all components of the M6800 μP family—include the Minibug II firmware ROM (this is the same ROM supplied with Motorola's Evaluation Module II), the M6810 RAM as a scratchpad and the M6850 asynchronous communications interface adapter (ACIA) for connection to the terminal.

MSI packages include the MC14411 bit-rate generator, the MC14025 gate package for ACIA address decoding and the MC1489/MC1488 pair, which provides the RS232 interface. If you use a TTY terminal requiring a 20-mA current loop, then a 4N33 optocoupler can act as the interface.

The ROM provides the program that recognizes both requests to perform standard operations and the routines that actually perform

	PRIMARY ADDRESS	ALIAS ADDRESS
μP VECTORS	EFFF,	FFFF
	EFF8,	FFF8
	EIFF,	FIFF
MINIBUG PROGRAM		
USER'S PROGRAM	EOOO,	FOOO
	COOO,	DOOO
MINIBUG RAM	AO7F,	BO75
	AOOO,	BOOO
MINIBUG ACIA	8007,	9007
	8004,	9004
USER'S RAM		
	OOOO,	IOOO

2. **The memory map shows wired addresses** and those used during system start-up.

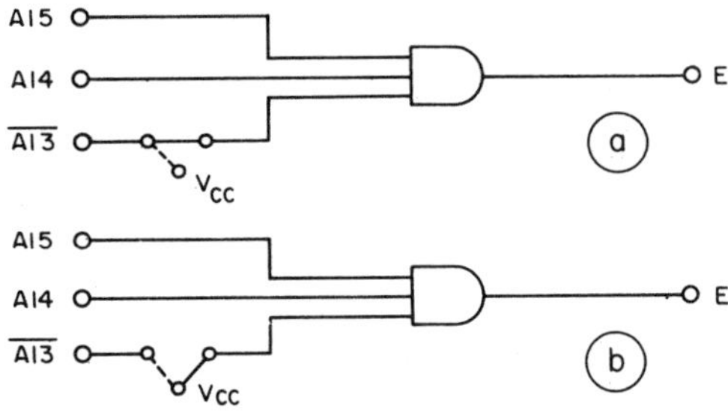

3. **Generation of system-enable signal:** in the TEST mode, firmware decodes C to generate an enable signal (a). Without TEST, C or E is decoded (b). Response is to CXXX or FXXX, depending on whether $\overline{A_{13}}$ or V_{cc} is connected.

them. The RAM—in addition to providing dedicated storage areas for stack, target, interrupt and data-enclosing vectors—also contains a small area that can hold limited test routines. Finally, the ACIA provides the serial-to-parallel interface to the terminal.

Connection of the test system is complicated by the μP-controlled start-up sequence. The μP's first action is to put all address lines, except A_0, at the HIGH level (hexadecimal address FFFE) and then look for the high-order byte of the program's starting address. Next, the μP puts A_0 HIGH (hex FFFF) and looks for the low-order starting-address byte.

When a program like the Minibug II is used, μP action must direct a vector to the start of the Minibug II ROM; when the operating system is used alone the same action must point to the start of the system ROM. Similar requirements exist for the interrupt vectors located at FFF8 through FFFD.

Equalizing the addresses

The Minibug ROM is wired to respond to address EXXX, but it must also respond to FXXX at system start-up. To see how this can be accom-

plished, you must interpret these locations in terms of the actual address lines. Hex E and F are equal to binary 1110 and 1111, respectively. The corresponding address line configurations are A_{15}, A_{14}, A_{13}, A_{12} and A_{15}, A_{14}, A_{13}, A_{12} respectively.

To make addresses E and F react equally, you need only make A_{12} an X, or a Don't Care. Then the Minibug II ROM—though wired as EXXX—will respond to FXXX.

As shown in Fig. 2, the Minibug II program also reserves AXXX for its RAM and 8XXX for its ACIA. With A_{12} as a Don't Care, the BXXX and 9XXX are unavailable without additional decoding. Since the low-order addresses usually are reserved for peripherals and program RAMs, the CXXX (or DXXX) 2-k byte area is only recommended for programs in small systems; more than 2-k bytes of program call for additional hardware decoding.

When you compare hex F (binary 1111) and hex C (binary 1100), and realize that you have already made A_{12} a Don't Care, you see that F and C differ only in A_{13}. Take advantage of this situation: Hook-up a single-pole, double-throw switch to determine whether the system is in the Minibug II or system-ROM program. Figure 3 shows how to generate the system-enable signal, E. The signal responds to CXXX when $\overline{A_{13}}$ is connected and to either CXXX or FXXX when V_{cc} is connected.

In operation, the system calls those functions that accomplish the desired end. These functions include:
- Read a memory location to a printer.
- Write into any memory location from an external keyboard.
- Write into memory from tape.
- Print a designated section of memory on either printer or tape (with computed checksum).
- Vector to a target program.
- Memory test (five patterns and a walking-bit test).
- Punch and load binary tape.

The memory-test function allows exhaustive testing of any block of memory the designer may designate by use of the M function. The tests are as follows:
- A Walking address.
- B Write FF into all locations and verify.
- C Write AA into all locations and verify.
- D Write 55 into all locations and verify.
- E Write 00 into all locations and verify.
- W Write a single walking bit through the entire memory.

As each test is completed, the corresponding letter is typed—if a test fails, the user knows immediately which one.

The function, "Punch binary tape," allows punching the exact contents of memory on tape

Table 1. Memory examine-and-change sequences

ENTER (Command)	RESPONSE
M	Space
XXXX (4 Hex digit memory loc.)	Space XX (2 Hex digit of memory contents.)
XX (2 Hex digit of new data.)	
C.R. or L.F. or ↑	1) C.R. stores data and responds with* 2) L.F. stores data, increments address and opens that location. 3) ↑ stores data, decrements address and opens that location.

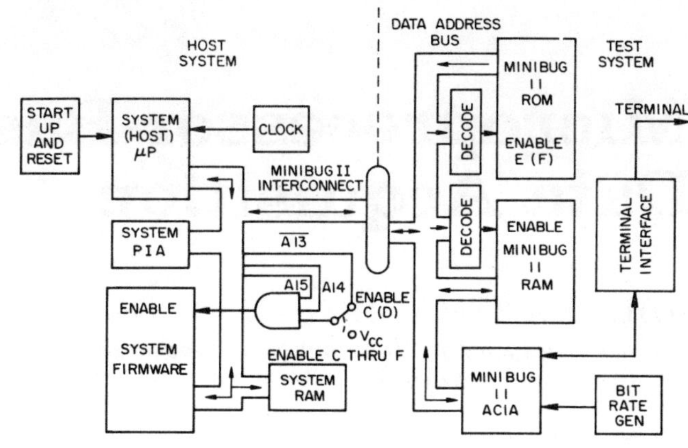

4. **How test system connects to host** µ**P** system. Little hardware change usually is needed to interconnect the two systems. A TTY terminal can be used.

Table 2. Test system response and command

ENTER (Command)	RESPONSE	ENTER	RESPONSE
G	Space	XXXX (4 Hex digit users starting address)	Goes to user's program and executes instruction sequence.
DISPLAY REGISTERS			
R			Prints register contents as follows: condition code ACCB ACCA INDEX P COUNTER STACK XX XX XX XXXX XXXX XXXX
MEMORY TEST FUNCTION			
W	Space		A B C D E W, carriage returns, prints*.
PUNCH BINARY TAPE			
Y			Tape is punched, carriage returns and prints*.
READ BINARY TAPE			
Z			Memory is read to printer, carriage returns, prints*.

—no ASCII II conversion is made, as is when talking with a printer. A tape header is generated that includes the word count and starting address. Record length is 256 words. If the record is longer, another header is inserted after each 256-word sector.

The "Read binary tape" function is exactly the inverse of the punch binary tape function—the record is written into memory at the starting address contained in the tape header.

Note that, with the test system, the memory-examine-and-change sequence should be learned first, because this sequence sets up portions of other commands (Table 1).

With the test system and a terminal both properly connected to your system (Fig. 4), and with the power on, a press of the system reset or restart button causes the terminal to respond with a carriage return, line feed and a printed asterisk. The system is now ready to accept commands from the terminal.

To load tape into memory, first load a formatted tape into the terminal and set the tape reader to Auto. Then just enter the command "L" following the asterisk, and the tape is loaded. To print out the memory contents or punch a formatted tape, first enter the high and low-order starting-print address into memory locations A002 and A003. Then enter into locations A004 and A005 the high and low-order END print address. After the asterisk appears, enter the command "P." The response is printout or recording of the formatted data.

To use the program-interrupt sequences, enter the assigned addresses into the test system as follows: at memory locations A001 and A002, the high and low-order hardware-interrupt vector; at A006 and A007, the nonmaskable interrupt; and at A00C and A00D, the software-interrupt vector.

The various commands associated with the user's program are given in Table 2.

Microprocessor-Based Data Acquisition

JOHN KAUFMANN
*Software Engineer, Motorola Semiconductor
Products, Inc., Phoenix*

You can keep an eye on various physical parameters or monitor a number of other analog voltages with a microprocessor-based system. Built around the 6800 μP and an a/d converter subsystem, the system can monitor and display any of four switch-selected voltages or various software-controlled functions (see table).

The monitor can interface to a main control system or operate as a stand-alone system. And, if necessary, a large number of parameters—with certain restrictions—can be monitored. These restrictions stem from the finite scan frequency, which is inversely proportional to the number of parameters.

Also, the scan frequency affects the type of parameter to be monitored since, for reliable conversion, the sensed quantity should not vary appreciably between conversion periods. Usually, though, physical quantities like temperature and pressure vary so slowly that a single a/d converter can monitor a large number of sensors.

In addition to the basic CPU, the system uses a peripheral interface adapter (PIA), such as the MC6820, and memory for the control program. Fig. 1 shows the allocation of the PIA register and control lines. To interface all the required operations of the display board through one PIA, the BCD inputs to the display decoder/drivers are multiplexed.

Also, all the ramp control lines for the a/d subsystems are tied to a single line in the register that interfaces the comparator outputs of the a/d to the CPU. This configuration allows up to seven a/d subsystems per PIA register to be interfaced to the CPU.

Higher voltage improves S/N

Hardware external to the CPU mounts on the display board. Included are the display select switch, the a/d subsystem chips (MC1405), display latch/decoder/drivers (MC14511), and seven-segment LED displays (Fig. 2). The a/d chips are powered by a 12-V supply, permitting a higher integrator-capacitor peak voltage than would

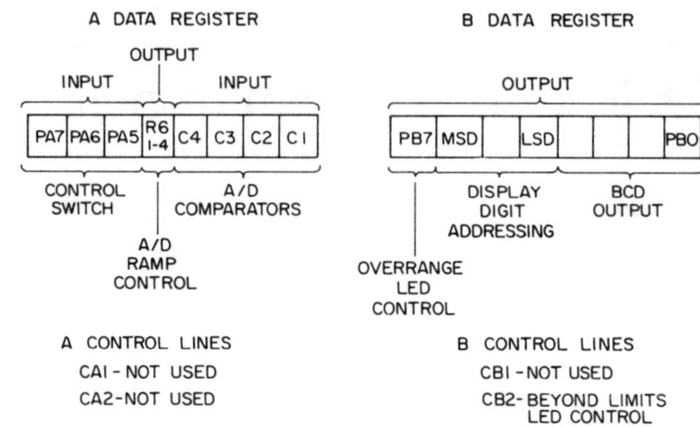

1. With multiplexing, just one PIA is needed to couple the display board to the μP. PIA allocations are shown.

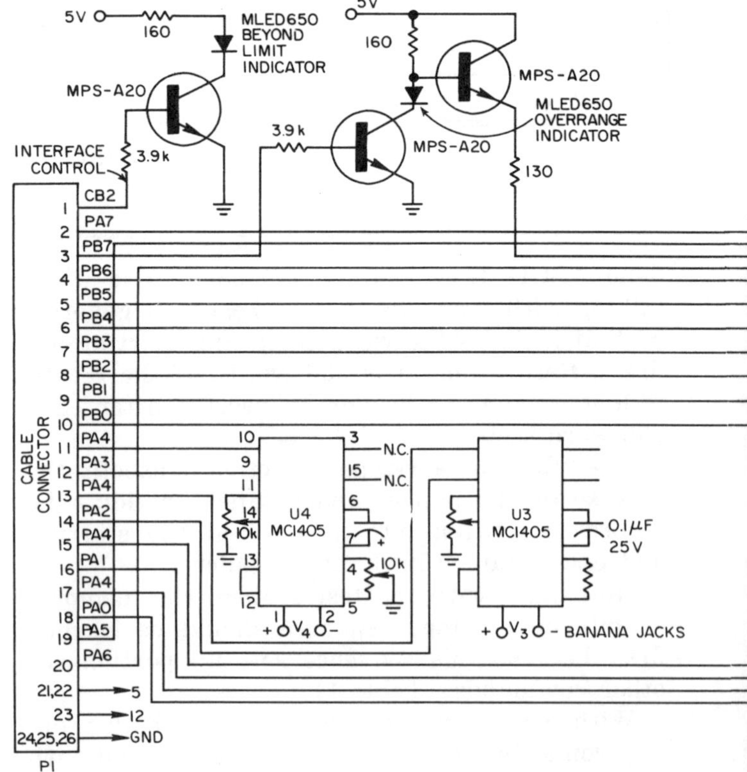

NOTE: PAO TO PA7 FORM I/O PORT I.
PBO TO PB7 FORM I/O PORT 2

a 5-V excitation. This improves the signal-to-noise ratio. The other parts on the display board are powered by a 5-V source.

After it initializes the system, the control program reads the control switch, performs the necessary a/d conversions, does any required calculations and displays the result. Since the object is to represent an analog voltage digitally, the main segment of the program is the routine that controls the MC1405s and performs the analog-to-digital conversion (Fig. 3). The assembly-language coding for the conversion is listed in Fig. 4.

The a/d routine is entered with (1) the addresses of the appropriate limits in the X register; and (2) a bit set in the B accumulator corresponding to the PIA register line that carries the comparator input signal.

The routine first stores the limit addresses and loads the X register with the address of that PIA register interfacing with the MC1405. After the routine loads the A accumulator with 99—one less than the value of 100 required as a base count for a 2-1/2-digit conversion—it checks to see if the comparator output is low. If it isn't low the routine waits until it is. Otherwise, a false conversion value would be obtained. When a low occurs, the routine sets the ramp control high and waits until the comparator output goes high.

When the high appears, the routine begins its base count: It decrements the A accumulator in a loop from 99 to 0 to produce the basic a/d-conversion time interval. The BIT B O,X and NOP instructions act as "filler" in the base-count loop so the time per decrement equals the time per increment in the conversion-count loop.

Table. Display-select switch settings

Position	Display
1	V_1
2	V_2
3	V_3
4	V_4
5	$V_1{}^2$
6	$V_1 + V_2$
7	$|V_1 - V_2|$
8	$V_1 \cdot V_2$

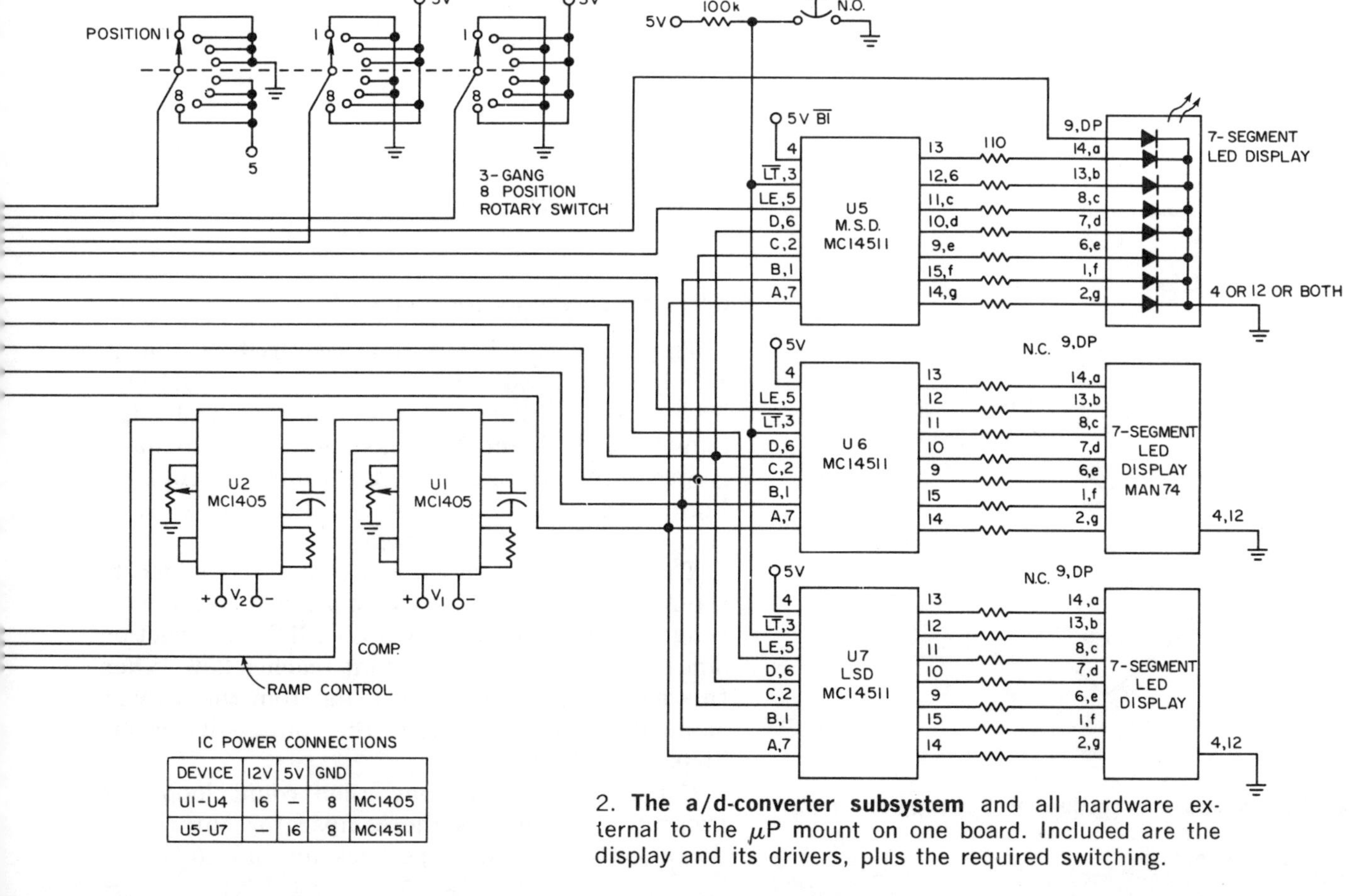

DEVICE	12V	5V	GND	
U1–U4	16	–	8	MC1405
U5–U7	–	16	8	MC14511

2. **The a/d-converter subsystem** and all hardware external to the μP mount on one board. Included are the display and its drivers, plus the required switching.

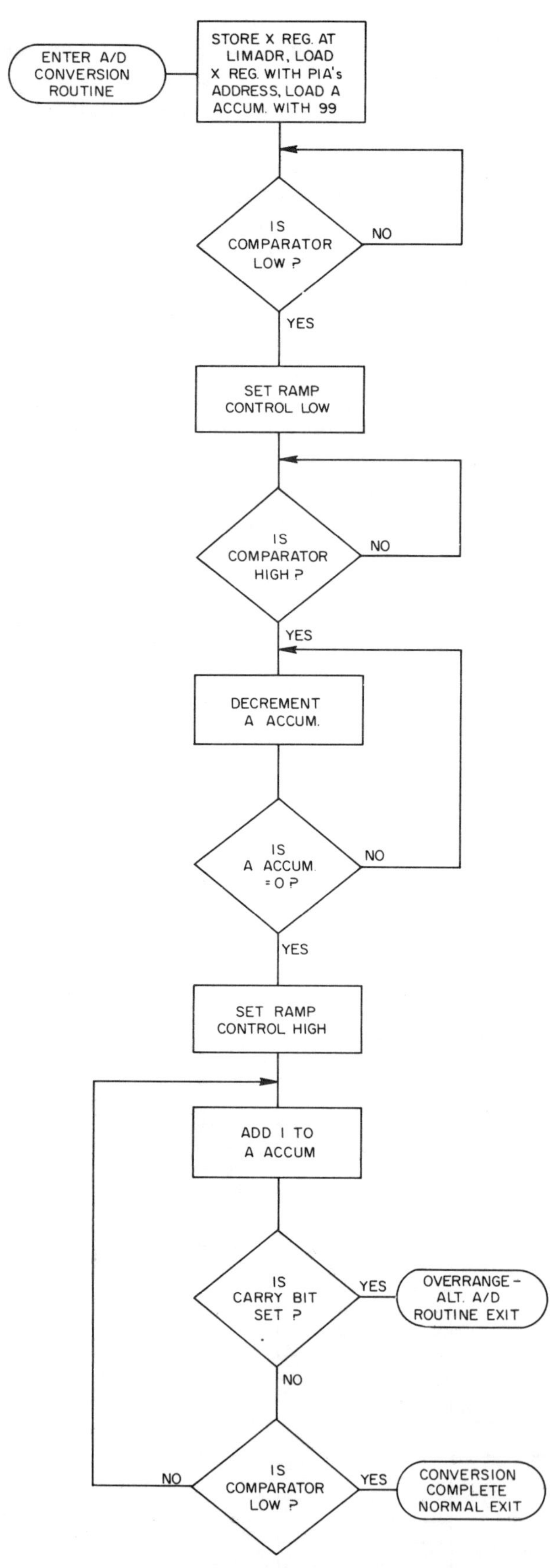

3. **Flow chart shows the section of the program** that controls the converter chips and performs the analog-to-digital conversion routine.

A2DRTN	STX	LIMADR	Save address of limits
	LDX	#PIAADR	Get PIA address
	LDA A	#99	
LOWC	BIT B	O,X	Is the comparator low?
	BNE	LOWC	No—Check it again
	CLR	O,X	Yes—Set ramp control low
HIGHC	BIT B	O,X	Is the comparator high?
	BEQ	HIGHC	No—Check it again
CNTDWN	BIT B	O,X	Yes—Countdown 100
	NOP		
	NOP		
	DEC A		A = 0?
	BNE	CNTDWN	No—Decrement A again
RCHIGH	NOP		Yes—Set ramp control high
	NOP		
	NOP		
	CLR A		
	COM	O,X	
CNTLP	ADD A	#1	Then do conversion count
	BCS	OVRRNG	Exit if count = 256
	BIT B	O,X	Is the comparator low?
	BNE	CNTLP	No—Continue counting
	SUB A	#10	Yes—Adjust count

4. **Assembly-language coding** for the analog-to-digital conversion. The routine takes about 4.6 ms.

Carry bit serves as overrange

The hundredth count time required for the 2-1 2-digit conversion is provided by the COM O,X instruction, which sets the ramp control high and the CLR A and NOP instructions immediately preceding. In this way, the ramp control goes high at the end of the base count and the conversion count immediately begins.

To perform the conversion count, 1 is added to the A accumulator. The carry bit acts as an overrange detector for the BCS OVRRNG instruction since the bit is set if the count reaches 256. When this happens, the program exits from the conversion-count loop and goes to the voltage-overrange display routine.

Continuing in the conversion count loop, the program next checks the comparator output. To do this, the routine loops back up and adds 1 to

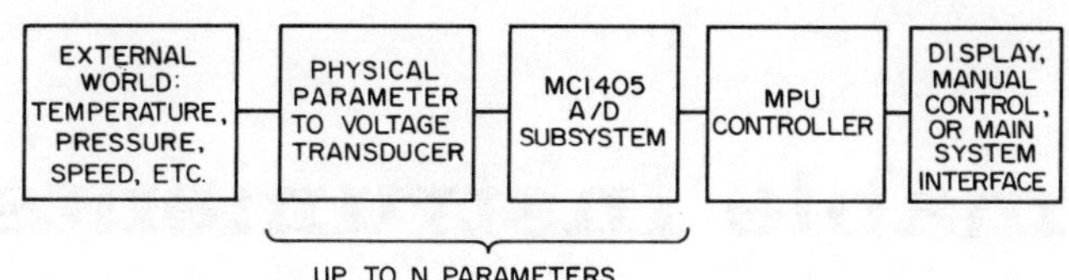

5. In a typical application, the μP controlled system monitors physical parameters, such as pressure, and provides a digital readout of a desired value.

the A accumulator if the comparator output is still high. When the output goes low, the program exits from the conversion-count loop and corrects the conversion value by subtraction of 10 as the MC1405 requires.

The value now in the A accumulator is the digital representation of the analog input voltage. Since the conversion-count loop requires 15 CPU clock cycles per count, at a CPU clock frequency of 1 MHz for a full scale conversion, the a/d routine requires 15 μs count $\times$ (100 + 199 + 10) counts $=$ 4.64 ms plus the comparator check time.

For use in a parameter sensing system, the outlined routine can be easily converted to a subroutine independent of the PIA address. Just put the first two instructions before the subroutine call and begin the subroutine with the LDA A #99 instruction. No other modifications are required since the routine is already independent of the PIA data register line on which the comparator signal appears.

If you do convert to a subroutine you can retain the overrange-detect feature by setting a flag before returning from the subroutine and after the conversion has gone to overrange. A check of the conversion value against preprogrammed limits can also be included in the subroutine. In this way, you can apply the subroutine to a μP controlled, parameter-sensing system (Fig. 5).

Controlling Programmable Instruments

OLIVER HOLT AND
FREDERICK SHIRLEY
*Sanders Associates, Inc.,
Nashua, New Hampshire*

Add a μP to programmable test equipment, and you can speed measurements while boosting accuracy. For example, you can automatically measure and plot the linearity of a voltage-controlled oscillator (VCO) in about five minutes—about six times faster than with manual methods. Because the procedure is automatic, you avoid misread meters or arithmetic tabulating errors.

To do the same tests manually, you adjust the reference voltage, read a power meter, read a frequency counter and record the readings for each of several reference voltages. All of this can be done without human intervention.

The μP—in this case, a Motorola 6800—steps the reference voltage through the VCO control range and prints and plots the results respectively on a teletypewriter and X/Y plotter (Fig. 1). Designing, constructing, programming and debugging such a μP test system should take about five weeks.

After the VCO is connected, operation starts with a teletypewriter command. The μP resets its own counters, prints a table heading on the teletypewriter and then begins a series of 40 VCO measurement cycles (Fig. 2).

Three steps to linearity

The first step in each measurement cycle updates the reference generator supplying the control voltage to the VCO under test. The μP does this by sending the proper binary number to the voltage generator (Fig. 3).

The second step measures the VCO response. The μP reads the frequency counter in IEEE Standard 488 format and converts the received ASCII data to binary for further processing (Fig. 4).[1] It also reads the power meter and converts both the power data and the voltage generator data to ASCII for later printout at the teletypewriter.

The third step is to draw a curve segment on the X/Y plotter. The μP calculates a differential frequency value by subtracting the predetermined

1. **With a μP connected to** programmable instruments through interface adapters, a VCO's linearity can be measured and plotted in only five minutes.

desired frequency from the measured frequency. The differential-frequency signal then goes to a Y-axis DAC, and simultaneously the reference voltage goes to an X-axis DAC (Fig. 5).

The analog outputs of the DACs drive the X/Y plotter to draw the line segment. Figure 6 shows a typical X/Y plotter curve.

Next, an entry is printed into the teletypewriter data table. The μP uses the Motorola MIKBUG interface routines to print sequentially the voltage, frequency and power data (Fig. 7).

Finally, the μP updates its counters and checks to see if the entire test has been completed. If testing is incomplete, the μP returns to the first step and begins another measurement cycle.

The μP communicates with the test equipment through a Peripheral Interface Adapter (PIA), a programmable IC that permits all handshake and data movements to be software controlled by the

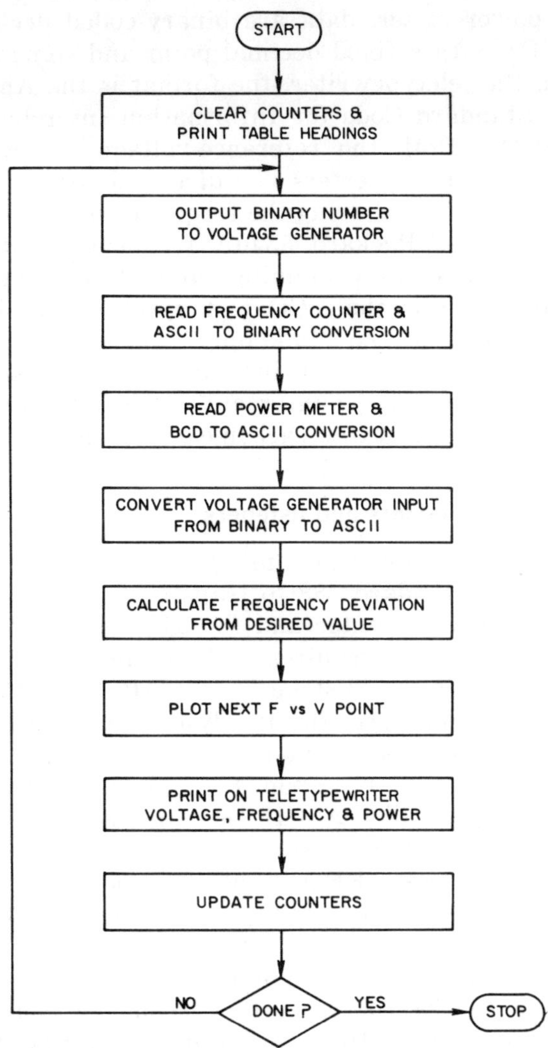

2. **Operational sequence of the automatic** test system starts with a teletypewriter command. The VCO is driven over its functional range of input voltages, and the corresponding output frequencies are read and recorded.

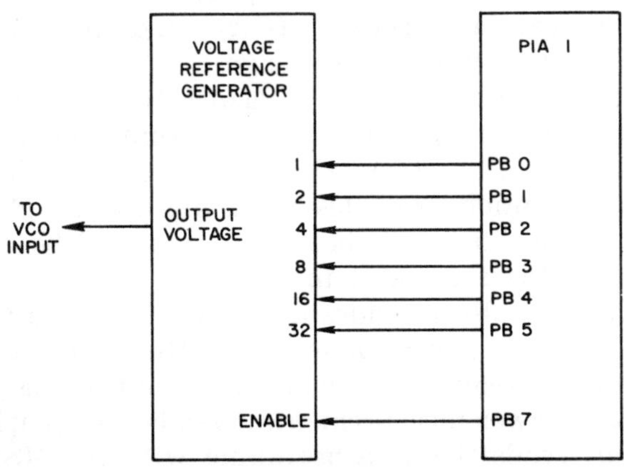

3. **The reference-voltage generator receives** its digital commands through a peripheral interface adapter (PIA). Six bits of binary code set the generator output level, which controls the VCO under test.

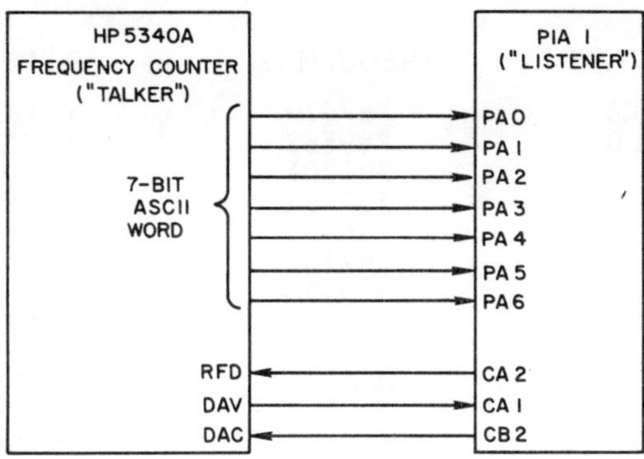

4. **A PIA also interfaces the system counter** to the μP. The counter works in a "talk" mode only and delivers the frequency automatically after each measurement.

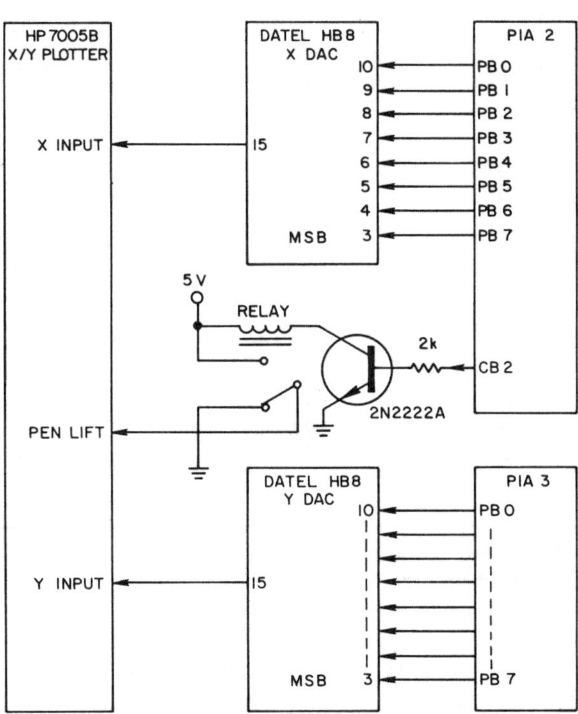

5. **To draw test results on an X/Y plotter,** both the frequency information and the reference voltage are put into analog form by d/a converters.

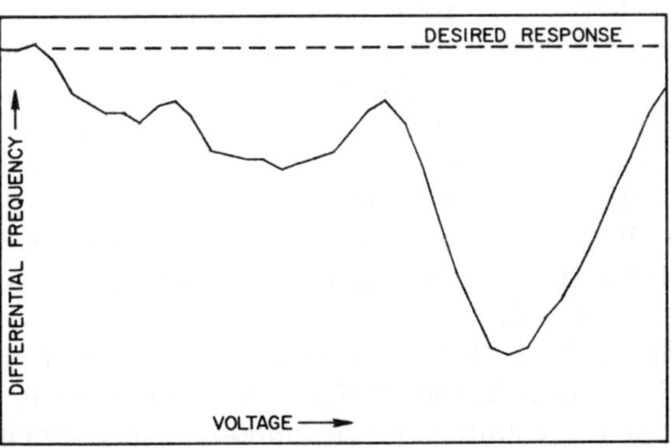

6. **Typical test results:** The VCO's linearity is plotted as differential frequency error vs. input level.

VOLTAGE	FREQUENCY	POWER
0.5	787579	0.023
1.0	789552	0.020
1.5	791501	0.019
2.0	793507	0.015
2.5	795593	0.019
3.0	797708	0.014
3.5	799838	0.011
4.0	801977	0.015
4.5	804139	0.019
5.0	806270	0.012
5.5	808382	0.013
6.0	810527	0.014
6.5	812752	0.016
7.0	814986	0.018
7.5	817234	0.022
8.0	819490	0.025
8.5	821769	0.028
9.0	824036	0.029
9.5	826293	0.027
10.0	828527	0.024
10.5	830715	0.022
11.0	832850	0.020
11.5	834965	0.020
12.0	837124	0.021
12.5	839407	0.022
13.0	841817	0.022
13.5	844355	0.022
14.0	846994	0.020
14.5	849729	0.019
15.0	852481	0.017
15.5	855212	0.017
16.0	857872	0.019
16.5	860473	0.021
17.0	863012	0.023
17.5	865462	0.024
18.0	867804	0.024
18.5	870057	0.022
19.0	872212	0.020
19.5	874300	0.017
20.0	876311	0.012

7. Tabulated results, as printed on a teletypewriter, include input voltage, output frequency and power.

μP.[2] The μP sets up communications links to all external devices by proper commands to the PIAs.

PIAs are the go-betweens

Each PIA consists of two 8-bit, bidirectional data ports and four handshake lines (Fig. 8). The 8-bit data ports are addressed independently and can transfer information in either direction; however, Motorola recommends a standard convention with the "A" port used for inputs and the "B" port for outputs. Two handshake lines are allotted to each port. One line is bidirectional under software control, while the other serves as an input only.

Since the PIA is programmable, it can be used with many different types of devices, such as the frequency counter, power meter, teletypewriter, reference-voltage generator and X/Y plotter.

Data format from the frequency counter con-

forms to IEEE Interface Standard 488; from the power meter, data are binary-coded decimal (BCD) with a fixed decimal point and sign; and from the teletypewriter, the format is the American Standard Code for Information Interchange (ASCII). Both the reference-voltage generator and the d/a converters use direct binary.

The job of measuring the frequency output falls to a Hewlett-Packard 5340A frequency counter with remote programming and digital-output capability. For the VCO test application, place the counter in the "talk only" mode using the external switch on the instrument's rear panel. In this mode, the counter automatically delivers data to the bus after each measurement.

Roles of the talkers and listeners

Figure 9 shows the timing sequence required by IEEE Standard 488 to transfer data between the frequency counter and the μP. As the "talker," the counter requires a different logic flow from that of the "listener"—the μP (Fig. 10).

The μP generates the Ready-For-Data (RFD) signal to tell the counter it is ready to accept data. The counter responds by placing data on the 7-bit, parallel ASCII bus and sending the Data Valid (DAV) signal.

The μP resets RFD, reads the data bus and sends the Data Accepted (DAC) signal back to the counter, which responds by removing DAV. The μP answers by removing DAC.

Data to the μP from the frequency counter take the form of 16 seven-bit ASCII words. The first three 7-bit words are preliminary data that signal the counter's status. Words 4 through 11 give the frequency count, with the most significant digit (MSD) first and all blank digits represented by zeroes.

Words 12 to 14 represent the letter "E," a plus sign, and a digit between 0 and 6 to indicate the power-of-ten multiplier. The last two words—carriage return (CR) and line feed (LF)—specify end of message.

To measure the power, a Pacific Measurements Model 1009 samples the VCO's output and sends BCD data to two PIAs (Fig 11). The 1009's data port, an option, provides 3-1/2 digits—the MSD is a single line, and the tenths, hundredths and thousandths are coded in BCD.

The port also provides a polarity signal so you can measure power in units of dBm. No handshaking is required with the 1009. When the μP needs a power measurement, it reads the polarity signal; reads the data beginning with the MSD; converts the data to ASCII; and transfers the data for printing.

How the X/Y plotter interfaces to the μP PIAs is shown in Fig. 5. Two 8-bit d/a converters provide the analog form needed by the plotter. The

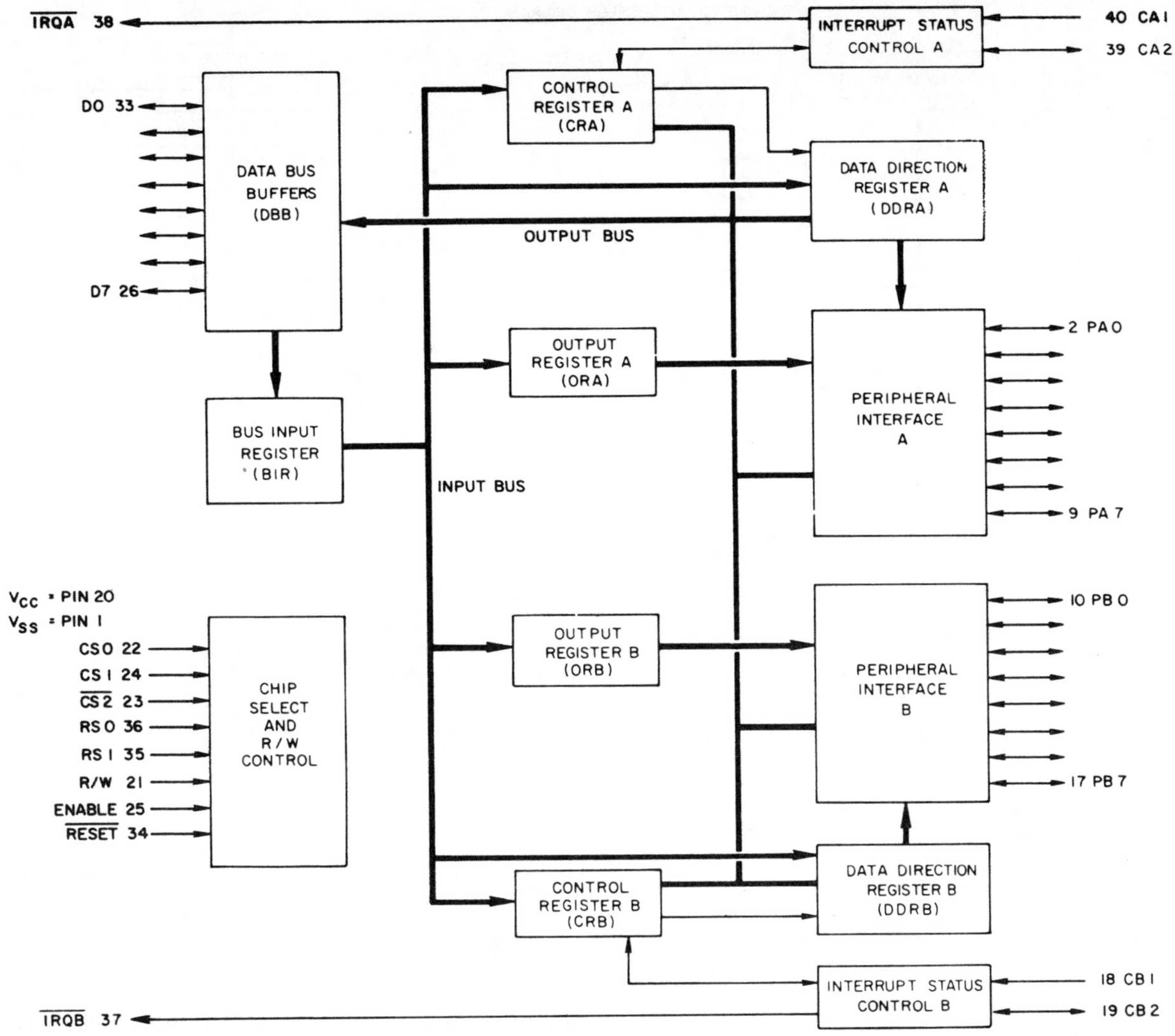

IRQA 38
INTERRUPT STATUS CONTROL A
40 CA1
39 CA2
DO 33
D7 26
DATA BUS BUFFERS (DBB)
CONTROL REGISTER A (CRA)
DATA DIRECTION REGISTER A (DDRA)
OUTPUT BUS
OUTPUT REGISTER A (ORA)
PERIPHERAL INTERFACE A
2 PA0
9 PA 7
BUS INPUT REGISTER (BIR)
INPUT BUS
Vcc = PIN 20
Vss = PIN 1
CS0 22
CS1 24
CS2 23
RS0 36
RS1 35
R/W 21
ENABLE 25
RESET 34
CHIP SELECT AND R/W CONTROL
OUTPUT REGISTER B (ORB)
PERIPHERAL INTERFACE B
10 PB 0
17 PB 7
DATA DIRECTION REGISTER B (DDRB)
CONTROL REGISTER B (CRB)
INTERRUPT STATUS CONTROL B
18 CB1
19 CB2
IRQB 37

8. **The PIAs used in the VCO tester** provide two 8-bit data ports, over which information flows in either direction. Four handshake lines are also available. Usually port "A" is used for μP inputs, "B" to outputs.

DATA (PARALLEL WORD)
DAV (DATA VALID)
RFD (READY FOR DATA)
DAC (DATA ACCEPTED)
t-1
t0
t1
t2
t3

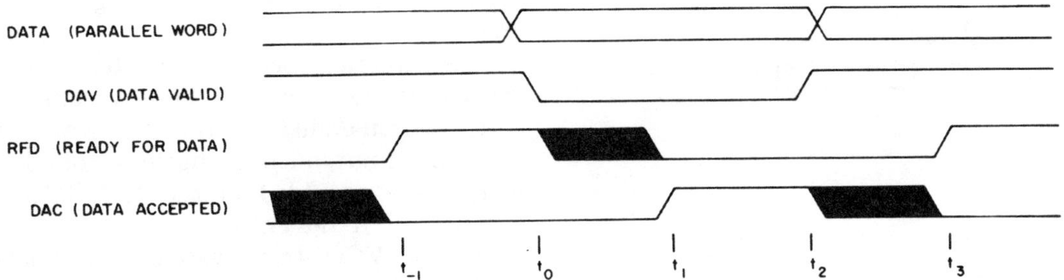

9. **Transfer of data between the μP** and the counter conforms to IEEE 488, the recently adopted interface standard for programmable instrumentation. Shown here is the required timing sequence for the interface bus.

MSB on each converter (pin 3) connects to PB7 on each PIA. The only handshake signal required is the pen-position command, which lifts the pen between curves. This signal is applied to the plotter through a simple transistor drive and a relay.

Because of the high resolution required for the VCO test, the μP commands the X/Y plotter to draw a curve of differential-frequency error vs. voltage. To do so, the desired response is typed into the μP, and the response is then normalized to a straight line across the center of the plotter.

The μP reads all frequency measurements and compares the results with the desired response to get the differential-error curve.

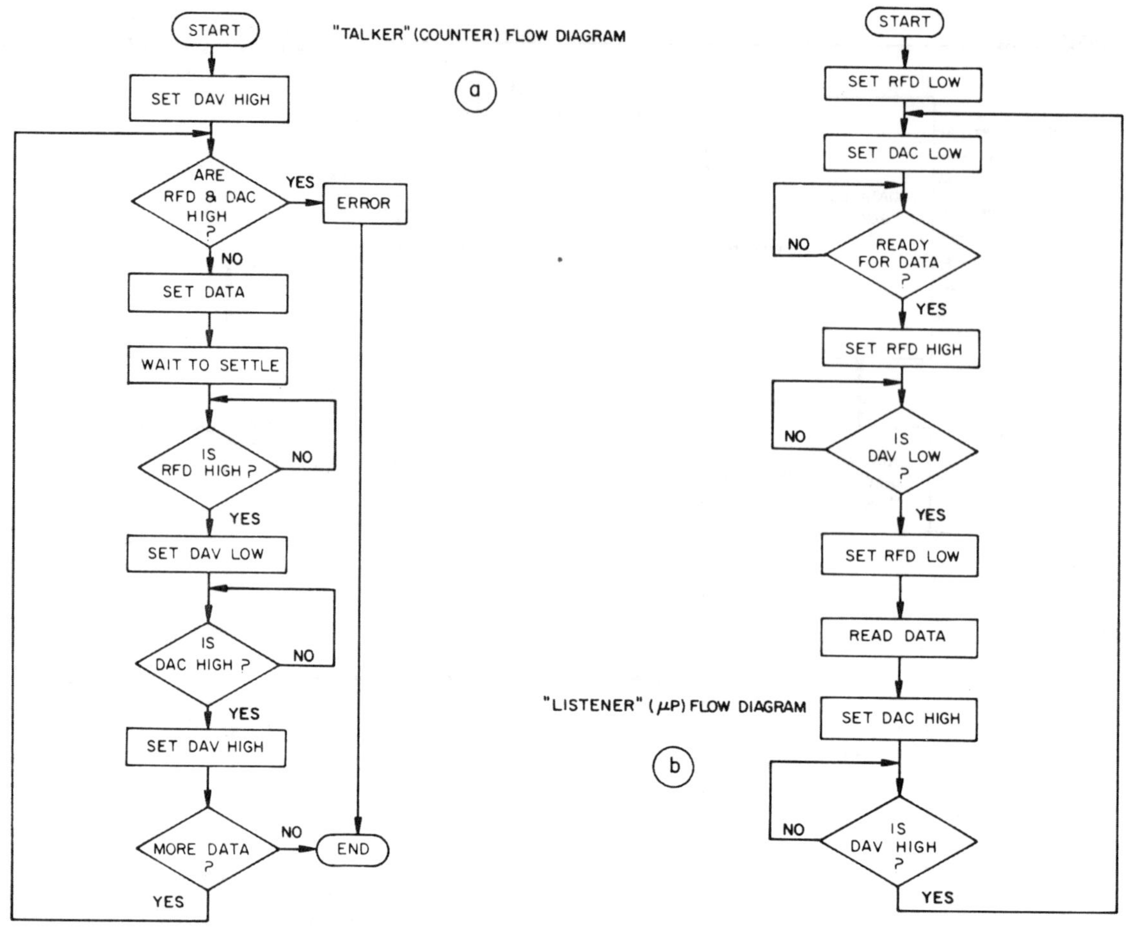

10. **How the counter and** μP **transfer data:** the counter "talks" (a), while the μP "listens" (b).

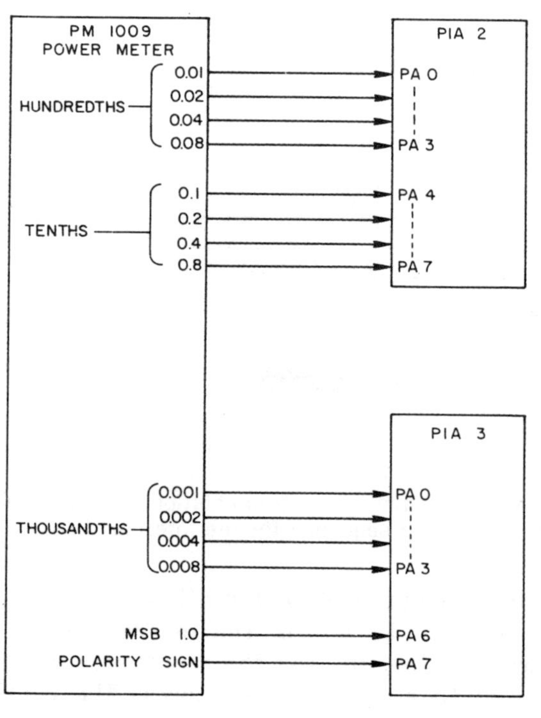

11. **Power measurements are sent out** on the system data bus with 3-1/2-digit resolution. No handshaking is necessary with the power meter.

To drive the VCO, the digitally controlled generator delivers 0.5 to 20 V in 0.5-V steps with a 6-bit straight binary input. Binary 0 produces the minimum level, binary 39 the maximum. The only handshake requirement is an enable signal, which switches the output from a high-impedance off state to the specified voltage at low impedance.

The interface between the teletypewriter and the μP is the standard 20-mA current-loop circuit recommended in the Motorola application manual. Input/output routines for the teletypewriter are provided in the MIKBUG firmware, a 1 k × 8 ROM chip.

In the VCO test system, the teletypewriter serves as both an input device and a printer. You, the system operator, type in the voltage range for the VCO under test, the desired frequency-vs.-voltage curve and the VCO identification number. Then you get things moving with the teletypewriter which, shortly, becomes the system printer.

References

1. *IEEE Standard Digital Interface for Programmable Instrumentation*, The Institute of Electrical and Electronic Engineers, Inc., New York, NY, 1975, IEEE Standard 488-1975.

2. *M6800 Microprocessor Applications Manual*, Motorola Inc., Phoenix, AZ, 1975.

SECTION VI
Designing with the F8

The F8 system, introduced by Fairchild, has become popular among those engineers designing low-cost systems that require relatively low performance—video games, for example. The system requires just two NMOS chips, the 3850 CPU and the 3851 program-storage unit, to form a complete 8-bit microcomputer that is capable of handling most routine control tasks.

Mostek is a licensed second source for the F8. Recently both Fairchild and Mostek announced single-chip versions. These should expand the range of possible applications and enhance the appeal of the system.

The first article gives a comprehensive description of the F8 chips and support circuits. Guidelines are given for expansion of the basic system; a cash-register application is illustrated. Other articles show how to use F8 microprocessors in multiprocessor control systems and for multi-channel synchro conversion.

Build Compact Systems with the F8

LARRY SULLIVAN
Application Engineer, Mostek,
Carrollton, Texas

Unlike most other microprocessors, the F8 uses two chips rather than one. But because of features not found in other μPs, the F8 can actually lead to more compact systems than those based on single-chip μPs.

By a special grouping of functional elements, the F8 eliminates the address bus, equalizes chip size, and reduces pin and parts count (Fig. 1). This partitioning also simplifies and speeds instruction execution.

The result: the two-chip system has sufficient RAM, ROM, interrupt and I/O capability to handle most control applications.

System structure allows easy expansion

A minimum F8 system consists of the 3850 central processing unit (CPU) and the 3851 program-storage unit (PSU), both of which come in 40-pin packages. Expanded RAM, ROM, PROM and I/O can be obtained with additional components, as indicated in a cash-register application (Fig. 2).

The F8 relies on two busses. A time-multiplexed 8-bit bus handles all data-addressing functions, and a 7-bit control bus coordinates and synchronizes the activity of the remaining F8-system components.

A significant number of pins for I/O and interrupt operations is available on the primary devices. The CPU and PSU have a total of 38 pins dedicated to these functions, accounting for more than 47% of the pins. Thus, as system requirements increase in complexity, the F8 allows a corresponding increase in the number of I/O lines and interrupt levels.

Each PSU provides 1024 bytes of ROM and 16 lines of TTL and CMOS-compatible, output-latched I/O that operates in a bidirectional manner. The PSU also features a programmable timer.

Additional savings in the number of packages accrue from the inclusion of a system-clock generator and power-on-reset function on the CPU. Also, for a number of applications, the CPU's 64-byte scratchpad memory is large enough to avoid the use of external RAM.

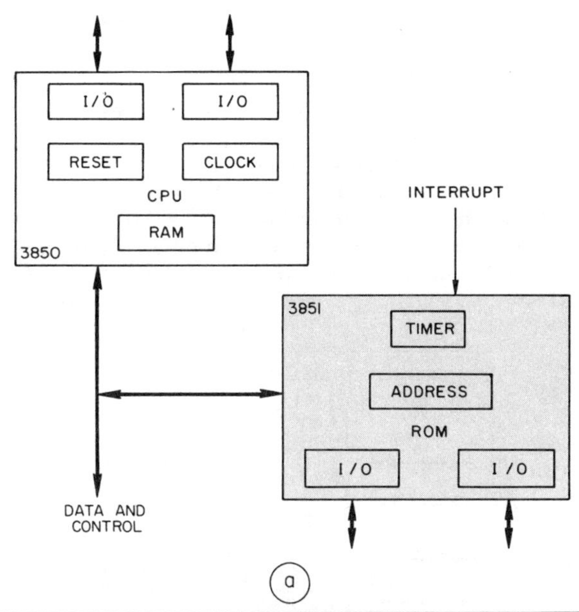

1. **Two LSI chips comprise the minimum F8 system** (a). One chip is the 3850 CPU, and the other is the 3851 program-storage unit. The latter performs all addressing functions, eliminating the need for an address bus and permitting the extra pins on both circuits to be used for I/O. The capabilities of the two-chip system can satisfy the bulk of control applications (b).

In most other microcomputers, the CPU contains the following: program counter, memory pointer, and the logic to save essential registers and to handle interrupts. However, with the F8 set, these are located in the PSU since they nor-

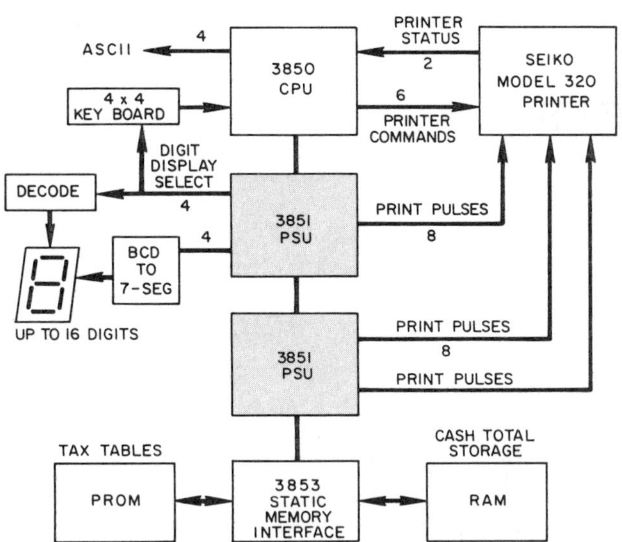

2. **A cash-register application uses the F8.** Interval timers internal to the PSU permit an orderly scanning of the display, keyboard and printer, without using software timing loops. Cash totals stored in RAM may be polled by a remote data-processing system via the ASCII interface.

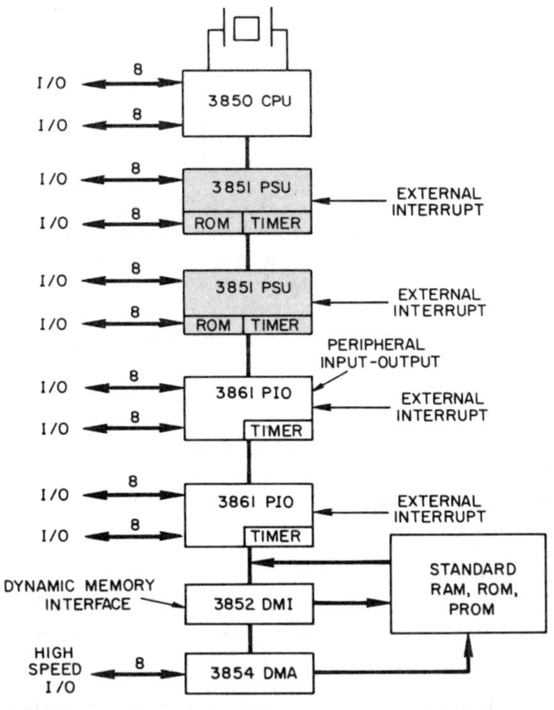

3. **The F8 system can be readily expanded** beyond the two-chip minimum by adding special support circuits. These may be connected directly together and to peripheral devices, often without interface hardware.

mally operate on the program store and data memory as well as each other. This "all-memory" referencing and addressing frees available pins for I/O.

A system with multiple PSUs has, of course, multiple program counters. However, only one PSU will respond with an 8-bit instruction at the beginning of any cycle. Page selection within the PSU maintains an orderly flow of instructions.

Applications calling for extensive memory can make use of the 3852 dynamic and 3853 static memory-interface chips (Fig. 3). These devices create a 16-bit address bus that permits the memory-interface chips to range through 64-k words of memory. The devices also incorporate read/write control. As a result, any combination of standard ROM, PROM or RAM may be used for program or data storage when internal memory isn't large enough.

Similarly, for systems requiring extensive I/O, the interface chips allow a mix of PSU and PIO (peripheral input-output) circuits to satisfy system-communications requirements.

For peripheral-to-memory direct-memory access (DMA), the 3854 offers DMA control when used in conjunction with the 3852 memory-interface chip. With the F8, DMA is "transparent" to the CPU, so DMA transfers don't degrade system performance. Once initialized by the CPU. the DMA and memory-interface chips maintain both memory-refresh requirements and transfer control, independent of the processor.

Internal RAM speeds operation

The 3850 CPU chip contains the usual arithmetic logic unit, 16-bit accumulator, and status registers found on most 8-bit central processing units (Fig. 4). The CPU's 64 × 8-bit scratchpad memory operates 2.5 times faster than external memory would on a bus. The lower 12 of the 64 scratchpad registers are directly addressable, though all 64 registers are indirectly addressable by the 6-bit ISAR (indirect scratchpad address register).

Several scratchpad registers are controlled by specific instructions that link the program counter, stack register, status register, and data counter to the scratchpad. The data paths allowed between elements appear in Fig. 4b.

The CPU's 16 bidirectional I/O lines can be connected directly to standard-TTL devices. All outputs are internally latched. CPU I/O transfers require 4 μs, or half the time needed by other I/O ports in the system. The chip-port addresses are fixed in firmware, and the ports are referenced with In and Out program instructions.

The CPU's clock may be driven by an external source, or controlled by a crystal or RC network. The power-on-reset function gets the system up and running in a "known-state" by initializing the program counter and disabling interrupts. The latter occurs by a resetting of the ICB (interrupt-control bit) in the status register.

The 8-bit bidirectional data bus transmits data and control-port information from the CPU. Special ROM-control lines define 1 of 32 possible states that the system can have during any instruction-cycle sequence. A decoding of these bits by microcontrollers on other members of the F8 family maintain system synchronization.

PSU requires mask programming

The MK 3851 PSU is a mask-programmable memory element (Fig. 5). All of its memory-reference pointers—such as program counter and data counter—are 16-bit registers. Inclusion of the pointers for data and program store eliminates the need for a system address bus. Also, their 16-bit length implies that up to 64 PSU or PIO circuits may be used together.

The F8 I/O lines feature electrical compatibility with TTL and CMOS logic families. Output drivers can source 100 μA and sink 2.0 mA. The PSU output drivers may also be configured with open drains or as a 1.0-mA source. Outputs are latched without the need for external hardware. The CPU, PSU, and PIO chips each provide 16 lines of I/O arranged as two 8-bit ports.

The CPU ports should be used when I/O speed is most important. The ports are serviced with single-byte instructions requiring only two machine cycles—4 μs. Servicing of all other ports requires 8 μs.

The F8 allows multilevel vectored interrupts. An interrupt may be generated by the external peripherals, by software, or by internal interval timers. A PSU or static-memory-interface chip provides one level of external interrupt and one interval timer. The level of priority associated with an interrupt is determined by the interconnection of priority-in and priority-out signal lines on the F8 chips. Thus, priorities are set in a "daisy-chain" fashion. Individual interrupt levels also may be selectively enabled or disabled under program control.

Responding to interrupts

When an interrupt occurs, the affected chip notifies the CPU via an interrupt request. If the interrupt system is armed, and a higher level interrupt is not pending, the affected chip's interrupt circuitry is enabled. When the CPU acknowledges the interrupt, the program counter vectors to the address specified by the chip receiving the interrupt. Though the interrupt vectors of the PSUs are mask programmed, that of the memory-interface chip is under program control and may be altered with I/O instructions.

Interrupt inputs are compatible with most logic families and they operate as edge-triggered sig-

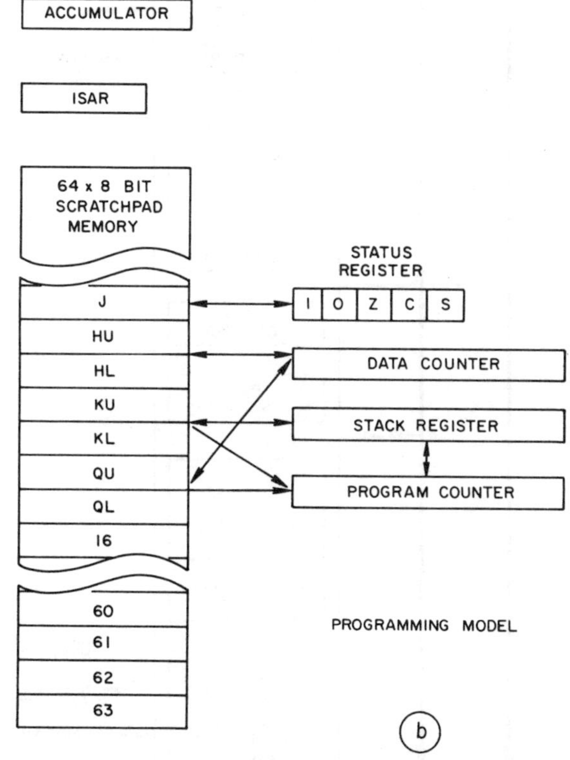

4. **The CPU chip contains a 64 × 8-bit RAM,** two 8-bit I/O ports and internal clock (a). It also has a power-on reset function and 16 TTL-compatible I/O lines. All 64 registers may be accessed indirectly through ISAR (indirect scratchpad address register), and 12 may be addressed directly (b).

nals. In most cases, these features eliminate the need for additional circuitry.

In other microcomputers, timing intervals are often generated by software timing loops. Only repetitive tasks that can be fitted into the timing loops may be executed.

The F8's programmable timers, however, free the microprocessor from such tasks and allow the processor to solve other problems. In effect, the F8 can perform several tasks simultaneously. In a system with several timers it is possible to have each timer pace a separate peripheral while the main program executes a more complex problem.

If the F8 is implemented with a 2-MHz clock, the timers are programmable in 15.5-μs increments up to about 4 ms. When the programmed interval has elapsed, the timer generates a vectored interrupt. The timer counter is viewed by the program as another I/O port; I/O instructions program the timer.

Design aids speed development

The F8 Survival Kit offers a quick and easy way to get the microprocessor system up and running. An assembled kit constitutes an evaluation/ development microcomputer with the features indicated in Fig. 6.

To operate the micro, simply attach a 110 or 300-baud ASCII terminal (such as a teletypewriter or CRT monitor system) and 5 and 12-V power supplies. By using DDT-1—designers development tool, the kit's software package—you can load, debug, and modify your own software in the 1-k byte of RAM provided (Fig. 6b). Also included in the kit is a Fortran IV cross-assembler.

An emulator for the PSU can be used to develop and design F8-based systems that employ one or more 3851 circuits. The Emulator is electrically equivalent to the PSU but is field programmable. Thus a user can perform a hardware verification of all PSU programming prior to ordering custom PSU chips.

Also, the Emulator even "plugs in" like a PSU chip (via a male, 40-pin connector on the end of an umbilical cord). Thus prototype systems can be converted to final production status by simply unplugging the Emulator and plugging in the corresponding custom PSU.

The ROM section of the Emulator uses either four 256 × 8-bit ultraviolet-erasable PROMs or a single 1-k × 8-bit UV-erasable PROM to pro-

5. **The 3851 program-storage unit,** a mask-programmable IC, has memory-reference functions.

24-bits of I/O arranged in three 8-bit ports
Full duplex TTY interface (20-mA loop)
Crystal control clock
Automatic power on reset
Hardware reset
1024 bytes of Random Access Memory
Nonvolatile operating system in PSU firmware called Designers Development Tool 1 (DDT-1)

(a)

Load command—loads memory from paper tape
Dump command—formats data and output to paper tape punch
Type command—examines blocks of memory from one location to another
Copy command—moves blocks of memory from one location to another.
Memory display and Modify Command—examines and modifies memory one byte at a time
Port commands—displays and modifies the 24 I/O lines
Hexadecimal and arithmetic commands
Execute command—directs program execution to a specific location
Breakpoint command—debugs users software

(b)

6. **An assembled Survival Kit** forms a compact F8 microcomputer with the features indicated (a). Application software can be written and executed by using commands stored in the PSU (b). The kit comes with a Fortran IV cross-assembler.

Set breakpoint address
Copy memory arrays
Dump memory onto paper tape
Execute at specified address
Load program (data) into memory
Display (and optionally modify) specified memory addresses
Display (and optionally modify) specified I/O ports
Initiate single-step mode at specified address
Type specified memory area

7. A software-development board's supervising system allows debugging commands like these.

vide nonvolatile storage of a user's program. The PROMs should be programmed prior to installation on the Emulator. Six ROM-address select switches can then be used to establish the location of the PROM in the system memory map. I/O ports on the Emulator employ an actual PSU.

A complete development system can be obtained by combining an RS-232 terminal with an F8 software-development board (SDB) and an application-interface module (AIM). The SDB contains an F8 system that can be used in two ways.

As a stand-alone computer system, the SDB offers debugging and assembly software. An engineer designing a microprocessor-based system can begin by developing and debugging his software on the SDB.

Secondly, after his hardware is ready, the SDB (in conjunction with an AIM) can be employed to control the user's target system (the system under development), thus imparting to it the debugging capability of the SDB. It should be noted that the control path is established by replacing the target-system's PSUs with AIMs. In this case, AIMs emulate PSUs but have the added capability of communicating with the SDB supervising system via DDT-2, designers development tool (Fig. 7).

From the control console—teletypewriter or equivalent—the programmer can now perform several tasks associated with system debugging.

Usually the target system is breadboarded in the actual system configuration with empty sockets substituted for each 3851 PSU chip to be used. AIMs are connected to the system through interface cables. The AIMs are then inserted into a standard F8 development system that contains a single SDB for monitoring, controlling and loading each of the ROM boards. Final test and checkout complete the design, and custom masks can be ordered for each PSU.

Multiprocessing with Microprocessors

DAVID CHUNG
General Manager, Research and Development,
Microsystems Div., Fairchild Camera and
Instrument, Mountain View, California

Because of the complexity of microprocessors, their early applications have been the most obvious ones. Mostly they have replaced minicomputers or hardwired logic. But a significant bonus can be realized when several microprocessors are linked together to form an intelligent network.

Intelligent networks perform many tasks

The concept of multiprocessor networks is well suited for MOS microprocessors (μPs). First, microprocessors are able to perform many dedicated functions at low cost without the use of supporting electronics or special I/O chips. They can be used as a universal standard component for literally any definable task, particularly data gathering.

Second, the MOS microprocessor, unlike its hardwired predecessor, is capable of generalized data manipulation, information storage and retrieval, and message communications. These attributes allow two or more microprocessors to be teamed to perform tasks requiring cooperation between dedicated and message-handling functions.

Suppose, for example, that microprocessor A is used as a controller for an in-plant telephone switchboard, and microprocessor B is used to control the temperature of the plant. If these two machines are linked we will have the added capability of both transmitting temperature data and controlling the temperature via a telephone line. The added benefits of such a coupled-microprocessor system are derived from the communications link.

A microprocessor network with common memory may perform the same functions as a single large-scale computer. The network provides an efficient information exchange between its constituent microprocessors. For example:

Suppose there are four microprocessors in a

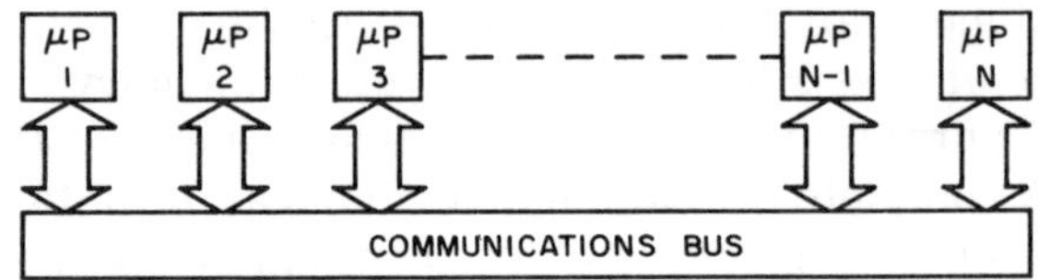

1. Microprocessors linked by a 2-wire bus have the lowest cost communications.

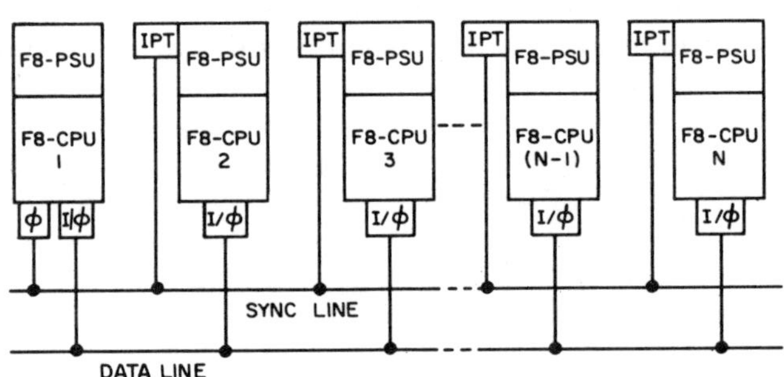

2. With several linked F8 μPs, No. 1 controls data transmission by driving the asynchronous interrupt inputs of the other μPs.

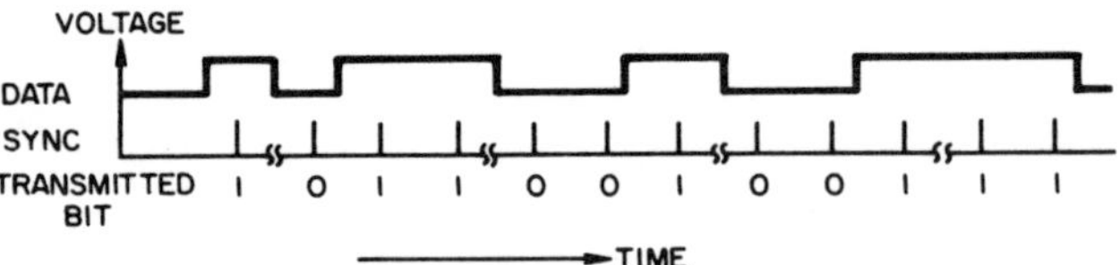

3. A timing diagram illustrates the serial and asynchronous method of transferring data.

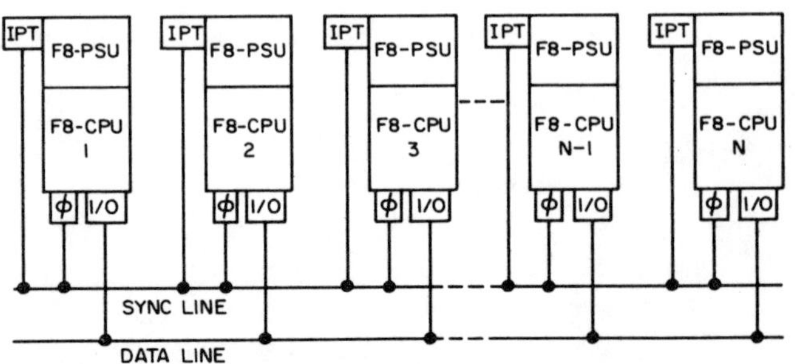

4. Data bus controllers can be dynamically reassigned so that if one device fails another may take over, still allowing the system to function.

certain manufacturing company; A handles the order entry; B controls the manufacturing and inventory; C processes the receivables and payables; and D keeps track of shipping and returned goods. Since each μP only has access to a portion of the company's total data base, none is capable of compiling a comprehensive month-end profit and loss statement.

But if these μPs were arranged to share the same memory, any one of the four would be capable of preparing the statement because each would have immediate access to all relevant data, without human intervention. The network also provides a modular arrangement that eases hardware implementation and software partitioning, and simplifies debugging.

Supervision by a fixed bus controller

Fig. 1 shows a group of μPs linked together via a serial-communications bus, the most inexpensive way possible. Processor-to-processor communications may use any suitable protocol.

Fig. 2 shows an example of such a network, using F8 μPs. In this case, μP No. 1 is considered the communications-bus controller. The entire communications bus is made up of only two wires (Fig. 3), one being a bidirectional data line, the other a synchronizing line to strobe the data.

The sync line is also controlled by μP No. 1, which drives the Interrupt inputs of all the other μPs in the network and may be completely asynchronous to CPU operation. All the other μPs have access to any transmitted message.

Messages should be formatted to take advantage of the best practices of communications discipline. They should have a header field with the addresses of the transmitter and receiver, a control field, a data field, and a cycle-redundancy check field. In fact, even the synchronous-data-link control (SDLC) protocol can be employed if desired. Since each microprocessor on the network is capable of receiving the check fields and understanding the message format, reliable message transmission and reception is assured.

Periodically, μP No. 1 will permit one of the other microprocessors to send out a message on the bus. In that case, sync timing is still provided by the bus controller, and the message may address any member of the network.

It would be useful to specify a maximum time interval between two consecutive sync pulses. A period of silence from the bus controller would then mark the beginning of a new message, and spurious pulses at power-on would be disregarded. F8 μPs have no difficulty in determining the time interval between interrupts because they are equipped with on-board timers. There are many possible improvements that can be made to this

The trade-offs compared

When MOS microprocessors first became available some three years ago, they were used as if they were inexpensive minicomputers. Then various peripheral controllers were built to supplement the single μP. That tended to reduce the cost advantage of using the μP in the first place.

In a single microprocessor system, the CPU has to assume a variety of different tasks, which gives rise to two undesirable consequences: it has neither hardware nor software modularity, and it tends to force the μP architecture to mimic minicomputer architecture. These trends run counter to the most important advantages offered by LSI technology, namely, low cost and large volume.

The microprocessor possesses two important features that gainfully exploit LSI technology. It takes a minimum number of chips to configure a dedicated function. Also, it permits the easy formation of microprocessor networks.

There are many systems now using a single processor/memory approach that are ripe for a multiprocessor application. Such systems include point-of-sale terminals, electronic automobile control and airborne-warfare control.

If the multiprocessor approach is used, unique controllers, sensors and long wire runs to the CPU for each input could be replaced by a more modular arrangement. The heavy load on a single CPU could be replaced by light loads on multiple CPUs. Software would be simplified in some cases and shorter runs at the lower data-transfer rates used purely for the exchange of processed-data could be substituted.

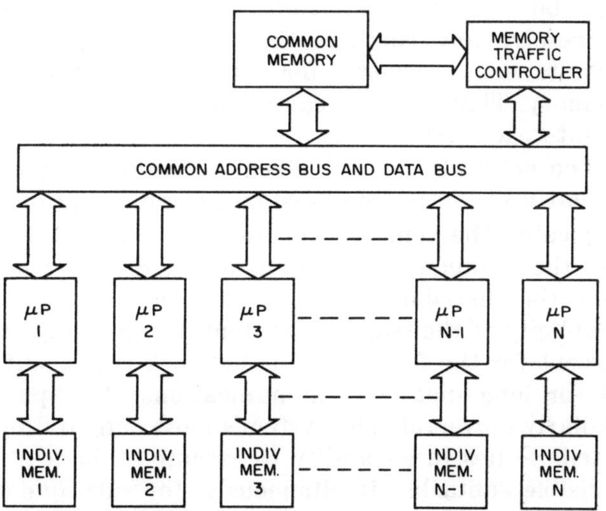

5. Microprocessors may have access to a common memory for general data, and an individual memory for program execution.

basic system. The data rate can clearly be increased by increasing the number of data lines, for example.

Supervision by distributed bus controllers

A more reliable system is shown in Fig. 4. A symmetrically wired system permits the role of the bus controller to be dynamically reassigned. Thus, the failure of one bus controller will not deprive the rest of the network of its ability to communicate, and reliability is improved.

Such a network is especially useful where the individual μPs are separated from each other by large distances. The two-wire network is ideally suited for controlling a large aircraft. Because of its physical simplicity, a duplicate system forms a practical backup.

A distributed system of the type described above has the following features:
- Simplicity of communication,
- Localized intelligence,
- Modularity,
- High reliability, but is not efficiently organized for multitask operations that must have access to a common memory.

Multiprocessors with individual and shared memories

A μP network may use a common memory (Fig. 5). Since each μP may also have its own separate memory in addition to the common storage, each one executes its own program without waiting for others. The data that have common interest can be written into the group memory and read out from it. Obviously the common memory is a highly accessible medium for information exchange.

Structurally, all μPs in the network are wired to the group memory via the common address and data bus. The memory traffic controller is needed to resolve any conflicts that might arise from simultaneous requests for use of the common memory. That function can be incorporated readily into each μP.

The network just described is simple and particularly suited for long-distance communications. Typically, the common address bus has 16 lines, and the common data bus has eight, so it is clear that the distributed system does not have the simplicity of the two-wire system shown in Fig. 2. Except for the fact that this network is not suited for long distance communications, it is particularly powerful. The system's most outstanding attribute lies in its ability to execute all logically divisible subtasks simultaneously, for subsequent correlation. The ability is especially compatible with low-cost MOS μPs.

Fig. 6 shows how several F8 μPs gain access to a common memory through the use of a

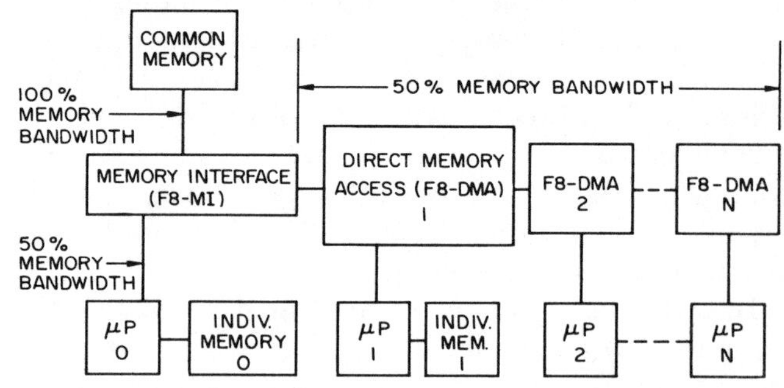

6. **A high-speed system may be constructed** if individual microprocessors can access common memory through DMA (Direct Memory Access).

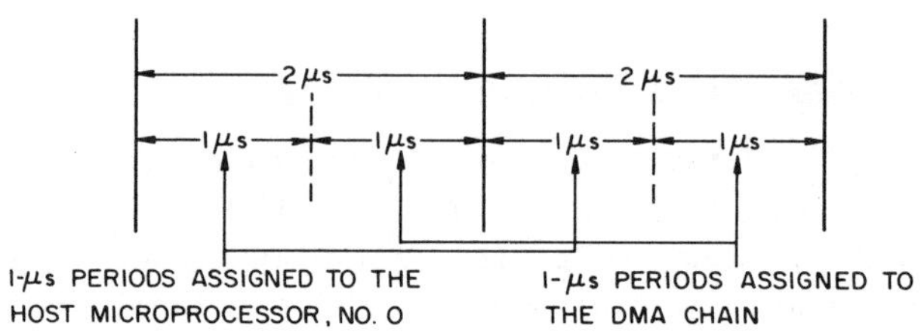

7. **Memory time slices are allocated alternately** to the host microprocessor and to the remaining processors.

memory-interface chip, the F8-MI, and a direct-memory-access chip, the F8-DMA. Since modern RAM chips are much faster than μPs, memory also may be accessed by other devices.

Typically, the cycle time of the available RAM chips ranges from 100 to 500 ns, and the shortest execution cycle of the available MOS microprocessors ranges from 1 to 2 μs. The memory-interface chip takes advantage of the memory's inherent bandwidth. (If a memory has a cycle time of 1 μs, then one million bytes per second may be transferred.)

The F8-MI also splits a 2 μs period in two, half for the host μP, No. 0, and half for the DMA chain. The host μP may access the common memory once every 2 μs, consuming half the bandwidth or 500-k byte/s.

Since the shortest execution time for most microprocessors, including the F8, is 2 μs, the memory allotment is more than sufficient for the host microprocessor's maximum needs. The remaining 50% of the bandwidth is distributed on the direct-memory-access chain, having also an assigned bandwidth of 500-k byte/s.

Because the μPs in the network have individual memories, their operations are continuous and independent of the bandwidth assigned to the shared memory.

Each DMA has an assigned task. If μP No. 1 is used as a floppy-disc controller (Fig. 8), DMA No. 1 must be able to accommodate a maximum data-transfer rate of 250-k bit/s or 31.25-k bytes/s. Microprocessor No. 2 might then control a serial-duplex-data link with a transfer rate of 14-k bytes/s. Then, DMA Nos. 3 through N have a worst-case aggregate bandwidth of $500 - 31.25 - 14$ equals 454.75-k byte/s, a rate that can accommodate many high-speed devices.

The network used in the example, using low-cost F8 μPs, is capable of performing several functions simultaneously. Microprocessor No. 1 specifies locations in the common memory from which data are transferred to or from the floppy disc. These locations in common memory cannot be specified as part of the μP's own instruction memory space.

In other words, the DMA method of accessing the common memory involves an intermediate step of data buffering. That step is quite desirable if a peripheral device such as a floppy disc or a CRT screen is involved, but is extraneous if information fetched from common memory is an instruction executed by the μP. In that case, a network such as the one shown in Fig. 9 is the most suitable.

Multiprocessors with just common memory

In the network of Fig. 9, all central-processing units share the same common memory. The block designated as the memory interface provides an orderly means for several contending CPUs to use the common memory. The procedure is called a "one-port" memory system, because only one CPU can use the common memory at one time.

The maximum speed is determined by the access time of the common memory. Theoretically, the optimum CPU execution rate should be N times the memory access period, where N is the number of μP chips in the network. The optimum rate provides the perfect match between the memory and the CPU speeds—but if the CPU speed is comparable to the memory speed, a multiport memory system should be constructed (Fig. 10).

In a multiport system, any CPU can have access to any module of the common memory. The block designated as the memory interface is a gigantic cross-bar switch with a built-in conflict resolver. But this type of switch is rarely used, except in very large computing systems, because it involves a lot of hardware.

A good compromise is available if every μP is autonomous and has its own private memory (Fig. 11). The compromise pre-empts the memory conflict presented in a network that only has a common memory. It nevertheless may have access to a common memory through a pair of isolating buffers controlled by a system-conflict resolver that permits only one μP at a time to use the common memory. Each μP then gains access to the common memory and treats it as a part of its own memory space. Such a system pro-

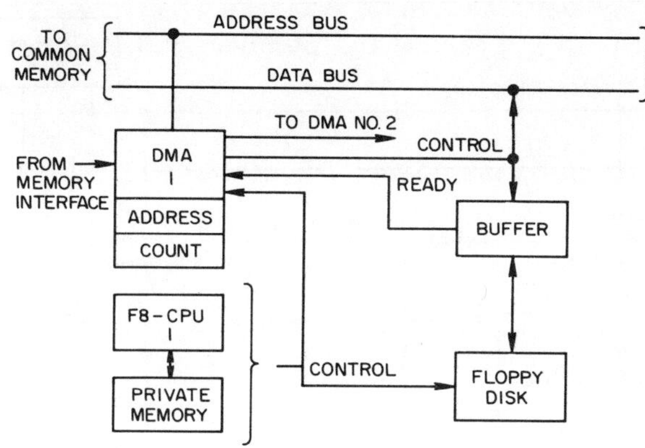

8. **A floppy-disc controller** requires that data be buffered before use by the microprocessor.

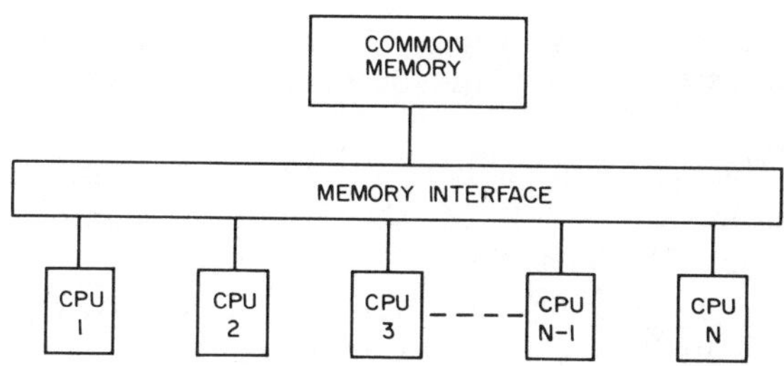

9. **Microprocessors sharing a common memory** for instructions and data may operate too slowly if CPU speed is comparable to memory speed.

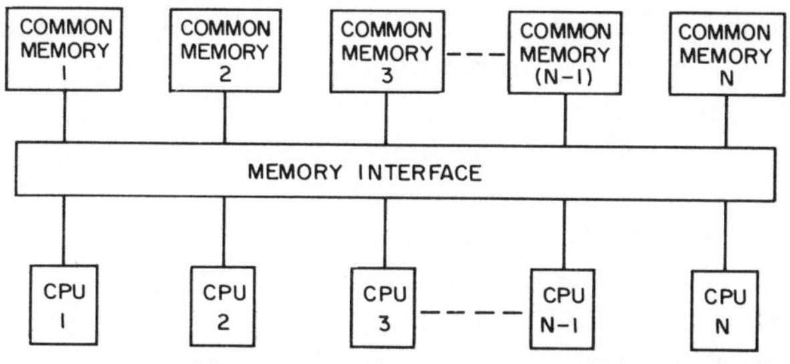

10. **Systems that have individual subports of common memory** allow fast operation, but require complex memory interface circuitry.

vides a simple but elegant synergism between a set of simultaneously operating μPs.

Communication through electronic mailboxes

In a common-memory network, communications between any two microprocessors require no special hardware. Instead, a simple software protocol may be adopted, the "mailbox" system. One μP is designated as the "coordinator;" every other μP in the network has two sets (mailboxes) of memory locations in the common memory, for message exchange with the coordinator. Let us say that μP No. 1 is the coordinator

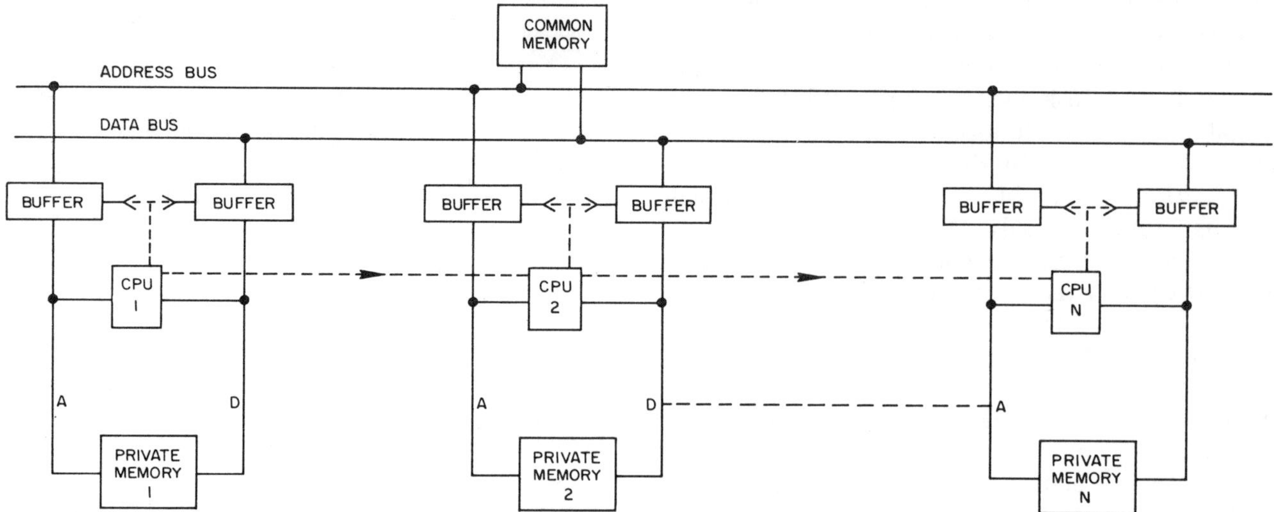

11. Either common memory or dedicated memories may be accessed by the microprocessors in the same address space. Buffers allow only one CPU to access the common memory in one time period.

for the network in Fig. 11. We may then designate locations 0-9 in the common memory as Mailbox 12. That is, microprocessor No. 1 uses these ten memory locations to pass instructions to machine No. 2. Data will reside in locations 1000 and higher.

Similarly, we may designate locations, 10-19, as Mailbox 21, which is used by μP No. 2 to deposite messages intended for μP No. 1.

An example may clarify how this mailbox system works. In a certain application of the network shown in Fig. 11, μPs No. 1, 2 and 3 are respectively the coordinator, the floppy-disc controller, and the data-link controller.

Suppose the coordinator wishes to transmit a record currently stored in floppy-disc 8, track 4, and record 17, to a distant city. It will manipulate the mailboxes in the following way:

1. The coordinator deposits a message in Mailbox 12 saying that μP No. 2 is to fetch the proper record (disc 8, track 4, record 17) to common memory locations 1000-1127.

2. On a periodic scan of its own mailbox (12), μP No. 2 discovers the above message. It promptly executes the instruction and leaves a message in Mailbox 21 stating that the operation is concluded.

3. In one of its periodic scans of Mailbox 21, the coordinator spots the record in locations 1000-1127. It then issues an order to μP No. 3 (the data-controller) via Mailbox 13. In the or-

der, the coordinator states that the record is presently in locations 1000-1127, and that it is to be sent by a specific coding scheme such as by-sync or SDLC.

4. Microprocessor No. 3, having understood the message in Mailbox 13, transmits the data in locations 1000-1127 with the specified format. It then signals the completion of the data-link operation by leaving an appropriate message for the coordinator in Mailbox 31.

5. The message in Mailbox 31 is read by the coordinator, which marks the end of the transfer.

The entire operation consumes only a few milliseconds. The significant point of the above example is that each microprocessor is almost totally independent except for the simple "Mailbox" convention. The program of each μP can be independently developed and debugged without regard to the programs of the other microprocessors on the same network. This system is an important development in computing technology, especially in view of the high availability and low cost of modern MOS μPs such as the F8.

As we've seen, there are two basic types of microprocessor networks, communications oriented, and common-memory oriented. Out of these two forms, we can derive many hybrid networks using different combinations and hierarchies. It is safe to predict that many tasks long the private domain of large computers will be handled in the future by microprocessor networks.

Multi-Channel Synchro Conversion

ARTHUR BERG
Project Engineer, Micro Networks,
Worcester, Massachusetts

Using a microprocessor, you can convert eight synchro or resolver channels to digital angles with four-arc-minutes accuracy in a package roughly the same size as a single-channel converter system—with only a bit more power consumption and at nearly the same cost. For example, in a complete modular system, the MN7200 from Micro Networks, a microprocessor controls sequencing and performs data conversions. The result is a converter capable of handling up to eight synchro or resolver inputs, whose accuracy is guaranteed over the full operating temperature range of 0 to 70 C.

There is one drawback, however. The μP-based instrument is limited to maximum transducer speeds of 10 deg/s.

Synchro/resolver converter basics

The conventional converter system (Fig. 1) requires six distinct steps to convert either a synchro or resolver signal into digital angles:

- Converting the three-phase synchro signal into a two-phase resolver signal with either a Scott-T transformer or op amps. One phase of the resolver signal is proportional to the angle's sine, and the other phase to the angle's cosine.

- Demodulating both these signals with respect to the synchro's ac reference signal with an ac/dc converter, to get dc levels proportional to the sine and cosine of the input angle.

- Detecting, from the dc signal, the quadrant or octant in which the input angle lies, and digitizing the angle. Table 1 shows the bit weights for a binary sequence of angles.

- Feeding the binary-angle information to an up-down counter.

- Multiplying the counter's output by the dc signals with two multiplying d/a converters— one for the sine signal and one for the cosine signal—to get two results: sin θ cos ϕ, and cos θ sin ϕ, where θ is the angle in the counter and ϕ the input angle.

Binary weights of angles in the coding method employed in the MN7200

Bit number	Degrees	Degrees, minutes		Radians
1	180	180	0	3.141593
2	90	90	0	1.570796
3	45	45	0	0.785398
4	22.5	22	30	0.392699
5	11.25	11	15	0.196349
6	5.625	5	37.5	0.098175
7	2.8125	2	48.75	0.049087
8	1.40625	1	24.38	0.024544
9	0.70312	0	42.19	0.012272
10	0.35156	0	21.09	0.006136
11	0.17578	0	10.55	0.003068
12	0.08789	0	5.27	0.001534
13	0.04395	0	2.64	0.000767
14	0.02197	0	1.32	0.000383
15	0.01099	0	0.66	0.000192
16	0.00549	0	0.33	0.000096

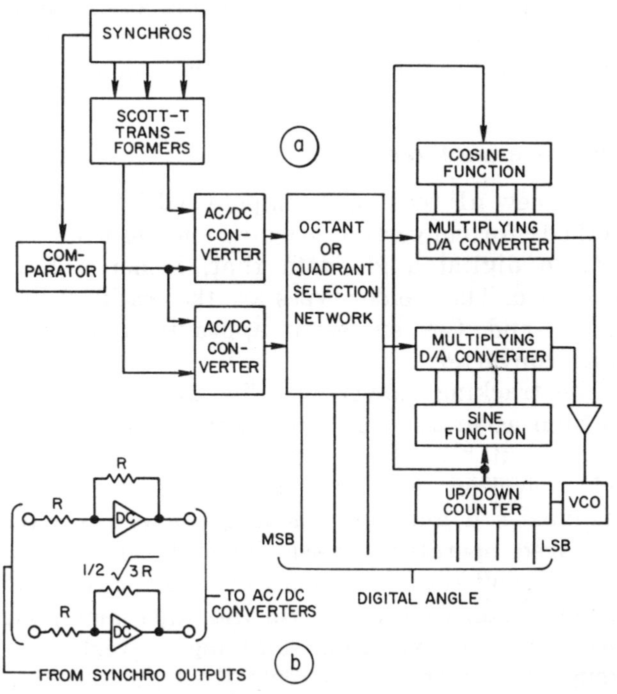

1. **Conventional multichannel converters** (a) use many linear components. You can replace the Scott-T transformer with an electronic Scott-T converter (b).

■ Subtracting, in an op amp, to get the difference between the two converter outputs, and adjusting the frequency of a gated voltage-controlled oscillator (VCO) with the result. The VCO's output pulses the up-down counter to the correct digital angle—the digital equivalent of nulling in an analog system. When the counter contains the exact input angle, the subtraction result is zero, and the process is complete.

The disadvantages inherent in this six-step process are obvious. Too much circuitry is re-

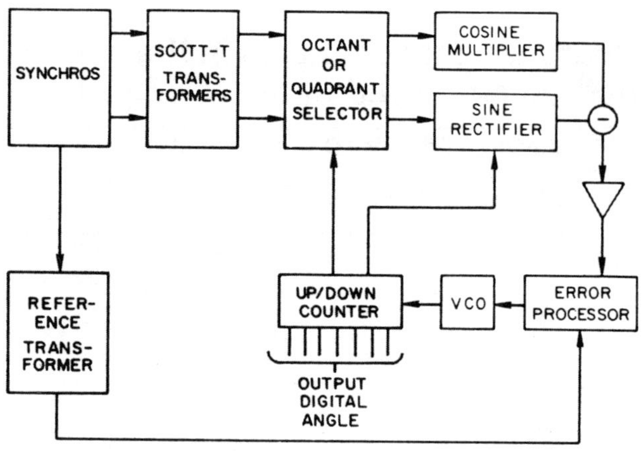

2. The popular tracking converters are accurate but limited to converting only a few channels. Successive-approximation sampling converters are useful for converting several channels in a multiplexed system, but have serious accuracy problems.

quired, principally for quadrant or octant selection and angle determination, and analog signals are carried too far—right up to the final counter.

Now there are three

The new μP technique competes with two other methods for converting synchro and resolver signals to digital angle data that, hitherto, have been used. These older types are the tracking converter and the successive-approximation sampling converter.

The tracking converter (Fig. 2) is noted for its high accuracy even with noisy signals. Noise cancels out because of ratio rather than amplitude detection. But, even though some recently available s/d and r/d tracking converters have improved operating speeds, most tracking converters can't track a synchro or resolver rotating at more than four rev/s. On the other hand, the successive-approximation sampling converter, although a higher-speed circuit than the tracking converter, becomes inaccurate with noise or distortion.

Tracking converters are used primarily when a limited number of channels is to be converted ac-

curately, and sampling converters when six or more multiplexed channels are to be converted at high speed.

The third method for s/d conversion, the microprocessor-based system, as used in the MN7200 is intended for multichannel applications. Accuracy (even in the presence of noise), low cost, small size and low power consumption make the μP-based system attractive for many applications, in spite of its low speed.

The new circuit (Fig. 3) is made up of eight dual ac/dc converters, a 16-channel data-acquisition system, and a microprocessor.

The microprocessor, a Fairchild Semiconductor F8, is a two-chip unit that consists of the CPU, and the Program Storage Unit (PSU). Besides being μP-based, the MN7200 circuitry differs from conventional s/d and r/d circuits because it has a minimum number of custom-linear circuits and, thus, is cheaper. Octant selection (0 to 45 degrees) is performed digitally with the microprocessor. And the hybrid circuits used, such as the ac/dc demodulators, multiplexers, and a/d converters are all standard products.

The system converts eight resolver (or with the addition of Scott-T transformers, synchro) channels into 14-bit digital form.

Multiplexing the inputs

While conventional multichannel converters typically require an a/d for each channel, only a single a/d is used in this circuit: It accepts up to eight pairs of sequential inputs from the multiplexer.

Synchro outputs from the Scott-T transformers or resolver outputs V_x ac and V_y ac are converted to dc voltages V_x and V_y by two ac/dc demodulators—one each for sine and cosine (Fig. 3). A multiplexer connects these dc signals sequentially —one per conversion period (approximately 2 ms) —to the a/d converter that converts them into the binary signals X and Y. After conversion, the binary X and Y signals are stored in RAM. The microprocessor then executes the conversion equation,

$$\theta = \tan^{-1} \frac{Y}{X},$$

and the result is placed on the output-data lines and stored in RAM. Up to 8 channels are thus converted and stored in 16 RAM locations. A conversion cycle takes 2 ms.

A fetch cycle takes 50 μs from the time the data-output line is triggered. The system has two externally controlled channel-selection modes. In the sequential mode, a counter is incremented after each channel is converted. In the random mode, each channel may be selected by the channel-select inputs and triggered by the load line.

The circuit differs from conventional s/d and

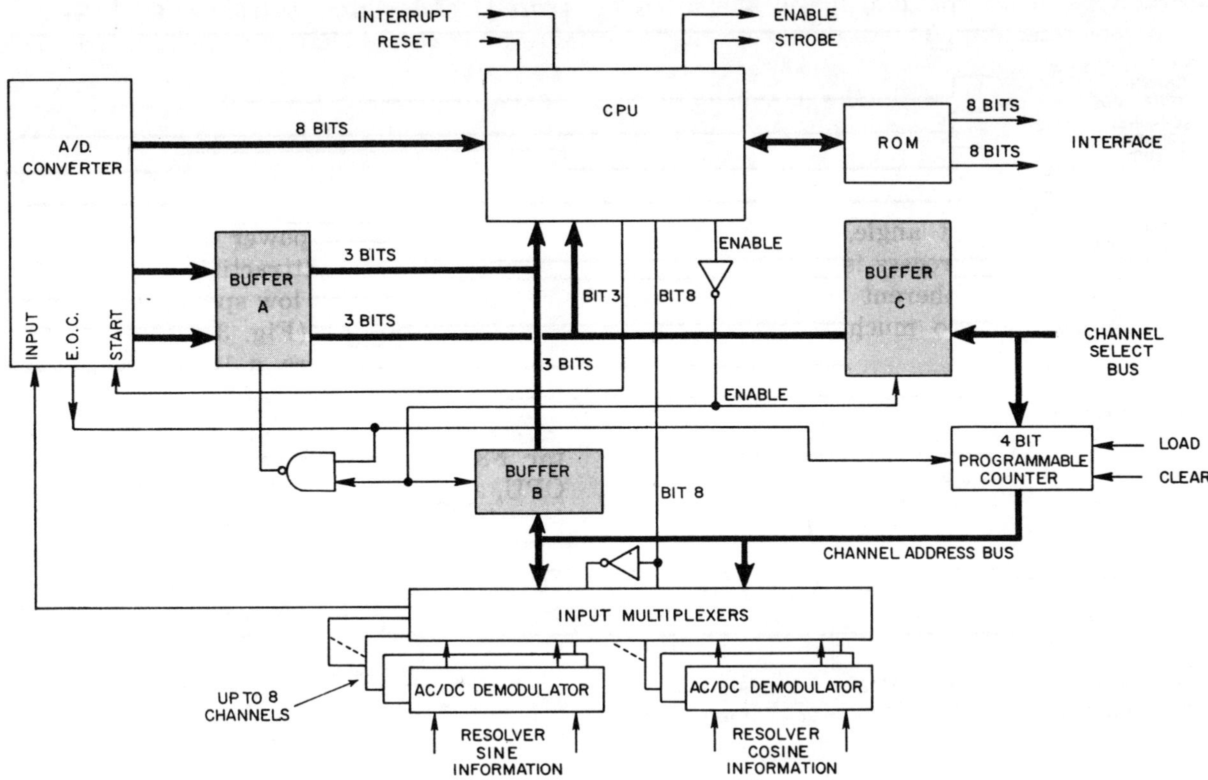

3. The MN7200 resolver-to-digital converter circuit differs from conventional ones in that it allows for low-cost multichannel (eight, in this case) conversions in a compact, low-power-dissipating configuration.

r/d converters in that all its data are converted to digital form at the input a/d converters, whereas much of the information in conventional designs remains subject to error in analog form, right up to the final digital counter.

Canceling nonlinearities

The 12-bit a/d converter in the circuit (Fig. 3) performs both sine-proportional and cosine-proportional signal conversions, so errors caused by using separate a/d's are eliminated. By ratioing, the microprocessor eliminates the potential error source due to amplitude changes of the sine or cosine-input signals.

Two data I/O ports connect the 12-bit a/d converter's output and the microprocessor's CPU. Two 8-bit ports deliver 12 bits to the CPU in 2 bytes. One port inputs eight bits, the other only four.

With buffer A on and buffers B and C off, a/d data goes to the CPU. With buffers A & C off and B on, the address of the channel being converted is sent to the CPU. When operating in the interrupt or data-fetch modes with C on and A and B off, an external address can be sent to the CPU to address the memory for data.

In addition to the data bus that links the PSU and the CPU, two other 8-bit I/O ports are used as a single 14-bit output port, with all eight bits active in one and only six active in the other.

This arrangement allows simple interfacing with either 16-bit minicomputers or 8-bit microcomputers.

After the synchro or resolver angle is computed, the microprocessor system stores the resulting 14-bit word in the registers of the PSU's two I/O ports, until the word is replaced by a new result.

The 4-bit programmable counter, which addresses the input multiplexers sequentially, is connected to the channel-select bus to receive direct-set inputs from an external channel-selector circuit. The 3-bit, channel-address bus links the input multiplexers to the programmable counter and the CPU via buffer B.

It all starts with reset input

Operation begins when a reset input initializes the CPU. The system is clocked by bit 7 of the CPU's I/O port, which drives the start input of the a/d. The a/d then outputs EOC (end of clock), which drives the programmable address counter. Bit 8 enables the input multiplexers to pass the channel addressed by the programmable counter. In all, 6 bits are used for data entry to the CPU.

The multiplexer's sine inputs are enabled by bit 8. Its complement, $\overline{\text{bit 8}}$, enables the cosine inputs so only one set of inputs, either sine or cosine, is active at a given time.

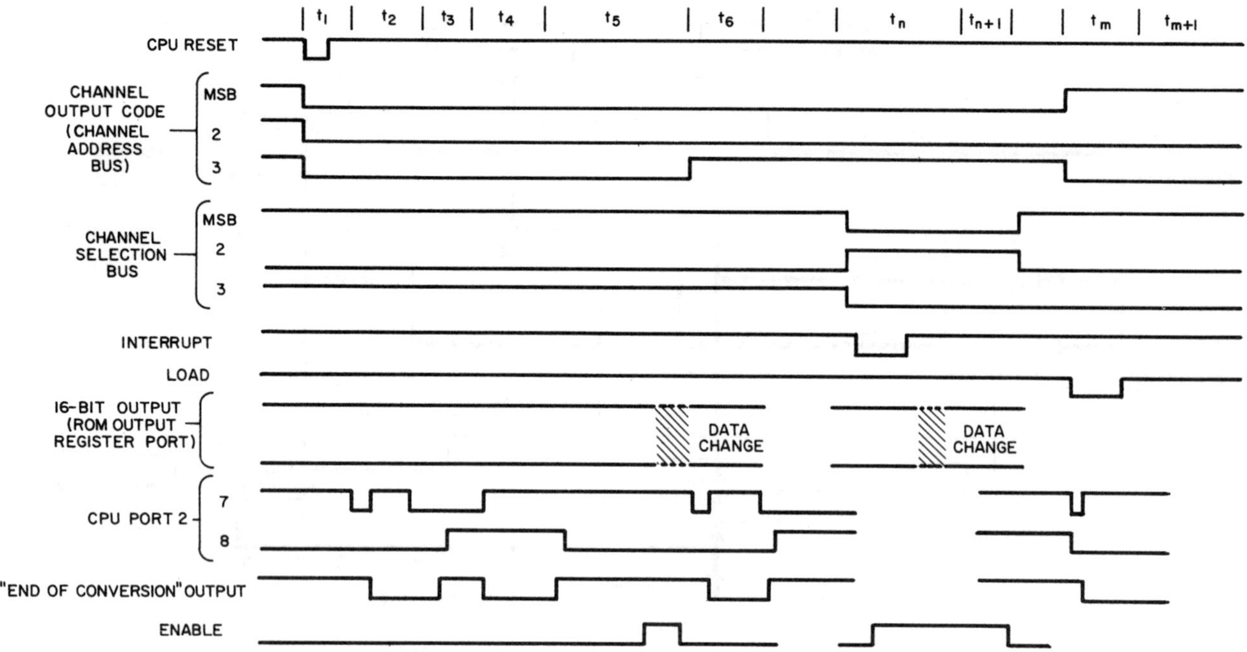

4. The converter's six timing states are repeated as it cycles through each of eight channels. For fewer than eight channels, the last active channel is followed by channel 0 and the sequence repeats.

The CPU's enable-output line indicates that an interrupt signal has been received or data are changing. Normally, this line (low) disables buffers B and C. Buffer A is enabled after the a/d conversion is finished (EOC high). (An enabled buffer A permits data transfer from the a/d converter to the microprocessor's CPU.)

After an interrupt signal, the enable goes high, which activates buffers B and C and disables buffer A. The interrupt stops the normal operation of the microprocessor and requests that stored data from the addressed channel be transferred to the output lines.

The reset line to the CPU resets the program counter in the PSU. The load line allows the programmable counter to be set to the channel chosen by the channel-select data bus. The clear line resets the programmable counter.

Look at the timing diagram

Operation starts at t_1 with a pulse on the CPU's reset line (and the programmable counter's clear line). This pulse clears both the program counter in the ROM and the programmable counter to ZERO (see Fig. 4). The ROM's program counter is started by CPU clock signals. The channel-select line is still inactive, and all three bits on the channel-address bus are ZEROs.

The sine input of channel 0 then passes from its dedicated demodulator through the input multiplexer into the a/d converter.

At t_2, the a/d converter's start line and the programmable counter's clock line are pulsed, which starts conversion in the a/d converter and blocks buffer stage A. During t_2, the EOC line clocks the programmable counter, but does not change the address to the multiplexers. This line changes only the LSB, which is not on the channel-address bus.

When the counter first accesses a channel, the address LSB is always ZERO. The multiplexer, therefore, always samples the selected channel's sine input first. The LSB is then toggled to a ONE, and the cosine input sampled. The LSB is then retoggled to ZERO. This time the 3-bit address is incremented, which accesses the next channel, starting with its sine input.

Also during t_2, the PSU's internal timer is set for a time interval slightly longer than the conversion time needed by the a/d. This timer stops the program counter in the CPU and restarts it at the end of the preset time interval. Meanwhile, the a/d converter completes its conversion cycle, and the EOC enables buffer A.

The a/d converter's 12 bits are routed in two parts—eight bits through data-port 1, and four bits through data-port 2. The first bit (MSB) indicates signal polarity. The remaining three bits are amplitude data and are stored in RAM by a program in ROM.

At t_3, bit 8 changes state, which both disables the sine multiplexer and enables the cosine multiplexer.

At t_4, conversion starts in the a/d and the EOC output blocks buffer stage A. The multiplexer connects the dc analog of the cosine input to the a/d converter, and an all-ZERO address is again connected to the multiplexer. The ROM's internal timer starts again, and the a/d converts the cosine analog of input-channel 0 to digital form. At the conversion's end, EOC reverses the state of the buffers so that the cosine is at the CPU's I/O ports. At the end of the timer's interval, the program is restarted, and the cosine goes into RAM. Therefore, after t_i, values for both the sine and cosine of a channel's input angle are in the RAM.

A branch point can occur

Next, the μP computes the angle (answer) from its sine and cosine values. The MSBs of the sine and the answer are the same. For a ZERO MSB, the answer is between 0 and 180 degrees, and here the program has a branch point. If the sine's MSB is ZERO (sine positive), the cosine's MSB becomes the answer's next bit. For the sine's MSB, a ONE (sine negative), the complement of the cosine's MSB is the second MSB in the answer.

The answer's third MSB is determined by subtracting the sine's 11 amplitude bits from the cosine's. A positive result makes the third MSB a ONE, a negative result ZERO.

Now the μP can divide the larger 11-bit number into the smaller to get the angle's tangent. The ROM contains a tangent-to-angle table. To minimize the size of this table, only 64 values and the slopes to the next value are provided for the tangent function. Therefore, only the tangent's six MSBs are used to address the table; the remaining five bits are multiplied by the slope.

The final answer is the sum of two values; the first an 11-bit word that the tangent's six MSBs fetch from ROM. The second summed value is the product of the five remaining bits multiplied by a slope value that is also accessed by the six MSBs.

The enable line is held high to indicate changing output data. Buffers B and C are enabled, buffer A is disabled. The channel address, along with the program's instructions, select a pair of RAM addresses in which to store the 14-bit answer. The 14-bit answer also remains at the ROM's output register port.

At t_6, the programmable counter is clocked, which changes the second LSB of the three-bit address. The multiplexers pass to the next channel. The a/d converter starts, which begins the sequence for the next input channel. This process continues until the digital angles for all inputs are in storage, when the CPU's main program counter and the programmable counter are zeroed and started over again. Words stored in RAM are replaced by updated words as new information is processed and received.

The digital-angle data are in binary-angle form rather than in degrees. The MSB indicates which half-circle the angle is in, the next MSB indicates which quarter, the next MSB indicates which oc-

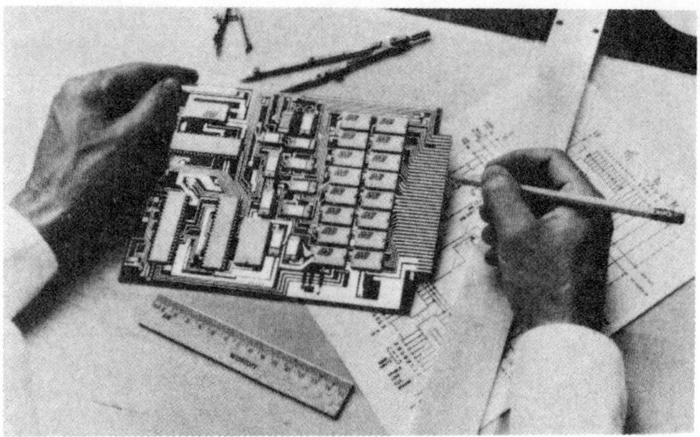

5. **The entire μP-based r/d converter** consists of 32 DIPs on a 6 × 8-in. board.

tant, and so on. Code conversion, say, to binary or degrees is easily added here.

At t_n (Fig. 4), an interrupt signal inhibits buffer A, enables buffers B and C, and stops the ROM's program counter. The three bits that are now manually entered onto the channel-select bus address the RAM through buffer C and port 2. This 3-bit code addresses one of eight 14-bit angles in the RAM. The addressed angle appears at the ROM's output-register port. At the end of the interrupt, the main program counter picks up again, and the program continues from where it was interrupted.

At t_m, a load signal jams the address on the channel-select bus into the programmable counter. The CPU's reset line then resets the CPU and clears the main program counter to ZERO. The program then picks up by using the channel selected on the channel-select bus as the first channel, and proceeds in sequence thereafter.

Interrupt, therefore, provides the latest stored data for a selected channel, while load and reset cause new data to be processed starting with the selected channel.

The Scott-T transformers and ac/dc demodulators in the input circuit are conventional components. So are the IC multiplexers. The 12-bit a/d converter needs only a parallel output, something available in a variety of commercial components. Three-state buffers A, B, and C are merely used as on-off switches in the data paths to permit time-sharing of the CPU I/O ports. While the programmable counter is shown in Fig. 3 as a 4-bit unit, a 3-bit unit is adequate. The fourth bit is used to divide by 2, thereby maintaining the same channel address as the sine and cosine input multiplexers are successively enabled.

In the two-chip F8 microprocessor, one chip houses the CPU (including the control logic for RAM and ALU) and clock-generating circuitry, and the other chip, the PSU, houses the ROM.

A look-up table, for converting the tangent function to angular data, is burned into the microprocessor's nonvolatile ROM.

SECTION VII
Designing with the PACE

As one of the few 16-bit microprocessors available, National Semiconductor's PACE is widely used by those engineers who need "number-crunching" capability approaching that of a minicomputer, but who find themselves able to live with the relatively slow speeds characteristic of PMOS chips. One advantage of the p-channel fabrication is that the circuits for the PACE system are relatively inexpensive. Because PACE has been in production for several years, it is supported by a broader range of peripheral circuits than newer 16-bit systems. Another reason for PACE's popularity is that engineers who are familiar with minicomputers find it easy to work with because its architecture is similar to that of Data General's Nova-1200.

Though Rockwell International is licensed to manufacture National's microprocessors, the company has not yet started to sell PACE. A faster n-channel version is under development at National and is scheduled for introduction during 1977. A second source for this version is under negotiation.

The first article provides all the information an engineer needs to start designing with PACE. In the next article, the author shows how, paradoxically, PACE can complement a minicomputer instead of replacing it. The last article describes some applications of microprocessors in industrial control; the examples are not restricted to PACE, though the emphasis is on 16-bit machines.

Keep the PACE Up and Running

FRANK LYNCH
PACE Product Manager,
National Semiconductor, Santa Clara

The PACE microprocessor is one of the few 16-bit μPs available, and the only one made with a low-cost PMOS process. It can operate with just a single-phase clock (both true and complement signals) and still deliver much of the performance formerly requiring a minicomputer.

A hardware stack, six vectored interrupts and six addressing modes work together to make the PACE easy to apply. The support circuits available (Table 1) also help during system design. A system timing element (STE) and three bi-directional transceiver elements (BTE) combine to provide a fully buffered and clocked processor (Fig. 1). The 16-bit data and address bus can drive 30 TTL loads, as can all the flag and strobe lines when buffered with BTEs.

Data flow easily on the bus

All data transfers between the PACE and external memories or peripherals take place over the 16 data lines. The transfers are synchronized by the NADS (negative true address strobe) IDS (input data strobe), ODS (output data strobe) and EXTEND (extended data transfer) signals.

Timing for address or data signals on the bus is shown in Fig. 2a. Where the signal timing is referenced to the clock signals, the reference is to valid logic ONE or ZERO clock levels. Cross-hatched areas indicate either uncertainty of output transitions or don't-care states for data inputs. Address data become valid one clock phase prior to the NADS signal and remain valid for one clock phase afterwards. Typically, the NADS signal strobes the address data into a set of latches that are either internal or external to the memory chips, or clocks decoded peripheral addresses into a control flip-flop.

PACE-address drivers go into a high-impedance state during the data-input interval (see Fig. 2a). The IDS signal can disable the output sense amplifiers and enable the three-state input buffers. Typically, this timing permits maximum speed of the μP in a system only if the memory access is less than two clock periods. The fastest commercial PACE has a 500-ns cycle time, so memories that access in 1 μs or faster work fine.

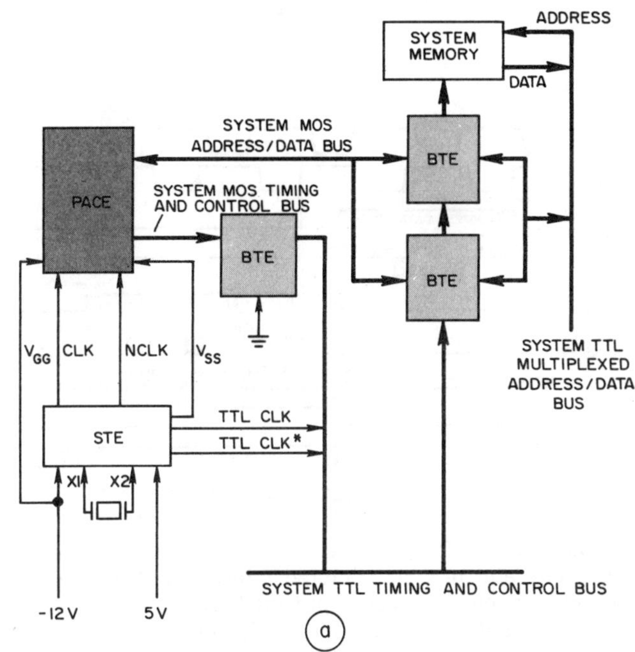

1. A minimal operating system can be built from the PACE, three BTEs, one STE and any amount of RAM or ROM (a). All input/output lines of the system can handle 30 TTL loads. A simple development system (b) uses three BTEs and simple TTL. Either the self-contained keyboard or a teletypewriter can be used.

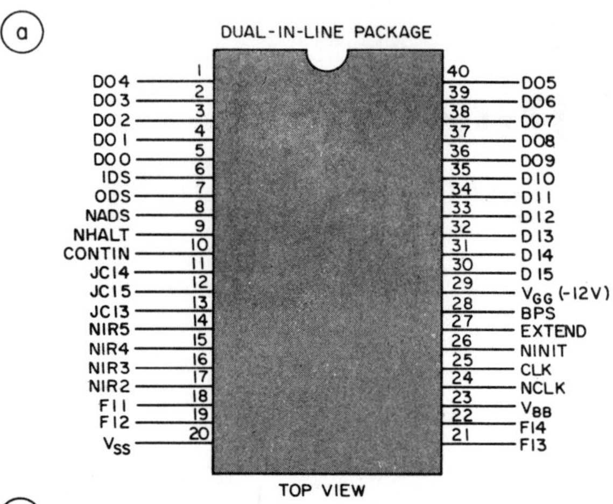

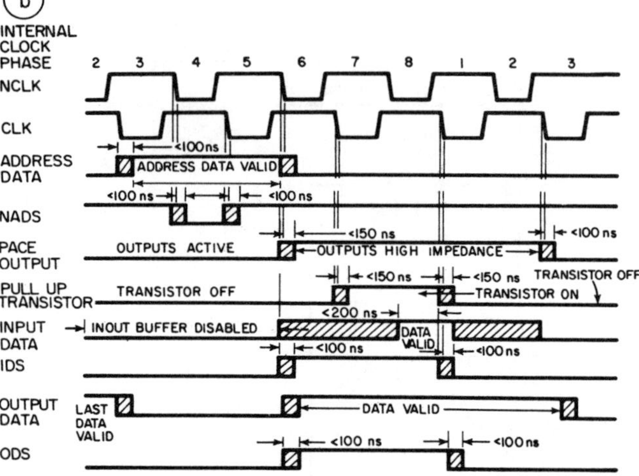

2. **The PACE** μ**P** (a) uses a multiplexed data and address bus and has six vectored interrupts. The two non-overlapping clock phases, provided by the STE, control the PACE μP (b). TTL-level clock signals (not shown) are also generated by the STE.

To use memories that have a longer access time, either the clock frequency can be reduced or the input/output (I/O)-cycle extend feature can be used.

Four serial inputs and four serial outputs are available via the flag, jump and continue lines. In all, there are 12 control lines on the PACE (not including the flag and jump lines) that can simplify many of the possible interface applications. The Extend input, employed by slow memories or peripherals to temporarily increase the time duration of data I/O transfers, can also be used to suspend I/O operations if applied at the end of an ODS or IDS pulse.

The three Jump Condition inputs (JC13, 14, 15) are user-specified inputs that can be tested with the Branch-on-Condition (BOC) instructions. These JC inputs are useful for testing external device status or receiving serial data. Four flag outputs (F11, 12, 13, 14), which can be either set by a Set-Flag instruction or pulsed or reset by a Pulse-Flag instruction, can provide direct control of a system function or serve as individual serial output ports.

Table 1. PACE support circuits

Model number	Pins	Description	Cost (100-up)
IPC-16A/500D	40	PACE CPU, 500-ns cycle time	$60.00
IPC-16A/520D	40	PACE CPU, 750-ns cycle time	$40.00
DP 8302D	16	System timing element	$6.50
DP 8300N	24	Bidirectional transceiver element	$5.10
DP 8301N	28	Multidirectional interface latch element	to be announced
MM 2101	22	256 × 4 static MOS RAM, 500-to-1000-ns access	$3.20
MM 2102	16	1 k × 1 static MOS RAM, 500-to-1000-ns access	$2.30
MM 2112	16	256 × 4 static MOS RAM, 650-to-1000-ns access	$3.20
MM 5269	22	256 × 4 static MOS RAM, with address latches, 1000-ns access	$3.20
MM 5271	18	4 k × 1 dynamic MOS RAM, 250-ns access TTL compatible	$12.00
MM 5281	22	4 k × 1 dynamic MOS RAM, 250-ns access TTL compatible	$15.00
MM 5214	24	512 × 8 MOS ROM, 1000-ns access	*
MM 5242	24	1 k × 8 MOS ROM, 500-ns access	*
MM 5246	24	2 k × 8 MOS ROM, 500-ns access	*
MM 5204	24	512 × 8 electrically programmable MOS ROM, 1000-ns access	$29.50

* consult factory

A dozen control lines do everything

Four lines are used as Negative-True Interrupt Request lines (NIR2, 3, 4, 5). Holding these lines LOW for one clock period (minimum) sets the associated internal-interrupt-request latch—but only if the corresponding interrupt enable has been set by the user's program. The interrupt is serviced after the current instruction is completed if the Master Interrupt Enable is set. The four interrupt lines are given differing priorities with NIR5 having the lowest priority.

The NHALT (Negative-True Halt) line, acting as an input or output signal, can be driven LOW by external logic to "stall" the μP or initiate a Level-$\emptyset$ interrupt, depending on the timing of the CONTIN (continue) signal. When not controlled by external logic, NHALT can be driven LOW by the PACE software for 7/8 duty cycle while a programmed halt condition exists. A programmed halt initiated by the Halt instruction can be terminated by using external logic to pulse the CONTIN line.

The CONTIN also acts as an input/output line. As an input line, it can terminate a programmed halt, exercise a μP stall and level-$\emptyset$ interrupt or initiate a jump condition that can be tested with a BOC instruction. As an output line,

Internal architecture of the PACE microprocessor

The PACE central processor, a single PMOS IC, uses a shared data and address bus to manipulate 16-bit wide data and instructions. All 45 instructions use a single-word, 16-bit format that keeps memory accesses and program-storage requirements to a minimum.

Data transfers between the PACE μP and the memory or peripheral devices take place on the 16-bit parallel address/data bus. Inside the chip, the data bus interfaces through a set of buffers to the operand bus and the instruction register. Connected to the operand bus are seven registers and a 10-word last-in, first-out stack. Four of the registers, AC0 to AC3, are available as general purpose accumulators. The other three registers include the program counter and two scratch pad registers, temp reg. 1 and temp reg. 2.

The contents of the registers or stack are routed to either the A or B inputs of the arithmetic and logic unit (ALU) and shifter. The ALU output can then be returned to any of the registers or stack by way of the result bus. Aside from performing the arithmetic, the ALU also sets the status flags, in accordance with the data length (8 or 16 bits) selected by the state of the byte-status flag. All status information is stored in a 16-bit status-and-control-flag register that can also be loaded onto or from the operand bus. The 14 status and control flags can be individually set, pulsed or reset under software control.

Instructions are stored in the instruction register as they are to be executed and are inter-

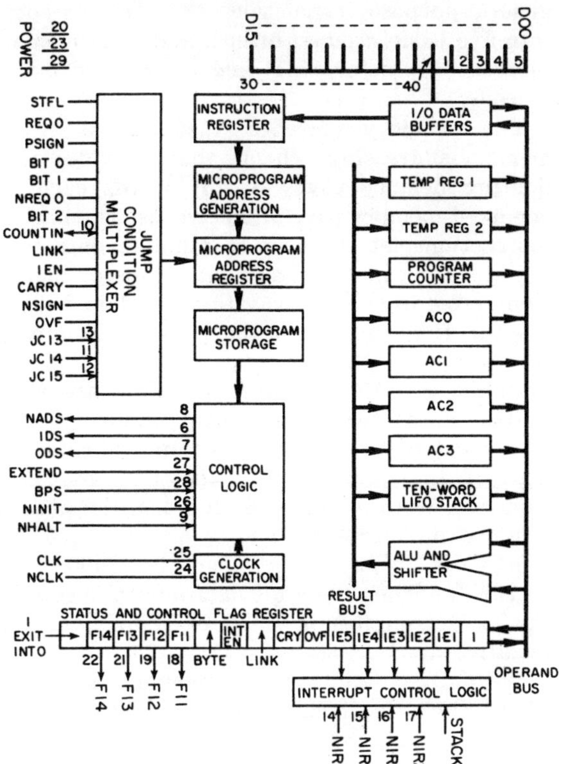

preted and executed by a microprogram stored in a 75-word-$\times$-20-bit ROM. Actual execution time is determined by the particular instruction and clock frequency.

CONTIN transmits a pulse to acknowledge an active interrupt input.

Two other input lines, the BPS (Base-Page Select) and the NINIT (Negative-True Initialize), are also available. The BPS signal enables one of two base-page addressing schemes. When BPS is LOW, the first 256 words of memory constitute the base page (page zero). When BPS is HIGH, however, the first 128 memory words and the last 128 memory words constitute the base page.

When the NINIT signal is LOW, all μP operation is suspended, and IDS/ODS signals are set to an inactive state. After NINIT completes a LOW-to-HIGH transition, the program counter is set to zero, the internal stack pointer is cleared and all flags and interrupt enables except the Level-0 interrupt enable are set LOW. The Level 0 is set HIGH. All other registers can contain arbitrary values.

With its six-level priority interrupt structure, the PACE μP keeps the circuitry for interrupt-driven systems simple. Each level of interrupt has its own Interrupt Enable (IEN). A master

IEN is provided for all five lower-priority levels at once. The master IEN is an input to the μP's internal jump-condition multiplexer. The state of the interrupt is tested by the PACE during the instruction-fetch routine (internal to the PACE) executed after each instruction is completed. Thus, an interrupt that is HIGH is automatically serviced.

During the interrupt sequence, an address is formed by the output of the priority encoder. This address is used to access the interrupt pointer, which in turn gives the highest priority interrupt request. The pointer specifies the starting address of the interrupt service routine for the particular interrupt level, except for a Level-0 interrupt (IR0), which is used primarily for alarm interrupts and control panel displays.

Surrounding the PACE are four circuits (Fig. 3), at the most, that need be used to make a complete operating system. The 24-pin STE (Fig. 3a), together with an external crystal and +5 and −12 V supplies generates the nonoverlapping MOS clock signals and the substrate bias necessary for PACE operation. A TTL-level

PACE addressing schemes and instruction set

The PACE microprocessor has a mix of 45 general-purpose instructions that can be sorted into five basic groups: branch and skip, memory-reference, register, shift and rotate, and miscellaneous.

The memory-reference instructions use a memory-addressing scheme that provides three floating-memory pages of 256 words each and one fixed-memory page of 256 words. The register instructions let the user manipulate data without accessing memory, and data-transfer instructions provide an easy way to move data between the functional blocks of the PACE microprocessor system.

In the PACE microprocessor, data are represented in the two's-complement number system. The most-significant-bit position indicates the sign of the number, 0 for positive and 1 for negative. With a single 16-bit word, the greatest positive number is $7FFF_{(16)}$ or $32,767_{(10)}$, and the most negative number is $8000_{(16)}$ or $32,768_{(10)}$. When the 8-bit data length is selected, the largest number is $7F_{(16)}$ or $127_{(10)}$, the most negative number, $80_{(16)}$ or $128_{(10)}$.

Both direct and indirect memory addressing instructions are included in the PACE instruction set. Direct-memory addressing has three available modes: base-page; program-counter (PC) relative; and indexed. The addressing mode is specified by the xr field of the instruc-

tion as shown in Fig. A.

When the xr field is 00, base-page (page 0) addressing is specified. However, two types of base-page addressing are available, and the type selected is determined by the state of the base-page select-signal (BPS) input. When BPS is LOW (ZERO), the 16-bit memory address is formed by setting bits 8 through 15 to ZERO and using the 8-bit displacement (DISP) field for bits 0 through 7. Thus, the first 256 words of memory (locations 0 to 255) can be addressed.

If BPS is HIGH (ONE), the 16-bit memory address is formed by setting bits 8 through 15 equal to bit 7 of the DISP field and using DISP for bits 0 through 7. Thus, the first 128 words (0000 to $007F$) and the last 128 words (FF80 to FFFF) of memory can be addressed. This technique is useful for splitting the base page between RAM and ROM or between memory and peripheral devices. Consequently, base-page addressing permits easy access of the data or peripherals.

When the xr field is 01, addressing relative to the contents of the PC is specified. During the PC-relative addressing mode, the memory address is formed by adding the contents of PC to the value of the DISP field, which is interpreted as a signed number. (The 8-bit DISP field is interpreted as a 16-bit value with the bit 7 value used for bits 8 through 15, which permits

clock and its complement are also generated to ease over-all system design.

Simple circuits support the PACE

On the STE, a MOS buffer provides two sets of clock signals. One set (CLK and NCLK) is damped by on-chip 43 Ω resistors and should be used for printed-circuit runs of no more than 2 in. The other output set (CK and NCK) is undamped to permit user-optimization.

The BTE circuit (Fig. 3b) in a 24-pin DIP provides input and output buffering between the PACE MOS I/O lines and the TTL world. Each BTE line has a fanout of up to 30 TTL loads. The four BTE mode-control function lines decode input control signals and, in turn, produce signals that set the TTL receiver/buffer and the MOS sense amplifier/driver into one of three operating modes: it can act as a driver, receiver or appear as a high impedance.

The PACE is also supported by the multidirectional interface latch element (MILE), a bidirectional 8-bit wide latch. The MILE comes in a 28 pin DIP and requires only a single supply due to

its CMOS structure. On the chip are four select lines and a strobe that permit up to 16 MILEs to be put on a single bus. Outputs of the MILE are three state and can drive eight TTL loads. Also included are several status flag lines to provide handshaking.

With the MILE, almost any memory can be used with the PACE. But for a minimal system, the MM5269—a 256×4 static RAM with built-in latches—fits in very nicely. The MM5269 has an access time of 1 μs and is housed in a 22-pin DIP; three are needed for a minimal system.

System support: The choice is wide

Supporting the PACE μP are a wide range of hardware and software products (Table 2). For simple hardware integration and basic program development, the PACE LCDS provides an inexpensive starting point. The LCDS system comes with a keyboard, display and a fully expandable common bus. Machine-language routines can be developed easily for it without a teletypewriter.

In all, three major levels of design support are available to PACE users:

representation of numbers ranging from -128 through 127.)

After the memory address is formed, the PC is incremented and contains an address value that is one greater than the location of the current instruction. Thus, memory addresses that can be referenced range from 127 locations below through 128 locations above the address of the current instruction.

The indexed (or accumulator-relative) mode of addressing permits any memory location within the 65,536 word address space to be referenced. The DISP field, as in PC-relative addressing, is interpreted as a signed value ranging from -128 through 127. The memory address is formed by adding DISP to the contents of either accumulator AC2 (when $xr = 1\emptyset$) or accumulator AC3 (when $xr = 11$).

Indirect addressing consists of first establishing an address in the same manner as direct addressing (by either the base-page, PC relative, or indexed mode). The contents of the memory location at the selected address are then used as the operand address.

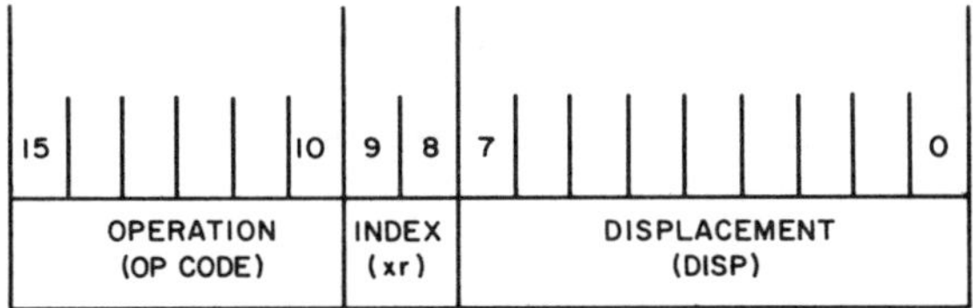

• A program written in National's extended Basic language quickly checks the feasibility of any design scheme and provides assembly-language subroutine calls and direct I/O control.

• The PACE Resident Software Package provides a full set of utility programs, including a macro-assembler.

• A full disc-operating system permits easy handling of large programs.

Hardware support includes a full range of peripherals, memory cards, cables and utility boards, as well as a source-statement translator that can convert older IMP-16 software to PACE software and reduce development time.

Designing with PACE is simple

A good example of a PACE design is an all-digital servo that would typically require four 4-bit up/down counters (74193) and four 4-bit comparators (7485) as well as some control logic to be simulated by a short subroutine.

The logic part of a servo includes a 16-bit position input that is initialized to a zero reference. An external servo element provides one clock

Mne-monic	Format 15	8, 7	disp 	01	Description
Branch and skip instructions					
BOC	0100	cc		disp	Branch-on condition
JMP	000110	xr		disp	Jump
JMP	100110	xr		disp	Jump indirect
JSR	000101	xr		disp	Jump to subroutine
JSR@	100101	xr		disp	Jump to subroutine indirect
RTS	100000	00		disp	Return from subroutine
RTI	011111	00		disp	Return from interrupt
SKNE	1111 r	xr		disp	Skip if not equal
SKG	100111	xr		disp	Skip if greater
SKAZ	101110	xr		disp	Skip if AND is zero
ISZ	100011	xr		disp	Increment and skip if zero
DSZ	101011	xr		disp	Decrement and skip if zero
AISZ	011110	r		disp	Add immediate, skip if zero
Memory data-transfer and operate instructions					
LD	1100 r	xr		disp	Load
LD@	101000	xr		disp	Load indirect
ST	1101 r	xr		disp	Store
ST@	101100	xr		disp	Store indirect
LSEX	101111	xr		disp	Load with sign extended
AND	101010	xr		disp	logic AND
OR	101001	xr		disp	logic OR
ADD	1110 r	xr		disp	Add
SUBB	100100	xr		disp	Subtract with borrow
DECA	100010	xr		disp	Decimal add
Register data-transfer and operate instructions					
LI	010100	r		disp	Load immediate
RCPY	010111	dr	sr	000000	Register copy
RXCH	011011	dr	sr	000000	Register exchange
XCHRS	000111	r	00	000000	Exchange register and stack
CFR	000001	r	00	000000	Copy flags into register
CRF	000010	r	00	000000	Copy register into flags
PUSH	011000	r	00	000000	Push register onto stack
PULL	011001	r	00	000000	Pull stack into register
PUSHF	000011	00	00	000000	Push flags onto stack
PULLF	000100	00	00	000000	Pull stack into flags
RADD	011010	dr	sr	000000	Register add
RADC	011101	dr	sr	000000	Register add with carry
RAND	010101	dr	sr	000000	Register AND
RXOR	010110	dr	sr	000000	Register EXCLUSIVE OR
CAI	011100	r		disp	Complement and add immediate
Shift and rotate instructions					
SHL	001010	r	n	ℓ	Shift left
SHR	001011	r	n	ℓ	Shift right
ROL	001000	r	n	ℓ	Rotate left
ROR	001001	r	n	ℓ	Rotate right
Miscellaneous instructions					
HALT	000000	000	0000000		Halt
SFLG	0011	fc	1	0000000	Set flag
PFLG	0011	fc	0	0000000	Pulse flag

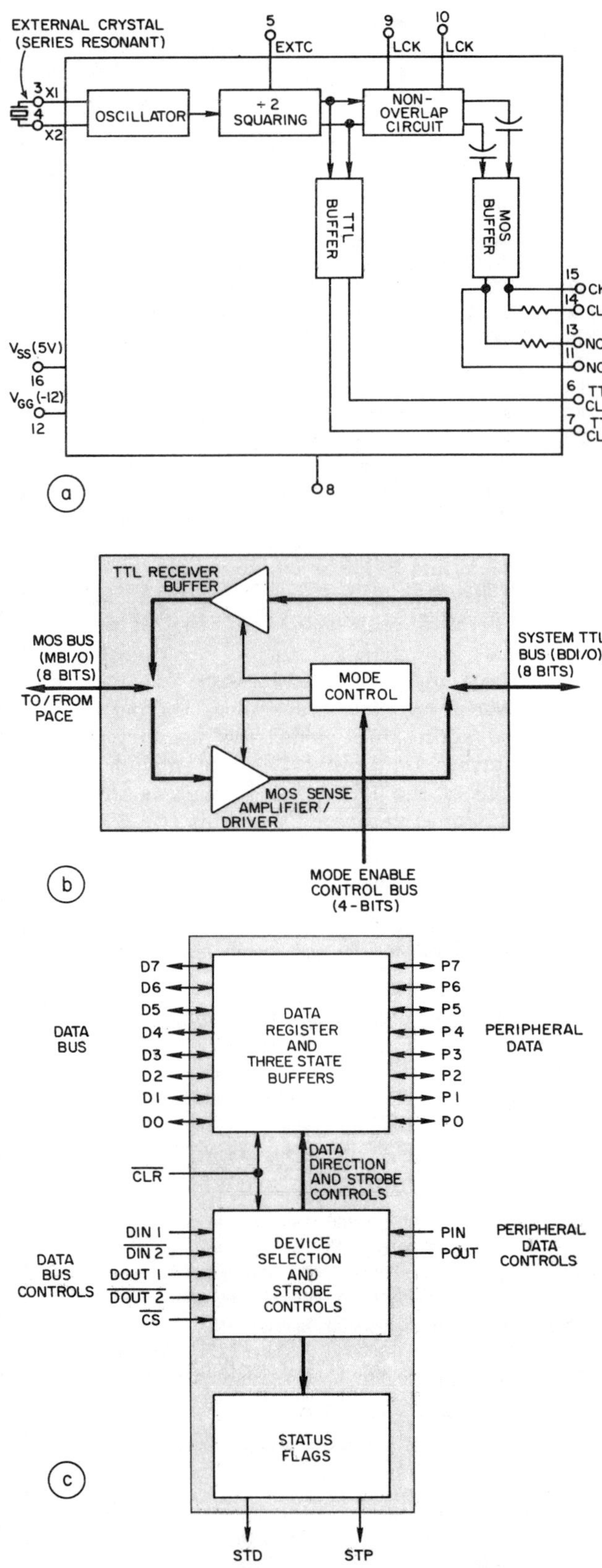

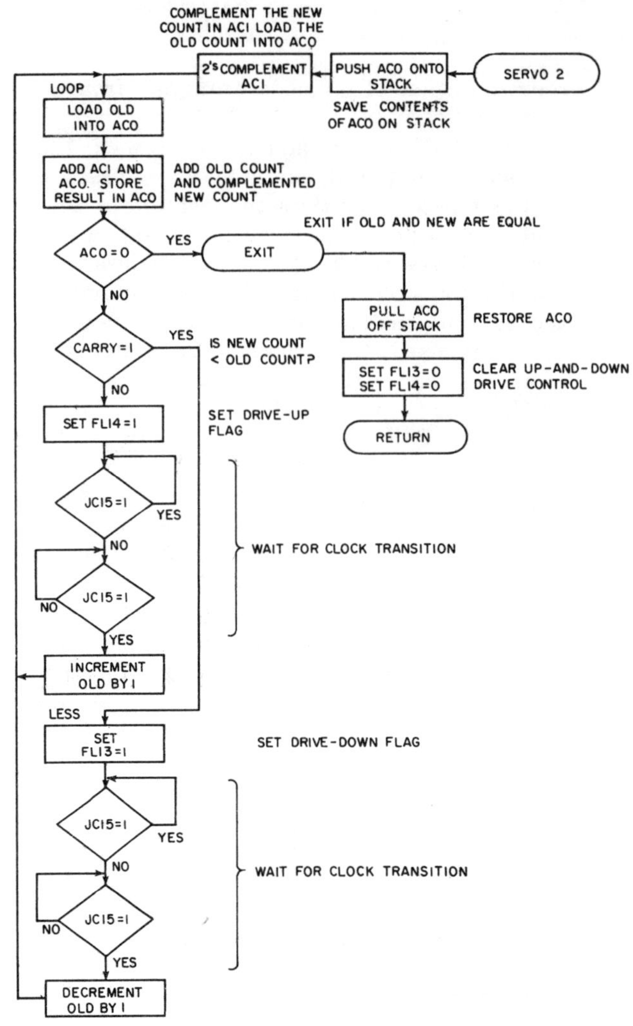


```
 1                    ;           DIGITAL SERVO
 2       0000    AC0    =        0
 3       0001    AC1    =        1
 4       000A    CRY    =        10              ;CARRY
 5       000D    FL13   =        13              ;DRIVE DOWN FLAG
 6       000E    FL14   =        14              ;DRIVE UP FLAG
 7       000F    JC15   =        15              ;CLOCK
 8 0000  6000  A SERVO: PUSH     AC0             ;SAVE AC0 ON STACK
 9 0001  7101  A        CAI      AC1,1           ;2S COMPLEMENT NEW COUNT
10 0002  C113  A LOOP:  LD       AC0,OLD         ;LOAD OLD COUNT INTO AC0
11 0003  6840  A        RADD     AC1,AC0         ;(AC0) -- (AC1) → (AC0)
12 0004  410D  A        BOC      1,EXIT          ;EXIT IF NEW = OLD
13 0005  4A06  A        BOC      CRY,LESS        ;BRANCH IF NEW < OLD
14             ;                NEW COUNT GREATER THAN OLD COUNT
15 0006  3E80  A        SFLG     FL14            ;SET DRIVE UP FLAG
16 0007  4FFF  A        BOC      JC15,.+0        ;WAIT FOR CLOCK TO GO LO
17 0008  4F01  A        BOC      JC15,.+2        ;WAIT FOR CLOCK TO GO HI
18 0009  19FE  A        JMP      .-1             ;
19 000A  8D0B  A        ISZ      OLD             ;INCREMENT OLD BY 1
20 000B  19F6  A        JMP      LOOP            ;CONTINUE ASSUME NO SKIP
21             ;                NEW COUNT LESS THAN OLD COUNT
22 000C  3D80  A LESS:  SFLG     FL13            ;SET DRIVE DOWN FLAG
23 000D  4FFF  A        BOC      JC15,.+0        ;WAIT FOR CLOCK TO GO LO
24 000E  4F01  A        BOC      JC15,.+2        ;WAIT FOR CLOCK TO GO HI
25 000F  19FE  A        JMP      .-1             ;
26 0010  AD05  A        DSZ      OLD             ;DECREMENT OLD BY 1
27 0011  19F0  A        JMP      LOOP            ;CONTINUE IF OLD NOT 0
28 0012  6400  A EXIT:  PULL     AC0             ;RESTORE AC0
29 0013  3D00  A        PFLG     FL13            ;CLEAR DRIVE DOWN FLAG
30 0014  3E00  A        PFLG     FL14            ;CLEAR DRIVE UP FLAG
31 0015  8000  A        RTS                      ;RETURN
32 0016  0000  A OLD:   . WORD   0               ;OLD COUNT
33       0000           . END
```

3. Providing all system timing, the STE delivers both MOS and TTL clocks (a). To buffer both incoming and outgoing data, the BTE can drive up to 30 TTL loads and has three-state outputs to the TTL bus (b). The MILE 8-bit latch element (c) provides the address or data storage for memories and peripheral devices while the μP bus switches from the address mode to the data mode of operation.

4. To make the PACE μP simulate a servo, use one of the JC inputs and two of the flag lines and some of the accumulators (top). The actual simulation program (bottom) requires only about 30 lines of code.

Table 2. System-level support

Model number	Description	Cost (unit qty)
IPC-16P/108	PACE development system with 8 k × 16 memory	$4910.00
IPC-16P/840	PACE disc operating system	$4500.00
IPC-16P/301	PACE low-cost development system with keyboard and display	$ 585.00
IPC-16C/100	PACE CPU card 500-ns cycle	$ 300.00
IPC-16C/001	PACE 1 k × 16 RAM card	$ 170.00
IPC-16C/011	PACE 1 k × 16 RAM common bus card	$ 170.00
IPC-16C/002	PACE 2 k × 16 ROM/PROM card	$ 495.00
IPC-16C/012	PACE 2 k × 16 ROM/PROM common bus card	$ 495.00
IPC-16C/801	Utility wrapped-wire card	$ 32.00
IPC-16P/802	Bus extender cable card	$ 120.00
IPC-16S/101	PACE/IMP cross-assembler	$ 100.00
IPC-16S/102P	PACE Fortran cross-assembler	$ 495.00
IPC-16S/901	PACE resident software package including assemblers, editor, loaders, debugger and diagnostics	from $100.
IPC-16S/902	PACE disc resident software package including assemblers, editor, loader, debugger and diagnostics	$ 200.00
IPC-16S/201	PACE Basic interpreter	$ 100.00
IPC-16A/928	PACE system design manual	*
IPC-16A/927	PACE logic designers guide to TTL equivalents	*
IPC-16S/969Y	PACE assembly-language programming manual	*

* available from local sales office

pulse for each increment of motion in either the up or down direction. With "normal" operation the A > B, A < B and A = B outputs serve to drive the servo element to the position indicated by the 16-bit position input.

If, for example, the position input has a greater value than the output of the counter, the A < B output lets the servo be driven in the up direction by the incoming counter pulses. When the counter has reached its position value, the A < B output goes LOW and the A = B output goes HIGH to stop the servo simulation. The servo will hold its current position until the value of the position input is increased or decreased.

For the flow chart and program listing based on this example (Fig. 4), the following assumptions are made:

■ Specified memory locations are dedicated for the storage of the current and desired servo positions.

■ Accumulator AC1 is used both as an input-data register for desired servo position value and as a working register (along with AC0) to determine when the servo is at the desired position.

■ Input and output assignments are as follows: Clock = JC15, A > B = flag 13 set (drive servo down), A < B = flag 14 (drive servo up) and A = B = flag 14 set and 14 reset (stop servo).

The comparison function is accomplished by taking the two's complement of AC1 after AC0 is stored in the stack and then loading OLD into AC0 and adding the contents of AC0 and AC1. In effect, this comparison function is a standard binary subtraction that does not alter the contents of AC1. If the subtraction's result is zero, the servo is in the desired position. If not, the state of the carry flag indicates whether the servo needs to be driven up (carry = flag reset) or down (carry = flag set).

When the servo must be driven, flag 13 or 14 must be set and the JC15 input tested to detect the positive going clock edge of the pulse input. Upon detection of the positive-going edge, the contents of OLD are incremented or decremented, as appropriate, and the subroutine returns to the loop address. This compare-and-count loop then gets repeated until the servo arrives at the desired position (the contents of OLD are the same as NEW).

When the servo does arrive, bit 0 of AC0 is HIGH, and the compare-and-count loop is terminated by the branch to the EXIT address. The original contents of AC0 then get restored from the stack and flags 13 and 14 get reset to terminate servo action. An RTS instruction can return to the main program.

Using Microprocessors in Minicomputer Systems

DAVID JONES
Senior Electronic Technician,
Los Alamos Scientific Laboratory

E. RAY MARTIN
Staff Physicist,
Los Alamos Scientific Laboratory

You can design a fast, powerful, yet inexpensive minicomputer-based system by including a microprocessor (Fig. 1). Let the μP replace much of the support hardware for the mini, and perform the simpler computer functions, while you reserve the mini itself for complex calculations, data taking and functions too slowly executed by the μP. Consequently, computation—the mini's most powerful capability—will be more readily available to the system. Also, you will avoid the mass of custom-designed interface logic usually needed. You will even be able to use the mini to compile the μP's programs.

All this can be done at a reasonable price. To keep costs down, you must select the right μP and its associated support circuitry. Also, you should use the mini wherever possible for programming, debugging and checking out the system's μP section.

Although the specific mini/micro system to be covered here is for nuclear-safeguards instrumentation, the features to be described are applicable to many mini-based systems—especially in real-time, on-line work. The following is a typical design example.

1. **The over-all system** with PACE on the left, mini and display-scope in the center and terminal at right.

Choosing a microprocessor

Select a suitable μP to link to the mini. The need for efficient programming, simple interrupt servicing, direct memory access (DMA) and compatibility with 16-bit minicomputers—such as Data General's Nova series—makes the 16-bit PACE by National Semiconductor a good choice. In this case, packaging considerations, over-all cost and system efficiency call for the use of chips rather than boards or complete systems.

The chips used in our example are:

- microprocessor (PACE).
- system timing element (STE).
- bidirectional transceiver element (BTE/8).
- address latch element (ALE/16).
- interface latch element (ILE/8).
- random access memory (RAM 256 $\times$ 4).
- programmable read-only memory (PROM 512 $\times$ 8).

All except the PACE and the memories, are available only in hybrid form, but, according to the manufacturer, they will soon be replaced by monolithic versions.

Selecting memory size and structure

Next, examine our memory requirements. The semiconductor RAM storage of a μP system is volatile—programs are lost whenever power is shut down. Hence, ROMs or PROMs are used for permanent storage of instructions. The stored control program is called firmware.

Of course, when using a μP for the control and overhead support of a mini-based system, you don't want to use too much memory. A 4-k word memory is appropriate—using 16-bit words, of course. We can use 2-k of PROM, for firmware, at the bottom of the address space and 2-k of RAM contiguous to the PROM: Then input-output addressing can occupy the high end of the addressing space. And for input-output transfers, you can split page zero (that area which can be directly addressed) between the first 128-PROM

Mnemonic	Operation Code (octal)	Action
AISZ	074000	add immediate, skip if zero
LI	050000	load immediate
CAI	070000	complement and add immediate
JMP	014000	jump
JMP@	114000	jump indirect
JSR	120000	jump to subroutine
JSR@	112000	jump to subroutine indirect
SKG	116000	skip if greater
SKAZ	134000	skip if AND is zero
ISZ	106000	increment and skip if zero
DSZ	126000	decrement and skip if zero
LD@	120000	load indirect
ST@	130000	store indirect
LSEX	136000	load with sign extended
AND	124000	logical AND
OR	122000	logical OR
SUBB	110000	subtract with borrow
DECA	104000	decimal add
SKNE0	170000	skip if ac-0 not equal
SKNE1	172000	skip if ac-1 not equal
SKNE2	174000	skip if ac-2 not equal
SKNE3	176000	skip if ac-3 not equal
LD0	140000	load ac-0
LD1	142000	load ac-1
LD2	144000	load ac-2
LD3	146000	load ac-3
ST0	150000	store ac-0
ST1	152000	store ac-1
ST2	154000	store ac-2
ST3	156000	store ac-3
ADD0	160000	add to ac-0
ADD1	162000	add to ac-1
ADD2	164000	add to ac-2
ADD3	166000	add to ac-3
RTS	100000	return from subroutine
RTI	076000	return from interrupt
BOC0	040000	stack full
	040400	ac-0 = 0
	041000	ac-0 > 0
	041400	ac-0, bit 0 = 1
BOC1	042000	ac-0, bit 1 = 1
	042400	ac-0 ≠ 0
	043000	ac-0, bit 2 = 1
	043400	Contin = 1
BOC2	044000	Link = 1
	044400	IEN = 1
	045000	Carry = 1
	045400	ac-0 < 0
BOC3	046000	OVF = 1
	046400	JC-13 = 1
	047000	JC-14 = 1
	047400	JC-15 = 1
SHL	024000	shift-left
SHR	026000	shift-right
ROL	020000	roll-left
ROR	022000	roll-right

2. **Memory-reference instructions** for the PACE microprocessor showing octal operation codes and action descriptions.

locations and the upper 128 input-output locations.

Letting the mini test and code the μP

Use the mini, since it is available, to check out, program and debug the system's microprocessor-section. Then you won't have to invest in a μP-dedicated data terminal and an extensive control-panel.

It's a good idea to try rough programs in RAM before committing them into firmware. Temporarily substitute 3-k of RAM for the PROM-portion of memory. At start-up, the mini can now load test programs directly into this RAM via DMA. For large-block DMA transfers it is better to halt the PACE than to cycle-steal with the extend feature. After the software is debugged, the mini can punch out a bit-pattern tape for PROM programming.

Easing μP programming with an assembler

Most test routines are so simple that hand-loaded, machine-language instructions aren't too cumbersome. Of course, more substantial tasks will require the use of an assembly language. The resulting program, which converts mnemonic input into binary-bit machine code, is called an assembler. If code is produced by one machine for use on another, the control program for the host computer is called a cross-assembler.

The similarity in hardware of the PACE μP and Nova units—hence the similarity of many of their instructions—eases the job of generating a cross-assembler. Example: Both have four accumulators (with two available for index addressing) and essentially the same addressing modes.

Because of this similarity in addressing modes, the PACE instruction set can be separated conveniently into two parts. The larger part consists of Memory-Reference-type instructions which are the same or nearly the same as Nova's. The smaller part consists of Register-Reference and Miscellaneous-type instructions.

Memory-Reference instructions are the following:

- Register-Reference Immediate.
- Memory Reference Jump, Skip.
- Exchange Register Flags and Stacks.
- Branch.
- Return.
- Memory Data-Transfer.
- Memory Data-Operate.
- Shift and Rotate, slightly modified.

The PACE instruction SHR r, n, l specifies a shift right of n places in register r with the link set, if specified. If instead you use SHR r, n for a shift right of n/2 places in accumulator r and link only if n is odd, the cross-assembler is easier to write.

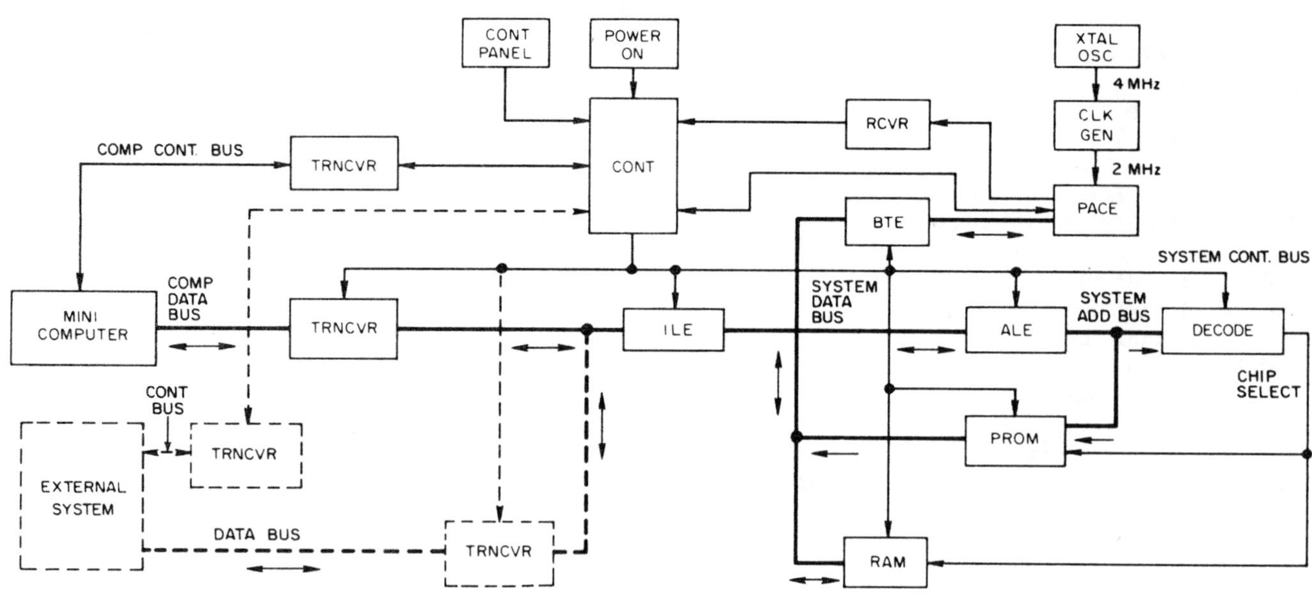

3. **System block diagram** shows data flow and control between mini and μP.

The format of the Memory-Reference-type instructions is:

15......10	9 8	7..............0
operation	index	displacement

This bit format is described in detail on pages 3-2 and 3-3 of the User's Manual.

The Miscellaneous-type instructions are:

- Register to Register Data-Transfer.
- Register to Register Data-Operate (except for CAI).
- Miscellaneous—HALT, SFLG, PUSH F, PULL F.

The cross-assembler must provide separately for each instruction in this category.

The cross-assembler first determines the type of a particular instruction. For the Memory-Reference type, the cross-assembler assigns the proper index and displacement. They are the same as Nova's except for indexed addresses using the program counter, which are one address larger in the PACE.

For the Miscellaneous type, the cross-assembler identifies the particular instruction and the register(s) or flag involved. Then it generates the required code. The list of PACE Memory-Reference instructions shown in Fig. 2 illustrates the procedure.

The cross-assembler occupies approximately 2-k words of the Nova's core.

Designing the logic

The relatively small amount of custom-designed logic needed to interface the PACE to the mini separates functionally as follows:

- *Data-transfer control.* Data passes from the

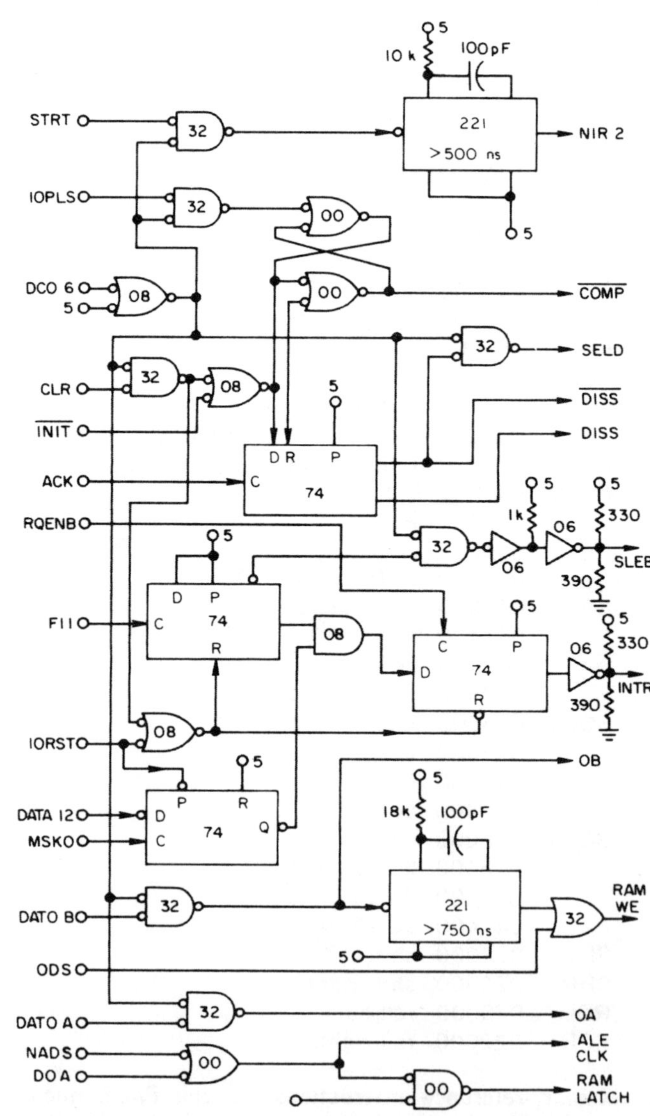

4. **Interrupt circuitry** for programmed transfer of data.

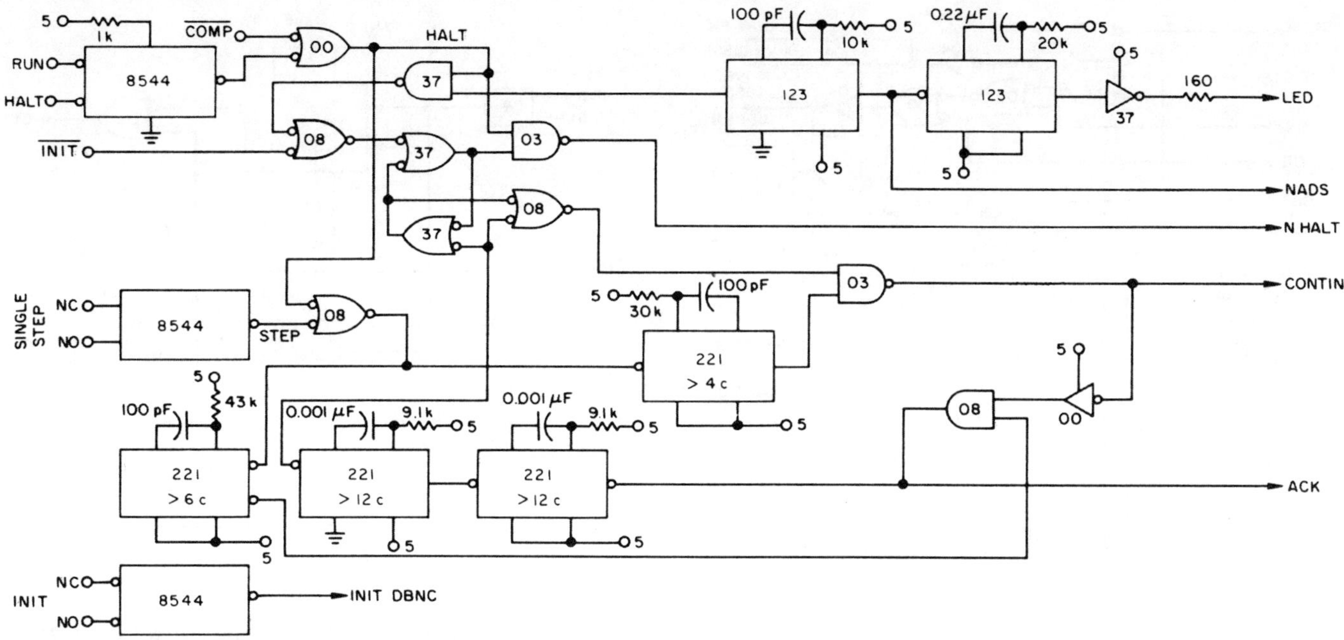

5. Halt/step control logic develops signals for starting, stopping and single-stepping PACE.

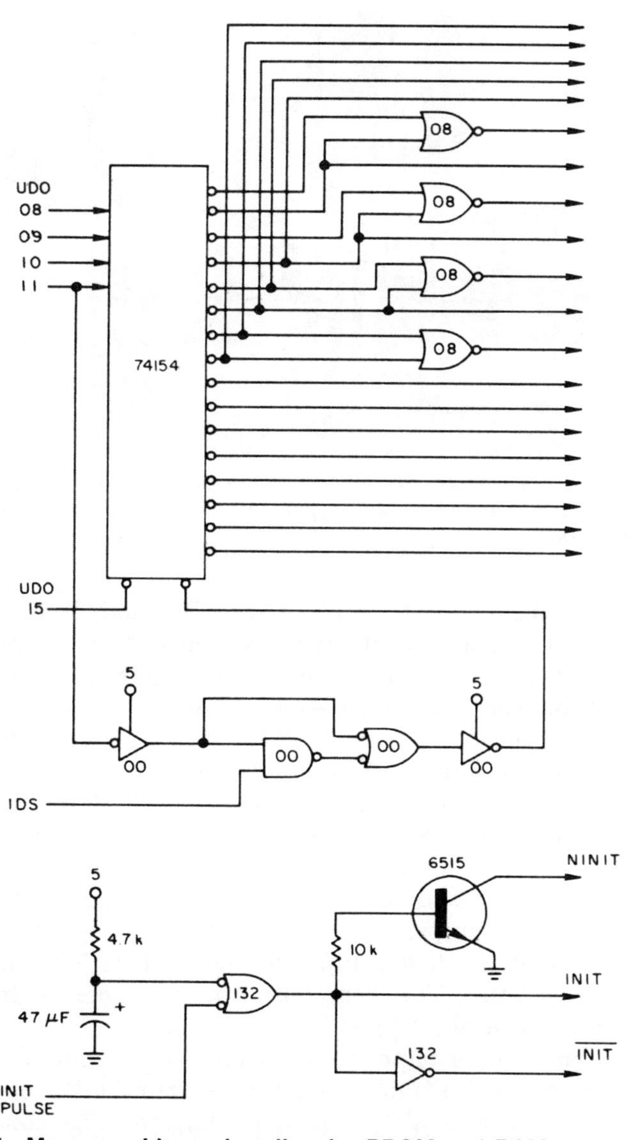

6. Memory address decoding for PROM and RAM.

mini to PACE via DMA, but passes bidirectionally between the μP and mini via programmed interrupts. Fig. 3 shows how the system and its busses handle the data. Fig. 4 describes the circuitry generating the required interrupts.

- *Halt/Step circuitry.* The bidirectional NHALT and CONTIN lines are used to halt or single-step the PACE (see Fig. 5). Caution is needed, however, because these are multiplexed lines. On NHALT, whereas an input halts PACE, an output indicates that a halt has been executed. On CONTIN, whereas an input causes PACE to resume operation, an output acknowledges that PACE is halted. Four one-shots provide correct timing for NHALT and CONTIN.

- *Memory-address decoding.* 2-k of PROM and 2-k of RAM are handled by the logic shown in Fig. 6. Circuitry to prevent writing into PROM is included, but must be disabled when you substitute RAM for PROM. Power-on initializing logic generates the INIT pulse, which resets the internal registers and starts the μP at memory-location ZERO.

- *Device-decode circuitry.* The mini addresses PACE with device-code ZERO (Fig. 7); the PACE addresses the mini with device-code SEVEN. Seven additional device codes are spares in each direction.

- *ILE control.* During a DMA transfer, two delays (see Fig. 7) allow data to pass through the ILE before latching into the ALE.

- *BTE delay circuitry.* The BTE's three-state outputs are put into the open-circuit mode for 300 ns prior to a change in drive direction by the circuitry in Fig. 8. This circuitry eliminates a high-current race caused by internal switching

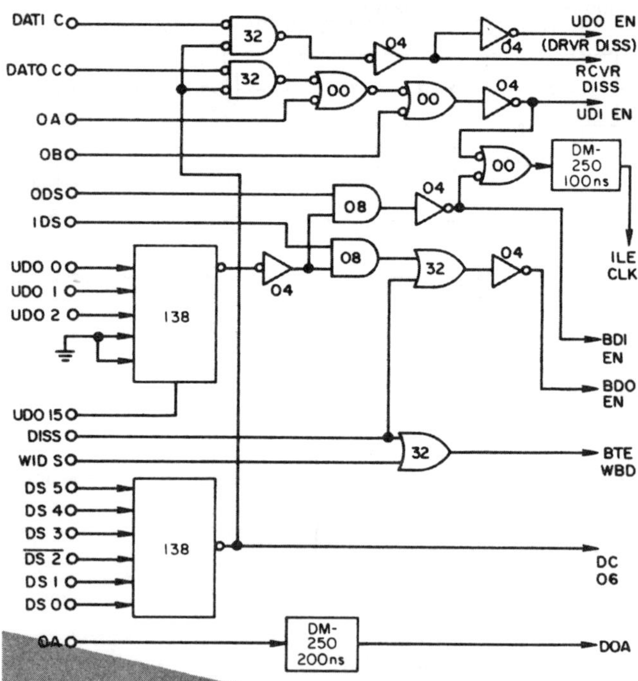

7. **Device decode** and ILE control logic.

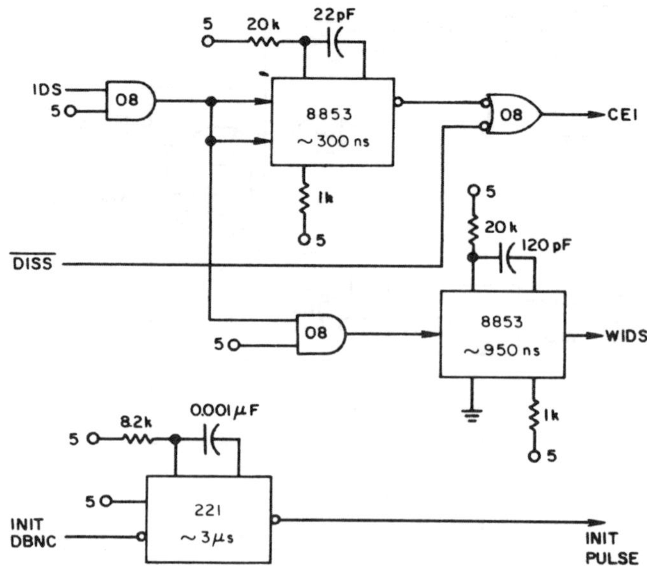

8. **BTE delay circuitry** is easily designed with one-shots.

9. **Microprocessor system hardware** consists of the μP and control panel in the upper bin and the interface in the lower bin.

between MOS and bipolar lines in the hybrids. The delay also allows the slow memory to release the bus before it is granted to the BTEs. The 3-μs one-shot shortens the INIT signal.

The signal sequences during data transfers (Figs. 3, 4) merit closer examination. A DMA data transfer begins with a HALT from the mini. PACE then halts, after completing its current instruction, and outputs an acknowledge that causes the interface to give the mini access to the bus. The mini then sends an address through the ILE, and the address is latched into the ALE and RAM address latches. Next, the mini sends a data word through the ILE into RAM. After the data transfer, the mini sends a continue signal to the μP. Note that PACE has only one bus, which is multiplexed for both addresses and data.

A programmed-interrupt data transfer starts when the sender latches a word into the ILE, and transmits an interrupt (INTR from PACE) to the receiver. When the receiver becomes responsive to the interrupt, it reads the word in the ILE.

The data from the ILE must be identified for either receiver to process it. A two-word format is practical; the first word identifies the data, and the second specifies its value.

No hardware is needed to prevent ambiguous information from appearing in the ILE when both units try to write into it simultaneously. Use a one-bit check in the software—LSB = PACE to mini; MSB = mini to PACE. Consequently, information transfer is limited to 14 bits for the first word only.

A final note about the N HALT line: Contrary to the information in the User's Manual, it produces no output. But since this output would be used only as a run indicator, an updating one-shot on the NADS line—as shown in Fig. 5—can do the job instead. The run indicator now stays on so long as address strobes occur.

The complete hardware for the PACE microprocessor system, including support chips, control panel, custom-designed interfacing and control logic, is shown in Fig. 9. The PACE, with its support chips, is in the upper bin, the interface is in the lower bin and the custom logic is in both bins. The complete control panel is in slot P-13 of the upper bin.

This control panel consists only of a "run" indicator, an "initialize" button, a "run-halt" toggle switch and a "single-step" button. The control panel is used primarily for system-test.

Microprocessors Simplify Industrial Control

ALAN J. WEISSBERGER
Applications Engineer,
National Semiconductor, Santa Clara

An increasingly popular use for LSI microprocessors is in industrial-control applications. The computer chips are cheaper than minicomputers, they're smaller and some are even more flexible.

Already, microprocessors have found their way into warehouse equipment, numerical and process controllers, and manufacturing machines. And future systems might well have microprocessors distributed throughout a plant. Individual processor-chip operations would be coordinated by a centralized minicomputer to form an integrated computer network.

Some of the hurdles

But the use of microprocessors in industrial equipment can entail special design techniques. The rigors of an industrial environment, for example, present several design hurdles. These include noise, physical distance between sources of variables, power consumption and dissipation, I/O interfacing, and future expansion plans.

Ambient electrical noise and line transients that typically occur in plant environments often require special circuitry and components to ensure reliable system operation. CMOS or high-threshold interface logic may be used to obtain adequate power-supply tolerance and noise immunity.

Further, opto-couplers can be employed to transform voltage signals originating in high-noise systems to light waves. These are transmitted through a fiber-optic "pipe" and then converted back to electrical signals. A phototransistor at the receiver detects the presence or absence of light. This simple detection and reconstruction scheme provides complete electrical isolation between the noisy industrial environment, subject to electromechanical radiation, and a noise-sensitive processor. Also, the light wave doesn't require a reference ground, as do electrical signals, which are susceptible to ground loops.

Distributed power supplies offer additional system benefits. Smaller supplies are easy to use and provide a reliability advantage over a centrally located supply. If one supply fails, the system won't shut down. Distributed supplies come in the form of voltage regulators or ferro-resonant supplies.

Cabling costs and noise pickup are high when the process variables are far from the processor. For this reason the variables should be "clustered" around the processor whenever possible. For one or two isolated variables—distances greater than 50 ft.—a two-wire transmitter can be used to convert the voltage to a current and send it along a twisted-pair cable. The same twisted-pair carries the required supply voltage from the processor to the two-wire transmitter. The current is converted back to an input voltage by the use of a precision resistor at the input.

MOS processors coupled with CMOS or low-power TTL logic minimize power consumption, dissipation and cooling requirements. This is an important consideration when physical size is limited or battery back-up operation is needed.

Interface logic and signal-conditioning circuitry are necessary for analog and digital I/O, control, timing, event counting, condition sensing and communication. Analog-scaling circuitry is usually needed to convert the output from a transducer, thermocouple or strain gauge to one that is compatible with an a/d converter. Low-level or high-level analog multiplexers may be required depending on the a/d input-voltage ranges. Voltage inputs or outputs must be converted to ONE and ZERO levels for the selected processor. In many cases, control can be simplified by the use of strobe or timing signals generated by the processor. Control-flag outputs provided on the microprocessor can be used, for example, to turn on a valve actuator, turbine, generator, pump, or to stop a motor via program control.

External event counters, interval timers and real-time clocks can be used to keep track of events and inform the processor when service is required. The processor can directly sense vari-

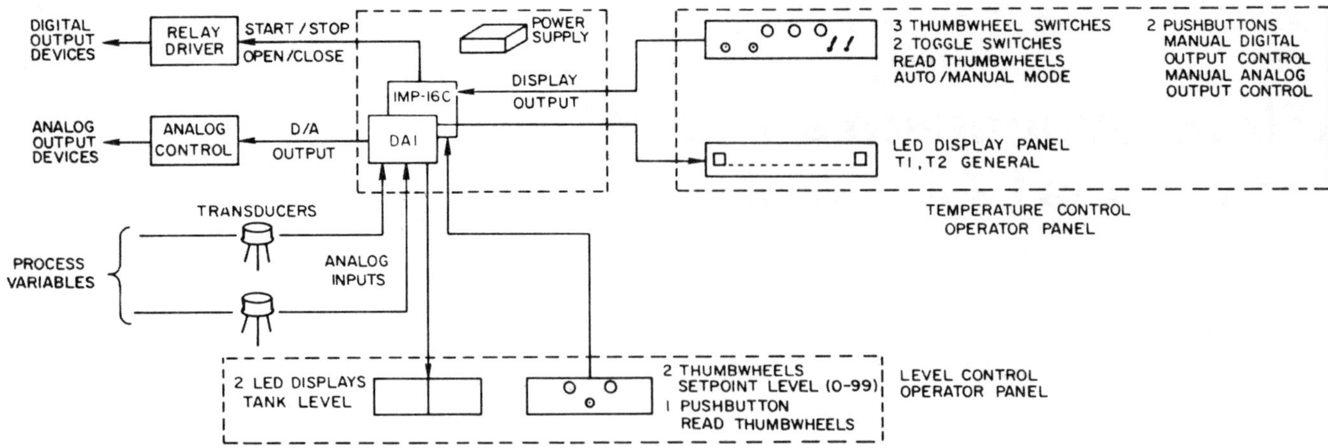

1. **A data-acquisition system** consists of two 8-1/2 × 11-in. PC boards: one for the IMP-16C microprocessor and the other for data-acquisition interface circuitry (DAI). The system uses two 256-word PROMs.

ous conditions by using branch-condition inputs. The status of a process loop and the completion of an a/d conversion are examples. A conditional branch or test-and-skip instruction checks the condition and specifies a memory location to branch to if the condition is true.

Communication requirements can be met with line drivers, line receivers, modems (when distance is over 10,000 ft.) or more elaborate communication controllers.

In the design of a microprocessor-based control system, distributed-task partitioning and software modularity are of paramount importance. If control points are added or removed homogeneously from a modularly designed system the impact on software will be minimal; the same routines and algorithms still apply. However if the data load exceeds the processor's capability or different control points or process variables are added, the problem becomes more complicated. One approach expands the number of microprocessors and redistributes control points and functions. Software complexity is then minimized along with system program and debug time.

A modular data-acquisition system can be built on two 8-1/2 × 11-in. PC boards (Fig. 1). A data-acquisition-interface (DAI) board contains analog and digital circuitry, and it simplifies the exchange of data and control signals to and from the microprocessor board (National Semiconductor's IMP-16C, a 16-bit unit). The microprocessor couples to pressure and temperature IC transducers.

Sensing the process variables

Process variables are sensed by the transducers and sent to the DAI board either directly or by means of two-wire transmitters, such as the LH0045. The DAI multiplexes the analog in-put signals and converts them to digital data which go to the microprocessor. The DAI also converts digital control signals from the processor to analog signals and sends them to the analog control points.

Changes in temperature and fluid level are two independent processes. The microprocessor receives the digitally encoded variables from the DAI and monitors the process via a program stored in PROMs on the microprocessor card. The temperature can be controlled either by this firmware program (auto mode) or by operator intervention through a local operator panel (manual mode). Tank-fluid level is controlled by operator entry of a setpoint level at a remote operator panel. The program then regulates pumps to achieve the entered setpoint.

Both operator panels consist of thumbwheel switches, pushbuttons, and LED displays. They are connected directly to the DAI and are serviced through CPU interrupts or by the testing of status conditions in the program. The CPU activates on/off and analog control points through relay drivers or power transistors.

Originally the system performed only temperature regulation. The incorporation of level sensing and pump control illustrates the minimal changes and fast redesign possible with a microprocessor. The firmware program was revised to acquire, process, and display the tank-fluid level and to control the pumps. The complete program is less than 256 words long and it resides in two PROMs.

The major hardware change was the substitution of a 4-to-16 decoder (Model 74154) for a 3-to-8 decoder (7442) to handle the increased number of functions. Other changes involved additional transistor circuitry to drive the pumps, scale the analog input, and decouple the control signals. All revisions took only one man-week to design, build and check. An equivalent hardwired

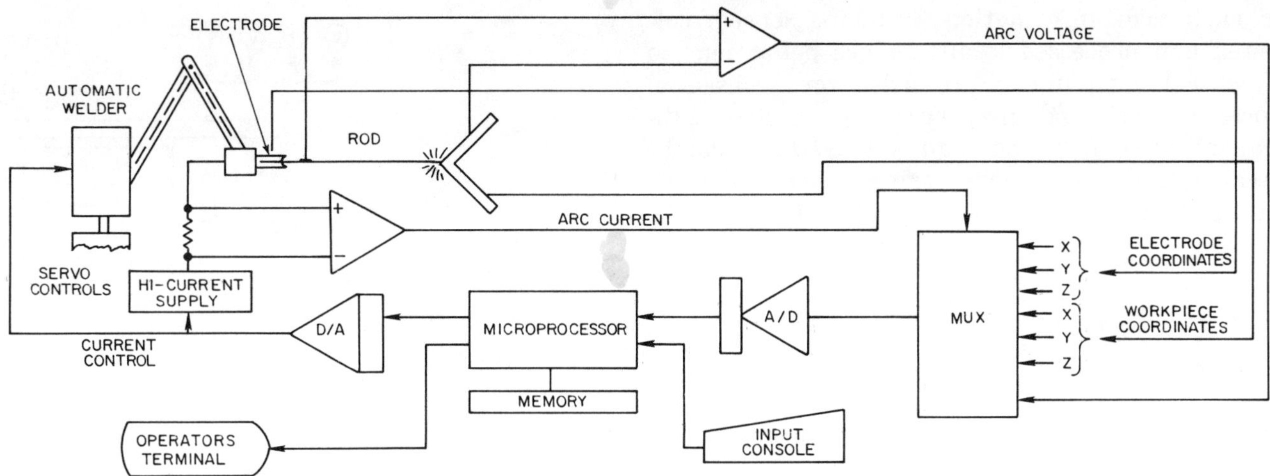

2. **A microprocessor forms the basis** for an automated manufacturing machine that welds and rivets.

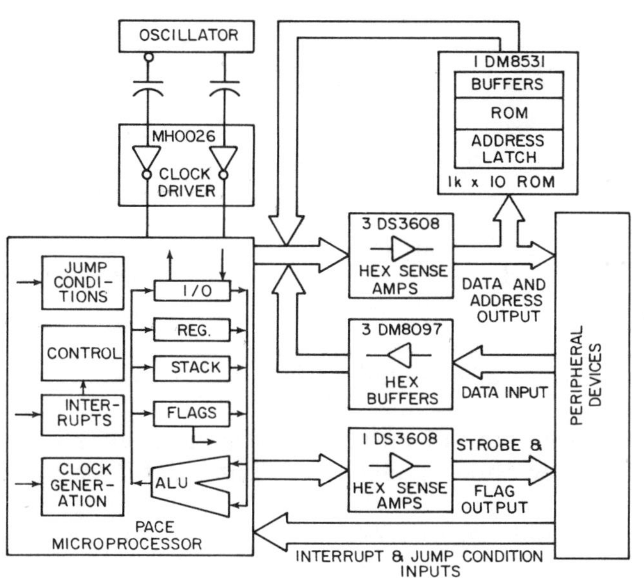

3. **Single-chip 16-bit microprocessors,** such as National's PACE chip, allow systems to be built with a minimal number of components.

control system would have taken many weeks to dismantle, rebuild and rewire.

Many relatively expensive analog components can be eliminated by the use of digital techniques. For example, RAM memory locations or registers internal to the microprocessor are used as programmable timers in the data-acquisition system described previously. Each analog variable to be scanned is assigned a memory location. These timer locations are initially set to a value proportional to the variable's response time.

At periodic intervals, an external oscillator interrupts the microprocessor. As a result, each timer is decremented and tested for zero (DSZ instruction) to determine if it is time to scan the variable. If it is, the corresponding subroutine is executed. The interrupt timer hardware consists of a D-type flip-flop (Model 7474) that saves the interrupt request from the oscilla-

tor. This prevents loss of the timer interrupt when the CPU is busy servicing another interrupt. The oscillator and flip-flop can be used to regulate any number of timers by use of DSZ instruction for each RAM timer.

Automatic welding and riveting

Another plant application employs a microprocessor in an automatic welder and riveter (Fig. 2). Both these systems require precise knowledge of the X, Y, and Z coordinates of both the workpiece and the rod or rivet tip. In the welding operation, the rod must be maintained at a precisely controlled distance from the weld surface: if the rod is too close, it sticks; if it is too far away, an open weld (or no weld at all) results.

By monitoring the current through the arc and voltage between the rod and workpiece, the microprocessor maintains precise, real-time, distance control. Similarly, the riveter head should exert the correct pressure on the workpiece, to prevent the rivet from being too loose or breaking during the fastening process. By monitoring the riveter head pressure against the work surface, the processor maintains it in the proper position at all times.

For process-control applications requiring a minimum number of component parts, new single-chip 16-bit microprocessors can be used. For example, National's Processing and Control Element (PACE) provides 16-bit instructions that can operate on 8 or 16-bit data length words (Fig. 3.). The benefits of this approach are lowered costs and decreased system size and dissipation.

A minimum microprocessor system could be installed at unmanned sites, such as a natural gas pipeline, water or power-distribution system, or an environmental or weather-monitoring station.

In each case, information would be sensed, collected and processed locally before being sent to a central computer or recorded on a cassette. Local control and preprocessing reduces data transmission costs and improves system security because only tested and verified data are sent. These systems could also run calibration and diagnostic tests of the remote instrumentation.

Plant security monitor

Single-chip 16-bit microprocessors can also replace a minicomputer or multiple dedicated microprocessors in complex control and data-processing applications. One example is a plant security monitoring system (Fig. 4) that monitors and, in some instances, controls an entire plant's operation.

One CPU chip acts as a data-acquisition/alarm scanner, while another CPU forms a central control/acknowledgement terminal. The functions monitored are plant power (peak demand, total consumption and output) and environmental quality (air contaminants, temperature and air flow). Various transducers, thermocouples and sensing devices measure the required analog variables and provide inputs to an analog multiplexer. The CPU scans these input points at preselected time intervals by supplying an address to the analog-multiplexer and starting the a/d conversions.

When the conversion is completed, data are read, processed, and checked against alarm limits. Critical deviations from normal operating conditions are detected and alarms are sent to the control/acknowledgement terminal. The CPU at the terminal formats and routes the alarm data to an operator's display panel. The operator on duty observes the detected alarm and takes the necessary steps to correct the problem.

Alarms corresponding to "crisis" situations, can be detected directly by limit switches, circuit-continuity breaks or by the manual depression of a button. Examples include floods, fire, burglary or accidents. These conditions require immediate

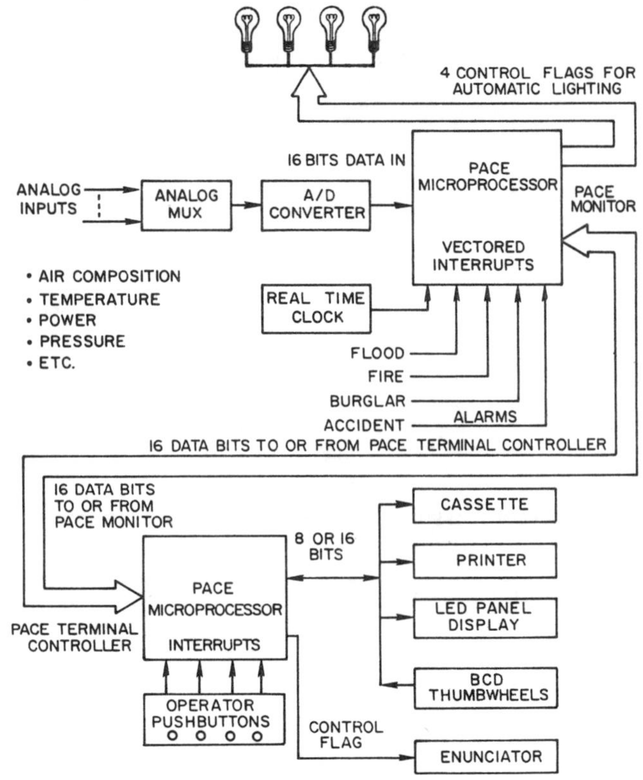

4. **A plant-security monitor** employs two PACE chips. The one at the top acquires data, while the other performs terminal operations.

attention and would therefore be assigned as priority vector interrupts in the CPU monitor. The sounding of an annunciator horn at the control terminal guarantees immediate operator notification.

In addition to monitoring chores, one or more simple control functions could be provided. For automatic light control, a real-time clock generates interrupt signals at fixed, preset, intervals. The processor recognizes the time of each interrupt, and it can dim the lights or turn them off to conserve electricity. Light-control commands employ flag bits provided by the CPU chip. Another function might be the temperature control of the building through the regulation of heaters and air conditioners.

SECTION VIII
Designing with the IMP Chip Set

Before the introduction of PACE and other 16-bit microprocessors, engineers who needed word lengths longer than 8 bits were forced to use either a minicomputer or a "bit-slice" chip set such as National Semiconductor's IMP. The most popular configuration, the IMP-16, requires five chips—four 4-bit slices plus a control chip. Today, we find that much of the useful literature on microprocessor applications specifies the IMP-16 or IMP-8. Though the PMOS IMP chips are rarely considered for new designs, many of the techniques described in the articles are easily transferred to other microprocessors, such as PACE.

The architecture of the IMP-16 simplifies microprogramming. The first article explains how and why this is done. The other articles use IMP systems to illustrate solutions to such common problems as fast multiplication, interfacing with analog circuits, and interfacing with data displays.

Microprogramming Extends Microprocessor Capabilities

GEORGE REYLING, JR.
Project Manager, National Semiconductor Corp.,
Santa Clara

Microprogramming techniques offer designers many advantages: They allow an LSI-microprocessor system to be tailored to a specific application. They also permit the same hardware to be optimized for two dissimilar applications, such as text manipulation and process control.

Any microprocessor has advantages over hardwired logic. For example, a microprocessor-controlled benchtop tester might be programmed to test a family of MSI integrated circuits. Then by a change of programs, the same hardware could be used to test a different class of circuits, such as memories.

But microprogramming extends the programmable characteristic one level further (see box). It represents one of several large-computer features that have been incorporated into current or planned LSI processors. Others include large register arrays, multiprocessing and virtual memory. However, of all the new capabilities, microprogramming appears to have the most universal application.

Some of the benefits

Increased execution speed represents one of the major benefits of microprogramming. Designers can achieve a more efficient or more extensive instruction set. Other benefits include a proprietary design that cannot be duplicated easily, an instruction set tailored to reduce system memory requirements, and possible emulation of other computers.

In addition, basic features of the system architecture can be modified. These include data length, register allocation, interrupt structure and data input-output operations. And sometimes the entire application program can be written at the microprogram level. Thus it's possible to eliminate the memory required to store machine instructions, the time needed to access and decode them, and the registers required to address and store them.

Increased speed leads directly to improved system throughput, or system response time. An

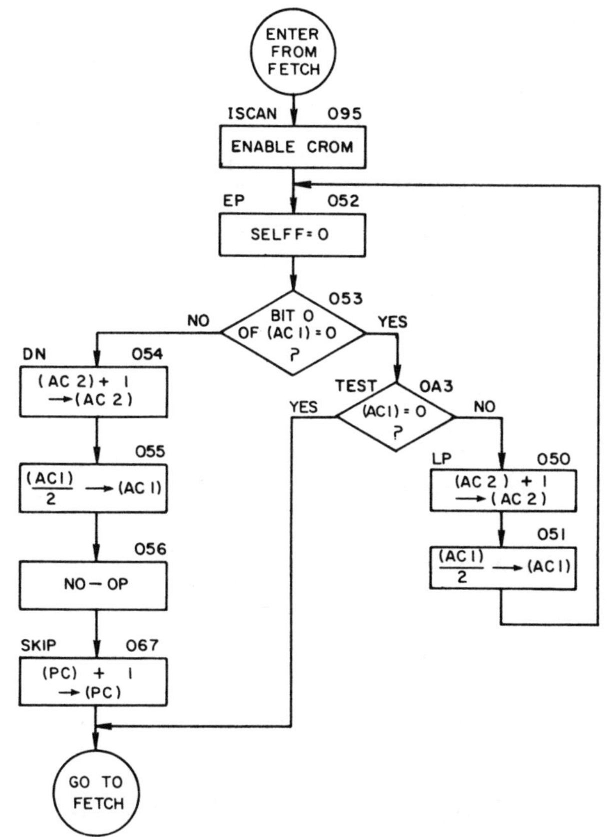

1. **The flow chart outlines an interrupt-scan routine** (ISCAN) that can be microcoded into a single machine instruction. A series of test and skip operations follow a clearing of the select flag (SELFF = 0). Register AC1 should be loaded with the interrupt-select status word, and AC2, with the base address of a pointer array for the service routines. PC refers to the program counter.

important response-time parameter in many systems is the total time required to detect an interrupt, to identify the interrupting device and to branch to the device's service routine. Without microprogramming, this time can become excessive when polling techniques are used, and when the system employs a large number of interrupting devices.

For example, the following interrupt scheme prevails in some applications that use a 16-bit

```
000   000000   *ISCAN   INTERRUPT SCAN INSTRUCTION
000   000000   *
000   000000   *        AC1 = INT STATUS WORD
000   000000   *        AC2 = STARTING ADDRESS OF INTERRUPT TABLE MINUS ONE
000   000000   *               (OR CURRENT INTERRUPT SCAN ADDRESS).
000   000000   *        IF AC1 = 0 THERE IS NO CHANGE IN AC1 OR AC2 AND THE NEXT INST
000   000000   *               IS EXECUTED.
000   000000   *        IF AC1 .NE. 0 THEN AC1 IS SHIFTED RIGHT UNTIL A 1 IS SHIFTED
000   000000   *               OUT OF BIT 0. THE SHIFT COUNT IS ADDED TO AC2 AND THE
000   000000   *               NEXT INSTRUCTION IS SKIPPED.
000   000000   *
095   000000            ORG X'95
095   000000   *        ASSEMBLER DIRECTIVE SETS MICROPROGRAM COUNTER TO HEX ADDRESS 95.
095   229405   ISCAN    B        EP,RE
096   000000   *        LOC X'95 IS THE ENTRY POINT FOR ISCAN.
096   000000   *        BRANCH TO THE LOCATION LABELLED EP, ENABLE CROM FOR EXECUTION.
050   000000            ORG X'50
050   00DB40   LP       ADD,AC2,,AC2   CIN
051   000000   *        INCREMENT THE CONTENTS OF AC2 (REGISTER 6)
051   351610            OR,,AC1,AC1    SHR
052   000000   *        SHIFT THE CONTENTS OF AC1 (REGISTER 5) RIGHT ONE BIT.
052   00A290   EP       RFLG,SELFF,AC1    OR,CMPA    DC WITH 46(ALSO 42,56)
053   000000   *        CLEAR THE SELECT CONTROL FLAG (SO THE LINK IS NOT INCLUDED
053   000000   *            IN SHIFTS). PLACE THE COMPLEMENTED CONTENTS OF AC1 ON THE
053   000000   *            RESULT BUS SO BIT ZERO MAY BE TESTED.
053   2518C4            B,BIT0         TEST       AC1 ON R BUS
054   000000   *        IF BIT ZERO OF THE RESULT OF THE PREVIOUS MICROINSTRUCTION
054   000000   *            IS TRUE, BRANCH TO THE LOCATION LABELLED TEST (OTHERWISE
054   000000   *            NEXT ADDRESS). PLACE THE CONTENTS OF AC1 ON THE R BUS.
054   00DB40   DN       ADD,AC2,,AC2   CIN         DC WITH 50               DC
055   000000   *        INCREMENT THE CONTENTS OF AC2.
055   351610            OR,,AC1,AC1    SHR                                   DC
056   000000   *        SHIFT THE CONTENTS OF AC1 RIGHT ONE BIT.
056   00A290            RFLG,SELFF,AC1    OR,CMPA    REQD FOR DC AT 52       DC
057   000000   *        CAUSES THE SAME FUNCTION AS THE INSTRUCTION AT LOCATION 52, BUT
057   000000   *            IS INCLUDED AS AN EFFECTIVE NO-OP TO ALLOW PHYSICAL
057   000000   *            MINIMIZATION OF THE MICROPROGRAM STORAGE PLA.
057   002748   SKIP     ADD,PC,,PC     CIN,IF                               DC
058   000000   *        INCREMENT THE CONTENTS OF THE PROGRAM COUNTER AND BRANCH
058   000000   *            TO THE INSTRUCTION FETCH ROUTINE.
0A3   000000            ORG X'A3
0A3   22814C   TEST     B,NREQ0    LP,IF
0A4   000000   *        BRANCH TO LOCATION 50 (LABELLED LP) IF THE RESULT OF THE
0A4   000000   *            PREVIOUS MICROINSTRUCTION WAS ZERO. OTHERWISE BRANCH TO
0A4   000000   *            THE INSTRUCTION FETCH ROUTINE.
```

2. **The assembly-language listing** details the microcoded scan instruction outlined in Fig. 1.

What is microprogramming?

In a microprogrammed processor, operations on the fundamental register-transfer level can be programmed. These basic operations are the elements of conventional machine instructions.

With minicomputers or large-scale computers, microprogramming employs a single high-speed memory whose outputs control the data paths in the systems either directly or through decoding logic. This memory is then programmed—in a manner analogous to conventional machine or assembly-language coding—to provide the functions needed for the processor's instruction set.

The microprogram provides a "fetch" phase to form an address, to access the machine instruction from the system memory (external to the CPU) and store it in the CPU instruction register. Also the microprogram has an "interpret" or "execute" phase to carry out the operations specified by the instruction. Microprogramming techniques can be extended to other programmable storage means besides conventional memories and to systems that include a number of programmable control sections operating in parallel or in a hierarchy.

In the case of microprocessors, microprogrammable units probably have evolved as much from programmable logic arrays for the control section of calculators as it has from an extension of conventional microprogramming techniques. In fact two current microprogrammable microprocessors use programmable arrays, rather than conventional ROMs for microprogram storage.

microprocessor (the IMP-16) from National Semiconductor, Santa Clara, Calif.: An interrupt causes the processor to issue a command to all devices to supply simultaneously their interrupt-request status over an assigned bit on the system data bus. The microprocessor scans the resulting 16-bit data word (if you assume 16 or fewer devices can interrupt) to determine which devices are interrupting and then services them. To perform this operation, a routine, consisting of shift and test instructions, requires 32 memory locations and takes 530 μs to scan all 16 bits.

But with a microcoded version of a single machine instruction, the same operation occurs in 112 μs. A flow chart of the microprogram appears in Fig. 1, and the listing is shown in Fig. 2. (The microcoded instruction, along with a variety of others, comes in an optional chip for the IMP-16.)

Another example occurs with the multiply function. The machine-instruction version of this routine requires 11 memory locations and executes in 678 μs (not including system memory-access delays or subroutine call and return delays). However, the microcoded version executes in 171 μs, for a 4:1 speed improvement. The ratio approaches 6:1 in a system with a 1-μs memory when the multiply routine is used as a subroutine and memory-cycle delays are included.

Typically, microprograms provide direct improvements in microprocessor performance. However, the technique can be employed indirectly to monitor system operation. Information obtained from the monitor microprogram can then be used to improve processor efficiency.

For example, a microprogram might be written to count the number of executions of each instruction in an application. The resulting information forms the basis for improvements in system throughput. Changes in the microcode for each instruction can be evaluated, and the effects of new instructions can be estimated.

Some of the problems

The heightened development costs and increased development times represent the major disadvantages of microprogramming. Development times increase because two program levels are encountered—one at the micro-instruction level and one at the machine-instruction level.

Furthermore the microprogram development is more complex. It requires a very detailed knowledge of the internal logic and timing of the microprocessor. And when machine instructions are changed from the standard set, software development aids offered by the manufacturer can no longer be used.

One way to cut down on some of these costs is to obtain an initial design that uses the manufac-

turer's fixed instruction set. Then an additional control chip can be microcoded to provide tailored instructions. This method also allows use of available software development aids.

The cost of a custom-masked control chip is considerably higher than that for a read-only memory, primarily because of the increased complexity. As a result, total over-all costs tend to discourage use of microprogramming in low-volume applications or experimental system designs. However, microprogram development systems are being offered for these applications.

Which micros are microprogrammable?

LSI microprocessors that are microprogrammable have been developed by American Microsystems of Santa Clara, Calif., and Computer Automation of Newport Beach, Calif., in addition to National Semiconductor. Other current microprocessors could undoubtedly be considered microprogrammable, but they have not been so promoted. And still other LSI processors expected shortly are described as microprogrammable.

Microprogrammable processors generally employ two basic LSI chips. A complete central-processing unit is formed by the addition of standard ICs for clock generation, data buffering and control.

One of the two chips, dedicated to system control, contains the microprogram storage and control logic. Generally called a CROM (control read-only memory), it accesses the correct microcoded routine for each machine instruction fetched, sequences through the microroutine, and provides the data-manipulation control signals to the second basic chip. This second chip, sometimes called an RALU (register and arithmetic logic unit), provides data storage and processing. It comes in a bit-slice configuration, so that several can be combined to form processors with word lengths that are multiples of the basic bit-slice length.

A block diagram of a 16-bit system using National Semiconductor's IMP chips appears in Fig. 3. The RALU provides a 4-bit slice of each of the following functions: seven data registers, a four-function ALU with complementing input, a data shifter, a status register, a 16-word last-in first-out stack and an input-output register. Up to eight of these chips can be used to build processors whose word lengths are multiples of four bits. All RALUs operate in parallel under control of the CROM to form a synchronous parallel processor.

The operational characteristics of the processor are primarily determined by a microprogram stored in the CROM. The microprogram specifies the assignment of the seven RALU registers, the instruction set used by the processor, and the

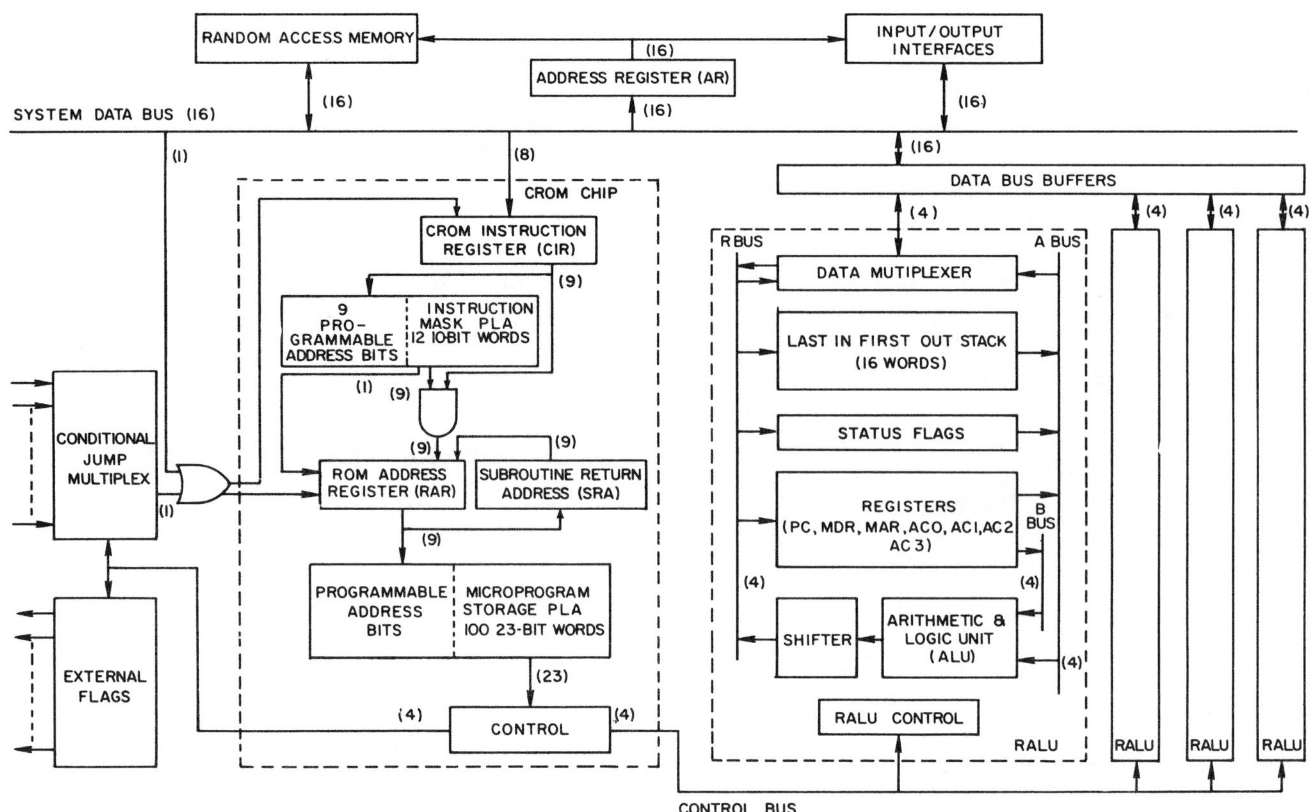

3. **A 16-bit LSI microprocessor** employs two basic building-block chips. The control read-only memory (CROM) contains the microprogram and control logic for the second chip, a register and arithmetic-logic unit (RALU) that processes data. From National Semiconductor, the unit also uses PLAs in the CROM.

timing and function of the control signals in the processor interface. It also makes possible the different word lengths that can be built with the RALU.

The CROM contains an instruction register that holds the current machine instruction to be executed. Also a programmable logic array (PLA) generates an instruction mask that is logically ANDed with the instruction microprogram address. The address provides the correct sequence of microcode for the current machine instruction.

Another PLA, with a capacity of 100 microinstructions, stores the microcode. The use of PLAs simplifies the translation of machine instructions to starting addresses, and it provides increased efficiency in the encoding and higher speed execution of some micro-instruction sequences.

Computer Automation's microprocessor chips, custom ICs contained in the company's Naked Mini product, resemble the IMP chips (Fig. 4). The 4-bit data-processing chip contains an arithmetic and logic unit, a file of seven data registers, status flags and an input-output interface. The control chip provides an instruction register, a sequence register and control logic plus a PLA for microprogram storage.

A significant architectural difference from the IMP control chip exists in the microprogram PLA addressing. In the Computer Automation chip, the PLA controls these functions: translation of instruction op codes to micro-routine addresses, testing of branch conditions and sequencing of micro-instructions. This provides higher-speed microprogram execution in some instances. However, a large PLA address decoding section is required.

The chip set proposed by American Microsystems differs somewhat from the other two (Fig. 5). Specifically the data-processing chip is an 8-bit slice and the control chip uses a read-only memory, rather than a PLA, for program storage. Also the microprogram capability appears to be intended primarily for the application program. However, the capability can also be used for machine instructions.

The 8-bit RALU chip provides 48 registers that can be employed as stacks or as general registers. The MIR (micro-instruction ROM) chip contains a 512-word memory, a seven-level microprogram address stack, and multilevel interrupt logic.

Developing microprograms

Ideally microprogram-level changes should have a short turn-around. This rules out mask-programmed control chips. Instead the functions

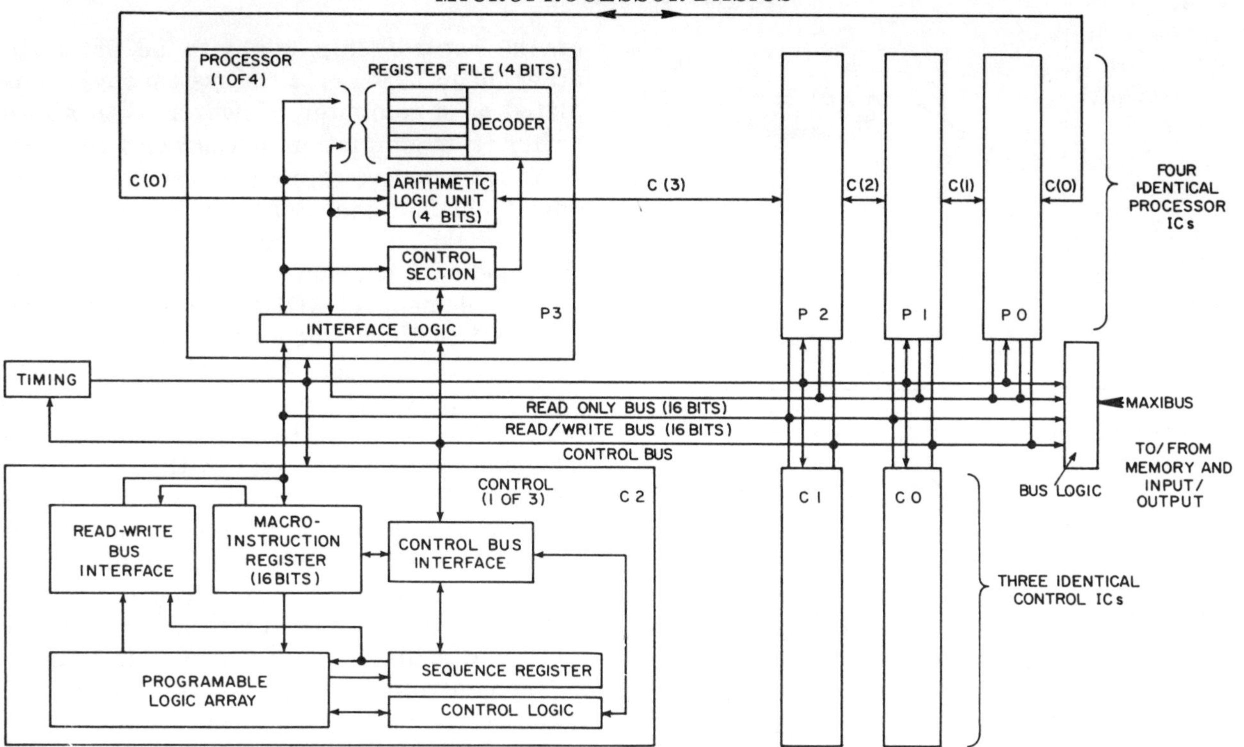

4. Custom microprocessor chips are used in Computer Automation's Naked Mini/LSI. The chips resemble the National Semiconductor's IMP series, in that one IC is devoted to data processing under the control of the second chip. However, the control chip has been organized for higher speed at a sacrifice in chip area.

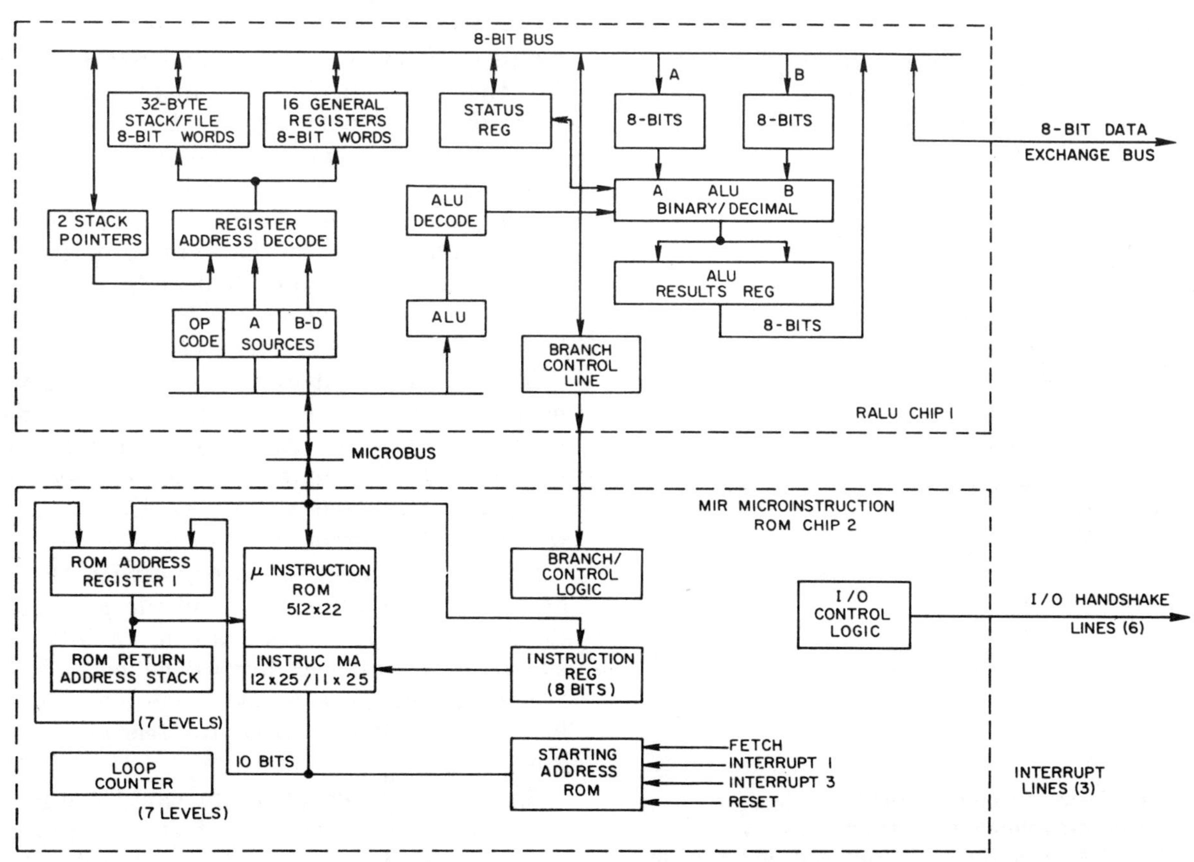

5. Another microprogrammable unit has been proposed by American Microsystems. Unlike the other units, this one employs an 8-bit slice, rather than 4 bits, and the control chip uses a ROM instead of a PLA.

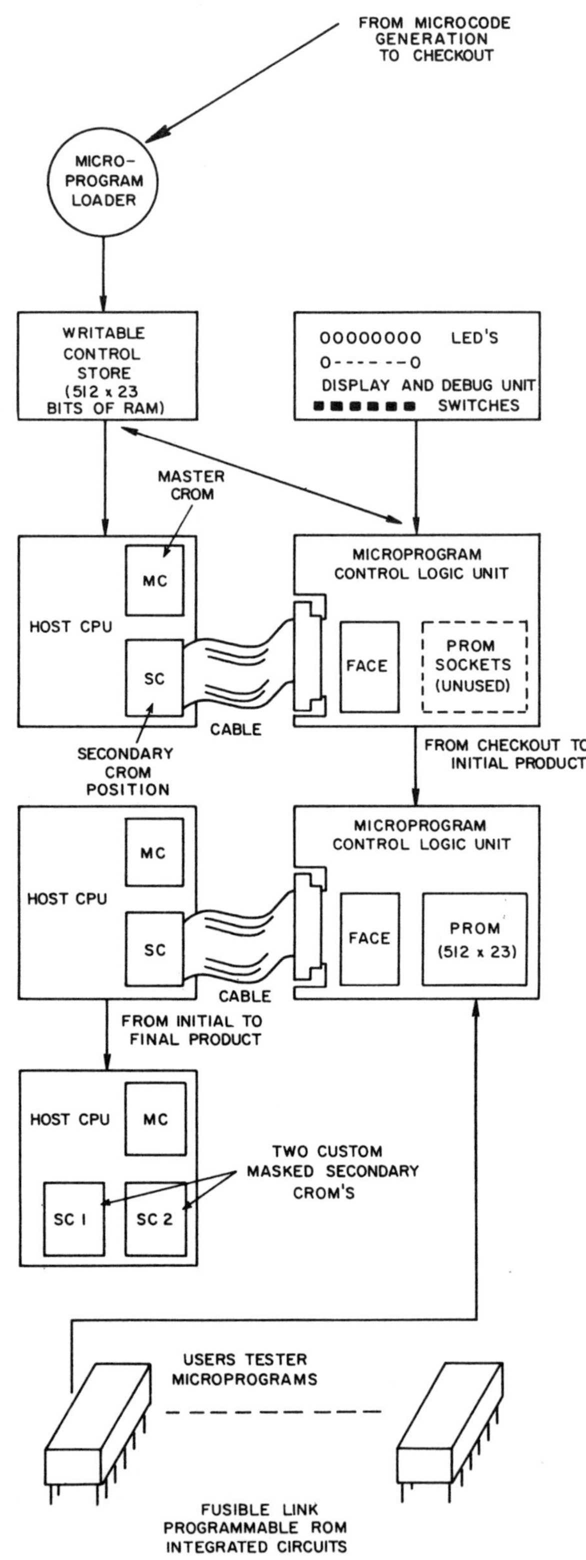

6. One development system for field microprogramming can be used in low-volume applications. The system employs a writable-control store, control-logic unit and display and debug unit. The FACE (field-alterable control element) chip in the control-logic unit constitutes the heart of the system. Functionally similar to a CROM, the FACE chip uses external memory for the microprogram store.

of the control chip ought to be obtained with other forms of logic, or the system ought to be simulated on a computer. However, both approaches suffer from simulation inaccuracies and high cost.

An alternative approach, presently available only from National Semiconductor, uses a modified CROM. Functionally identical to a CROM, the modified version is called a field-alterable control element (FACE). The chip differs from a CROM in that it doesn't contain the microprogram store. Rather, external RAMs, ROMs or pROMs are employed.

FACE represents the key element of a microprogram development system that can be applied economically to low-volume applications or for program development prior to specification of a custom CROM for high-volume applications. The complete development system consists of a microprogram control-logic unit, a writable control store and a display and debug unit (Fig. 6).

The control-logic unit contains the FACE chip and directly replaces a CROM. Optional programmable ROMs can be obtained to store the designer's microprogram. Also ROM inhibit logic permits memory bank switching, if needed. Other facilities simplify the mapping or transformation of instruction operation codes into microprogram addresses.

The writable-control store (WCS) consists of 512-words by 23-bits of high-speed, bipolar read/write memory. A serial "handshaking" interface for the WCS provides a universal I/O scheme that doesn't depend on the host system. Hence microprograms can be modified more quickly than when pROMS are used.

The display and bebug unit (DDU) traps, latches and displays the control signals of the user's microprogram. Through switches and LEDs on the board, errors in the microcode can be detected and corrected readily.

The development system can operate with the host processor either as a secondary control element, a master controller, or as a noncontrolling element. In this manner, the host system may employ a standard CROM as the basis to load the writable-control store.

The development steps begin with the writing of a microprogram in a symbolic language, then its assembly on a time-sharing facility. The resulting object microcode must be loaded into main memory, then into the WCS via a microprogram loader. The DDU is used for testing and debugging.

The tested microprogram can be stored more permanently in pROMs for test or pre-production systems. In the final product, the object microcode generates a custom mask-programmed CROM. The end result is a system that employs only one or more additional CROMs to achieve the custom instruction set.

Speeding Microprocessor Multiplication

HERMANN SCHMID
Senior Engineer-Computers,
General Electric Co., Binghamton

When required to multiply, microcomputers—LSI microprocessors plus support circuits and memories—may be too slow for a host of real-time control applications. Typically these applications require multiplication times of 5 to 50 μs. Microcomputers need several orders of magnitude longer. But with external circuitry—either a circuit that complements the CPU or a separate, peripheral multiplier—the speed limitations can be overcome.

The complementary-circuit approach requires a microprocessor that can be microprogrammed and has an externally accessible control bus. The circuitry differs from one processor to another. However, the approach yields the highest speed and least hardware complexity.

A separate peripheral multiplier can be used with any LSI processor. But it is less efficient from the standpoints of time and hardware: An 8×8-bit multiplier requires nine MSI circuits and at least four clock periods; for a 16×16-bit multiplier, these requirements are doubled.

A complementary circuit for National Semiconductor's IMP-16C microcomputer[1] can be built with 16 standard SSI and MSI circuits. And these can be interconnected on a 3×4-in. PC board that is mounted piggyback on the microcomputer.

The complementary circuit has been designed around the National unit, because it was the first available 16-bit model. Other models have been announced.

With the complementary circuit, the National microcomputer allows multiplication of two 16-bit unsigned operands in 16 microcycles, or 23 μs, with a 6.5-MHz clock. Thus the multiplication time is reduced by a factor of 30 from the relatively fast 700 μs needed by a conventional macro-software operation. It is reduced by a factor of seven from the 150 μs needed by an optional microprogrammed instruction offered by National.

Speed benefits also result when a complementary approach is used for division or square-root operations, or for multiplication of signed oper-

ands. The same hardware technique is used for these operations, but with some increase in ICs.

The design of the complementary circuit for multiplication assumes these three requirements: (1) The basic operation of the microcomputer will not be disturbed or impeded; (2) The additional circuitry will provide the necessary bipolar or MOS interface levels, and (3) No addi-

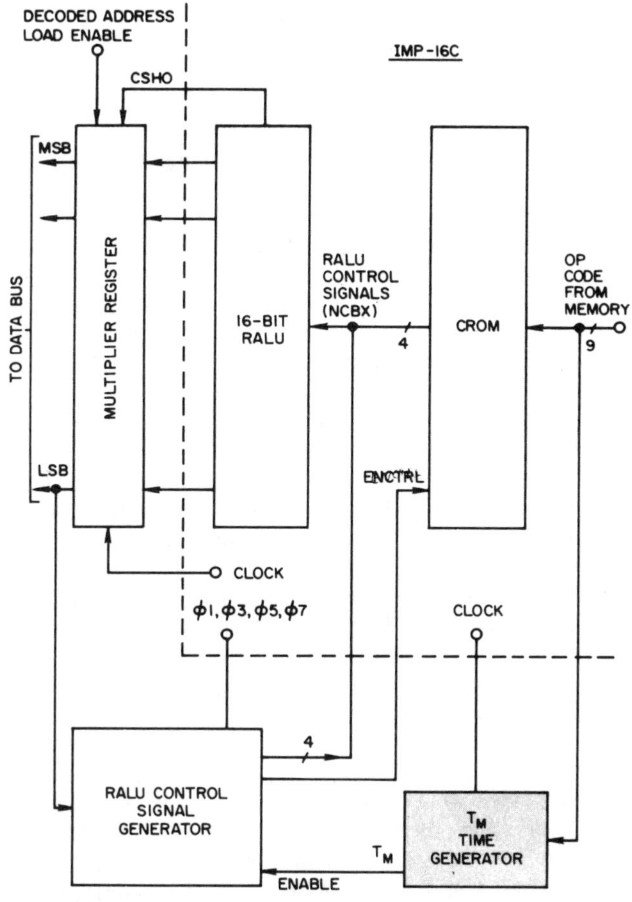

1. **In this CPU complementary multiplication circuit,** CROM outputs are replaced with special control signals that permit hardware multiplication operations. The additional circuit blocks consist of a time generator, signal generator and multiplier register.

tional power supplies will be used.

The major blocks of the multiplication circuitry are connected to the RALU (register and arithmetic logic unit) and CROM (control read-only memory) of the IMP-16C (Fig. 1). The external circuitry consists of the T_M time generator, the RALU control-signal generator and the multiplier register (MR).

Key microcomputer operations

In a typical microcomputer operation, the CROM receives a 9-bit operational (op) code from memory and processes it into the RALU control signals (NCBX). This time-sequenced 16-bit control word instructs the RALU what to do at each phase of a microcycle. At each clock phase, the four lines determine the following:

- During phase ϕ_1, which register (or stack) is connected to the "A" bus. The "A" and "B" buses constitute the two ALU input buses.
- During ϕ_3, which register is connected to the B bus and also whether to complement the A bus.
- During ϕ_5, which arithmetic logic and control operations are to be performed.
- During ϕ_7, which signal bus is to be connected to the "R" bus (the ALU output bus) and into which register (or stack) the R bus is to be loaded.

For multiplication, the RALU control signals from the CROM are replaced with separately generated control signals. These are a function of the least-significant MR register bit. The switchover in control signals occurs upon detection of a special multiplication op code—not in the instruction repertoire. The op code simply turns the CROM off and the T_M time generator on.

The time generator provides a period 16 microcycles long for a 16-bit multiplier, and it starts one microcycle after receipt of the multiplication op code. Also, T_M connects the shift clock to the MR register. A function of this register is to

---

Digital multiplication: The basics

The use of hardware multiplication to speed microcomputer computations also entails the writing of software. Though not a difficult task, digital multiplication could present problems to designers not familiar with the procedure.

A simple example (top right) will show how to develop a basic multiplication subroutine (bottom right).

Assume that two binary numbers, $X = 13$ and $Y = 11$, must be multiplied. X is called the multiplier and Y the multiplicand. The procedure requires that Y be added to the partial product Z_i whenever the least-significant multiplier bit X_i is 1. When $X_i = 0$, zero is added. After each addition, the partial product and the multiplier are shifted to the right by 1 bit. Thus after multiplication of two n-bit operands, a 2n-bit or double-precision product results.

Most microprocessors perform multiplication sequentially by software. A typical multiplication subroutine consists of three steps:

(1) Initialize,
(2) Loop and
(3) Finalize.

In Step 1, CPU registers AC0, AC2, AC3 are loaded with the operands X, Y and the index n; AC1 is reset to zero. In Step 2, we add Y into AC0 when the LSB of AC0 $\neq$ 0. We omit the addition when the LSB of AC0 $= 0$. The contents of AC0 and AC1 are shifted to the right 1 bit at a time, for each pass through the loop, while the index counter is decremented. In the last step we transfer the double-precision product from AC0 and AC1 to specified memory locations.

$$Y = 11 \qquad X = 13$$
$$1011 \quad \times \quad 1101$$

$$
\begin{aligned}
Z_0 = \ & 0000 \\
      & +1011 \\[4pt]
Z_1 = \ & 1011 \\
      & 1011 \longrightarrow \text{SHIFT RIGHT} \\
      & +00000 \\[4pt]
Z_2 = \ & 01011 \\
      & 1011 \longrightarrow \text{SHIFT RIGHT} \\
      & +101100 \\[4pt]
Z_3 = \ & 110111 \\
      & 110111 \longrightarrow \text{SHIFT RIGHT} \\
      & +1011000 \\[4pt]
Z_4 = \ & 1000111
\end{aligned}
$$

143 = DOUBLE-PRECISION ANSWER

```
OPERATIONS: AC1, AC0 ←——— AC0 x AC2
INITIALIZE: AC0 ← X, AC1 ← 0, AC2 ← Y,
            AC3 ← n
LP: JUMP +2 IF AC0 LSB = 0
    ADD AC1 ← AC1 + AC2
    RIGHT SHIFT AC1      LSB ——→ L
    RIGHT SHIFT AC0      L ——→ MSB
    DECREMENT COUNTER, SKIP IF ZERO
    JUMP TO LP
FINALIZE: STORE AC0 AND AC1 IN MEMORY
```

initially hold the 16-bit multiplier.

At each clock cycle, or microcycle, the multiplier shifts one bit to the right. And as the least-significant multiplier bit (MR−LSB) leaves the low side of the register, the least-significant product bit enters the top side. At the end of T_M, the MR register thus holds the 16 low-order product bits.

Use of an external register to store the multiplier operand eliminates the following:

- The need to shift through the "Link" flip-flop (CPU status flag), which would require two microinstructions.
- Testing of the multiplier LSB through software, which would require a conditional branch microinstruction.
- The need to establish, increment and test the index counter, which would require another two microinstructions.

The RALU control signals (NCBX) are generated with simple logic circuits and connected to the NCBX bus during T_M (Fig. 2). Only one transistor, four Tristate MOS buffers and six diodes are needed.

The multiplicand is loaded into accumulator AC2, and the multiplier into the external register. During each microcycle either the content of AC2 (MR − LSB = 1) or zero (MR − LSB = 0) is added to the content of AC0, which is initially zero. In addition the contents of the AC0 and MR registers shift 1 bit right, and the content of the least-significant AC0 stage shifts into the most-significant MR register stage. At the end of the multiplication operation, the most-significant product byte is in AC0 and the least-significant byte in the MR register.

For this design, a macroinstruction loads the multiplier operand into the MR register prior to the multiplication operation. Similarly another macroinstruction causes the 16 low-order product bits to be read out from the register after multiplication.

Obviously the T_M period and the RALU control signals can be extended, so these two operations are performed at the high speed of 1 microcycle each without additional software. But for simplicity, this approach is not used.

Control signal pattern easy to generate

To perform a hardware multiplication operation, two pseudo-microinstructions must be generated and then executed. These are the following:

$$(AC0) \leftarrow [(AC0) + 0] \, 2^{-1} \text{ if } MR - LSB = 0 \quad (1)$$
$$(AC0) \leftarrow [(AC0) + (AC2)] \, 2^{-1} \text{ if } MR - LSB = 1 \quad (2)$$

Translated, this means: (1) Add zero to the content of AC0 and shift the result 1 bit right if MR − LSB = 0; (2) Add the content of AC2

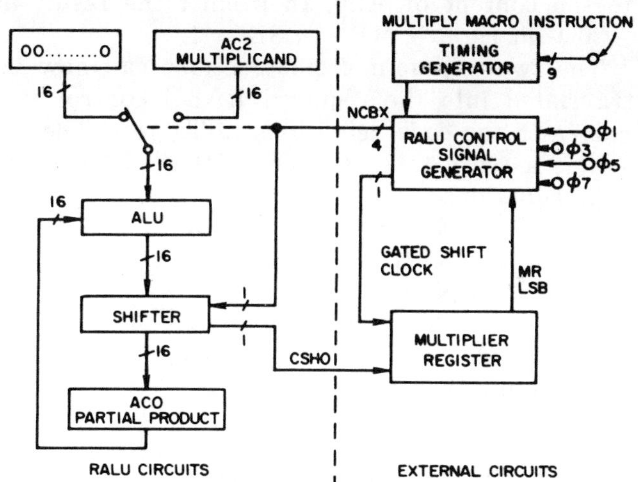

2. **The complementary circuit provides alternative** control signals, labeled NCBX, for the RALU. The technique can be used with the IMP-16C because it is a microprogrammable processor.

Table 1. Command codes for the RALU

ALU functions			Control functions		
NCB (1), (0) @ T5	Function		NCB (3), (2) @ T5	Function	
11	AND		11	None	
10	XOR		10	R-bus control	
01	OR		01	Shift left	
00	ADD		00	Shift right	

A, B and R-bus addresses			R-bus control		
NCB (2) (1), (0)	Address		I/O NCB(3) @ T7	BYTE (SININ @ T5)	R-bus value
111	ZEROS		1	0	Output of shifter
	FLAGS, STACK		1	1	Output of shifter
110	R1				
101	R2		0	0	Output of I/O mux
100	R3				
011	R4		0	1	Value of sign input on SININ @ T7
010	R5				
001	R6				
000	R7				

Table 2. RALU signal patterns that permit unsigned multiplication

	Time period	NCB3	NCB2	NCB1	NCB0	Operation
Multiplier MR − LSB = 0	ϕ_1	1	1	1	1	(A bus)←0
	ϕ_3	1	0	1	1	(B bus)←AC0
	ϕ_5	0	0	0	0	SHIFT RIGHT, ADD
	ϕ_7	1	0	1	1	(AC0)←(R bus)
Multiplier MR − LSB = 1	ϕ_1	1	0	0	1	(A bus)←(AC2)
	ϕ_3	1	0	1	1	(B bus)←(AC0)
	ϕ_5	0	0	0	0	SHIFT RIGHT, ADD
	ϕ_7	1	0	1	1	(AC0)←(R bus)

to the content of AC0, then shift the result in AC0 1 bit right if MR − LSB = 1.

The two pseudo-microinstructions can now be translated into the required RALU control signals with the code definitions in Table 1. The result is a truth table (Table 2) that yields these logic equations:

$$NCB0 = \phi_1 + \phi_3 + \phi_7$$
$$NCB1 = \phi_{1S} + \phi_3 + \phi_7$$
$$NCB2 = \phi_{1S}$$
$$NCB3 = \phi_1 + \phi_3 + \phi_7,$$

where ϕ_{1S} denotes the clock phase, ϕ_1, switched by the multiplier LSB.

The problem: Interfacing and timing

Implementing these logic equations in either TTL or MOS levels would be a cinch. However, the RALU and CROM have both types of inputs and outputs, even though the chips use MOS techniques. The outputs may be either the standard pull-up/pull-down types, open collector or Tristate.

As shown in Table 3, some of the RALU control signals perform different functions within the eight time periods of 1 microcycle. For example, CSHO (carry-shift-zero) accepts a carry input during period T_5 and outputs the shift pulse during T_x. Also, the NCBX signals are always driven to logic ZERO during even clock phases.

The timing of these signals is very critical. For example, the carry output signal (CSHO) is guaranteed to be available only during the last 70 ns of T_x. Similarly the pseudo-NCBX signal cannot be delayed by more than 85 ns from the start of the clock phase.

Consequently logic levels, impedances and the

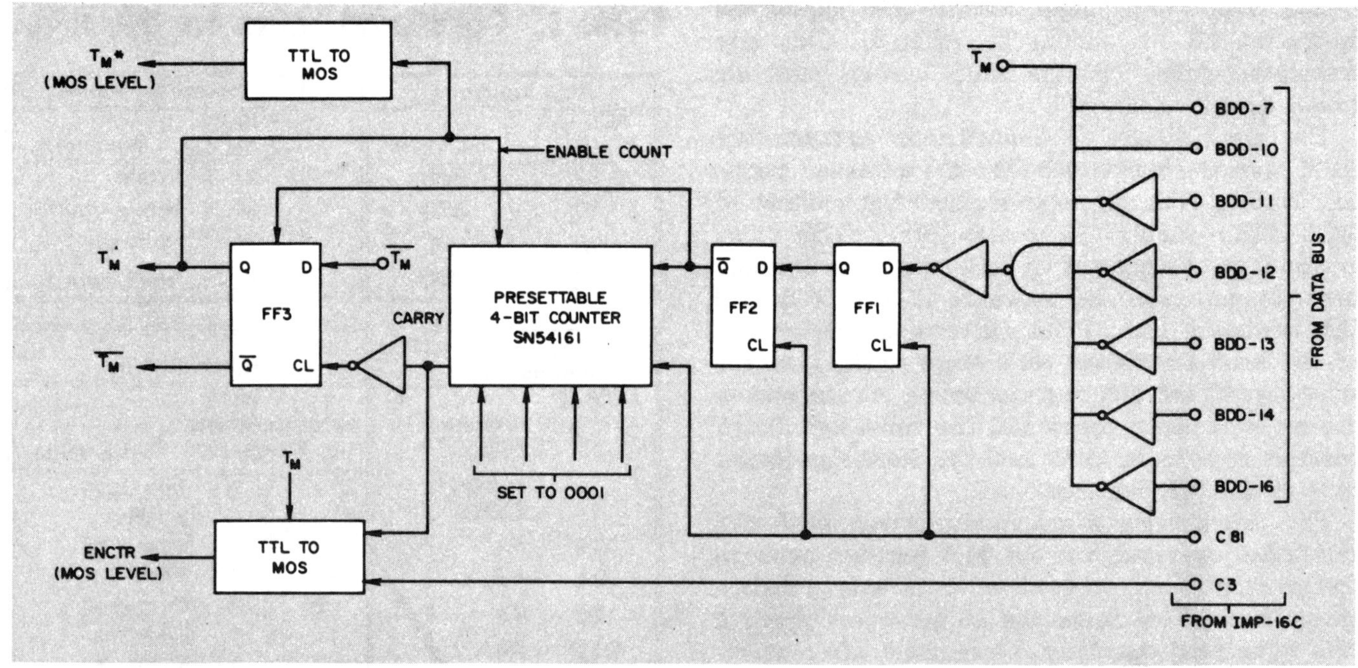

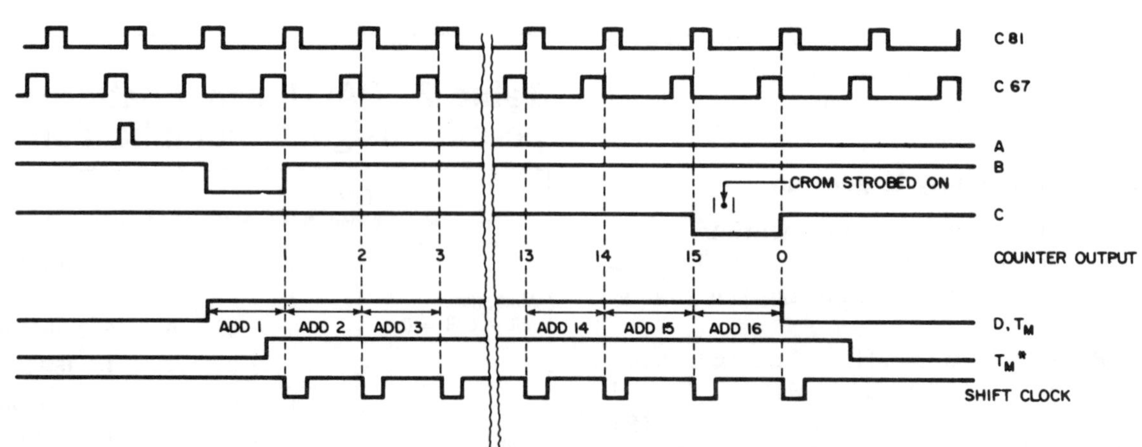

3. **The 16-clock T_M period** is generated when the multiplication op code is detected. FF2 provides an inverted pulse that presets the counter to 0001. Unless otherwise indicated, TTL circuits and levels are implied.

Table 3. Critical timing for the RALU

Signals	Logic levels	T_1	T_2	T_3	T_4	T_5	T_6	T_7	T_8	Pin function	Pin No.
Clocks　ϕ_1	MOS									IN	2
ϕ_2	MOS									IN	1
ϕ_3	MOS									IN	23
ϕ_4	MOS									IN	22
Command											
NCB(0)	MOS	$\overline{A0}$	"0"	$\overline{B0}$	"0"	$\overline{ALU0}$	"0"	$\overline{R0}$	"0"	IN	21
NCB(1)	MOS	$\overline{A1}$	"0"	$\overline{B1}$	"0"	$\overline{ALU1}$	"0"	$\overline{R1}$	"0"	IN	19
NCB(2)	MOS	$\overline{A2}$	"0"	$\overline{B2}$	"0"	$\overline{CTL0}$	"0"	$\overline{R2}$	"0"	IN	18
NCB(3)	MOS	$\overline{STACK}$	"0"	$\overline{COMP}$	"0"	$\overline{CTL1}$	"0"	$\overline{I/O}$	"0"	IN	20
Data											
DATA(0),(1),(2),(3)	TTL	R BUS (OUT)		A BUS(OUT)		"1" (OUT)[3]		DATA INPUT	"1" (OUT)	I/O	17, 5, 4, 7
Control											
FLAG	TTL	FLAG		"1"						OUT	16
Misc											
SININ	MOS T5 TTL T7	Don't Care (DC)				BYTE	DC	SIGN	DC	IN	10
CSH0	MOS	"1" (OUT)	HIGH IMPEDANCE[2]			CARRY (IN)	"1" (OUT)	$\overline{SHIFT}$ I/O		I/O	14
CSH3	MOS	$\overline{OVCEN}$ (IN)	HIGH IMPEDANCE		"0" (OUT)	CARRY (OUT)	"1" (OUT)	$\overline{SHIFT}$ I/O		I/O	11

Note 1. A positive true logic convention is used for all signals—"1" = more positive voltage, "0" = more negative voltage. Signal names beginning with N are complementd signals.

Note 2. CSH0 and CSH3 high impedance states for intervals T_2 through T_4 are Tristate mode for output drivers.

Note 3. "1" (OUT) means RALU is driving this node to the "1" logic level during the defined interval. For bidirectional I/O lines the logic state is defined as "in" or "out."

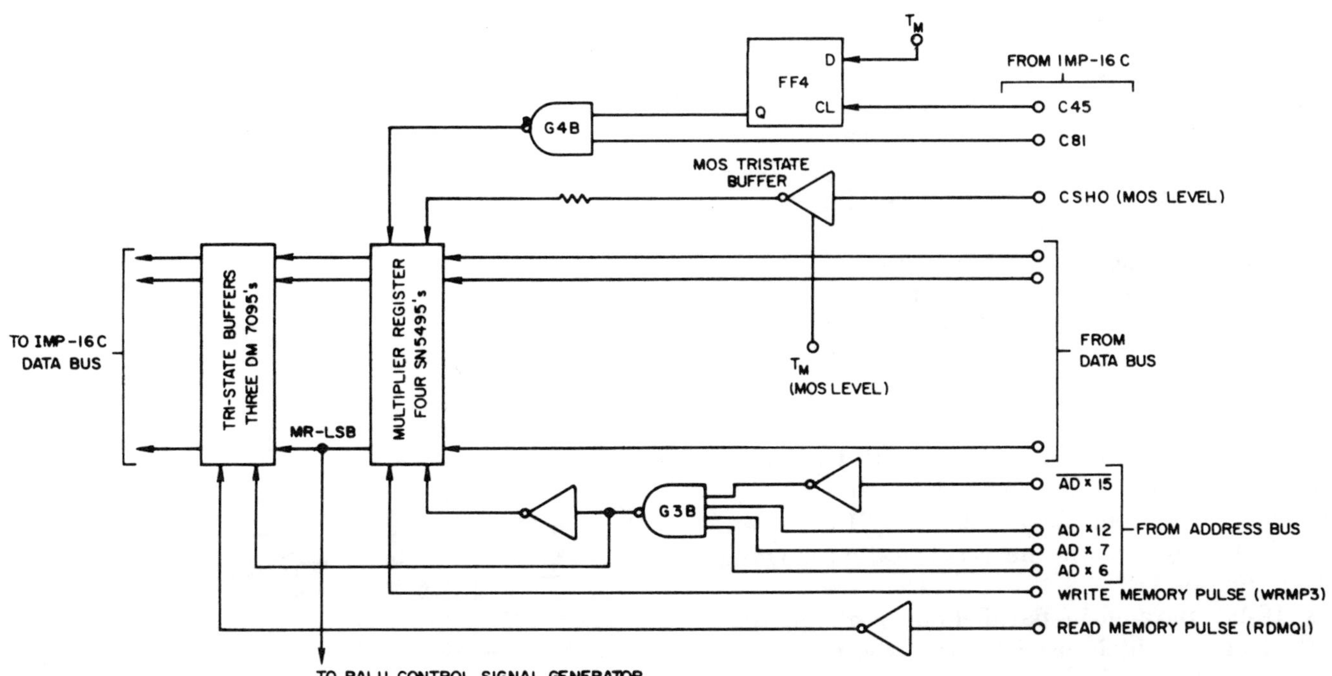

4. **The external multiplier register** first stores the multiplier operand, then shifts it right 1 bit per microcycle, and then injects the least-significant partial product bits. After 16 microcycles, the register contains the 16 LSB double-precision product. The multiplier register employs four 4-bit universal shift registers.

timing of all signals to and from the IMP-16C play a critical role in the hardware multiplication operation. The problem is aggravated by the fact that the speed required—a 6.5-MHz clock—is beyond the capabilities of most available standard SSI and MSI/MOS circuits.

To bridge this interface gap, one MOS-to-TTL and four TTL-to-MOS converters are needed, all of which must switch in less than 50 ns. The MOS-to-TTL conversion is relatively simple; it can be accomplished with a standard CMOS inverter. The TTL-to-MOS—+5 to −12 V—converters require capability to AND two TTL-input signals and to have an open-collector output that pulls low.

The NCBX line drivers present another interface problem. The signals must have MOS levels, and they must be connected to the bus only during T_M. Yet they must switch in less than 50 ns. The Motorola MC 14502 strobed hex inverter provides three-state output, the +5 to −12 V levels and the high speed.

The solution

The timing generator is initiated when the multiplication op code appears on the data bus (Fig. 3). Data bits 7, 10, $\overline{11}$, $\overline{12}$, $\overline{13}$, $\overline{14}$ and $\overline{15}$ are ANDed at the data input of a two-stage shift register (FF1 and FF2), which is clocked with the leading edge of clock period C_{81} (waveform A). The Q output of FF2 is thus an inverted pulse, exactly 1 microcycle wide and starting 1 microcycle after the decoded op code is clocked into FF1 (waveform B).

The inverted pulse presets the 4-bit counter to 0001 and FF3 to $Q = 1$. Thereafter the counter increments with every C_{81} pulse until count 15 is reached and a carry is generated (waveform C). The trailing edge of the carry pulse resets the FF3 Q output and the period T_M back to zero (waveform D). Thus the T_M interval is exactly 16 microcycles wide. To produce the clock pulses for shifting the MR register, T_M is reclocked with C_{45} and gated with C_{81}.

The enable control pulse (ENCTL) is produced by gating ϕ_3 with the carry pulse, but it is connected to the ENCTL line only during T_M. Its purpose is to turn the CROM back on so it will fetch the next instruction and continue with the macro program. The three flip-flops, FF1 to FF3, are reset by the system clear pulse, SYCLR, to ensure that they are in the reset state following power turn on.

A 16-bit parallel-in/parallel-out register that shifts to the right is used to store the multiplier (Fig. 4). Its functions are to store the multiplier operand, to shift it 1 bit right every microcycle and to shift the low-order product bit on the CSHO line into the register. After 16 micro-

cycles, the register contains the 16 least-significant bits of the double-precision product.

The register employs four 4-bit universal shift registers and three Tristate hex buffers. The multiplier operand is loaded into the MR register prior to the actual multiplication operation (before T_M), with a macro STORE instruction that addresses the register as if it were another memory location. The use of specific memory addresses for peripheral devices has an advantage: The access is faster, and all memory-reference instructions can be used.

The output of the address-decoding gate (G3B) connects to the mode-control input (pin 6) of the four 4-bit shift registers. When the registers are addressed, the mode control signal is high, and when the clock-2 signal (WRMP3) switches from ONE to ZERO, the registers perform a parallel-load operation. This loads the multiplier operand into the MR register.

The gated clock signal at the G4B output shifts the MR register content 1 bit right at the leading edge of the C_{81} timing pulse. The signal (MR − LSB) on the least-significant MR register output line thus constitutes the multiplier operand in serial-binary form.

The contents of the multiplier register must be loaded back into accumulator 1 of the RALU following completion of multiplication. For that purpose, a memory LOAD operation must be executed. The register is addressed as in the STORE operation. But when the read-memory pulse (RDMQ1) occurs, the MR contents are sent to

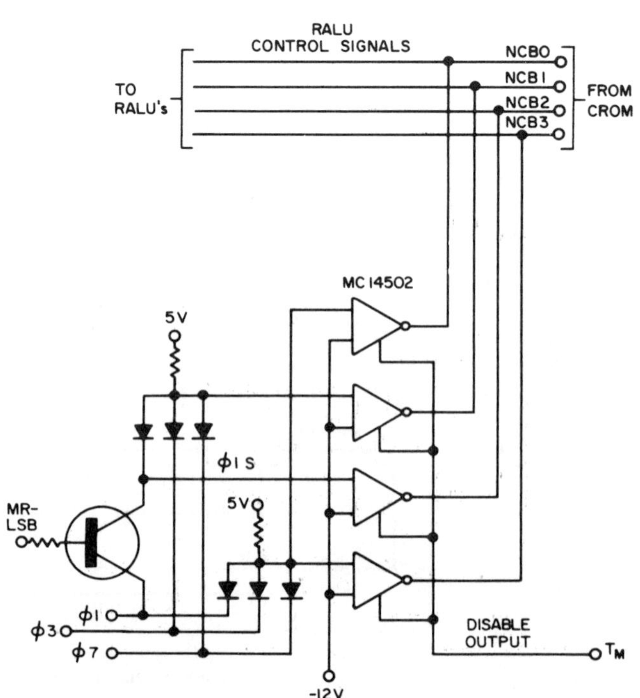

5. The control-signal generator produces pseudo microinstructions that will execute the required add and shift operations in the RALU.

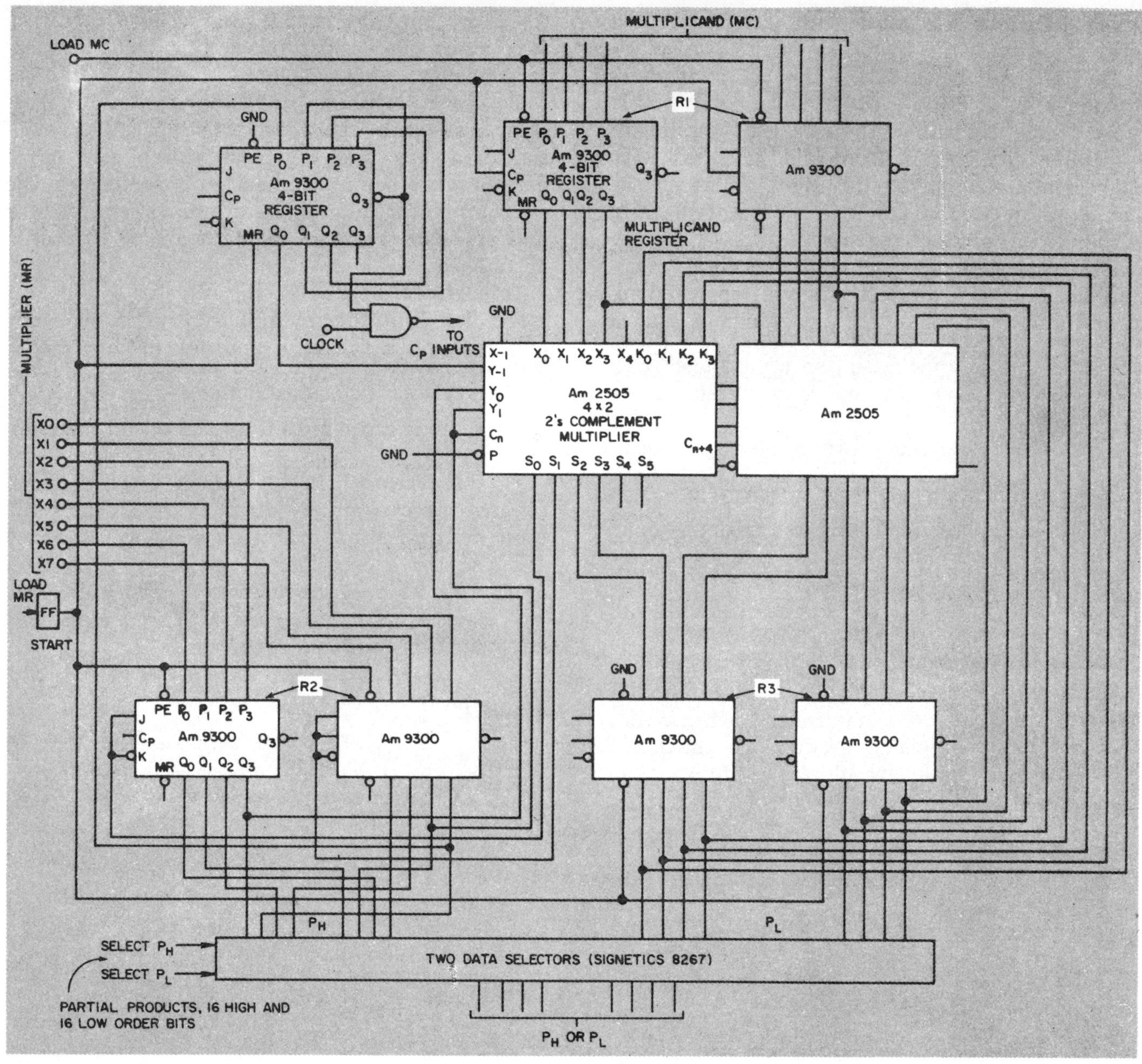

6. Two 4 × 2-bit IC multipliers sequentially add the 8-bit parallel multiplicand into the partial product register. Control of the operation is provided by the two least significant multiplier bits.

the data bus by a set of three noninverting Tristate buffers. These buffers are enabled by the decoded address and the RDMQ1 pulse.

The RALU control signal generator produces four time-multiplexed NCBX signals (Fig. 5). The signals control the RALU, so it executes the required add and shift operations. The circuit consists of a transistor switch, two diode-OR gates and four strobed inverters.

The transistor connects the ϕ_1 clock pulse to the diode-OR gate when MR − LSB = 1. The six diodes form two three-input OR gates that combine the ϕ_3 and ϕ_7 clock pulses with either ϕ_1 or the switched clock pulse, ϕ_{1S}. The strobed MOS inverters are Tristate devices that connect the NCBX signal to the RALU control bus only during T_M.

Though peripheral multipliers can be built with a number of available MSI ICs, only serial-parallel (rather than all-parallel) multipliers are cost and speed-compatible with microprocessors. The 4 × 2-bit IC multiplier[2] in Fig. 6 is an example.

The 8 × 8-bit peripheral multiplier consists of three single-length registers, a 2 × 8-bit multiplier, an output data selector and some addressing and control logic. Register R_1 holds the multiplicand, while register R_2 holds the multiplier. Double-precision products are stored in registers R_2 and R_3.

At the start of multiplication, the multiplicand and multiplier are loaded into registers R_1 and R_2, respectively. During an operation the multiplier is shifted out, 2 bits at a time, and the empty locations are filled with partial product bits.

The two Advanced Micro Devices multipliers provide a 2 × 8-bit product during each clock cycle. Under control of the two least-significant multiplier bits, the multiplicand is added with appropriate weights to the eight LSBs of the partial product. The result is then stored again in the partial-product register.

The multiplier operand and the eight most-significant partial product bits are separated into odd and even parts, each of which is loaded into one 4-bit shift register. A shift of two places can thus be obtained with one clock pulse, with each register providing one least-significant bit as an output.

Four shift operations are needed to execute 8 × 8-bit operations. This means that the basic multiplication execution time is four clock periods. Since these MSI circuits easily can operate at a clock rate of 4 MHz, the complete multiplication can be performed in 1 μs.

Extending the technique

The technique can be extended easily to handle 16-bit multiplicand and multiplier operands and a 32-bit double-precision product. In the latter case, however, the length of all registers and of the actual multiplier must be doubled. Similarly the execution time also increases by a factor of two, since eight shift operations must be performed now.

To use a peripheral multiplier in a microprocessor system, the multiplier must operate through the data bus and be treated like any other peripheral. When multiplication is performed, the microprocessor addresses a multiplier register and specifies whether the data are to be stored or fetched.

In a typical operation, the register would first store the multiplicand and multiplier operands and then fetch the high and low product bytes. This necessitates two output and two input operations, or four macroinstructions, and this would require much more time than the actual multiplication.

In the National IMP-16, each I/O operation requires approximately 10 μs. Consequently the total multiplication execution time would be 40 μs. And for a complete 16 × 16-bit peripheral multiplier, with all the address decoding and control logic, approximately 18 MSI and eight SSI integrated circuits are required.

References

1. IMP-16C Application Manual, 4200021B, National Semiconductor Corp., Santa Clara, CA, 1973.
2. Ghest, R. C., "A Two's Complement Digital Multiplier," Application Note, Advanced Micro Devices Corp., Sunnyvale, CA, 1971.

Mating Microprocessors with Converters

HERMANN SCHMID
Senior Engineer,
General Electric Co., Binghamton

GEORGE MROZOWSKI
Design Engineer,
General Electric Co., Binghamton

Interfacing data-acquisition and data-decoding systems with a microprocessor is easy. But you must be familiar with all hardware components, the software requirements (programming) and circuit timing needs.

Use of a microprocessor in a control system that has analog sensors and. analog actuators or displays requires the analog signals from the sensors be digitized and the processor outputs be converted to analog form.

With over a dozen different microprocessor chip sets and hundreds of different analog-to-digital and digital-to-analog converters available, complex tradeoffs between software and hardware are needed. Ideally you should try to minimize processor execution time and the processor-to-converter interface hardware.

But how would you begin in a system like the one in Fig. 1? It consists of a National IMP-16C microprocessor,[1,2] a Micro Networks MN-7000 data-acquisition module[3] and a Burr-Brown DAC-85 d/a converter.[4] To put the system together, follow three basic guidelines:

■ A/d and d/a converters should be addressed as part of the main memory, because they can respond just as quickly.

■ A software-initiated converter-to-processor transfer requires little interface hardware and a minimum of processor time, and the method introduces the least delay on the signal.

■ A chain consisting of a processor, a d/a and an a/d permits very simple end-to-end system testing for self-calibration and performance checking.

Converters: Small, fast peripherals

Peripherals such as tape readers or typewriter terminals. are usually slow devices. They communicate with the computer over a separate data bus tied into the computer bus with a set of switches. In the conventional approach, a special set of instructions must be used to fetch data from or load data into the peripherals. For the required input/output operations (I/O), a con-

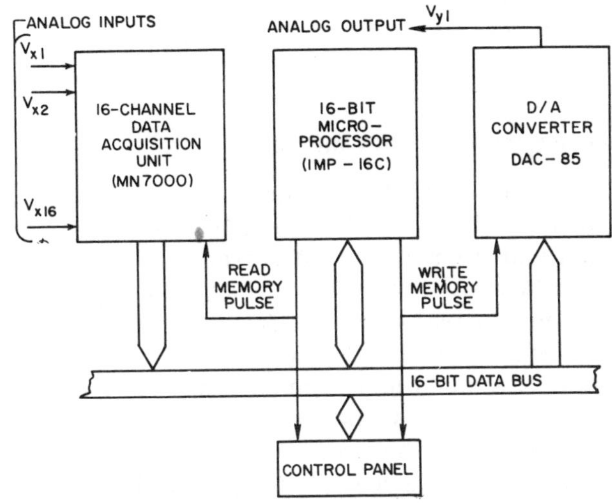

1. **This basic microprocessor-controlled data-acquisition system** consists of a 16-channel a/d converter, a 12-bit d/a converter and a processing unit, all connected through the data bus.

trol word—similar to an address word—is first transmitted to the peripheral. Approximately one microcycle later the data word is either fetched or sent.

A/d and d/a converters differ from the common type of peripheral because they are small, fast and usually placed close to the computer. Some converters also have built-in storage: A/d's for storing the converted data and d/a's for holding the computer data word until the convert signal is given.

To the processor, an a/d or d/a converter can be made to appear as a memory location, with data being fetched from the a/d or stored in the d/a. This approach offers the following benefits:

■ The memory-reference operations are faster than conventional I/O operations.

■ No separate I/O bus is required.

■ No additional bus switching circuits are needed.

■ All memory-reference instructions can be used; the operand can be added directly to any of the computer's accumulators.

However, to access the converter directly a

suitable address must be provided for the converters. Thus part of the memory should be allocated to these special peripherals. Let's assume that within the IMP-16C computer we have 64 k words of memory available, and let's divide the memory up as follows:

- Read-only-memory (ROM) locations (32 k): B15 = 1, B14 = 0.
- Peripheral locations (16 k): B15 = 0, B14 = 1.
- Random-access-memory (RAM) locations (16 k): B15 = 0, B14 = 0.

Now a 16-bit converter address can be formed, where B14 and B15 select the peripherals out of memory, B8 to B11 their mode of operation, B6 and B7 the type of peripheral and B$\emptyset$ to B3 the desired device or the channel in a multichannel system (Fig. 2).

Transferring data isn't difficult

Once the converter is addressed as a memory location, outputting data to a d/a or inputting data from an a/d is straightforward. D/a converters are easy to control—just execute a store operation to transfer data from the processor to the desired converter. Multichannel a/d converters are much more complex, since the desired channel must first be selected and conversion initiated before the processor can fetch the data.

D/a converters are easy to control—just use a store operation and then transfer the data in the memory location to the desired peripheral. Three conventional methods are used to fetch converter data from a multichannel a/d. In each, the converter initiates the transfer of data.

1. Interrupt-initiated transfer.
2. Direct-memory access (DMA) transfer.
3. Auxiliary memory transfer.

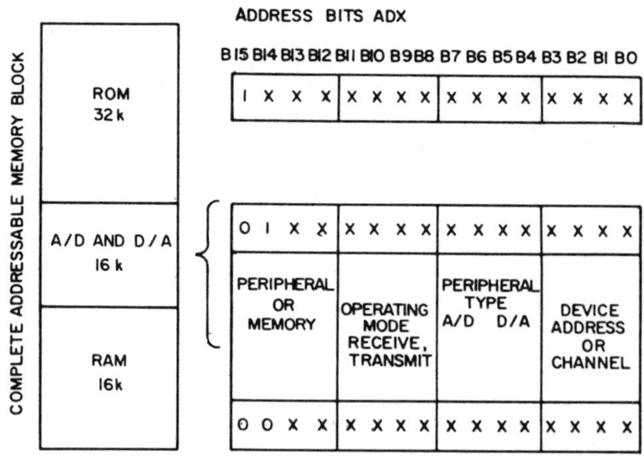

2. **The 64 k words of directly addressable memory** can be separated into three sections (a). Each address word is divided into four 4-bit control bytes (b).

The interrupt method first addresses the a/d converter, selects the desired input channel and initiates the conversion process. When the conversion process is complete, the converter's end-of-convert (EOC) signal interrupts the processor, which in turn fetches the converter data. This method requires little additional interface hardware, but it does need plenty of processor time and up to 12 macro instructions that must be stored in the computer memory.

Direct memory access permits the converter to run continuously, and after each conversion the EOC signal initiates a transfer of the converted signal to the main storage. Unfortunately this transfer can take place only when the data bus is not being used by the processor. Thus additional interface hardware is needed and large delays are introduced (up to one iteration period), but no processor time is lost.

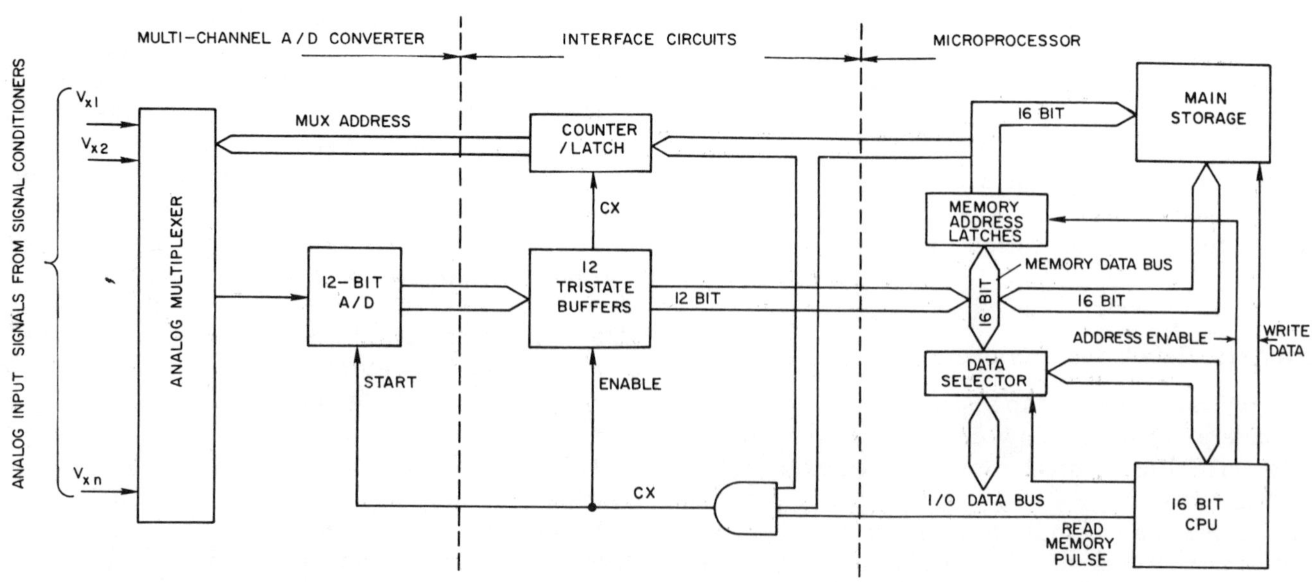

3. **Converter-to-processor interface circuits** connect the multichannel a/d converter to the processor, address the desired channel and buffer the a/d output signals so the next sample can be worked on.

A look inside the three building blocks

What's inside the three major building blocks used in the accompanying article to form the microprocessor-based data-collection and control system?

The National IMP-16C is a 16-bit microprocessor mounted on a printed-circuit card. It consists of a central processing unit made from five LSI chips, a 256 × 16-bit random-access memory, a 512 × 16-bit read-only memory, clock and timing circuits, bus control logic and some other control circuits (Fig. A).

The central processor has four 4-bit registers, arithmetic and logic (RALU) units and a control read-only memory that stores the microprogram and controls the operation of the processor. All data to and from the processor travel over a time-multiplexed 16-bit parallel data bus. The bus, in turn, is controlled by a four-phase clock and micro and macro programs.

There are 43 macro instructions, including various memory, register-to-register, branch and input-output commands.

The MN-7000 a/d converter subsystem from Micro Networks contains a 16-chanel multiplexer, a differential buffer amplifier, a sample-and-hold circuit, a high-speed, 12-bit successive-approximation a/d converter, a reference supply, a clock and control logic (Fig. B). The converter operation starts with control signals from the processor or internally generated trigger pulses. After the desired channel is selected from the multiplexer, the actual conversion begins.

After 12 clock periods, the conversion is completed, and the result is stored in the successive-approximation register. The "end of convert" signal is also generated when the data word is stored.

Burr-Brown's DAC85 d/a converter is a 12-bit hybrid-IC unit in a 24-pin metal dual in-line package (Fig. C). It is relatively high-speed (1 to 5 μs), and it has an internal reference and output amplifier. The unit accepts a wide variety of input codes just by pin-jumping, and you also have a choice of output ranges.

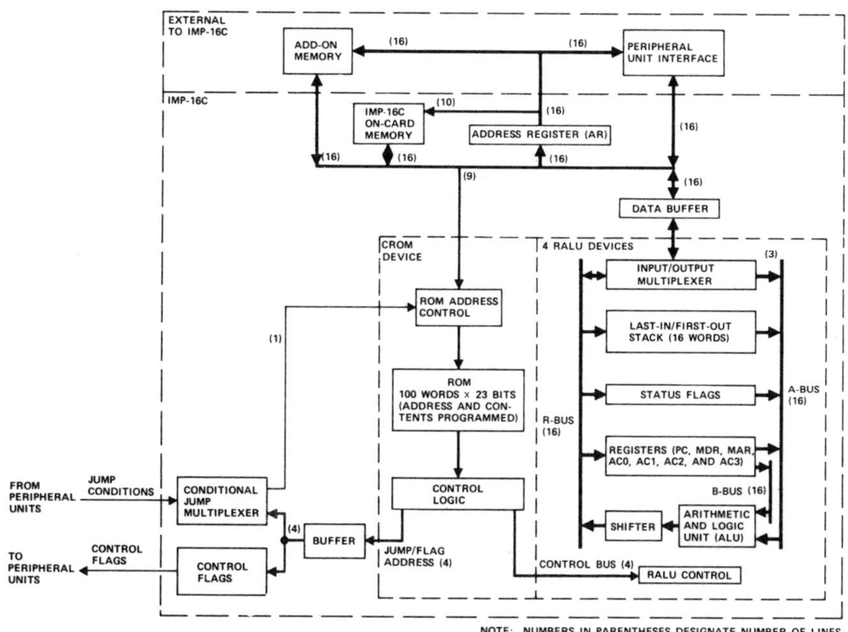

(a)

(b)

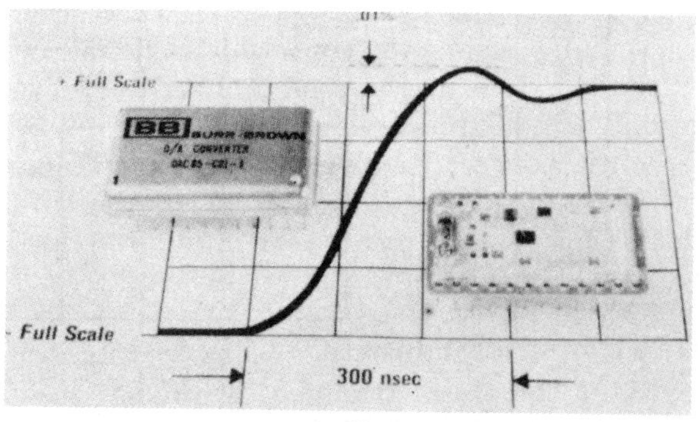

(c)

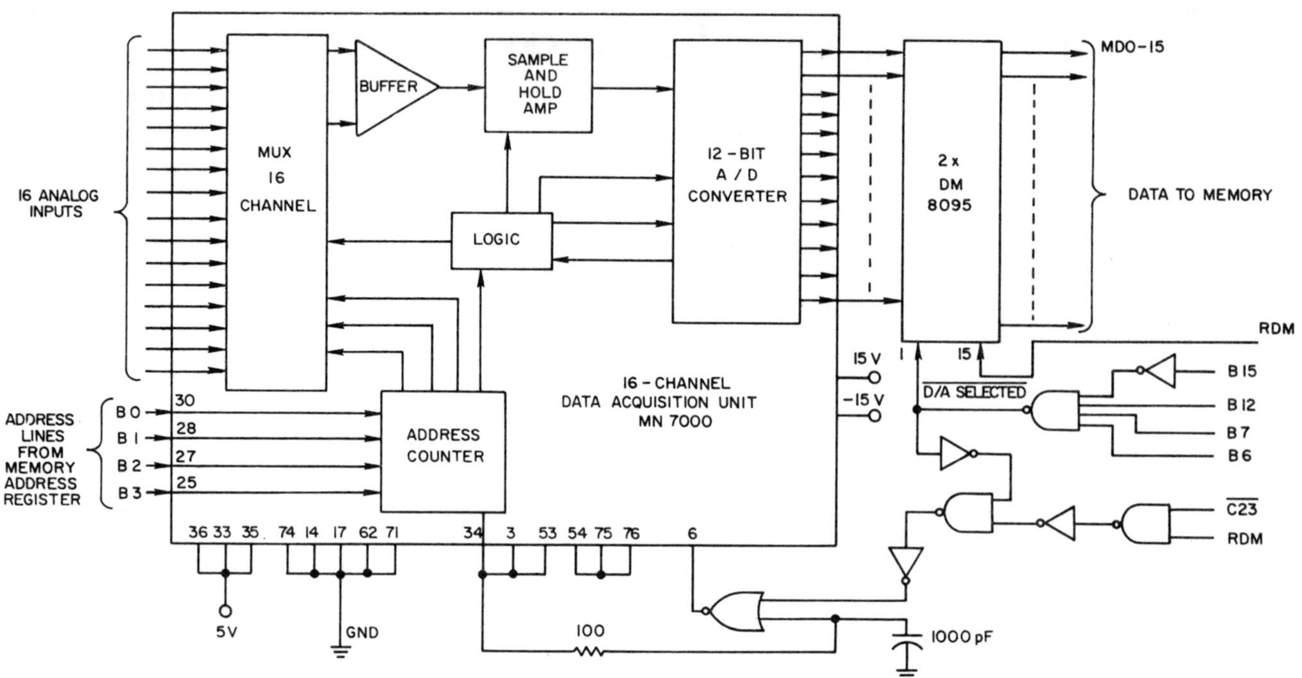

4. **Logic circuits needed to control** the Micro Networks MN-7000 data-acquisition module are very simple. They provide complete processor control of the system under software command.

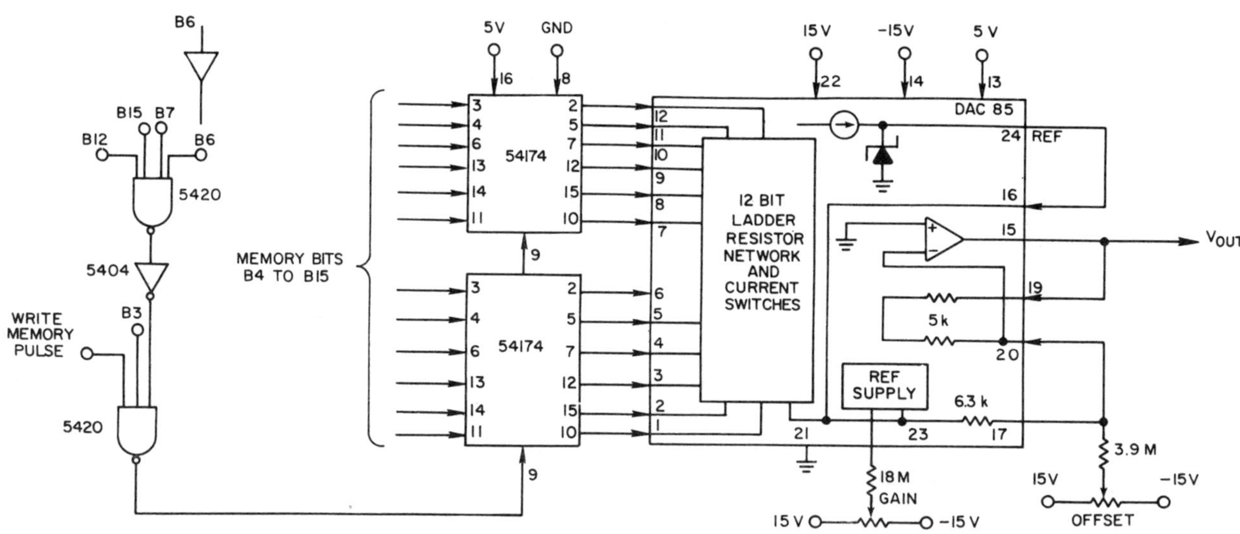

5. **D/a converters can be interfaced** easier than a/d's. All you need are several gates to enable two hex D flip-flops, which then transfer the data, into the d/a converter weighting network or buffer register.

Auxiliary memory transfer works in the same way, except that the converter data are stored in an auxiliary memory, from which the processor reads the data. If the read and write cycles require only a half microcycle, they can be interlaced so little control hardware is needed. Processor time is also kept low, but delays are introduced,. since the signals to be measured are sampled only once each iteration period.

Software initiates the transfer

In each of the three transfer techniques discussed so far, the transfer of data is controlled by the converter. But starting the data transfer with the processor program boosts system efficiency and yields the following benefits:

- Only one instruction is needed to select, initiate and transfer.
- Processor time is minimal, since the converter must be accessed only once.
- No interrupt subroutine must be stored and executed.
- Any memory-reference instruction can be used to transfer.
- No address and data bus switching are needed.
- The processor always receives the most up-to-date data with minimum delay.

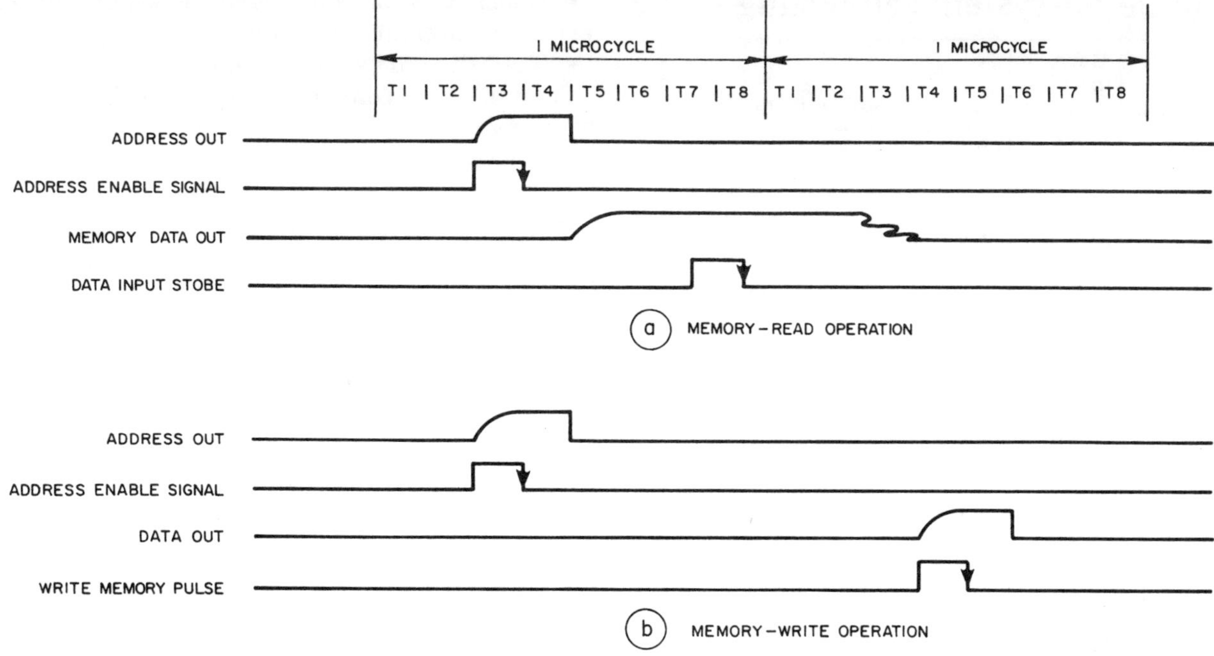

6. **Microprocessor timing pulses** for the memory-read (a) and memory-write (b) operations control inputs from a/d's and outputs to d/a's. The timing pulses are initiated by software store or read commands.

The system in Fig. 3 operates the a/d converter under software control and addresses it like a memory location. Macro programs contain instructions to fetch converter data. Each time such an instruction is executed, the processor first outputs an address. The address, which selects the channel to be converted, starts the conversion process and fetches the previously converted word.

When the system operates, the central processor (CPU) transmits a 16-bit memory address, which is strobed into the memory address latches by the address-enable pulse. The latch output signals—B6, B7, B14 and B15 (for the code shown in Fig. 2) and the read-memory flag pulse are ANDed into an over-all control signal, CX. This signal performs three functions:

1. It presets the four least-significant memory address latch outputs B∅ to B3 into the multiplexer address counter.

2. It starts the a/d conversion process.

3. It loads the a/d output data from the previous conversion onto the memory data bus by enabling the 12 three-state buffers.

Once the a/d outputs are fed to the data bus, they can be loaded into any CPU register, as directed by the specific instruction executed.

There are, though, disadvantages to this software approach:

■ The input signal-sampling rate varies proportionately with the speed of program execution, especially when branching operations occur.

■ An additional burden is placed on the programmer; the processor must fetch the previously converted data while addressing the data needed next.

Interfacing circuits are simple

To interface the a/d with a processor, you need only initiate the operation with the decoded address signal and connect the converter output briefly to the memory data bus. Two hex three-state buffers (DM-8095) and a few logic gates are all that's needed (Fig. 4).

When the selected address and the "read memory" pulse are present, the three-state buffers are enabled. Simultaneously the "a/d selected" line and the "read memory" signal start the converter operation, and load the 4-bit channel address into the counter latch of the MN-7000.

The converter output data are then connected to the CPU input data bus with four 4-bit data selectors (DM-8123), just as if they were memory data in the IMP-16C.

To interface the processor with a d/a, store the computer output at the proper time and hold it until it is replaced by a new value. This can be achieved simply with two hex D-type flip-flop ICs (SN54174) and a few gates for decoding the address (Fig. 5).

Note that the address is stored in the address register of the microprocessor, just as when a memory store operation takes place. The data for the d/a are available from the start of T_4 ON (Fig. 6). When the write memory pulse signal goes low with the T_4 of the next microcycle, the computer output is loaded into the set of D flip-

Subroutine for system self-testing

Task	Address	Machine instruction	Mnemonic	Comments
I	80	10C0	per Addr.	
	81	0400	R1N	Input x + mux addr
	82	0880	PFLG 8	
	83	89FC	LD2, −4	Load AC2 with per addr
	84	5000	CAIO	Complement ACO (x̄)
	85	A00A	STO M10	d/a addr
	86	A2C2	STO, D/A	
II	87	850B	LD1, +9	Load mask into AC1
	88	3483	RANDO, 1	Mux addr
	89	3200	RADD2, 0	a/d addr = per add + mux addr
	8A	A80C	ST2, M12	
III	8B	8200	LDO, AD-X	Initiate a/d operation
	8C	A008	STO, M11	
IV	8D	C00A	ADDO, M10	x = a/d − x
	8E	5CFC	SHR SELO	Right justify result
	8F	0600	ROUT	Output result
	90	21EE	JMP-16	JMP to repeat conv.
	91	000F	MASK	

flops and held there until it is replaced by a different value. The d/a produces an analog voltage that is proportional to the value stored, and thus the voltage changes when the new value replaces the old one.

Troubleshooting the system

You've completed the wiring, turned on the power, but the system doesn't work. Now what?

Here are some simple steps you can follow to troubleshoot such a microprocessor-based data-acquisition system.

■ Check the microprocessor without any converter or interface circuits.

■ Test the converters alone.

Testing the converters alone calls for the following:

1. Jumping the a/d output to the d/a input.

2. Connecting +5 V or ground to the address inputs, as required by the converter address.

3. Using an external pulse generator to start the a/d and a delayed pulse to strobe the d/a input latches.

4. Connecting a dc voltage to the addressed a/d input line and comparing the d/a output with the input voltage. Repeat this for several voltage levels.

Once the system is set up, you can test the a/d and d/a converters with the microprocessor and a simple software routine.

The subroutine lets you select, with the control panel, each a/d converter channel and the test voltage (see table). The number representing the test voltage is stored in the d/a memory. The difference between the input number, X, and the a/d output is displayed on the panel. The program performs four major tasks:

1. Fetches the number X from the control panel and loads the d/a converter.

2. Fetches the multiplexer address from the control panel and selects the input channel.

3. Reads and stores the a/d output.

4. Calculates and displays the error.

References

1. Data sheet for IMP-16C microprocessor set, National Semiconductor, Santa Clara, CA 95051.

2. Reyling, G., "Extend LSI-Processor Capabilities," *Electronic Design* No. 22, Oct. 25, 1974, pp. 90-95.

3. Data sheet for the MN-7000 data-acquisition subsystem, Micro Networks, Worcester, MA 01604.

4. Data sheet for the DAC-85 12-bit d/a converter, Burr-Brown, Tucson, AZ 85706.

Generating Simultaneous Analog Outputs

JOHN CONNORS, HENRY BELL,
BERNARD NORDMANN, AND
DAVID WAINLAND
*Naval Surface Weapons Center,
White Oak, Maryland*

Interfacing digital-to-analog converters to a microprocessor is a straightforward job. Just connect them to the output bus and assign them channel numbers. Each converter will then deliver its analog output when addressed. But this isn't sufficient if you need several simultaneous output changes because individual addressing creates time delays between adjacent channel outputs.

You can avoid the time delays by first having the data for all channels stored in an array of buffer latches and then, after all channels are loaded, strobing the d/a converters so they all get the data at the same time.

A typical sequential system for multiple analog outputs has data transferred from the processor to the Channel-1 data latches using software commands and external control logic (Fig. 1). As soon as the data are latched, d/a conversion for Channel 1 begins.

The computer then generates a second set of software instructions that transfer data to Channel 2's data latches. When the new data are latched, conversion on Channel 2 begins. This process repeats until all data-output channels are accounted for.

For a given computer or microprocessor, the time interval between the beginning of the d/a conversion on one channel and that of the next channel can be calculated. All you need to assume is that all output data are already stored in the computer memory so that all transfer times are the same.

Let's use the National Semiconductor (Santa Clara, CA) IMP-16 microprocessor as a specific example of how the two data-output methods compare.

With conventional sequential addressing, to send data to an output channel requires three instructions for the first channel and two instructions for each additional channel. The first channel needs an instruction that identifies that channel's address. For all subsequent channels,

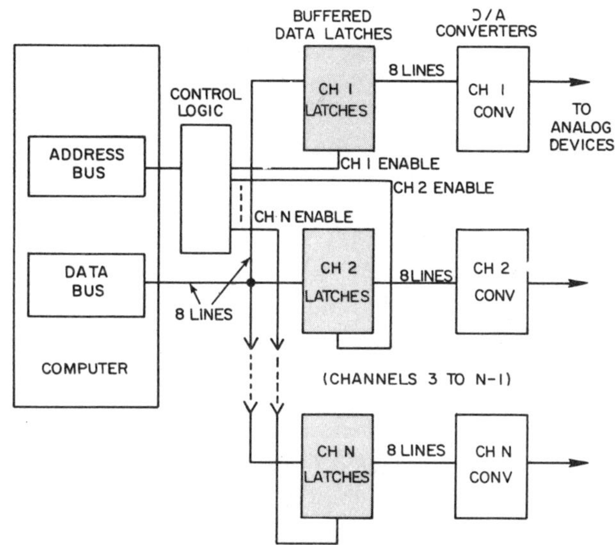

1. **A sequential-output d/a-converter interface** can delay the signals by approximately 20 μs for each channel fed by the computer.

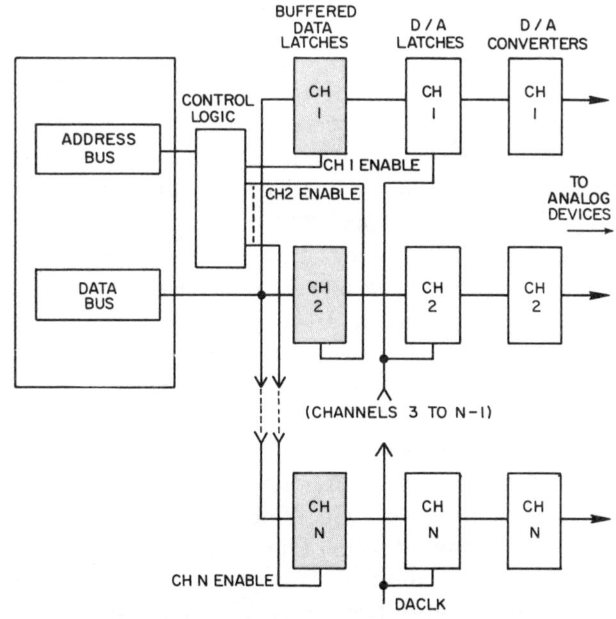

2. **To obtain simultaneous analog outputs** from a multichannel d/a converter system, use an extra set of latches to hold the digital words.

the new address can be entered as part of the output instruction.

The two main instructions required include the LD command, which takes the stored data and sends them to a location from which they can be transferred to the output channel selected. The other command, ROUT, transfers the data from the computer to the output channel. A simple output program for this sequence is shown in Table 1.

Execution time of the two instructions on the IMP-16 requires a little less than 20 μs. Therefore the time interval between the beginning of d/a conversion on one channel and on the next is 20 μs. Also, if there are N channels, the d/a conversion on the Nth channel would begin (N-1) $\times$ 20 μs after the first channel—a considerable delay if you need simultaneous changes.

Extra latches eliminate the delay

There is an alternative (Fig. 2) for applications where time delays like the one just described are intolerable. An additional set of data latches for each channel can be added to hold data before strobing the d/a converters. Data are transferred from the computer to the extra latches in the same way they were transferred to the converters, as explained earlier. However, the d/a converter latches are disabled. After data have been transferred to all N channels, a pulse from the computer or generated externally enables the d/a converter latches and transfers data to all converters simultaneously so that all converter outputs will change at the same time.

Let's see how this simultaneous interface circuit goes together for a dual-output system. Data transfer from the computer is accomplished by use of software instructions, a decoding circuit and the d/a converter interface. The software routine needed is shown in Table 2 and the decoding circuit and d/a interface are shown in Figs. 3 and 4, respectively.

The software places data on the computer's buffered 16-bit data-out bus (BDO), loads the correct address on the 16-bit address bus (ADX) and supplies the decoder and interface circuits with pulses to control the latches. Data that go to the BDO bus must originate in the IMP's accumulator $\emptyset$ (AC$\emptyset$).

The first instruction shown in Table 2 (line 1$\emptyset\emptyset$ loads data into AC$\emptyset$ from wherever they are currently being stored. The address sent to the ADX bus is the sum of the contents of accumulator 3 (AC3) and the seven-bit channel address specified in the output instruction, ROUT N.

You have the option of how to allocate the word for the address bus. In the system shown, bits 3

Table 1. Sequential output program

Program address	Label	Command		Comments
50	DATA1:	.WORD	75A6	
51	DATA2:	.WORD	6847	
52	DATA3:	.WORD	FF83	
53	DATA4:	.WORD	8000	
100	WAIT:	BOC	$\emptyset$D, WAIT	; Program is halted ; at line 100 until signal ; is received on condition ; bit "$\emptyset$D" indicating it ; is time for computer ; to output data.
101		LI	3, 18	; Places device address 3 ; + channel address $\emptyset$ in ; accumulator 3.
102		LD	$\emptyset$, DATA1	; Place contents of ; DATA1 in AC$\emptyset$
103		ROUT	$\emptyset$	; Data are output to ; channel 0 of device 3
104		LD	$\emptyset$, DATA2	; Contents of DATA2 ; are placed in AC$\emptyset$
105		ROUT	1	; Data are output to ; CM1 approx. 20 μs ; after data were output ; to CM$\emptyset$
106		LD	$\emptyset$, DATA3	
107		ROUT	2	; Data are output to ; CH2 approx. 40 μs ; after data were output ; to CH$\emptyset$
108		LD	$\emptyset$, DATA4	
109		ROUT	3	; Data are output to ; CH2 approx. 60 μs ; after data were ; output to CH$\emptyset$

Table 2. Simultaneous output program

Program address	Label	Command		Comments
50	DATA1:	.WORD	0125	; DATA1 & DATA2 are memory
51	DATA2:	.WORD	0672	; locations containing stored ; data
100		LD	$\emptyset$, DATA1	; Load AC$\emptyset$ with contents of DATA1
101		LI	3, 18	; Load AC3 with 18 hexadecimal
102		ROUT	$\emptyset$	; Add $\emptyset$ to AC3 and send the ; sum to ADX BUS, send con- ; tents of AC$\emptyset$ to BDO BUS, ; pulse WRP and WRPA lines.
103		LD	$\emptyset$, DATA2	; Load AC$\emptyset$ with contents of DATA2
104		ROUT	1	; Add 1 to AC3 and send sum ; to ADX BUS, send contents ; of AC$\emptyset$ to BDO BUS, pulse ; WRP and WRPA lines.

to 6 identify an interface device and permit up to 16 peripheral units. The three remaining bits, $\emptyset$ through 2, correspond to the channel code for a particular device. This lets each device handle up to eight channels. The nine bits remaining can be used for further system expansion should the need arise.

The address for the first channel is given on lines 1$\emptyset$1 and 1$\emptyset$2 of Table 2. The sum specifies channel $\emptyset$ of device 3 (the d/a interface). Execution of line 1$\emptyset$2 transfers this address to the

ADX bus, sends the contents of AC∅ to the BDO bus and provides two latching pulses, WRP and WRPA.

Program lines 1∅3 and 1∅4 repeat the process for Channel 1. Line 1∅3 loads the new data into AC∅ and line 1∅4 updates the address, sends the address and data to their respective busses and supplies the two latching pulses.

When the device and channel numbers are transferred to the ADX bus, they also appear on the input lines of the 74175 latches in the decoder circuit of Fig. 3. The WRP pulse latches the address, then the two 74154 decoders can enable the proper device-number and channel-number lines. A selected decoder line is LOW, while all unselected lines are HIGH. Decoder timing relationships are shown in Fig. 5a.

When data are transferred to the BDO bus they also appear at the input lines to the buffered

data latches of each channel. Latching the data to the proper channel's latches is the job of the control logic circuit of Fig. 4. This circuit prevents Channel 1 from receiving Channel ∅ data, and vice-versa.

Inputs to the control-logic circuit include the device-3 decoder line, Channel-∅ and Channel-1 decoder lines and the WRPA line. All the decoder lines are inverted and then the inverted lines for device 3 and Channel ∅ are NANDed with WRPA to provide an enabling pulse to lock Channel-∅ data into the latches. Similarly, the inverted Channel-3 line and the Channel-1 line are NANDed to enable the Channel-1 latches.

The timing sequence for latching in the data is shown in Fig. 5. When the inverted device and channel numbers and WRPA are all HIGH (starting at t_1), the NAND output goes LOW. About 100 ns later, at t_2, the WRPA line goes

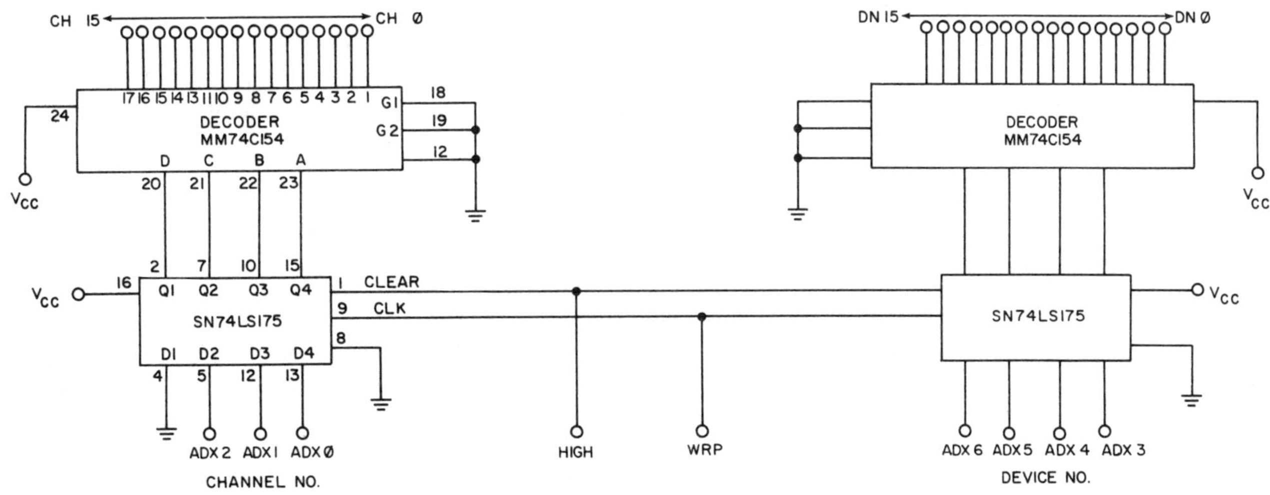

3. The channel and device number can be decoded by using a latch and a one-of-16 decoder. This system can be expanded for as many channels as you need, just by adding extra latches and decoders.

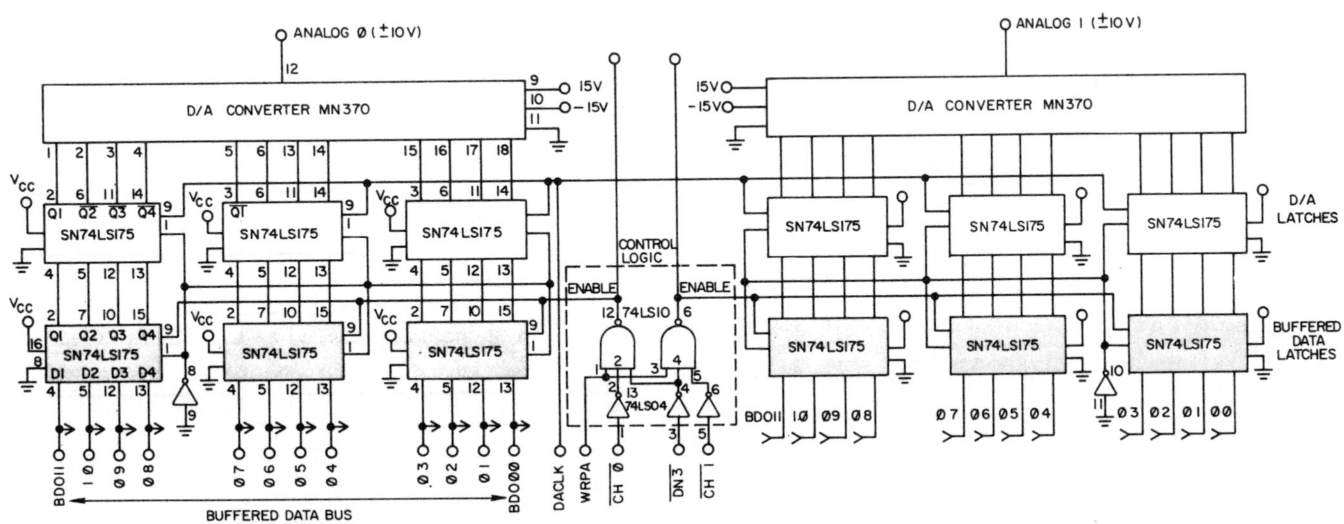

4. The d/a-converter interface circuit uses an extra set of data latches to buffer the computer data and store the data until all channels are loaded. A common strobe signal starts all the converters.

LOW and returns the NAND gate to a HIGH output. At the same time data on the BDO bus are latched into the data buffers.

Once all the data latches are loaded, the data can be transferred to the d/a converters by a pulse on the data clock line (DACLK). Since the data appear simultaneously (barring propagation delays) on all the converter inputs, all outputs will change simultaneously. All the d/a converter-latch outputs are inverted except for the most significant bit. This was done to convert the two's-complement format used in the IMP to the type of binary code required by the d/a converter selected, in this case a Micro Networks (Worcester, MA) MN370.

Since the circuit uses low-power, Schottky TTL, bypass capacitors should be included to eliminate any chance of faulty operation due to current spikes at the clock frequency. A 0.01-μF capacitor should be used across each package's supply leads and a 10-μF capacitor should be connected across the supply leads where they enter the circuit board.

The two-channel interface can easily be expanded to handle more channels. For instance, if eight channels are needed the following modifications must be made: For each new channel, connect up additional latches and d/a converters as shown for the two channels (in Fig. 4). Then, connect the NAND-gate inputs to the inverted decoder output of device 3, to WRPA and to a previously unused channel-decoder output, between 2 and 7.

There is an alternative to the additional data latches used for each converter (Fig. 6). Try using multiple sample-and-hold amplifiers to hold the analog signals. Since there are no latches, the d/a conversions all take place at different times. When the DACLK line is pulsed, data from d/a converters get locked into the amplifiers.

The costs of the s/h circuits are still higher than that of the extra latches, so this method really isn't economically feasible. Also, voltage offsets, drifts and decay are error sources for the s/h circuits.

Table 3. System self-test program

Program address	Label	Command		Comments
1	LOOP:	.WORD	0FFF	;12 bit counter to cycle ; through all possible codes.
2	START:	.WORD	07FF	; Represents positive full ; scale
3		LI	3, 018	; Select Device 3, CH 0.
4	LP1:	LD	2, LOOP	
5		LD	0, START	
6	LP2:	ROUT	0	; Dev. 3, CH 0.
7		ROUT	1	; Dev 3, CH 1.
8		PFLG	0	; Gate data into d/a.
9		AISZ	0, −1	; Decr d/a code.
10		RCPY	1, 1	
11		AISZ	2, −1	; Decr loop counter.
12		JMP	LP2	
13		JMP	LP1	
	.END			

Let the system check itself

Once you have the system up and running, every so often you can run a self-check to make sure the system is still operating properly. Table 3 lists a program that will test the operation of the d/a-converter interface. Each complete loop through the program provides a staircase output from each d/a converter. The range of each unit will vary from +10 to −10 V and if you continuously loop through the program you can see the converter outputs on an oscilloscope.

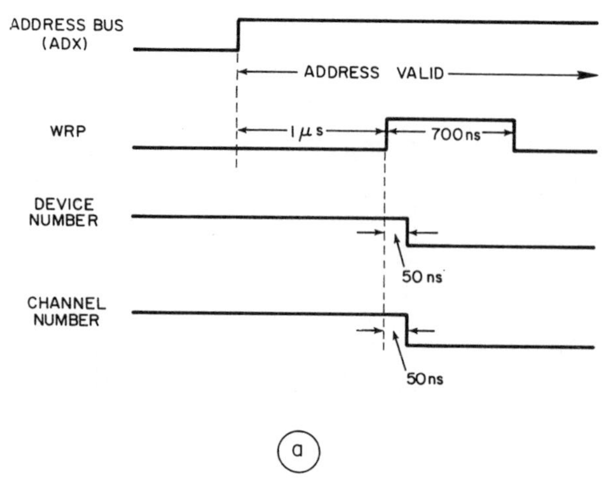

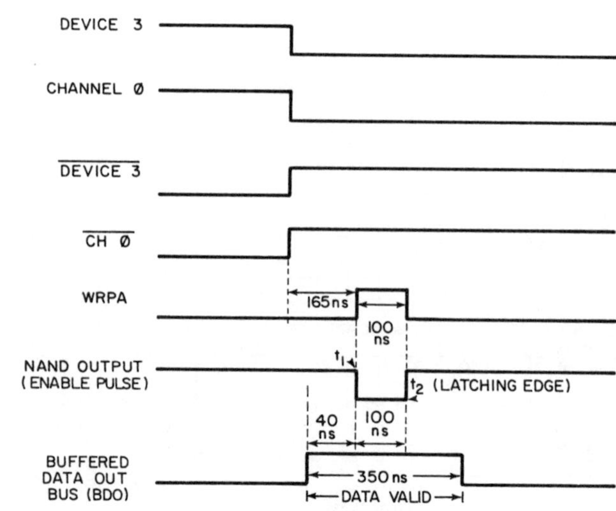

5. **Timing relationships** for the decoder circuit (a), and the d/a interface circuit (b), have no critical conditions.

After the device is selected, the enable pulse transfers data from the buffers to the converters.

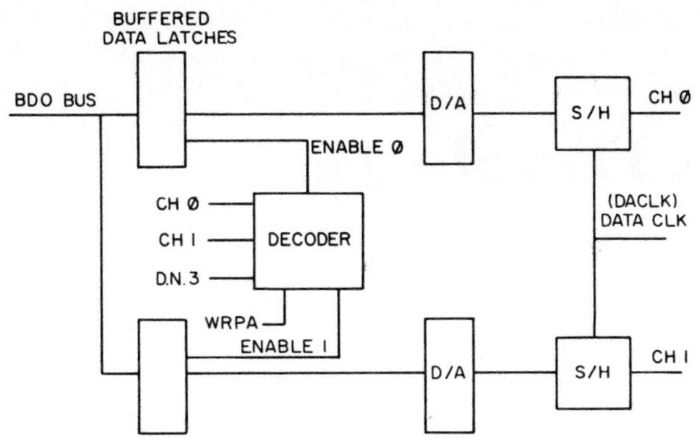

6. **An alternative to the extra data latches** uses multiple sample-and-hold amplifiers to store the analog outputs of the d/a converters.

Line 1 of the program is a memory location that contains the data word ØFFF which will be used to count the number of program cycles. (All numerical values in Table 3 are in hexadecimal notation.) Line 2 defines another location that contains the data word Ø7FF, which corresponds to the positive full-scale value of the d/a converter. The next program line (line 3) loads the code for device 3 and Channel Ø into AC3. Hex value 18 corresponds to device 3, Channel Ø. Line 4 loads the contents of LOOP (data word ØFFF) into accumulator 2 while the next line loads the contents of START (Ø7FF) into ACØ.

Lines 6 and 7 output the contents of ACØ into Channels Ø and 1, respectively. After these two instructions each channel's buffered latches contain the binary equivalent to 7FF. Line 8 pulses a computer flag that is connected to the DACLK line for test purposes. When the flag is pulsed, the 7FF data are transferred to the d/a converters and conversion begins.

The instruction given on line 9—add immediate, skip if zero (AISZ)—adds −1 to the contents of ACØ thus decrementing it by 1. In this way each cycle of the program will generate an analog signal that is decreasing in value, thus forming a descending staircase.

If the accumulator reaches zero, the program skips the next instruction and performs the instruction on line 11, which decrements the contents of AC2. Since AC2 originally contained ØFFF, the first time the instruction is followed the contents of AC2 reduce to ØFFE. Line 12 will then be executed, and this loops the program back to line 6. If the instruction of line 11 causes the AC2 to reach Ø, the d/a converter will output a −10-V signal and the program will loop back to line 4 instead of line 6.

Thus, this program generates all possible converter codes and produces a +10 to −10-V staircase. The program will cycle indefinitely and can only be stopped by pressing the Halt or Initialize switch on the computer front panel.

Interfacing with Data Displays

ROGER THOMPSON
Microprocessor Engineer,
National Semiconductor, Santa Clara

The data-handling capabilities of 8-bit microprocessors are both versatile and flexible enough to interface with displays that run the gamut from simple seven-segment digital types to complex CRT terminals.

A seven-segment digital display requires only infrequent updating, and when it is updated, very little information actually transfers to the display. A video-display terminal must be updated—or refreshed—very frequently (unless a storage tube is used), and that entails a large amount of data.

Data can be transferred from buffer memory to a display by various methods. The simplest is a software-controlled transfer, which uses minimal peripheral-interface hardware. However, the software approach may turn out to be the slowest one when performed on the usual macroprogram level. Higher data rates can be obtained through microprogramming.

A completely hardwired direct-memory-access (DMA) approach achieves the highest throughputs. A microprocessor like the IMP-8 (Fig. 1) allows these and other data-transfer methods.

Treat the display as a standard peripheral device

When you use the 8-bit microprocessor,[1,2] the display should be treated as a standard peripheral unit that attaches to the μP's bus in the same way that memory does. The IMP-8 instruction set contains no instructions specifically intended for peripheral operations. All peripheral transactions with the CPU are performed by standard memory-reference instructions, like Load Accumulator from memory and Store Accumulator in memory.

Two basic software-control methods—loop and in-line—may be employed on the macroprogram level.

The loop method executes a sequence of instructions over and over again (Fig. 2). This method has the advantage that only a few words of code are needed to transfer a large block of data from

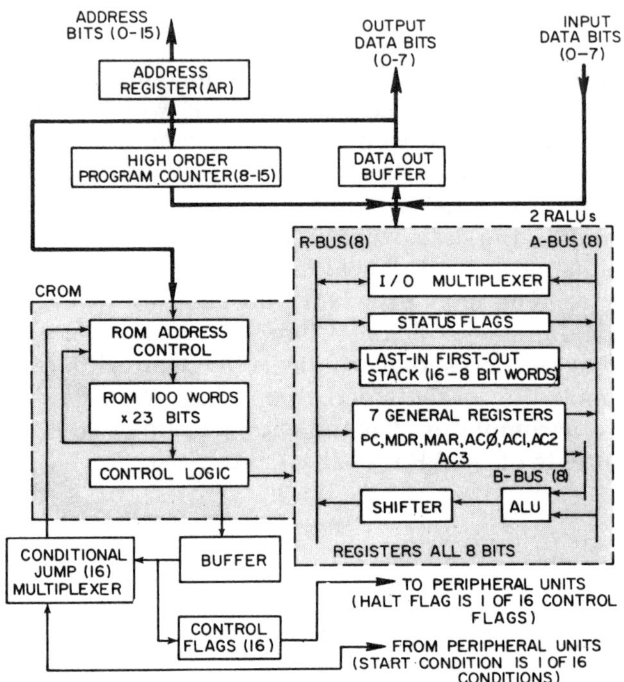

1. **The IMP-8, an 8-bit microprogrammable μP,** employs two 4-bit RALUs (register and arithmetic logic units) and one CROM (control read-only memory). The μP's instruction set can be changed by modifying the existing CROM or by adding extra CROMs in parallel.

memory to the peripheral. However, to keep track of the buffer word being processed, the pointers for the last-in, first-out stack must be incremented and tested continually. As a result, the actual rate of transmission is relatively slow.

In Fig. 2, BUF1 represents the starting address of the first buffer. AC3, the third accumulator, functions as the index register and increments once for each data word transferred. When AC3 becomes equal to zero, the loop will be terminated and the transfer of a second buffer can begin. For each pass through the loop, four machine instructions must be executed, requiring 44 machine cycles at 1.4 μs (minimum) per cycle. Hence, one 8-bit word can be transferred every 61.6 μs.

When only a few data words need be transferred to a peripheral, the data rate can be increased about 50 percent by using the in-line method (Fig. 3). This method eliminates the control loop and uses instead a separate Load and Store-instruction pair.

In Fig. 3, BUF1 is again the starting address and AC3 serves as the base index register. The short program increments the displacement value for each Load instruction. The method requires only the execution of two machine instructions for each data transfer, and these two instructions

tical to the structures of other members of the IMP family.[3] Each microinstruction specifies the exact function of the ALU and any external logic during that microcycle.

For example,

$$\text{ADD, AC3,, AC2   CIN}$$

specifies an Add operation. The A-bus operand is AC3, and the B-bus operand is undefined—and consequently is interpreted as all zeros. CIN indicates that the result will be incremented. In this example AC2 indicates that the final result

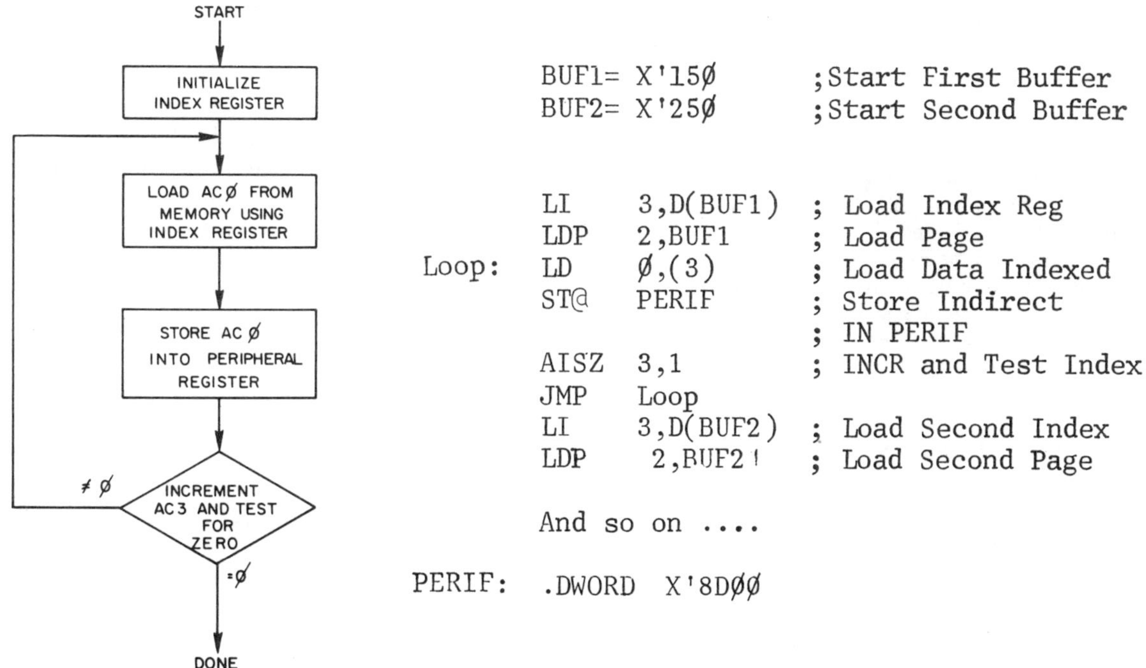


```
                          BUF1= X'15Ø        ;Start First Buffer
                          BUF2= X'25Ø        ;Start Second Buffer

                   LI     3,D(BUF1)   ; Load Index Reg
                   LDP    2,BUF1      ; Load Page
           Loop:   LD     Ø,(3)       ; Load Data Indexed
                   ST@    PERIF       ; Store Indirect
                                      ; IN PERIF
                   AISZ   3,1         ; INCR and Test Index
                   JMP    Loop
                   LI     3,D(BUF2)   ; Load Second Index
                   LDP    2,BUF2      ; Load Second Page

                   And so on ....

           PERIF:  .DWORD  X'8DØØ
```

2. The loop method uses only a few words of machine code to transfer an 8-bit word from memory to a peripheral display. However, each transfer takes a lengthy 62 μs since stack pointers in the RALUs must be continually tested and incremented. A speed-enhancing microprogrammed approach uses the same flow chart.

require only 26 machine cycles at 1.4 μs per cycle. Hence one 8-bit word can be transferred every 36 μs. However, the in-line method requires more memory to store the control program than does the loop method.

Microprogramming speeds data transfers

Other techniques for data transfer deal directly with the microprogram that controls the execution of each machine instruction. With the IMP-8 μP, you can add or delete portions of the microprogram to achieve an altered instruction set.

But microprogramming lengthens development time and costs, and it can entail additional CROMs (control and read-only memories). In general, this approach becomes economical only for high-volume applications.

IMP-8 microprogramming structures are iden-

(after incrementing) will be stored in that accumulator.

Several microinstructions are sequenced together to form a general subroutine. Each subroutine is executed as a response to a fetched and decoded macroinstruction from memory.

A microprogram-loop method like that discussed on the macroprogram level offers several advantages. First, the four-machine-instruction loop is replaced by a single machine instruction. And since all data are transferred within the execution of a single machine instruction, the over-all data rate can be reduced dramatically.

The example in Fig. 4 requires only 9.2 machine cycles per pass through the loop. Since each machine cycle requires only 1.4 μs, each word transmitted takes just 12.9 μs. That's about 1/5 the time needed by the macroprogrammed loop.

The in-line method, when applied on the micro-

```
       BUF1 = X'15Ø


       LI      3,D(BUF1)
       LDP     2,BUF1
START:
       LD      Ø,(3)    ;LOAD FIRST WORD
       ST@     PERIF    ;SEND TO PERIPHERAL
       LD      Ø,1(3)
       ST@     PERIF    ;SEND SECOND WORD
       LD      Ø,2(3)
       ST@     PERIF    ;SEND THIRD WORD


       AND SO ON .....


PERIF:.DWORD  X'8DØØ
```

3. The in-line method increases the data rate of the loop method by about 50 percent when only a few words need be transferred. The routine reads a memory location's data into accumulator zero and then outputs that data to the peripheral. It then reads the next memory location and transfers its data to the same peripheral. The routine continues to do so for each pair of Load and Store instructions.

program level, doesn't increase speed much over the microprogrammed-loop approach. Only two machine cycles can be saved per word transmitted. Everything else in the example remains the same. Thus, the transmission rate reduces to one word every 10 μs.

Because the total microprogram storage area is rather limited for the IMP-8, the in-line method should be employed only for very limited data transfers, even though a comparison between this method and the macroprogram in-line version shows a 3-to-1 speed advantage. It requires only one machine instruction, as opposed to two for each buffer-word transferred.

Hardware-controlled data transfers

In the clock-hold DMA method—a hardware implementation—the requesting peripheral must generate a clock-hold request whenever it requires data (Fig. 5). The request temporarily stops the CPU clocks for a maximum of 10 μs. During this period, the CPU address buffers are disabled, allowing the requesting peripheral to take control of the address bus.

Data rates are limited to the cycle rate of the memory. For example, with a memory having 1-μs access, up to 10 words of data could be transferred during a 10-μs clock-hold period.

Since no software control is needed, the peripheral's request can be serviced in less than 1 machine cycle, or 1.4 μs. However only a limited

number of data words per request can be transferred; the clocks can be held only for a short period of time each machine cycle.

An interrupt-controlled DMA doesn't rely on a stopping of clocks. Instead, the peripheral requiring data requests a CPU interrupt.

The interrupt must be serviced under program control. First the DMA interrupt-service routine executes a Halt instruction, which sets the CPU Halt flag. This flag and its complement then are used as the appropriate address-buffer enable disable signals. As was the case with the clock-hold method, data can be transferred at the cycle rate of the memory once the requesting peripheral obtains control of the address bus.

When data exchange has terminated, the requesting peripheral must raise the Start jump-condition input to the CPU. This in turn resets the Halt flag that established the original setting of the CPU address buffers. Once the Halt flag has been lowered, the Start input can be lowered, too. This returns control to the machine instruction that follows the Halt instruction in the interrupt-service routine.

Although the method doesn't handle data any faster than the clock-hold method, it can transfer as many words as required. However, an interrupt-latency time exists between the actual interrupt request and the time the first word is transferred. For the application described, the latency time is about 75 μs, corresponding to the time needed by the μP to prepare for its execution of the Halt instruction.

Organize a two-port memory

In all of the examples described, the buffer memory was presumed to be part of the main-system memory. But since data are all that are being transferred, there is no reason for the buffer memory to be organized the same way as the instruction memory. In fact, if the buffer is organized as a two-port memory, high data rates can be sustained for any length of time without the need for a μP interrupt. This, in turn, would eliminate the interrupt latency time, and allow transfer of data within one machine cycle or 1.4 μs on the standard IMP-8.

One port performs read-only operations, and is controlled directly by the peripheral. The second port, a write-only, is connected to the main μP I/O bus.

The μP generates data and stores it in the buffer memory, from which the peripheral takes data. However, the buffer memory does not acknowledge the transfer to the IMP-8 μP. After each write operation, the CPU must check the buffer to determine if it is in a DMA mode. Only when the buffer completes a data transfer can the μP write in new data.

```
*          MEMORY ADDRESS REGISTER(MAR) CONTAINS PERIPHERAL
*               PAGE ADDRESS.
*          MEMORY DATA REGISTER(MDR) CONTAINS PERIPHERAL
*               BYTE ADDRESS.
*          ACCUM 3 CONTAINS BUFFER PAGE ADDRESS.
*          ACCUM 2 CONTAINS BUFFER BYTE ADDRESS.
*
*
LOOP       PFLG,HI,MAR,,Ø        Ø        * SEND HIGH ORDER PERIF ADDRESS
           PFLG,LO,MDR,,Ø        Ø        * SEND LOW ORDER PERIF ADDRESS
           PFLG,WRITE,ACØ,,Ø     Ø        * WRITE DATA IN ACØ TO PERIF
           ADD,AC3,,AC3          CIN      * INCR AC3
           B,NREQØ              CONTINUE,FETCH   * TEST, IF BUFFER DONE
                                                 * FETCH NEXT MACHINE
                                                 * INSTRUCTION
    CONTINUE
           PFLG.HI,AC2,,Ø        Ø        * SEND BUFFER PAGE ADDRESS
           PFLG,READ,AC3,,ACØ   DATAIN    * SEND BUFFER BYTE ADDRESS, THEN
                                          * READ NEXT WORD IN BUFFER
                                          * SAVE IN ACØ FOR NEXT TRANSMISSION
           B                   LOOP       * REPEAT LOOP
```

4. A microprogram-control version of the loop method increases data rates by a factor of five. The listing, which shows the source code to a microassembler, implements the flow chart shown in Fig. 2. The first several lines essentially are comments that identify the locations of different pieces of information.

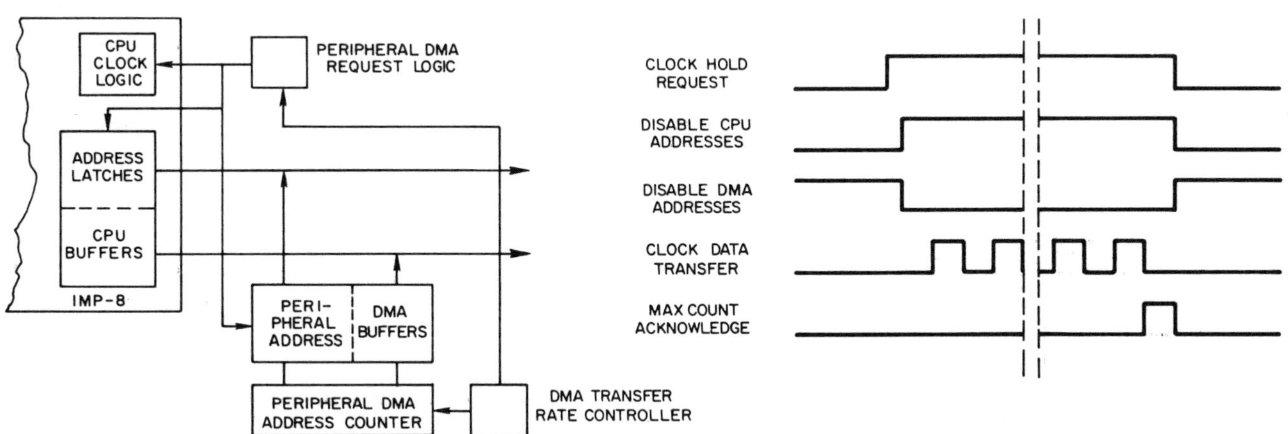

5. A completely hardwired transfer technique—clock-hold DMA—can service a peripheral's data request in less than one machine cycle, or 1.4 μs. But only a limited number of words can be transferred, because the clocks can be held only for a short period during each machine cycle.

When the peripheral requests data from the buffer, it must wait only until the completion of any previous μP write operation. Since this is always less than one machine cycle, the peripheral requesting data always gains access in less than one machine cycle.

The examples given in this article are by no means the only methods of transferring data from memory to peripherals. In fact, it may be possible to combine these methods to satisfy different application requirements. Also, the examples cover only the case of transferring blocks of data from memory to peripherals. The same concepts hold true, with minor modification, for transferring to the microprocessor's memory data from the peripheral device.

Moreover, the same methods can be used with the IMP-16, a 16-bit version of the IMP-8. In all cases, the rate of transmission will be comparable and the hardware required will be similar. The only significant difference is that 16-bit data words will be transferred where 8-bit words were before.

References

1. *IMP-8 Applications Manual*, Publication #4200032, National Semiconductor, Santa Clara, CA 95051.

2. *IMP-8 Programming Manual*, Publication #4200031, *ibid.*

3. *IMP Microprogramming Manual*, Publication #4200062, *ibid.*

SECTION IX

Some Recent Microprocessors

Though the microprocessors described here are too new to have generated a body of applications literature, each has important features that make it a contender for new designs.

The Signetics 2650 is an NMOS 8-bit CPU that can be used to build a completely static microcomputer system. It is easily interfaced with conventional TTL logic and avoids the synchronization problems of some microprocessors. Second-sourced by Intersil the 2650 is gaining popularity for relatively simple, low-cost applications.

RCA's second Cosmac microprocessor, the CDP1802, is one of the few CMOS microprocessors available. The 8-bit circuit's major advantages are low power dissipation, high speed, high noise immunity, and a wide operating-temperature range. The 1802 is second-sourced by Hughes, and a broad line of compatible support chips is available .

An unusual feature of Intersil's IM6100 is its 12-bit word length. Engineers find the 6100 easy to design with because its architecture is similar to Digital Equipment Corp's popular PDP-8/E minicomputer; much of the existing software is directly transferable to the microprocessor. Like RCA's 1802, the 6100 employs CMOS technology and shares many of the same advantages—low dissipation, high speed, etc. Harris Semiconductor is a licensed second source.

Using the 2650 Microprocessor

DAVID UIMARI
Microprocessor Product Marketing Manager,
Signetics, Sunnyvale

A completely static microcomputer system can be built with the 2650 microprocessor as its heart. You can easily interface logic circuits with the μP since every input and output can handle one TTL load. And, many of the multiple-sourced memory and support circuits can be connected without any extra interfacing—thus permitting you to design a low cost system.

The 2650 is a single-chip μP made using an ion-implanted, n-channel, silicon-gate process. It has a fixed command set of 75 instructions, operates on 8-bit parallel data and can address 32,768 bytes. A single +5-V power supply and single-phase TTL clock are all you need to get the μP up and running. All bus outputs of the 2650 are three-state and can drive either one 7400-type load, or four 74LS loads.

Both memory and input/output (I/O) lines operate asynchronously at any speed up to the maximum data transfer rate of the memory circuits without additional buffering. No external latching of data is needed.

Specialized support circuits cut complexity

Aside from the 40-pin μP IC there are many support circuits and development aids in the 2650 family (Tables 1 and 2). Some of the specialized interface circuits to be introduced include the 2651 programmable communication interface (PCI), which accepts program instructions from the μP and supports almost any serial-data communication mode. Another circuit, the 2655, is a programmable peripheral interface (PPI) that contains three bidirectional 8-bit I/O ports and an 8-bit data bus to communicate with the processor.

The 2650 has a maximum clock frequency of 1.25 MHz, giving a clock period of 800 ns. Each processor cycle requires three clock periods, and an instruction can require two, three or four processor cycles. Since the μP contains static rather than dynamic circuitry, the clock frequency can be dropped to zero without affecting

A complete microcomputer on a board, the 2650PC-1000, contains the 2650 μP, a control and R/W memory, an I/O port, a clock and all necessary interface circuits to get a system up and running.

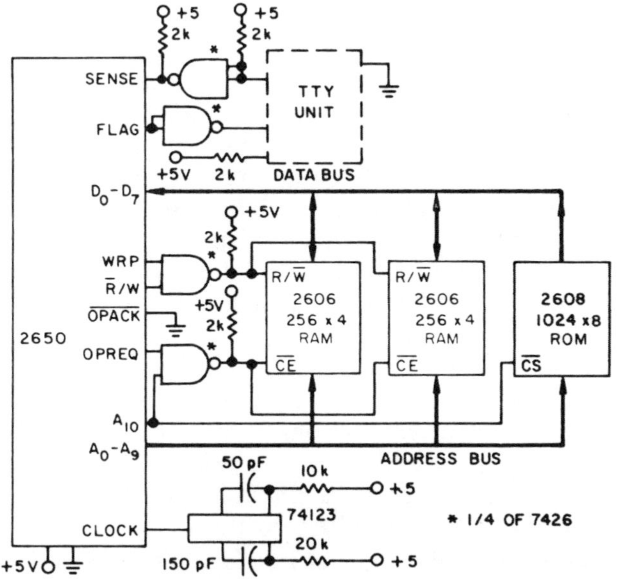

1. **You can put together a complete microcomputer** with only six ICs. The 2650 offers full TTL compatibility on every input and output line to ease the interface requirements to external circuits.

Table 1. System components for the 2650

Product	Description					Price (1-24)	
2650	8-Bit,	N-channel,	microprocessor			$26.50	
2651	Programmable communication interface					‡	
2655	Programmable peripheral interface					‡	
2102-1	1024 × 1,	N-channel,	500 ns	RAM		4.17	
2604	4096 × 1,	N-channel,	300 ns	RAM		22.00	
2606	256 × 4,	N-channel,	750 ns	RAM		5.00	
2606-1	256 × 4,	N-channel,	500 ns	RAM		5.50	
2608	1024 × 8,	N-channel,	650 ns	ROM		*	
82S10/11	1024 × 1,	Bipolar,	45 ns	RAM		24.60	
82S23/123	32 × 8,	Bipolar,	50 ns	PROM		6.45	
82S114	256 × 8,	Bipolar,	60 ns	PROM		39.00	
82S115	512 × 8,	Bipolar,	60 ns	PROM		40.00	
82S126/129	256 × 4,	Bipolar,	50 ns	PROM		8.20	
82S130/131	512 × 4,	Bipolar,	50 ns	PROM		15.05	
8T26	Three-state quad bus transceiver					4.29	
8T28	Three-state quad bus transceiver					4.29	
8T31	8-Bit bidirectional input-output port					13.20	
8T34	Quad three-state transceiver					3.63	
8T95/96	Hex three-state buffer					2.90	
8T97/98	Hex three-state buffer					2.90	
2650PC1001	Prototyping card					495.00	
2650PC2000	4-k byte memory board					395.00	
2650PC3000	Demonstration module					149.00	
2650KT9000	Prototyping kit					95.00	
2650S2000	Development/demonstration base with power supply					775.00	
2650BM1000	Manual set, including update service					40.00	
2650AS1000	PIPASM—Fortran IV batch cross assembler			(32-Bit)		1250.00	
2650AS1100	PIPASM—Fortran IV batch cross assembler			(16-Bit)		1250.00	
2650SM1000	PIPSIM—Fortran IV batch cross simulator			(32-Bit)		750.00	
2650SM1100	PIPSIM—Fortran IV batch cross simulator			(16-Bit)		750.00	
Training	Extensive three day seminar describing					375.00	(West Coast)
	2650 hardware, programming, and applications					425.00	(Other)
	One-day basic microprocessor seminar					40.00	
2650KT9500 ABC kit						190.00	
2650PC1500 ABC card						275.00	

* not available in unit-quantity bracket.
‡ to be announced.

any internal registers. The μP can then be manually stepped through a program for debugging.

A 2650-based microcomputer requires almost no external support circuits, save for a ROM or RAM, a clock and some line drivers (Fig. 1). All the ROMs or RAMs are connected to the data and address busses and up to five other control pins. The entire system is modularized and can be expanded in building-block fashion.

The three main interconnecting busses are the bidirectional data bus, which requires eight lines; the address bus, which requires up to 15 lines; and the memory-control bus, which requires up to five lines. In addition to the 8-bit bidirectional data bus on the 2650, a single-bit-wide I/O port for serial inputs is built into the μP.

Eight-bit wide I/O instructions either are one or two-byte commands. They are designated as nonextended (one byte) or extended (two byte). The nonextended I/O instructions can be directed to one of two I/O devices designated as either data or control. The data or control devices can be accessed from any general purpose register with a single-byte read or write instruction. Extended I/O instructions require two bytes and can be used simultaneously to select a device and transfer data to it.

Assembling a μC is easy

To get a 2650-based system operating, let's first look at all the control and signal pins on the μP (Fig. 2). The SENSE line (pin 1) is a direct input to one of the bits of the Program Status Word register in the 2650 (a special-purpose, 16-bit register that holds status and control bits; its abbreviation is PSW). This pin serves as a serial input port. The bit can be stored or tested by a software instruction.

Pins 2 through 14 represent the lower 13 bits of the address bus and can directly address 8-k bytes of memory. The $\overline{\text{ADREN}}$ (Address Enable)

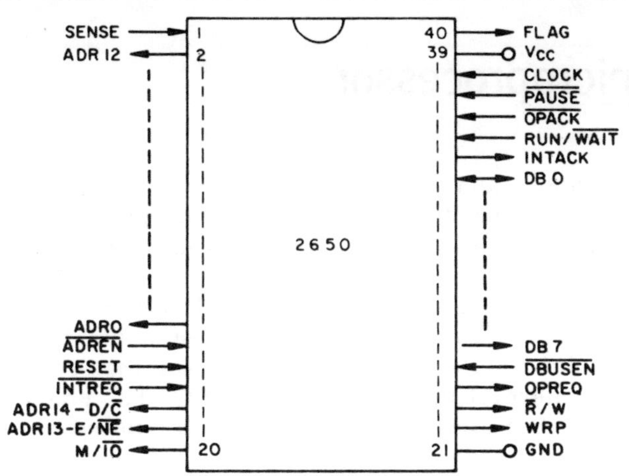

2. The different control lines on the 2650 provide handshaking responses to simplify the interface. Two of the memory-address lines serve the dual purpose of cutting the pin count and providing better control.

signal from pin 15 permits external control of the three-state address bus. When pin 15 is HIGH, the address-bus lines appear as high impedances; this permits wired-OR connections with other signal lines.

The RESET line (pin 16) is normally used to start the processor after power-up or to restart a program. When brought HIGH, RESET clears both the Interrupt Inhibit control bit of the PSW and the Internal Interrupt-Waiting signal, then sets the Instruction Address Register to zero.

Pin 17 is the $\overline{\text{INTREQ}}$ input (Interrupt Request) and is normally HIGH. By bringing the line LOW, an external device can change the program flow. When the processor recognizes an $\overline{\text{INTREQ}}$ input, it completes its current instruction, places a ZBSR (Zero Branch to Subroutine Relative) instruction into the instruction register, sets the Interrupt Inhibit bit in the PSW and responds with INTACK (Interrupt Acknowledge) and OPREQ (Operation Request) signals. These signals perform a "handshake" with the peripheral that initiated the interrupt.

Pins 18 and 19, the ADR14 and 13 (D/$\overline{\text{C}}$ and E/$\overline{\text{NE}}$ lines), serve dual functions and are controlled by the next line, pin 20 (the M/$\overline{\text{IO}}$ line). When pin 20 is HIGH (in the M state), pins 18 and 19 act as the higher-order bits of the memory address. However, when pin 20 is LOW, pin 18 is used to discriminate between two types of one-byte I/O instructions. When LOW, pin 18 indicates that either a Read or Write instruction to the I/O device (control) is to be executed; when HIGH, it indicates a Read or Write instruction to the I/O device (data).

The output from pin 19 defines whether a one or two byte I/O operation is being performed. When LOW, the instruction is a one-byte nonextended operation and when HIGH the instruction is a two-byte extended command.

The ground line, pin 21 is connected to the general system ground. The next line, pin 22, is the Write-Pulse output (WRP). It provides a

Table 2. Support hardware and software

Development software	
PIPASM	An assembly-language assembler written in Fortran IV. It operates in a two-pass mode to build a symbol table, issue helpful error messages, produce an easily readable program listing and output a computer readable object module. Two versions are available: The AS1000 for 32-bit machines and the AS1100 for 16-bit machines.
PIPSIM	A Fortran IV program you can use to simulate the execution of your program without using the 2650. PIPSIM maintains its own internal Fortran storage registers to describe the 2650 program, its registers, the ROM/RAM configuration and input data. There are two versions available: The SM1000 for 32-bit machines and the SM1100 for 16-bit units.
PLμS	The Signetics Higher Level Language allows you to program the 2650 in PL-type language and is available for both 16 and 32-bit machines. PLμS is also available from Signetics on mag tape or from NCSS and GE Timeshare Networks.
System development hardware	
TWIN	The Microprocessor Prototype Development System known as TWIN typically consists of three hardware elements: A prototype development computer (PDC), a floppy-disc storage subsystem and a system console. The PDC includes a MOS and bipolar PROM programmer and an in-circuit emulation/hardware debug facility. System software includes operating system file management, debug software, a text editor and a 2650 resident macro assembler.
ABC	The Adaptable Board Computer prototyping system ABC1500/9500, is a modular microcomputer containing a 2650 μP, memory, I/O ports and support circuitry. Included on the board are 512 bytes of RAM and 1-k byte of ROM, containing PIPBUG (a loader, editor and debug program).
KT9000	A microprocessor protoyping kit that contains a 2650 μP and enough circuits to build a single-board computer system.

Internal architecture of the 2650 microprocessor

The internal structure of the 2650 CPU is centered about the ROM and arithmetic-and-logic unit (ALU). An on-chip ROM contains the control microprograms for the ALU, which does the arithmetic, Boolean and combinatorial shifting functions. The ALU performs 8-bit parallel operations and uses carry-look-ahead logic for fast operation.

A second, small ALU is used to increment the instruction address register and to calculate the operand addresses for the indexed and relative addressing modes. This separate address adder permits complex addressing modes to be used with no increase in instruction execution time.

The general-purpose register stack and the subroutine-return address stack are built from static RAM cells to permit clock rates of the μP to be brought all the way down to dc. The register stack contains seven addressable 8-bit registers and the subroutine return-address stack can hold up to eight 15-bit addresses to permit up to eight subroutine nesting levels.

Since the subroutine stack is on the μP chip, very low package-count systems can be built. Separate 15-bit instruction and operand address registers are also included on the chip.

Within the μP is a special-purpose register called the Program Status Word (PSW) that holds the status and control bits of the processor. The PSW can be divided into two parts—an upper and lower half (PSU and PSL). All bits can be tested, loaded, stored, preset or cleared using commands from the fixed instruction set.

The 2650 has only a single level of hardware vectored interrupt. When an interrupt occurs, the μP finishes its current instruction and then sets the interrupt-inhibit bit in the PSW. The processor then executes a Zero Branch to Subroutine Relative instruction (ZBSR) and sends out Interrupt Acknowledge and Operation Request signals. When the interrupting device receives in INTACK signal, it inputs an 8-bit address (the interrupt vector) on the data bus.

The basic instruction cycle for the 2650 requires three clock periods. Direct instructions require from one to three processor cycles. The circuit only requires a single-phase clock that runs at a maximum speed of 1.25 MHz.

The processor is capable of directly addressing 32-k words of memory since there are 15 address lines. Two of the address lines also serve as control lines on a multiplexed basis. Both the ADR13 and ADR14 lines deliver address data when the M/$\overline{\text{IO}}$ line is in the M phase. The ADR13 line discriminates between extended or nonextended I/O instruction when M/$\overline{\text{IO}}$ is in the I/O phase. The ADR14 line discriminates between data and control I/O when M/$\overline{\text{IO}}$ is in the I/O phase. The dual functions of these pins help to keep the pin count to a minimum.

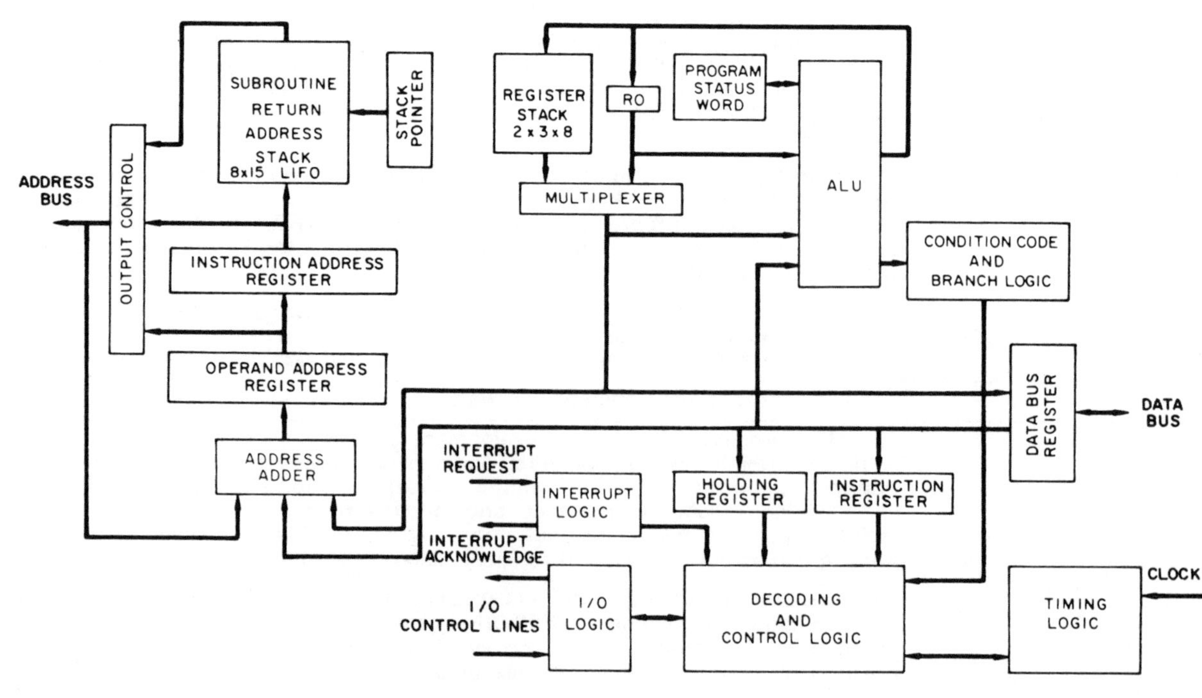

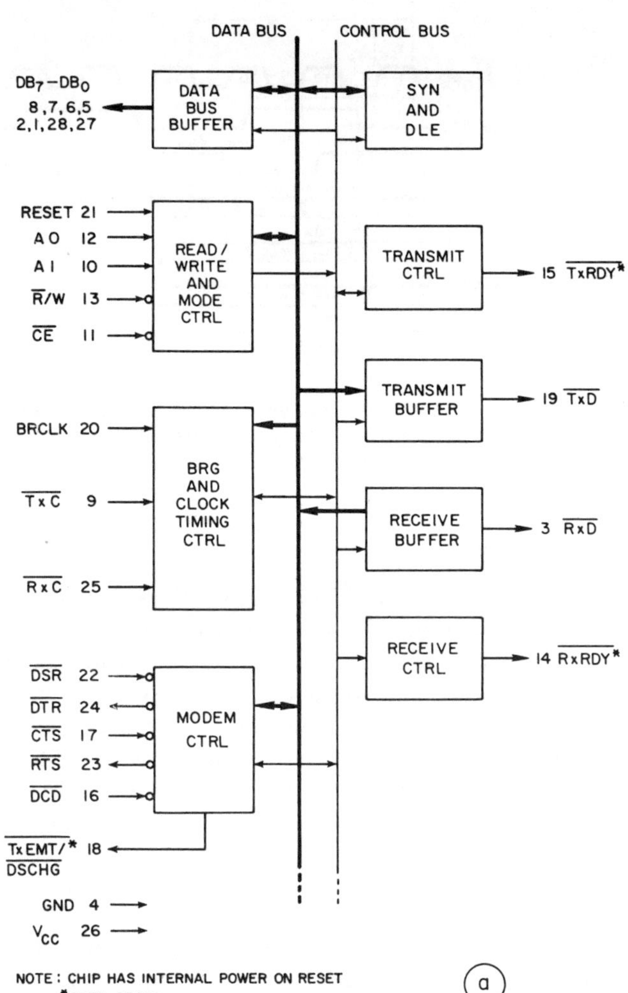

positive-going pulse in the middle of each requested write operation. During read operations the WRP line appears as a high impedance. The WRP line is designed to be used with the company's 2606 RAM to deliver timed Write signals.

On pin 23, the R/W (Read/Write) output defines whether an operation is Read or Write (HIGH corresponds to Write, LOW to Read). The OPREQ output line (Operation Request), pin 24, coordinates all external operations. When OPREQ is HIGH, the M/$\overline{\text{IO}}$, $\overline{\text{R}}$/W, E/$\overline{\text{NE}}$, D/$\overline{\text{C}}$ and IN-TACK lines describe the external operation being performed. When LOW, the OPREQ line indicates that the external operation is complete.

The $\overline{\text{DBUSEN}}$ (Data Bus Enable) line, pin 25, permits external control of the three-state data bus. When HIGH, pin 25 causes the data bus to appear as a high impedance; when LOW, the bus operates normally. The next eight pins, 26 to 33, form the 8-bit bidirectional data bus. Pin 23 indicates the flow of data on the bus. From pin 34, the INTACK line, a HIGH output indicates an interrupt request is being handled.

The RUN/$\overline{\text{WAIT}}$ output signal from pin 35 indicates the processor status. When the 2650 is executing an instruction, the line is HIGH (in the RUN state), and when the processor is halted by

3. By using the programmable serial (a) or parallel (b) interface circuits you can simplify the over-all circuit design. The serial interface has 16 programmable baud rates and the parallel interface has three 8-bit ports, one of which can also act as a serial port or timer.

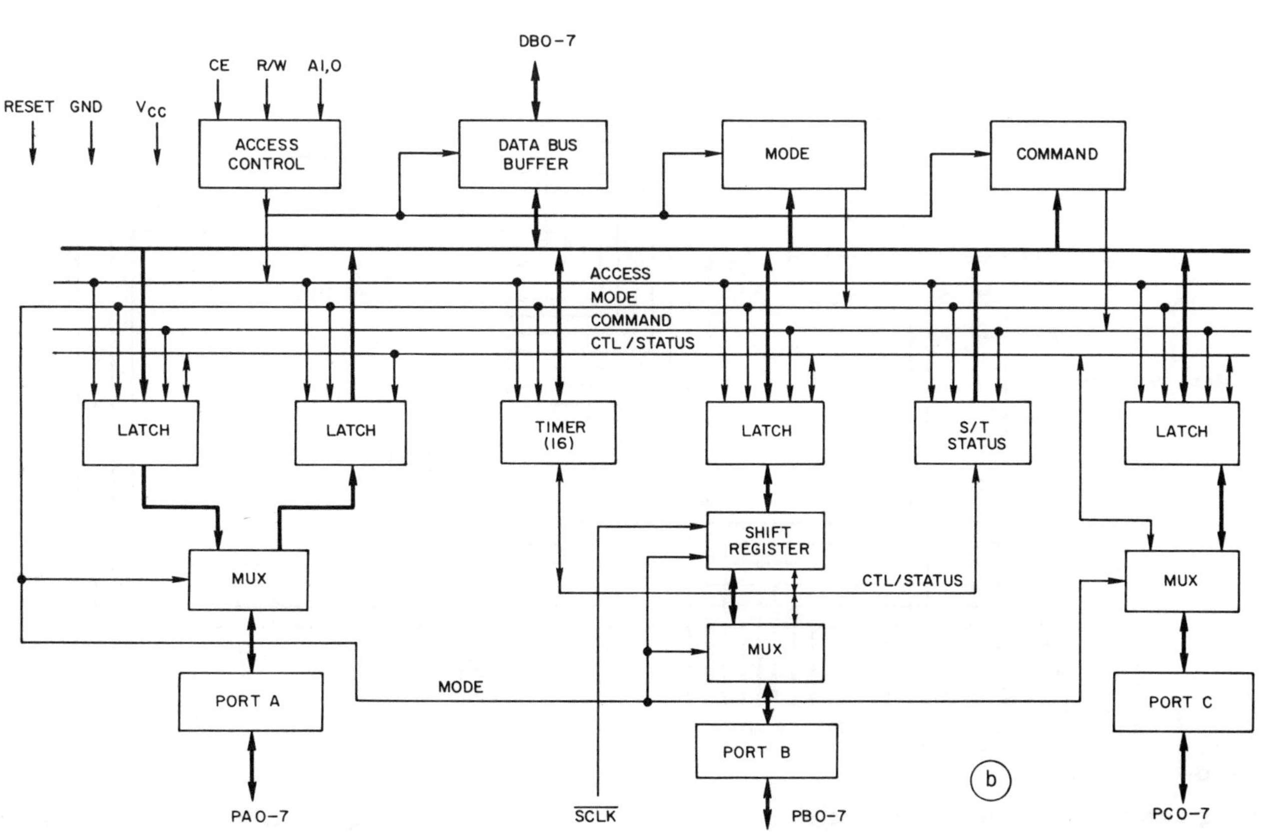

a pause instruction the line goes LOW ($\overline{\text{WAIT}}$ state).

Pin 36 is the $\overline{\text{OPACK}}$ (Operation Acknowledge) input line and it accepts inputs in response to the OPREQ signal. It is used to control timing sequences between different speed memories and the processor.

You can temporarily stop the processor with the $\overline{\text{PAUSE}}$ line (pin 36). When the line is driven LOW, the 2650 finishes its current instruction and enters the WAIT state.

The clock input of pin 38 accepts positive-going pulses. Three clock periods make up one processor cycle. Direct instructions are two, three or four processor cycles long and indirect addressing adds two more processor cycles to the direct instruction times.

A simple 5-V supply is all that has to be connected to pin 39. The last pin on the 2650, pin 40, is the FLAG output line. This output indicates the change of state of the FLAG bit in the PSW register.

Support circuitry is simple

Since all inputs and outputs of the 2650 are TTL compatible, standard logic circuits can be used for all interface requirements. The two specialized interface circuits mentioned earlier—the PCI and PPI—offer interfaces that are software alterable (rather than hardware alterable) for parallel and serial data applications.

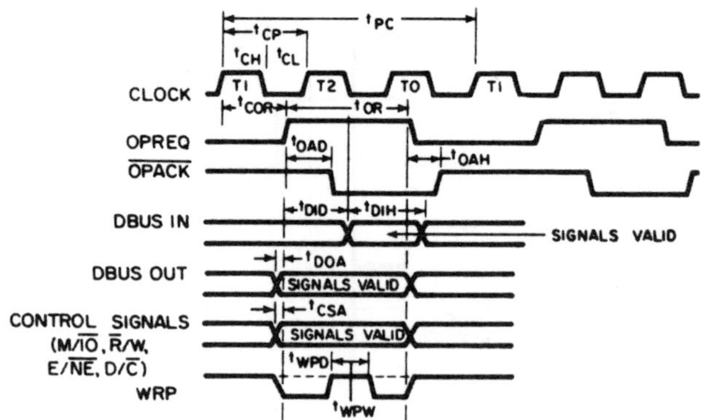

4. **There are only half-a-dozen signals** that are used to control the different memory circuits and peripherals that connect to the 2650.

The PCI (Model 2651) is a universal synchronous/asynchronous data-communications controller that supports almost any serial-data communications link in full-duplex or half-duplex modes (Fig. 3a). It accepts serial data from a peripheral and converts it to parallel data for the 2650. Inside the 2651 are a baud-rate generator, a modem controller, data-transmit and receive buffers and support control logic. The baud-rate generator has sixteen commonly used baud rates that are software selectable.

The transmitter and receiver sections of the 2651 can operate simultaneously and the baud-rate generator can accept external clocks or use

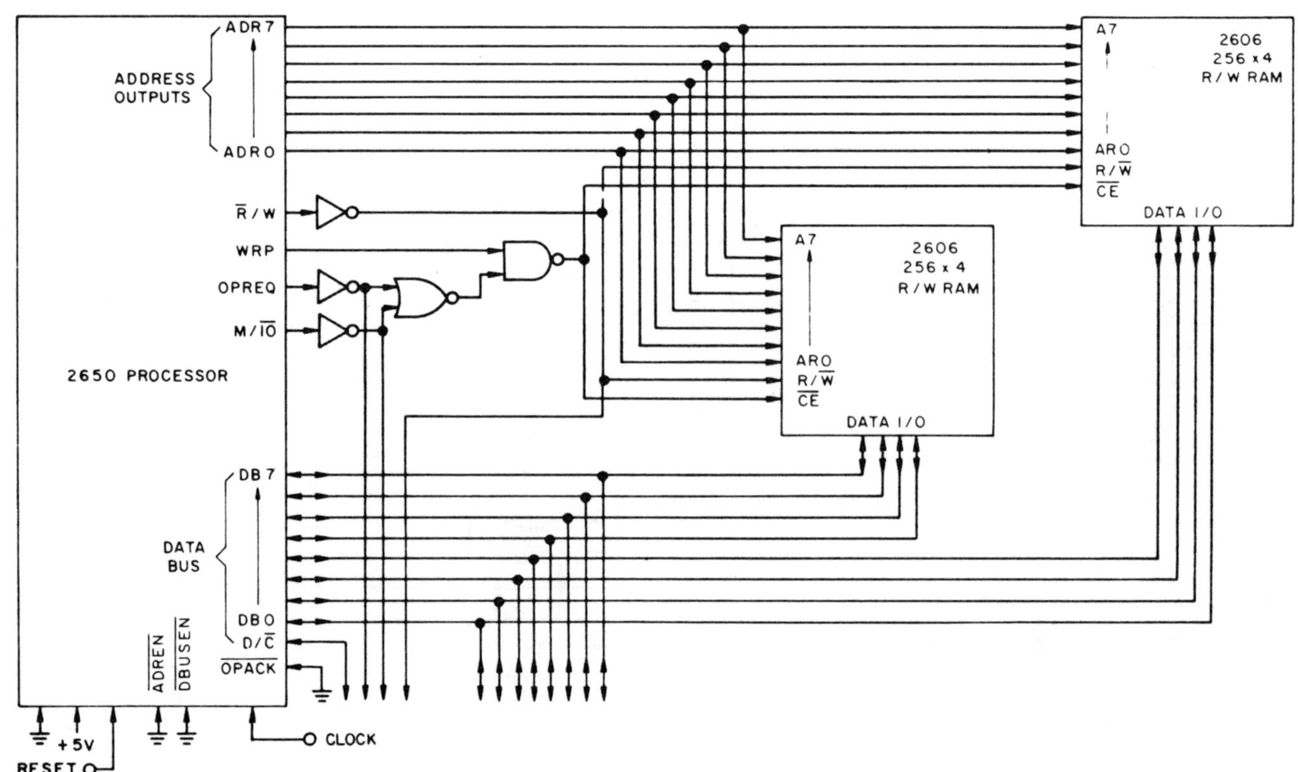

5. **Adding memory circuits to the 2650 is simple**—just connect the address and data busses to the circuits and the R/W, M/IO OPREQ and WRP lines; additional memory uses the higher-order address line.

its own internal clock for all timing. A 28-pin DIP houses the n-channel MOS device and only a 5-V supply is needed for circuit operation.

The PPI (Model 2655) contains three 8-bit quasi-bidirectional ports for I/O in a 40-pin DIP (Fig. 3b). All three ports are internally multiplexed to feed onto the 8-bit-wide bidirectional data bus of the 2650. Each port of the PPI can be software controlled to act as an input, output or bidirectional bus. The PPI can be programmed to function in five major I/O operating modes: static, strobed, bidirectional, serial or serial/timer.

One port of the 2655 can act as a serial I/O. A 3-MHz programmable timer or event counter is also available on the serial port to aid in timing external events. All lines are TTL-compatible.

To use either of these circuits, just set up the control words in your program and load the program into the 2650 memory. You can even change the port's function in mid program, depending upon your application. An interrupt request from

Instruction set and addressing schemes

The instruction set of the 2650 contains 75 instructions, about 40% of which are arithmetic. The arithmetic instructions include add, subtract, compare and Boolean operations, each of which can be executed using any one of eight different addressing modes. Another 30% of the instruction set contains branch operators that can be used with six of the addressing modes.

The remaining 30% of the instructions include I/O operations, status-register manipulation commands, a decimal-adjust instruction and a HALT directive.

The multiple addressing modes of the 2650 permit you to reduce the number of instructions needed to perform a desired operation. The different addressing modes include:

■ *Register addressing:* In this mode the first two bits of the instruction byte define the register and the other six bits contain the operation code.

■ *Immediate addressing:* The first byte of this two-byte instruction contains the operation code and register designation, and the second byte contains the data to be used as one of the operands during execution of the first byte operation code.

■ *Relative addressing* (direct and indirect modes): In this two-byte instruction, the first byte contains the operation code and the register address. The second byte contains the relative displacement from the current memory address in a seven-bit two's complement coding. The eighth bit of the second byte defines whether the address is direct or indirect.

■ *Absolute addressing* (nonbranch instructions, direct and indirect): This is a three-byte instruction, where the first byte holds the operation code in the six most significant bits and a two-bit Index or Argument register address in the remaining two bits. The second byte is divided into three parts: the highest order bit determines whether direct or indirect addressing is to be used, the next two bits determine how the effective address will be calculated—indexed only, indexed with auto increment/decrement, or nonindexed—and the lower five bits contain the uppermost part of a 13-bit address. The third byte contains the lower eight bits of the 13-bit address.

■ *Absolute addressing* (branch instructions, direct and indirect): This instruction is almost identical to the nonbranch instruction, except that there are no index control bits. The second byte contains the single control bit for direct or indirect addressing and the seven upper bits of a 15-bit address.

The fixed instructions permit true indexing and have optional auto increment/decrement. Each instruction requires one, two or three bytes to accomplish its task. However, I/O instructions only require one or two bytes.

The first, second and third bytes of instructions are read into the 2650 from the data bus and are loaded into the instruction register, holding register and data-bus register, respectively. An internal ROM and random logic decode the words. The first byte of each instruction always specifies the operation to be performed and the addressing mode to be used.

Automatic incrementing and decrementing of an index register can be done in the arithmetic indexed instructions. All branch instructions except indexed branching can be conditional. The interrupt is a single-level address-vectored interrupt. This means that the interrupting device can force the 2650 to execute code at a memory location determined by the device.

Register-to-register commands only require a one-byte directive; register-to-memory instructions are two or three bytes long. The two-byte commands use either the immediate or relative addressing modes.

a peripheral is one way to do this.

When an external interrupt occurs on the $\overline{\text{INTREQ}}$ line, the μP branches to any of 128 possible memory locations, as defined by an 8-bit vector supplied by the interrupting device.

Since the interrupting peripheral specifies the interrupt subroutines in a relative-address format, the vector can point to any location that is within +63 or −64 bytes of page zero, byte zero of memory. (Negative relative addresses wrap around the memory, so the address is contiguous.) The peripheral can also specify whether the subroutine address is direct or indirect.

System interconnects are straightforward

Aside from the connections to the data and address busses there are about half a dozen signal lines that make up the control bus (Fig. 4). For instance, during a memory-read operation, the OPREQ and M/$\overline{\text{IO}}$ lines go HIGH and the $\overline{\text{READ}/}$

Arithmetic operations		
Mnemonic		**Definition**
ADD	Z	Add to register zero w/wo carry
	I	Add immediate w/wo carry
	R	Add relative w/wo carry
	A	Add absolute w/wo carry
SUB	Z	Subtract from register zero w/wo borrow
	I	Subtract immediate w/wo borrow
	R	Subtract relative w/wo borrow
	A	Subtract absolute w/w borrow
DAR		Decimal adjust register
AND	Z	AND to register zero (r ≠ 0)
	I	AND immediate
	R	AND relative
	A	AND absolute
IOR	Z	Inclusive OR to register zero
	I	Inclusive OR immediate
	R	Inclusive OR relative
	A	Inclusive OR absolute
EOR	Z	Exclusive OR to register zero
	I	Exclusive OR immediate
	R	Exclusive OR relative
	A	Exclusive OR absolute
COM	Z	Compare to register zero arithmetic/logical
	I	Compare immediate arithmetic/logical
	R	Compare relative arithmetic/logical
	A	Compare absolute arithmetic/logical
RRR		Rotate register right w/wo carry
RRL		Rotate register left w/wo carry
Branch instructions		
BCT	R	Branch on condition true relative
	A	Branch on condition true absolute
BCF	R	Branch on condition false relative
	A	Branch on condition false absolute
BRN	R	Branch on register nonzero relative
	A	Branch on register nonzero absolute
BIR	R	Branch on incrementing register relative
	A	Branch on incrementing register absolute
BDR	R	Branch on decrementing register relative
	A	Branch on decrementing register absolute
ZBRR		Zero branch relative, unconditional
BXA		Branch indexed absolute, unconditional (see note)

BST	R	Branch to subroutine on condition true, relative
	A	Branch to subroutine on condition true, absolute
BSF	R	Branch to subroutine on condition false, relative
	A	Branch to subroutine on condition false, absolute
BSN	R	Branch to subroutine on nonzero register, relative
	A	Branch to subroutine on nonzero register, absolute
ZBSR		Zero branch to subroutine relative, unconditional
BSXA		Branch to subroutine, indexed absolute unconditional (see note)
RET	C	Return from subroutine, conditional
	E	Return from subroutine and enable interrupt, conditional
I/O, program status and load/store instructions		
WRTD		Write data
REDD		Read data
WRTC		Write control
REDC		Read control
WRTE		Write extended
REDE		Read extended
HALT		Halt, enter wait state
NOP		No operation
TMI		Test under mask immediate
LPS	U	Load program status, upper
	L	Load program status, lower
SPS	U	Store program status, upper
	L	Store program status, lower
CPS	U	Clear program status, upper, masked
	L	Clear program status, lower, masked
PPS	U	Preset program status, upper, masked
	L	Preset program status, lower, masked
TPS	U	Test program status, upper, masked
	L	Test program status, lower, masked
LOD	Z	Load register zero
	I	Load immediate
	R	Load relative
	A	Load absolute
STR	Z	Store register zero (r ≠ 0)
	R	Store relative
	A	Store absolute

Note: Index register must be register 3. or 3'.

WRITE line goes LOW. In return, the $\overline{\text{OPACK}}$ line from the memory goes LOW and then the data from the memory appear on the data bus. The OPACK line is a handshaking signal, and must be valid (HIGH) for the data to have meaning.

The FLAG and SENSE lines are I/O ports that can directly output or input one bit of data without any external address decoding or synchronizing signals. The circuit of Fig. 1 shows how these two lines can be used to sense character inputs from a TTY port. The FLAG can be used as a serial output channel, as an extra address bit for wider addressing range, as a switch or toggle output to control external logic or external functions or can be used as a pulse generator for polling applications. The SENSE line, of course, can be used as a serial input channel, a sense switch input, a break signal to a running program, or an input for a yes/no signalling routine from external devices.

The 2650 has a total addressing capability of 32,768 bytes of memory, but in most cases has a direct-addressing instruction range of 8192 bytes —using only the lower 13 bits of the address word. To make it possible to access the full 32-k bytes, a paging scheme is used to break the memory into four 8-k byte pages, where the ADR13 and 14 lines are used to determine the page.

Fig. 5 shows a complete interface between the 2650 and two 2606, 256 × 4 RAMs, organized as a 256 × 8 R/W memory. For a larger memory, the next few address lines can be bussed to the RAM inputs.

Almost any memory can be used

Available memory circuits include the 2602 (1 k × 1) and the 2606 (256 × 4) static RAMs, the 2608 (1-k × 8) ROM and the 82S115/123/129 (512 × 8, 32 × 8 and 256 × 4) PROMs. The RAMs are available with access times ranging from 500 ns to 1 μs, and are housed in 16-pin DIPs. The ROM has a 650 ns access time and comes in a 24-pin DIP. The PROMs, made using Schottky-TTL processing, have access times of 35 ns, typical. They are also available in 16 or 24-pin DIPs. Memories made by other companies can also be used with the 2650, but only memories with access times of less than 800 ns allow the μP to operate at its maximum speed.

The other support circuits include the 8T26 quad transceivers, the 8T31 8-bit bidirectional port and the 8T95, 96, 97 and 98 hex buffers/inverters. All of these support circuits offer pnp inputs and have currents of only 200 μA instead of the 1.6 mA that standard TTL offers. This permits more circuitry to be connected to the 2650

busses without overloading the internal sinks.

To help you with basic system development, Signetics offers several development aids for both hardware and software:

- The 2650PC1001: A microprocessor prototyping card that contains a complete microcomputer on a single printed-circuit card. On the board is the 2650 μP, a control and R/W memory, an I/O port, a clock and all necessary buffering and interface circuits.

- The 2650PC2000: A 4-k byte memory card that is compatible with the 1001. It contains 32, 21L02 1-k × 1 static RAMs. Decoding is provided to select any block of 1-k × 8 and to distinguish cards in a multicard system.

- The 2650DS2000: This is a complete μP demonstration system that can accept one PC1001 and one PC2000. It has a built-in power supply and serial interfaces for RS-232 and TTY inputs.

- The KT9000: This is a microprocessor prototyping kit that contains the 2650 μP and enough support circuits to permit the development of a small system.

- The ABC1500/9500: The adaptable board computer is a modular microcomputer that contains the μP, memory, I/O ports and support circuitry. It also permits user designed circuits to be directly wired on the board. Two forms of the ABC system are available: The 1500 fully assembled version and the 9500 kit.

For software development Signetics has the TWIN microcomputer. It has two central processors so that user-developed programs are kept completely separate from operating programs. This provides a completely "crash-proof" system —no accidental erasing or disruption of operating software can occur as a result of a mistake or accident.

For software support and development debugging several different programs are available:

- Assembler: The 2650 assembly language (PIPASM) is a symbolic language designed to simplify the writing of programs for the 2650. It is written in Fortran IV and is modular—it can be executed in an overlay mode if the processor memory can't handle the entire program. Two passes are used to generate the symbol table, issue error messages, produce a program listing and computer-readable object listing.

- Simulator: The 2650 simulator program (PIPSIM) is a Fortran IV simulation of how the 2650 operates.

- Signetics Higher Level Language (PLμS): A microprocessor programming language which the programmer uses to replace many lines of machine code with a single statement. The PLμS compiler is available in 16 or 32-bit formats and also on GE and NCSS time-sharing services.

Getting to Know the COSMAC 1802

ALEX YOUNG
Manager, Microprocessor Design Engineering,
RCA Solid State Division, Somerville

Unlike most other 8-bit microprocessors, which use multiple-byte instructions, the CDP1802 developed by RCA uses mostly single-byte commands. Only two instructions require two bytes. The μP is fabricated on a single chip with a self-aligned, silicon gate CMOS process. It can therefore operate over a 3-to-12-V supply range.

Because of its new, closed-CMOS structure, the 1802 offers many design advantages over n or p-channel devices:

- Wide operating temperature range. The μP can function over −55 to 125 C.

- High speed. Instruction times of 2.5 to 3.5 μs are possible when the 1802 is biased at 10 V. (All but two instructions require 2.5 μs.)

- High noise immunity. The design permits an immunity margin equal to 30% of the supply voltage.

- Low power dissipation. Maximum dissipation (50 mW with a 10-V supply and a 6.4-MHz clock) is about one tenth that of other μP families.

- Static operation. No minimum clock frequency or multiphase timing signals are needed. An on-chip oscillator circuit requires only an external crystal and resistor.

The 1802 contains all the logic necessary for fetching, interpreting, and executing instructions stored in memory. The 40-pin circuit minimizes the external I/O and memory-control circuitry (Fig. 1). Four directly testable input flags, an output flip-flop, an internal direct-memory access mode and flexible instructions all help reduce system complexity.

Get the most out of the 1802

For the 1802 to address its full 64-k word memory, two bytes must be sequentially loaded onto the memory address bus (pins 25 to 32), since the μP has only eight address lines. When the memory is addressed, the first byte, which represents the higher order part of the address, must be loaded into an external latch controlled

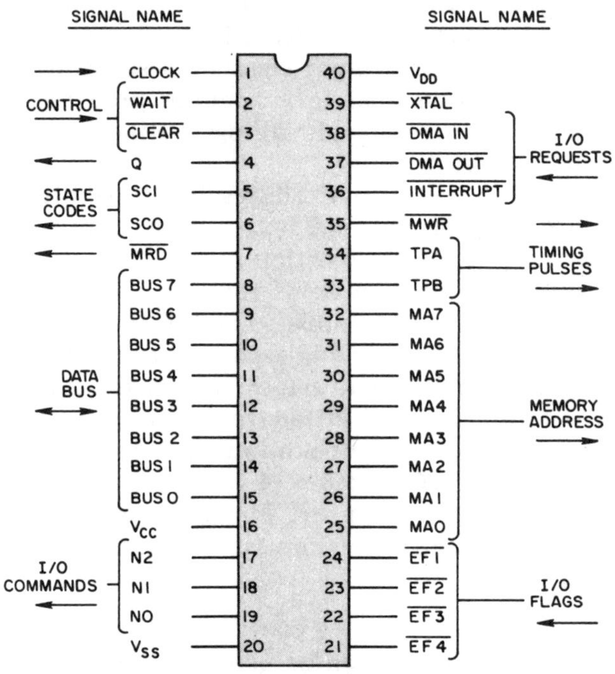

1. **The CPD1802 microprocessor** has an 8-bit data bus, an 8-bit address bus and 15 control lines. There are 91 instructions.

by the TPA line of the 1802. After the data are latched, the second address byte is moved onto the bus and then the memory is enabled. If 1800-series, read-only memory circuits are used, no external latches are needed; the ROMs have the latches on the chip.

The $\overline{\text{MRD}}$ and $\overline{\text{MWR}}$ lines (pins 7 and 35) of the 1802 control the memory operation. For a memory-read function, $\overline{\text{MRD}}$ must be LOW and $\overline{\text{MWR}}$ must be high. A memory-write operation is just the reverse, and a nonmemory operation is indicated by both lines HIGH.

During normal operation, the $\overline{\text{CLEAR}}$ and $\overline{\text{WAIT}}$ lines (pins 3 and 2) are both HIGH. When the $\overline{\text{CLEAR}}$ line goes LOW, the 1802 resets and initializes itself. If both lines are LOW, the μP enters its Load mode, which permits input bytes to be sequentially loaded into memory start-

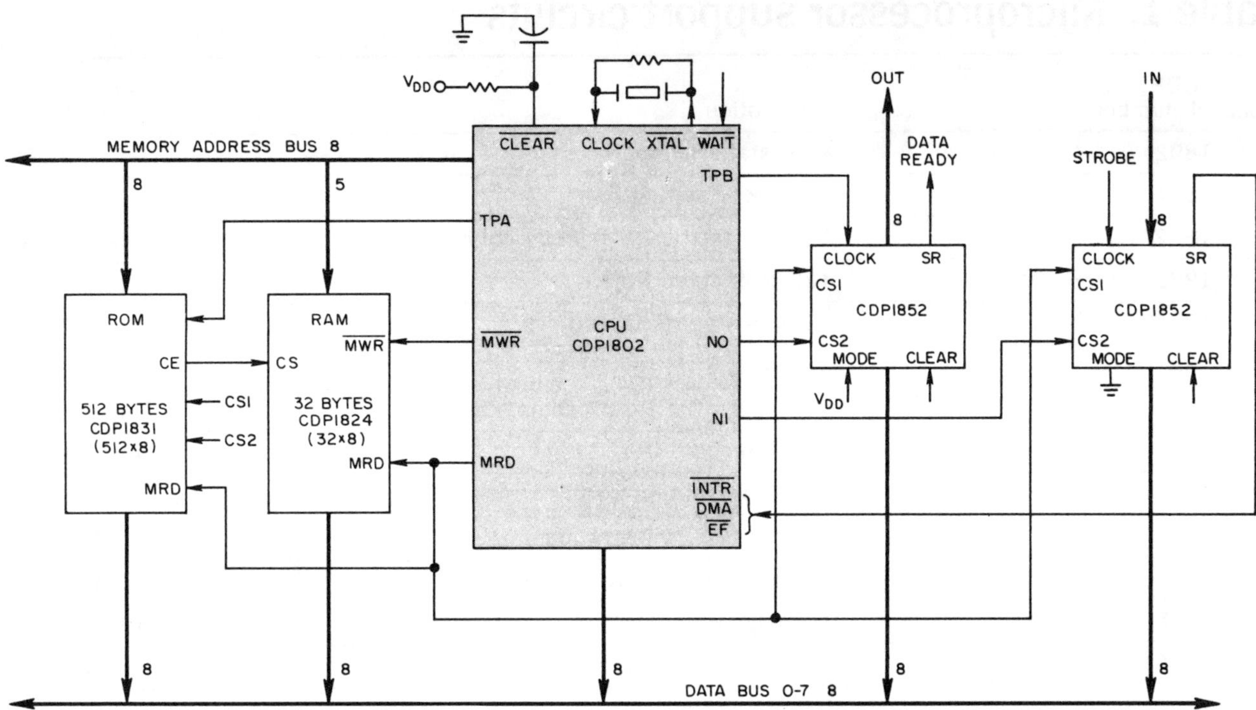

2. **A minimal operating system for the 1802** includes an I/O port and a small amount of RAM or ROM. If a large amount of memory is needed, an extra set of data latches must be used to deliver a 16-bit address.

ing at M(0000). This procedure permits direct program loading without the use of external "bootstrap" ROM programs.

When the $\overline{\text{WAIT}}$ line goes LOW (with the $\overline{\text{CLEAR}}$ line HIGH), the 1802 stops operation cleanly on the next negative transition of the clock. The 1802 resumes normal operation on the first negative transition of the clock after the $\overline{\text{WAIT}}$ line goes HIGH. The $\overline{\text{WAIT}}$ signal does not inhibit the on-chip clock, so all external timing is unaffected.

In the Run mode, when both the $\overline{\text{CLEAR}}$ and $\overline{\text{WAIT}}$ lines are HIGH, the 1802 can be in one of four processing states. The two state-code lines S0 and S1 (pins 5 and 6) indicate the processing mode: Instruction Fetch, Execute, DMA, or Interrupt. These lines can be used to display the mode on a front panel and to control a DMA or Interrupt operation.

Use internal or external system timing

All the timing functions are controlled by the 1802's internal clock or by an external clock fed into the μP (pins 1 and 39). The high-frequency clock is internally divided into 16 periods. The first eight are used to control the fetch cycle, and the second eight control the execute cycle.

The TPA and TPB output lines (pins 34 and 35) are timing signals that can latch memory address bits, transfer data, and set or reset I/O controller flip-flops. The Q output line (pin 4),

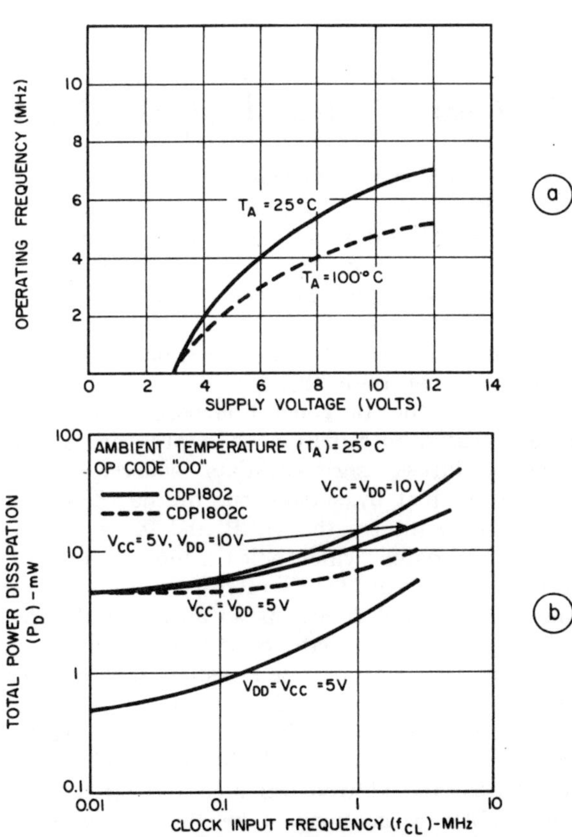

3. **To calculate the maximum operating frequency** of the microprocessor clock once you know the supply voltage, or vice-versa, you can locate one of the terms on its axis and find the other on the curve (a). Similarly, if you know the clock frequency or the power dissipation, you can find the other by using the family of supply-voltage curves developed at 25 C (b).

Table 1. Microprocessor support circuits

CDP model number	Description	Approximate cost (100-up)
1802	8-bit static microprocessor	$23.50
1821	1024 × 1 static RAM	$21
1822	256 × 4 static RAM (2101 equiv.)	To be announced
1823	128 × 8 static RAM	To be announced
1824	32 × 8 static RAM	$9.50
1831	512 × 8 ROM	Consult factory
1832	512 × 8 ROM (2407 compatible)	Consult factory
1851	Programmable I/O	To be announced
1852	Byte input/output port	$8.35
1853	Gated 3-to-8 N-line decoder	$6
1854	Asynchronous receiver/transmitter	$18
1855	Multiply/divide unit	To be announced
1856	Memory-bus buffer/separator	$6
1857	I/O-bus buffer	$6
1858	Address latch decoder	$6
1859	Address latch decoder	$6

Internal architecture of the Cosmac microprocessor

The RCA Cosmac microprocessor is a single-chip circuit handling 8-bit data. The CMOS μP comes in a 40-pin package and has an architecture based on an array of 16 general-purpose scratch-pad registers, each of which holds a 16-bit word (R registers). These registers can be used to point to data in memory, to point to programs, or to store data (two bytes per register).

Any of the 16 general-purpose registers can be designated to function as a program counter, memory-address register, data source, or data destination just by setting one of the three available 4-bit pointers, the N, P and X registers.

The D register, which holds 8 bits, buffers data transfers between the scratch-pad registers and the data bus and functions as an accumulator.

By changing the contents of the P register, you can point to a different R register (thus changing the program counter). The N register stores a variable pointer that is directed by the instruction. The other 4-bit register, X, stores a pointer that designates an address register during I/O and some ALU instructions. Like the P register, it can be loaded by a single instruction.

The use of the N, P and X registers to indirectly specify a 16-bit address is a key feature of the 1802 μP. In addition to the register arrays, the 1802 contains a conventional arithmetic and logic unit that performs operations between data stored in the D register and in memory, with the result stored in D. An overflow bit, DF, is also available and can be used for conditional branching.

Instruction cycles are divided into fetch and execute halves often referred to as machine cycles. During the fetch cycle, instructions are brought from the program memory, the four most-significant bits are placed in the I register, and the four least-significant bits are funneled into the N register. The I register designates a class of instructions, and the N register defines the specific processor operation.

The 15 lines of I/O interface offer some unique features:

- Four input flags, which can be tested by condition branch instructions.
- A serial output, which can be set and reset under program control and tested by conditional branch instructions.
- Programmed I/O data transfer, which uses the data in the N register as a device-select code, then transfers data between the selected device and memory.
- A maskable interrupt, which is activated by a single input. When an interrupt occurs, the old values of the P and X registers are automatically saved in a temporary register, T, and new values are jammed into the P and X registers.
- A DMA channel, which can be activated by either of two control lines, uses the R(0) register as a pointer. Each DMA request causes one ma-

combined with any of the four EF input lines (pins 21 to 24), forms a serial I/O interface. A software routine can interpret the logic levels and can assemble or disassemble the data into bytes or serial form.

Three I/O command lines, N0, N1 and N2 (pins 17 to 19) can be used, along with the $\overline{\text{MRD}}$ line, to directly select any of six possible ports. With a 3-to-8 decoder, up to seven input and seven output ports can be addressed. By using the 3-to-8 decoder, two CD4076s and an 8 to 256 decoder, any one of 1792 I/O ports can be selected.

Three I/O request lines (pins 36, 37 and 38) handle interrupts, DMA outputs and DMA inputs, respectively. A LOW condition on the Interrupt line initiates the interrupt. Inside the 1802 is a special Interrupt Enable (IE) register holding one bit. Normally it is kept in a ONE state; but when an interrupt command comes in, the IE register is set to ZERO and locks out any other interrupts. Software instructions can manipulate the IE register to control interrupt operation.

The only other lines on the 1802 are the 8-bit data bus (pins 8 to 15) and the power and ground leads (pins 16, 20 and 40). The data bus is bidirectional, but pull-up resistors should be used on the bus outputs to put it in a known state if it is allowed to float during the Wait mode.

Put a system together, simply

Designing a simple system based on the 1802 is straightforward. A parallel-I/O system can be built from only four ICs: the μP, two I/O ports and a RAM or ROM (Fig. 2). A family of ICs, designed for interface and memory use (Table 1), supports the 1802.

For a system requiring maximum performance, the operating speed must first be determined. The clock rate, in turn, fixes the instruction time at 16 clock periods for all commands except for long branch and long skips, which require 24 periods.

The maximum clock frequency is a function of supply voltage, and the graph of Fig. 3a can help determine one from the other. The frequency is also temperature dependent and must be decreased by 0.35%/°C from the calculated frequency at 25 C.

Power dissipation is composed of a frequency-

---

chine cycle to be stolen, generates appropriate memory address and control signals, and increments the pointer.

■ Timing signals, which provide synchronization to assist in data transfers and general system timing functions.

The 8-bit ALU performs all the arithmetic and logic operations. Operand bytes are pulled from the D register and from the memory (on the data bus).

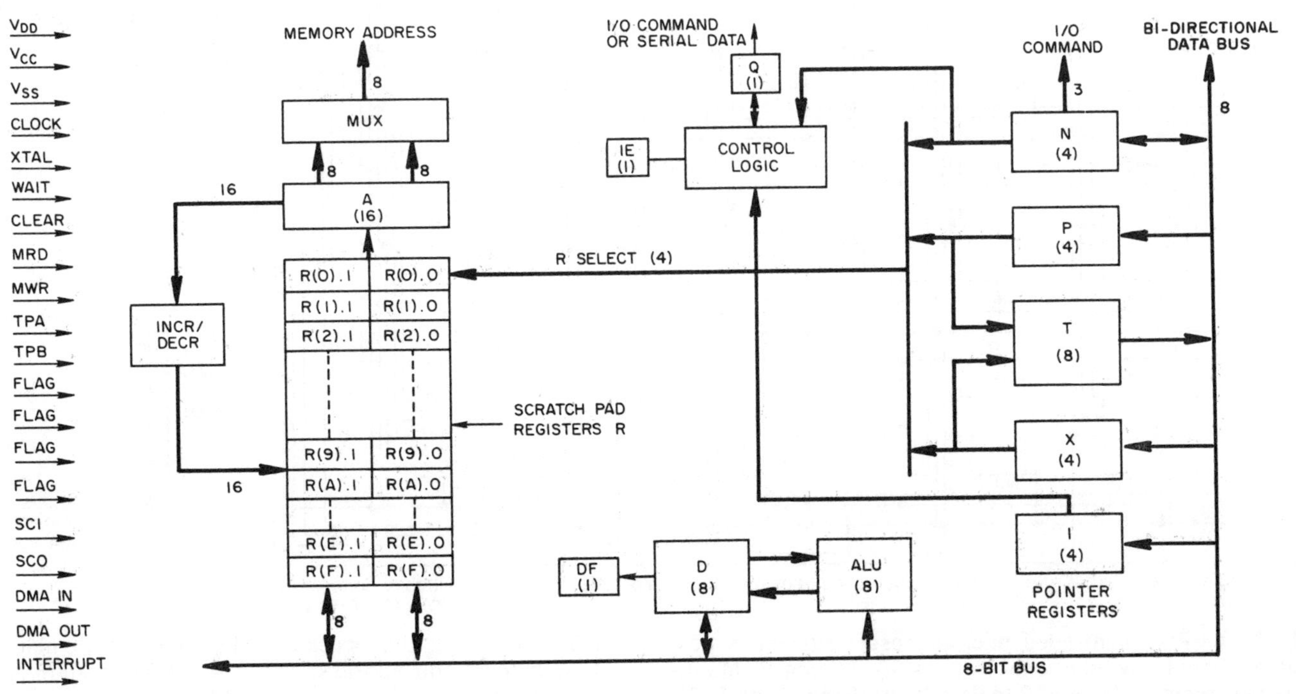

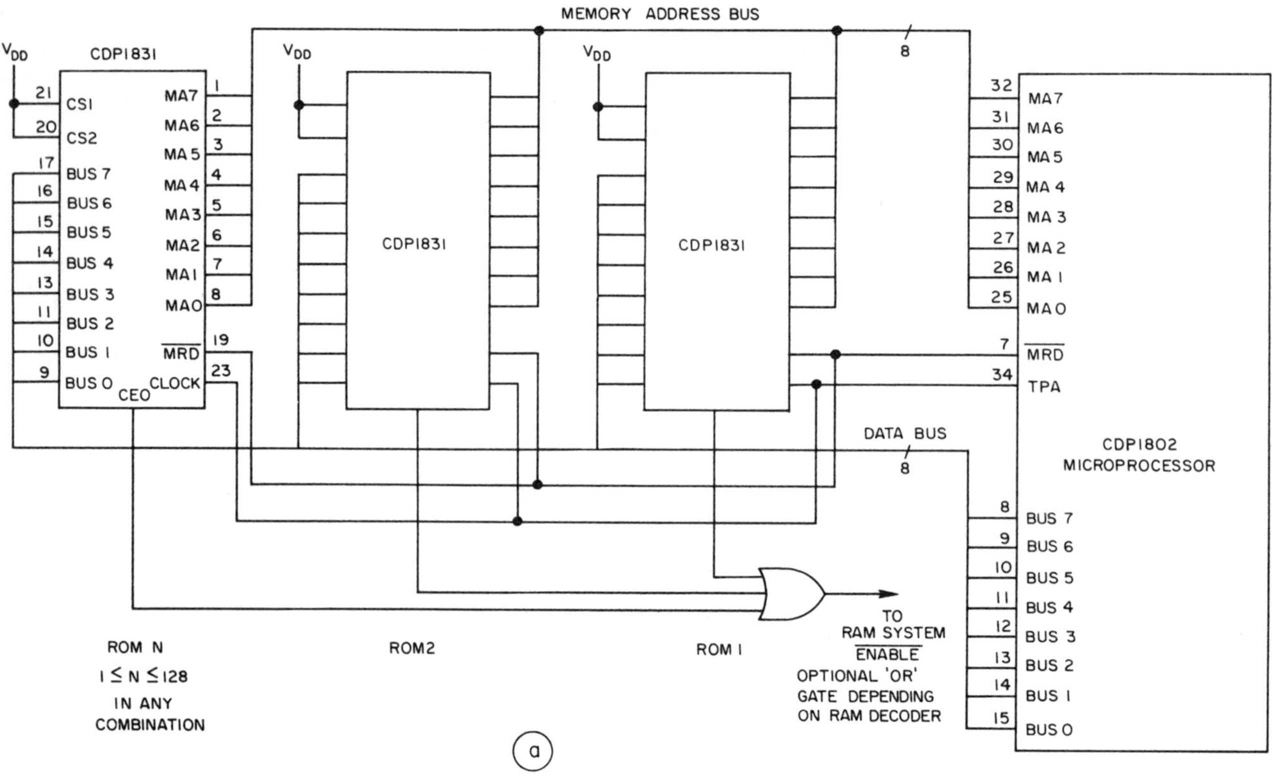

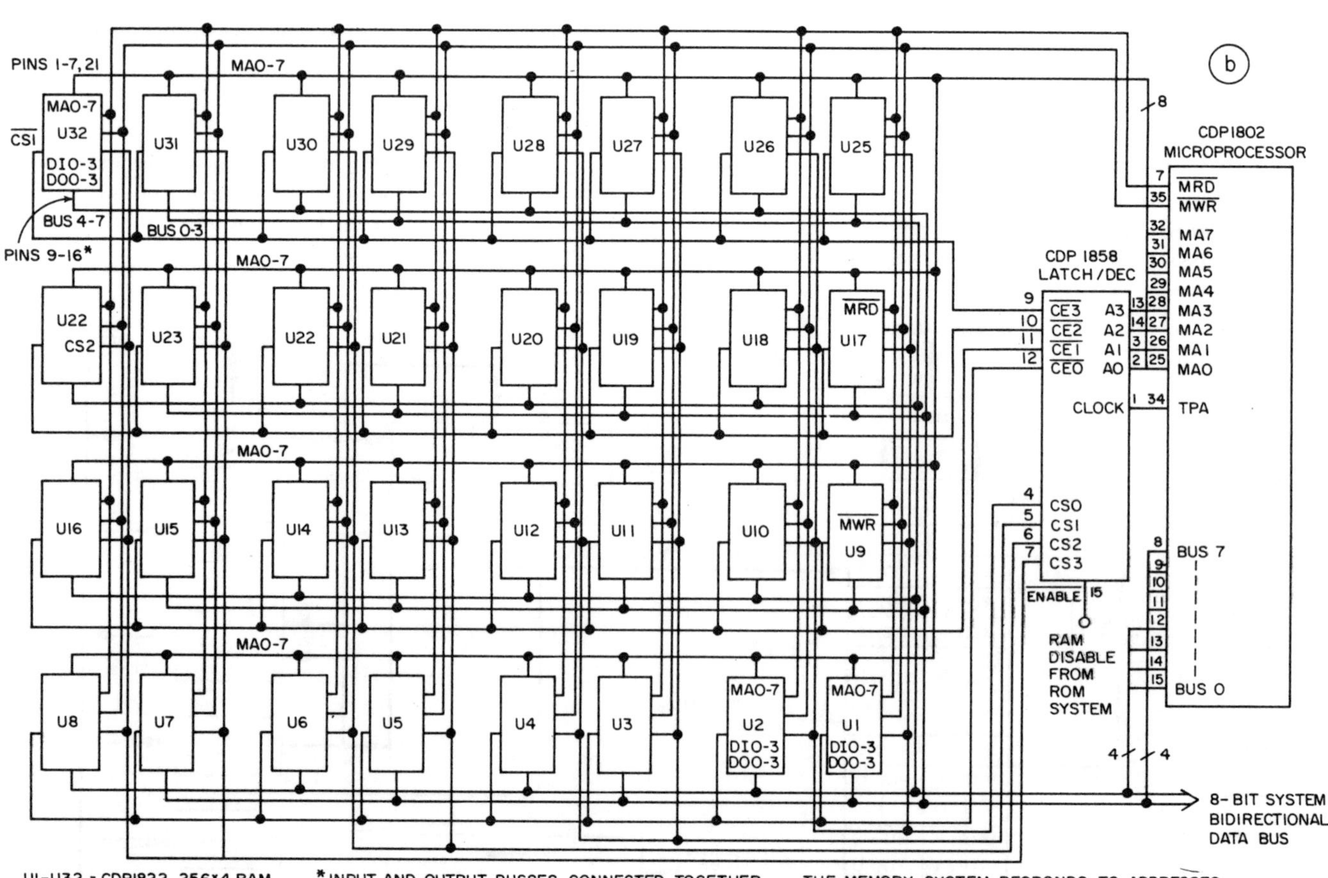

4. An all-ROM-controlled microprocessor system is possible without any additional circuits (a). Adding ROMs increases memory from 512 to 65-k bytes. Each of the 1831 ROMs contains the necessary data latches to hold the first byte of the address. For a 4-k RAM system, however, control circuitry must be added (b).

dependent dynamic term and a temperature-dependent quiescent term. The dynamic term can be calculated from the graph of Fig. 3b, and the quiescent term can be approximated by adding 20 μW to the dynamic term for every degree C above 25 C.

Consider a simple system design for a microcomputer that must add two 8-bit bytes in 8 μs, function over a 25-to-100-C range and operate from under 7 V. Since the processor must perform an ADD instruction, $M(R(X))$ to D, one command can meet the 8-μs time requirement.

For this system, the clock frequency can be determined by first dividing the instruction time by 16, then taking the reciprocal of the result:

$$(8 \, \mu s/16)^{-1} = 2 \text{ MHz}.$$

The μP must therefore be able to operate at 100 C—at a clock rate of 2 MHz. The curve of Fig. 3a can be used to find the minimum supply voltage: 4.8 V.

Assuming 5 V is used, the power dissipation can be read from Fig. 3b as 5 mW for the 1802D or as 9 mW for the 1802CD, at 25 C. At 100 C these values increase by 1.5 mW.

It's easy for the system to remember,

Almost any RAM or ROM circuit can be added to an 1802-based system. A small system with 32 bytes of RAM (CDP1824) and 512 bytes of ROM (CDP1831) requires no additional devices. You determine the address space for the memory when you write the program to be stored in ROM.

The 7-bit, user-specified sector address (the seven most significant bits of the 16-bit, multiplexed address bus) locates the ROM in one of the 128, 512-byte memory sectors. When the proper sector address is input to the ROM, the CEO output goes HIGH and disables the RAM. The RAM is enabled when the ROM is not selected.

Expanding the memory is simple. The circuit of Fig. 4a shows how to increase the ROM space from 512 bytes to 65-k bytes. The system needs no address decoding and is directly compatible with the 1802. A system with 4-k bytes of RAM uses the 1858 address latch/decoders and the 1822 RAMs (Fig. 4b). The 1824, 1822 and 1831 memories are directly compatible with the 1802, and the 1831 has the address latches built-in. If larger RAM or ROM circuits, made by other vendors, are used, the latches must be added externally.

The simplest way to bring data into the μP is through the four external flag inputs, EF1 to EF4. Each input can perform as an independent serial data link, under program control. Branch instructions can test the flag inputs and divert the program on the appropriate condition. Loops

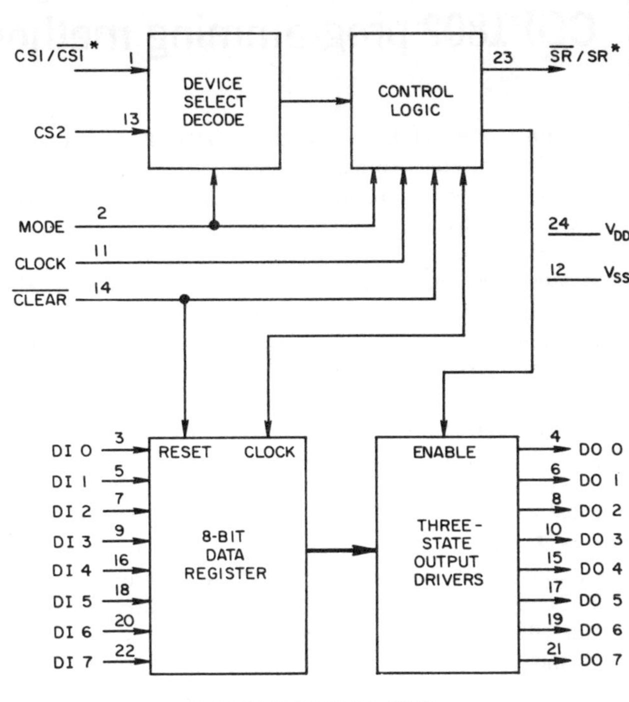

5. **The byte input/output port** handles data flowing into or out of the 1802 μP. It can be hard-wired to do either, but it is not software programmable. When available, the 1851 I/O port provides software control of data flow.

can be constructed to continually test the flag lines and manipulate the data as required.

The Q output of the 1802 serves as a control port or serial output. The Q bit can be set, reset and tested by branch instructions, or it can be used either as a pulse-width-modulated output or a variable-frequency output.

Programmed I/O data transfers can be used to directly select any of three possible peripherals. The instructions use a hexadecimal format of 6X, where the three LSBs of the code for X digit are routed to the N0, N1 and N2 pins of the μP to activate a device.

Even more peripherals (up to 14) can be selected if an 1853 N-bit decoder is used. If a two-level decoding scheme is used, the number of external devices is unlimited.

Memory selection isn't critical

RCA has designed several static RAMs and ROMs with the 1802 in mind. The smallest is the 1824, a 32 × 8 CMOS RAM housed in an 18-pin DIP. It provides sufficient working space and stack storage for systems requiring minimal storage.

The 1822 and 1823 CMOS RAMs are organized as 256 × 4 or 128 × 8, respectively. The 1822 is pin-compatible with the common 22-pin 2101 RAM.

Access times for the RAMs are 350-ns typical

CDP1802 programming methods and mnemonic definitions

The instruction set of the CDP1802 consists of 91 single-byte commands grouped into five basic types: register, memory and logic; arithmetic; branch, skip and control; and I/O byte transfer instructions.

Most instructions require two machine cycles (1 instruction period). The only exceptions are the long-branch and long-skip instructions, which require three cycles. Each machine cycle is internally divided into eight equal time intervals, T, so the instruction time is 16 T for two machine cycles and 24 T for three cycles.

There are four basic addressing modes of the Cosmac:

- Register. The operand's address is contained in the four lower-order bits of the instruction byte. This mode permits you to directly address any of the 16 scratch-pad registers so that you can count or move data in or out. Typical instructions might be Decrement (2N) and Get Low (8N).

- Register-Indirect. The address of the operand is stored in one of the 16-bit scratch pad registers. When you access one of the 16 registers it points to the location in memory where the operand is stored.

- Immediate. The operand is in the byte following the instruction. This mode permits you to extract data from the program stream without setting up special memory locations and pointers to them. Typical instructions include Add Immediate (FC) and Load Immediate (F8).

- Stack. One specific CPU register is implied as the pointer to memory. The stack is used as a last-in, first-out working area to store intermediate calculations and keep track of control transfers between parts of a program.

Each CPU instruction is fetched on the first machine cycle and executed during the second cycle, except for long-branch and long-skip instructions that require the first machine cycle to fetch the instruction on the second and third cycle to fetch the address (execute).

Each instruction is broken into two 4-bit hex digits, designated as I (the higher-order digit) and N (the lower-order digit). The I word specifies the instruction type, and the N word either designates the scratch-pad register to be used or acts as a special code.

Register operations include instructions that count or move data between internal 1802 registers. Memory reference commands provide directions to load or store a memory byte. Branching operations provide conditional and unconditional branch instructions that can either work in the current memory page or go to any location.

Arithmetic and Logic instructions provide many of the common operations: add, subtract, AND, OR, EX-OR and shift, while control and I/O com-mands take care of all the timing and data-transfer operations. The control functions facilitate pro-gram interrupt, operand selection, branch and link operations and control the Q flip-flop. The I/O functions handle memory loading and all data transfer operations into and out of the 1802.

Memory and logic instructions**

Instruction	Mne-monic	Op Code
Increment reg N	INC	1N
Decrement reg N	DEC	2N
Increment reg X	IRX	60
Get low reg N	GLO	8N
Put low reg N	PLO	AN
Get high reg N	GHI	9N
Put high reg N	PHI	**B**N
Load via N	LDN	0N
Load advance	LDA	4N
Load via X	LDX	F0
Load via X and advance	LDXA	72
Load immediate	LDI	F8
Store via N	STR	5N
Store via X and decrement	STXD	73
OR	OR	F1
OR immediate	ORI	F9
Exclusive OR	XOR	F3
Exclusive OR immediate	XR	FB
AND	AND	F2
AND immediate	ANI	FA
Shift right	SHR	F6
Shift right with carry	SHRC	76*
Ring shift right	RSHR	
Shift left	SHL	FE
Shift left with carry	SHLC	7E*
Ring shift left	RSHL	

Arithmetic instructions**

Add	ADD	F4
Add immediate	ADI	FC
Add with carry	ADC	74
Add with carry immediate	ADCI	7C
Subtract D	SD	F5
Subtract D immediate	SDI	FD
Subtract D with borrow	SDB	75
Subtract D with borrow, immediate	SDBI	7D
Subtract memory	SM	F7
Subtract memory immediate	SMI	FF
Subtract memory with borrow	SMB	77
Subtract memory with borrow, immediate	SMBI	7F

Branch instructions

Short branch	BR	30
No short branch (see SKP)	NBR	38*
Short branch if D = 0	BZ	32
Short branch if D not 0	BNZ ⎫	3A
Short branch if DF = 1	BDF ⎬	33*
Short branch if pos or zero	BPZ	
Short branch if equal or greater	BGE	
Short branch if DF = 0	BNF ⎫	3B*
Short branch if minus	BM ⎬	
Short branch if less	BL ⎭	
Short branch if Q = 1	BQ	31
Short branch if Q = 0	BNQ	39
Short branch if EF1 = 1	B1	34
Short branch if EF1 = 0	BN1	3C
Short branch if EF2 = 1	B2	35
Short branch if EF2 = 0	BN2	3D
Short branch if EF3 = 1	B3	36
Short branch if EF3 = 0	BN3	3E
Short branch if EF4 = 1	B4	37
Short branch if EF4 = 0	BN4	3F
Long branch	LBR	C0
No long branch (see LSKP)	NLBR	C8*
Long branch if D = 0	LBZ	C2
Long branch if D not 0	LBNZ	CA
Long branch if DF = 1	LBDF	C3
Long branch if DF = 0	LBNF	CB
Long branch if Q = 1	LBQ	C1
Long branch if Q = 0	LBNQ	C9

---

*Note: This instruction is associated with more than one mnemonic. Each mnemonic is inividually listed.

**Note: The arithmetic and logic instructions are the only instructions that can alter the DF.

Skip and control instructions

Short skip (see NBR)	SKP	38*
Long skip (see NLBR)	LSKP	C8*
Long skip if D = 0	LSZ	CE
Long skip if D not 0	LSNZ	C6
Long skip if DF = 1	LSDF	CF
Long skip if DF = 0	LSNF	C7
Long skip if Q = 1	LSQ	CD
Long skip if Q = 0	LSNQ	C5
Long skip if IE = 1	LSIE	CC
Idle	IDL	00
No operation	NOP	C4
Set P	SEP	DN
Set X	SEX	EN
Set Q	SEQ	7B
Reset Q	REQ	7A
Save	SAV	78
Push X,P to stack	MARK	79
Return	RET	70
Disable	DIS	71

Input/output byte transfer instructions

Output 1	OUT 1	61
Output 2	OUT 2	62
Output 3	OUT 3	63
Output 4	OUT 4	64
Output 5	OUT 5	65
Output 6	OUT 6	66
Output 7	OUT 7	67
Input 1	INP 1	69
Input 2	INP 2	6A
Input 3	INP 3	6B
Input 4	INP 4	6C
Input 5	INP 5	6D
Input 6	INP 6	6E
Input 7	INP 7	6F

for the 1822 with a 5-V supply, and 400-ns typical for the 1824, also with a 5-V supply. Since the RAMs are CMOS, typical power dissipation is only 500 μW for the 1824 and 8 mW for the 1822.

Available ROMs include the CDP1831 mask-programmable ROM, organized as 512 $\times$ 8. The ROM has a set of built-in data latches to hold the first word of the two-word address needed to locate a stored instruction. Because the latches are built-in, a ROM system of up to 64-k bytes can be designed and will require no extra decoding circuitry. Also included on the chip are three-state output buffers that are enabled by a combination of the three chip selects, CS1, CS2 and $\overline{\text{MRD}}$. The signal polarities of these select lines are user-selectable during mask programming.

Similar to the 1831 is the 1832 mask-programmable ROM. Its pin-out, however, matches the popular 2704, 512 $\times$ 8 erasable PROM's. The 1832 can be directly substituted into a 2704 socket without any circuit changes.

Specialized circuits support the memory

In addition to the RAMs and ROMs developed for the 1802, four special support circuits simplify the over-all system design. The 1858 and 1859 address-latch/decoder circuits provide all the control necessary to interface the 1802 with up to 4-k bytes of RAM. The 1858 is designed to work with 256 $\times$ 4 RAMs and the 1859 with 1024 $\times$ 1 RAMs.

An 8-bit address latch, the 1852, and a memory-bus buffer/separator, the 1856, are also available. The latch contains three-state drivers that connect to the bus, and the buffer/separator can split the memory bus for large-memory applications.

Generalized I/O support circuits are also available, and there are a few others still being developed. The 1852, 8-bit I/O port; the 1853, 3-to-8-line decoder; and the 1857 (an I/O bus buffer) will be available this year. The 1851 programmable I/O port, the 1854 universal asynchronous receiver/transmitter and the 1855 multiply/divide unit will be available soon.

The 1852 (Fig. 5) simplifies parallel data transfers to and from the 1802. The I/O circuit is semi-dedicated because it can function, via mode control, either as an input port (mode = 0) or as an output port (mode = 1). When the circuit is used as an input port, and data are strobed into its 8-bit register by a HIGH level on the clock line, the HIGH-to-LOW transition of the clock latches the data and sets the $\overline{\text{SR}}$ (Service Request) output to ZERO. The three-state output drivers are enabled by CS1$\cdot$CS2 = 1, and on the HIGH-to-LOW transition of CS1$\cdot$CS2, $\overline{\text{SR}}$ is reset to ONE.

When used as an output port, data are strobed

Table 2. Hardware and software support

Model	Description
CDP18S011	Cosmac Microtutor: a low-cost free-standing microcomputer designed for users with no previous knowledge of microprocessors.
CDP18S020	Evaluation kit: a complete microcomputer kit based on the 1802 μP. It contains 256 bytes of RAM, a utility program in ROM, built-in 20 mA TTY and RC232-C interfaces, and more—all on a 14 $\times$ 9.17-in. PC board.
CDP18S004	Development system: a complete microcomputer with editor, assembler and debug programs. It is designed for hands-on use and complete software development. The system is housed in a 19 $\times$ 11 $\times$ 5.5-in. rack-mountable card cage and comes with its own power supply, front panel and 4 k words of RAM. A floppy-disc system is also available.
CSDP —	Cosmac software development package: an assembler and simulator/debugger program available on General Electric Information Services International network or can be purchased in a Fortran IV version for in-house installation. It is available on magnetic tape (CDP18S910) or as a card deck (CDP18S911). An Editor program is also available.

into the circuit at CS1$\cdot$CS2$\cdot$Clock = 1, and are immediately available at the outputs. A Data-Ready pulse is generated when $\overline{\text{CS1}}\cdot$CS2 = 1 and is present (HIGH level) until the next HIGH-to-LOW clock transition. A built-in clear control resets the register and mode setting in the 1852.

The 1853 is a gated 3-to-8 N-line decoder that interfaces directly to the N0, N1 and N2 outputs of the 1802. It gates the decoded state with the interval between TPA and TPB pulses to select an I/O device during programmed data transfers. The 1857 buffers the data bus and can be used as a simple I/O port where data latching is not required.

Support the hardware with software

In addition to the hardware circuits available, various support systems can be used for learning, evaluating, prototyping and programming the the 1802 (Table 2). One of the newest units is the 18S011—the Cosmac Microtutor. This system is an inexpensive ($349), free-standing microcomputer designed for beginners.

Inputs are entered via eight toggle switches, and outputs are displayed on two LED hexadecimal displays. There are four auxiliary controls: Clear, Load, Start and Input. The Microtutor comes with 256 bytes of RAM and has an empty connector slot so that all processor signal lines can be examined. It also includes all the circuitry for clock and control signal generation, switch debouncing and general control.

The 18S020 evaluation kit, a more advanced microcomputer, contains the 1802 μP, 256 bytes of memory (expandable to 4 k), I/O circuitry, a display, and clock and control circuitry. A comprehensive utility program stored in ROM is included to permit communication over built-in 20-mA TTY and RS232-C interfaces. It also has built-in controls for Reset, Run-Program, Run-Utility and Single-Step functions as well as a self-adjusting communications interface for terminal rates of 110 to 1200 band.

The most advanced development system, the 18S004, is a full microcomputer with built-in Editor, Assembler and Debug programs for software development. The unit has its own power supply, 11 plug-in printed-circuit cards, room for 22 more cards, and a front panel for control and monitoring. It comes with paper tape, cassette, or floppy-disc versions of the Resident-Editor and Resident-Assembler programs. Only 4-k

words of RAM come with the system, but they are sufficient to hold the Editor program and provide a working buffer.

The Editor program permits such commands as Move Pointer, Delete, Append, Insert, Save, Search and Substitute, Type, and Output. The assembler is a multipass program that can output the results to paper tape, cassette, or floppy-disc. The 18S004 also has a floppy-disc option, the 18S800, with an operating system to facilitate storage and retrieval of programs.

Software development programs are also available in Fortran IV for direct purchase, or lease on the GE timesharing network. Two versions of an Assembler program are available. Level I refers to each instruction by name, and each statement defines a single instruction. Level II provides a variety of shorthand symbols, some Fortran-like features and more flexibility.

A simulator/debugger program, available on time-sharing systems, is quite handy for program development. The simulator mimics the actions of the 1802 for all instructions. The Debug programs permit you to set breakpoints; set, read or write guards for any memory address; set interrupts; inspect and modify any memory address or register; save machine state at any point; restore machine state; single step through program executive; and more. It can also halt and give diagnostic messages for invalid instructions.

Consider the 6100 for CMOS Systems

BRUCE GRIESHABER
Applications Engineer, Harris Semiconductor,
Melbourne, Florida

When the 6100 microprocessor was introduced about a year ago, it offered the user three advantages over most existing μP circuits: static CMOS circuitry, 12-bit word lengths and the use of an already existing and popular instruction set. It was and still is the only μP that can emulate the software operation of a full minicomputer—Digital Equipment Corporation's PDP-8/E.

The microprocessor is a single-chip CMOS circuit built with a self-aligned, silicon-gate process. Internal circuitry is completely static, and the μP can operate at any speed between dc and the maximum operating frequency (8 MHz). Only one supply, from 4 to 11 V, is required for operation, and the on-chip oscillator needs only an external crystal. While low power consumption (less than 10 mW with a 4 MHz clock and +5 V supply) is a standard feature of the CMOS processor, full MIL temperature range performance is an added bonus. All on-chip input and output buffers permit simple interfaces to all TTL logic families.

12-bit words add flexibility

Because the 6100 has a 12-bit data word, several advantages in data-acquisition applications are readily apparent. In many systems, 10 or 12-bit analog-to-digital converters are used to prepare signals for digital storage. However, most available μPs have 8-bit word lengths, and you must use at least two data words and some extra control circuitry and instructions to get the data. The 6100, however, requires only one instruction and only one memory location to store the data.

To keep the μP pin count to a reasonable 40, the address and data paths are multiplexed on the same 12-line bus (Fig. 1a). The 6100's timing and state control lines provide all external signals needed to communicate with memory and peripheral devices (Fig. 1b).

Many other available circuits are intended as direct support for the μP (Table 1): the 6402/3, a CMOS universal, asynchronous receiver/transmitter (UART); the 6101, a parallel interface element (PIE); the 6610, 6611 and 6612, 256 $\times$ 4 field-programmable CMOS PROMs; and the 6312, a 1024 $\times$ 12 mask-programmable ROM for program storage. Of course, you can choose from a wide selection of CMOS RAMs, including 256-$\times$-4 and 1024-$\times$-1 models.

Building a microcomputer based on the 6100 is straightforward. All the CMOS parts are static and require only a single supply. A complete system can be built with the μP, a ROM, a RAM and a PIE (Fig. 2). The ROM should be located in the higher part of memory, including 7777$_8$, to define the restart location after a reset. An output on the ROM, RSEL, defines the area in the 4-k memory field dedicated to RAM.

The ROMs and RAMs designed for the 6100 have address latches built onto their chips, so external parts won't be needed. The PIE has two read, two write and four sense lines to control inputs and outputs, as well as four programmable flag outputs. Only one sense line and two flag lines are used in the system shown in Fig. 2, which leaves two read, two write and three sense lines for external I/O control.

If a UART is added, the amount of programming for the serial I/O can be reduced. And since the UART has its own crystal for synchronization, it can operate independently of the system clock. To control the UART, the PIE needs one read, one write, and two sense lines, which leaves all the others for external control.

The PIE can also handle priority-vector interrupts. To add either two or more vector interrupts or more I/O control, additional PIEs can be connected to the system bus. Each PIE must have a different address, but up to 31 units can be connected in a system.

Software simplifies the control panel

One special feature of the 6100 is the provision for a dedicated control panel. The limited number of pins on the single-chip μP prevents the contents of internal registers from being read by displays without help from the software. Since a control-panel memory can be included the 6100 can display the registers without relying on the main memory. A 256 × 12 ROM and 16 × 12 RAM, separate from the main memory, are all that's needed to duplicate the full PDP-8/E control panel (Fig. 3).

The control panel communicates with the processor via the Control-Panel Request (CPREQ) line. This line functions somewhat like the Interrupt-Request (INTREQ) signal, but with some important differences: The CPREQ bypasses the interrupt-enable system and forces the processor

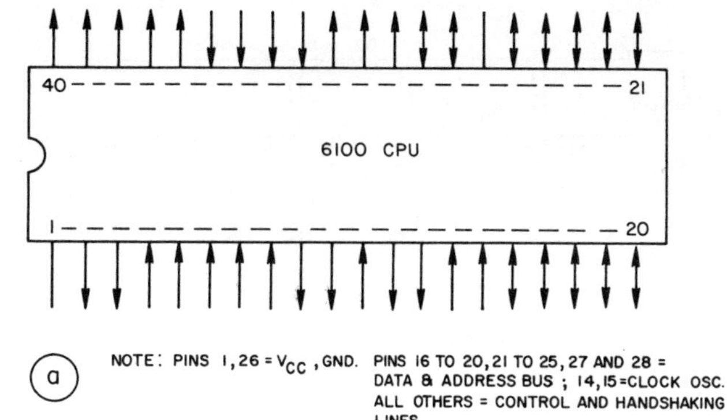

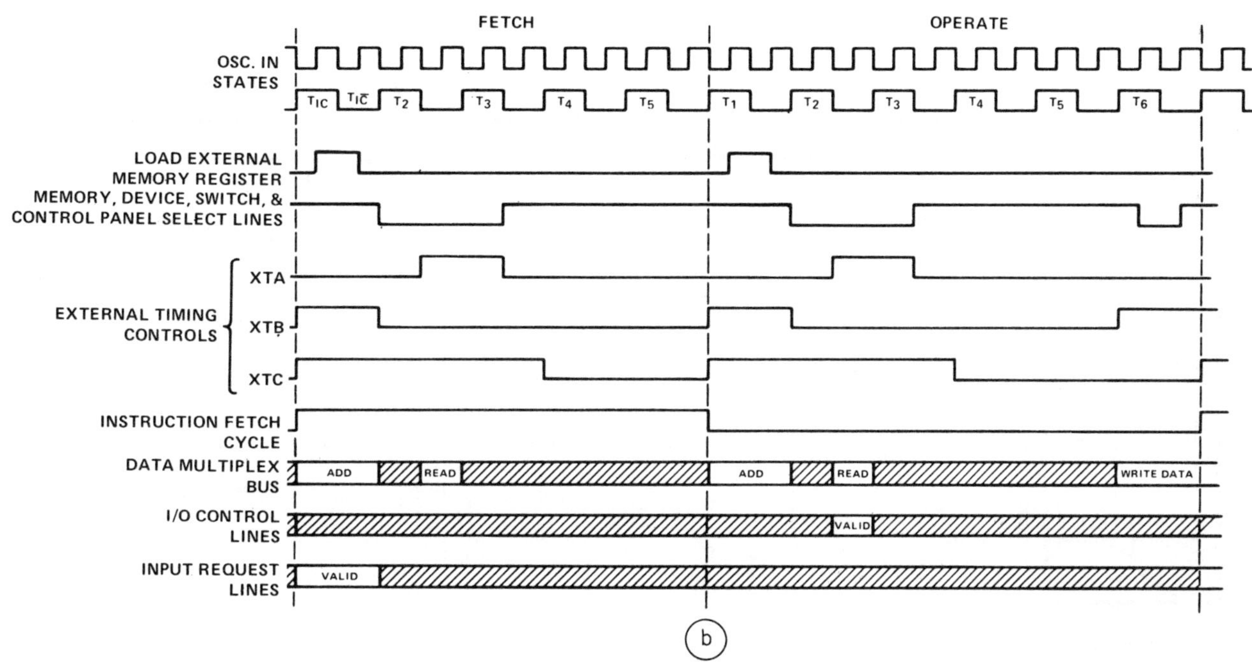

1. By using a shared address and data bus, the pin count of the 6100 μP can be kept to 40 (a). Timing waveforms are more complex than for many of the static μPs since the multiplexed bus must be controlled.

Table 1. System components for the 6100

Part number	Description	100-up price
HM-6100	12-Bit CMOS microprocessor (single chip)	$25.20
HD-6101	CMOS parallel interface element	$8.85
HD-6402/03	CMOS universal asynchronous receiver/transmitter	$6.95
HM-6312	1024 × 12 CMOS read-only memory	Consult factory
HM-6508	16-pin 1024 × 1 CMOS random-access memory	$6.80
HM-6518	18-pin 1024 × 1 " " " "	$6.80
HM-6501/51	22-pin 256 × 4 " " " "	$8.40
HM-6561	18-pin 256 × 4 " " " "	$6.80
HM-6562	16-pin 256 × 4 " " " "	$6.80
HM-6610/11	16-pin 256 × 4 CMOS field programmable read only memory	In development
HM-6612	18-pin 256 × 4 CMOS field programmable read only memory	In development

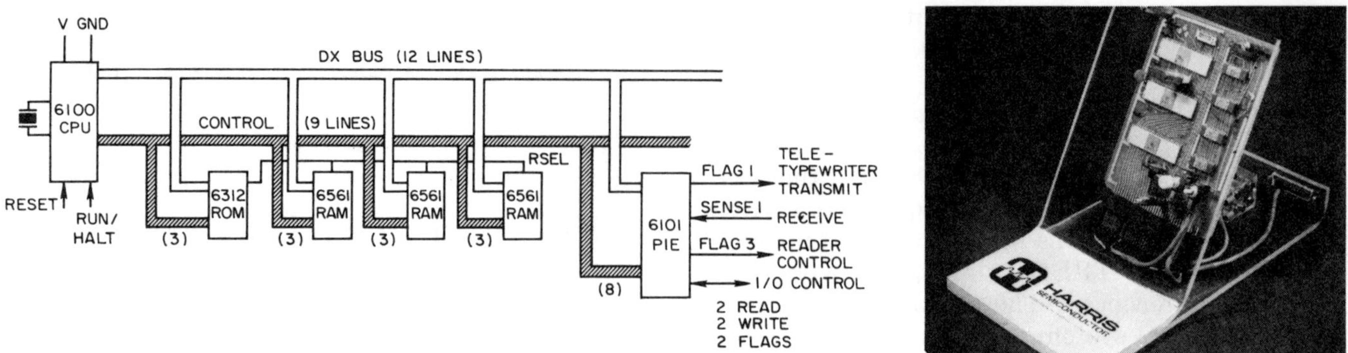

2. Just four circuits are needed to build a minimal operating system—the 6100, a ROM, a RAM and a PIE.

A bare-bones system can operate for a week on a set of flashlight batteries.

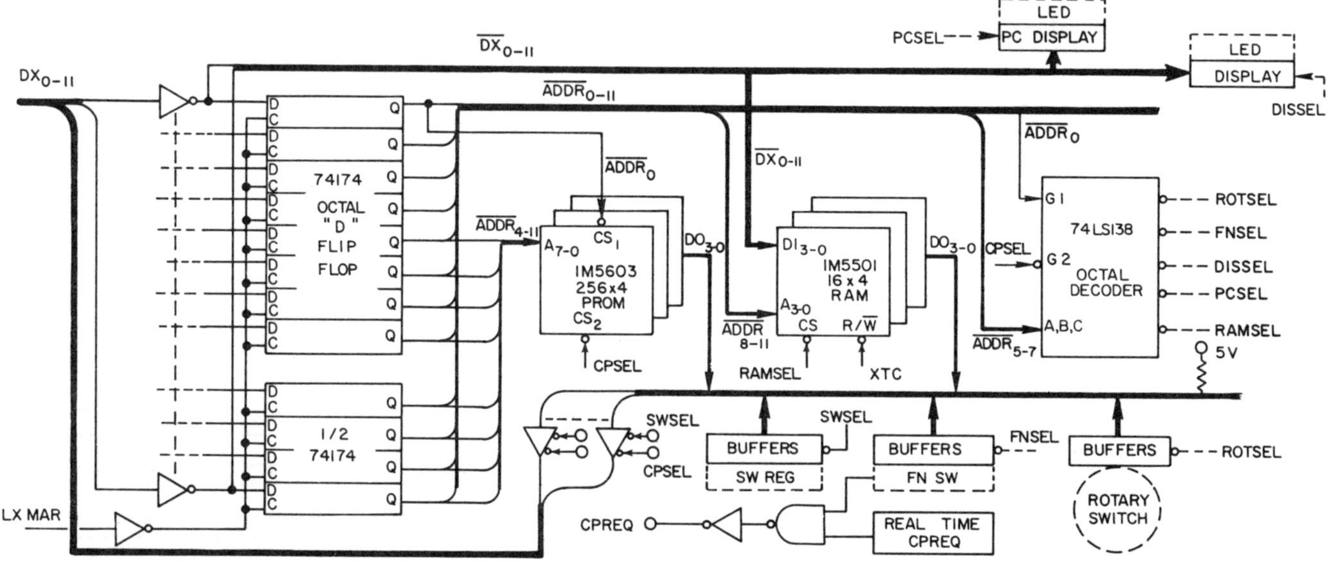

3. You can make a complete front panel for the 6100 by using a second memory system that does not require any space in the main memory. Even debug programs can be stored in the panel memory.

to ignore the IOT, ION and IOF instructions. Once a CPREQ is granted, the DMAREQ (direct-memory-access request) or INTREQ commands will not be recognized until the CPREQ instruction has been fully serviced.

When a CPREQ is granted, the value of the program counter is stored in location 0000_8 of the panel memory and resumes operation at location 7777_8 of the panel memory. The panel memory is a second RAM/ROM bank (4-k words, maximum) organized with RAMs in the lower pages and ROMs or PROMs in the higher pages. The service routine then can be easily stored in memory locations, starting with 7777_8.

While the CPU is in the panel mode, the control-panel memory select (CPSEL) line—not the main memory select (MEMSEL) line—is active. However, during the execute phase of indirectly addressed AND, TAD, ISZ or DCA instructions, the MEMSEL line activates, thus permitting access to the main memory. Therefore, the CPSEL line should be used as an indicator to distinguish between main and control-panel usage.

To exit from the control panel routine, simply have the 6100 execute the following sequence:

    ION

    JMP I 0000_8 (Loc 0000_8 in CPMEM).

The ION command resets the internal CPREQ, and the indirectly addressed location 0000_8 holds the count of the PC just before the CPREQ signal is acknowledged. The value in location 0000_8 returns to the 6100's PC, and the original program flow continues.

Several options, such as test, maintenance and diagnostic routines, can be added to the control panel program. The panel can also be considered a portable device that can be plugged into a socket on the processor board either to help troubleshoot a down system or simply to observe system operation.

Memory organization permits easy expansion

The 6100 has a basic addressing capacity of 4-k, 12-bit words. Each location has a unique four-digit octal address (from 0000_8 to 7777_8).

A look inside the 6100 microprocessor

Since the 6100 microprocessor was designed to emulate the PDP-8/E minicomputer made by Digital Equipment Corp., it should come as no surprise that the μP is also architecturally identical. The 6100 has six 12-bit registers, an arithmetic-and-logic unit (ALU), all the gating and timing logic, and the instruction-decode and control ROM.

The accumulator register (one of the six just mentioned) is the central focus point of the 6100. All the arithmetic and logic operations are performed in it. For any ALU operation, the data held in the accumulator and the data fetched from memory are combined and stored (temporarily) back in the accumulator. Under software control, the accumulator can be cleared, set, complemented, tested, incremented or rotated. The accumulator also serves as an input/output register since all I/O transfers must pass through it.

A one-bit extension called the link is built into the accumulator. It can be complemented with a carry out of the ALU or cleared, set, complemented, tested and rotated along with the rest of the accumulator—all under program control. The link also serves as the carry output for two's complement arithmetic.

The other 12-bit registers include the MQ, a programmable register that can be used as a temporary storage location. The TEMP register can be used for microprogram control and helps to avoid race conditions. The MAR register holds the current address of the memory location selected for reading or writing. And, of course, both arithmetic and logic operations are done in the 12-bit ALU, as well as shifting left or right.

The PC (program counter) register holds the address of the memory location from which the next instruction will be fetched. During normal operation (an instruction fetch), the contents of the PC are transferred to the MAR, and the PC gets incremented by one. Of course, a jump or skip instruction modifies the procedure. Also included on the chip is a 12-bit instruction register (IR) that holds the instruction to be executed.

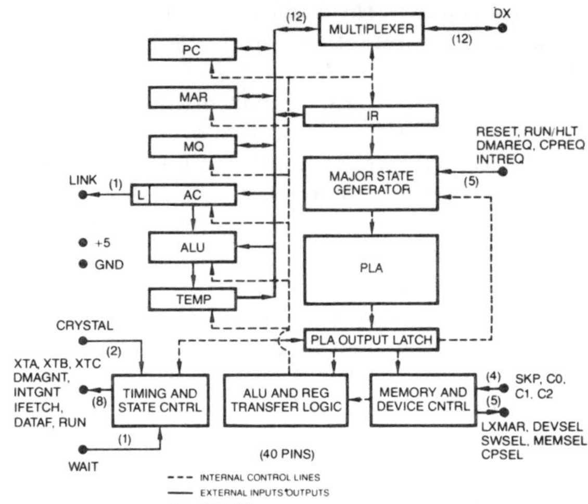

Data and addresses share a common 12-line bus that feeds directly into a 12-bit multiplexer. The multiplexer, in turn, is controlled by the major-state generator and control ROM. All timing and state signals needed by the 6100 are generated by an on-chip clock (only a 4-MHz crystal is required). An internal dividing circuit reduces the clock so that the internal states are 500 ns long.

Programmed data transfers, the easiest means of controlling data I/O, require the least hardware support. However, to use this form of I/O, the 6100 must remain in an idle state (wait loop), while the I/O device completes its last transfer and prepares for the next. Interrupts can reduce or totally eliminate the time waiting for device status signals.

Whenever the INTREQ input is driven LOW, the interrupt system permits external signals to divert the program to a preselected subroutine. If no higher priority requests for an interrupt exist, the current request is granted when the 6100 completes its current instruction. After reacting to an interrupt request, the Interrupt-Enable flip-flop in the 6100 gets reset so that no other interrupts can be acknowledged until the current interrupt is serviced and the system goes back to program control.

However, to make the memory space easier to operate, the locations are split into 37_8 pages, each with 177_8 addresses (in decimal notation, 32 pages of 128 locations each). The memory size can be extended to 32 k by using a memory-controller circuit to organize the memory as eight 4-k blocks called memory fields, 0_8 to 7_8. Defining a memory location then requires three bits from the controller to specify the field, the five most significant bits of the word for the page number, and the lower-order seven bits for the relative page address.

The 6100 is compatible with several ROMs and RAMs developed by both Harris and Intersil. The 6312 is a 12-k, mask-programmable ROM with an access time of 500 ns. Both the address and data lines are multiplexed on the same pins. Included on the ROM is a RAM-select output that defines an area in the memory-field dedicated to RAM. The ROM can operate over the full military temperature range with a supply of 4 to 11 V.

Instruction set and addressing schemes

Instructions of the 6100 are 12 bits long and can be broken into three major groups: memory reference instructions (MRI), operate instructions (OI) and input/output transfer instructions (IOT). All of the over 70 instructions are software compatible with the PDP-8/E command set. The basic PDP-8/E paper-tape soft..are supplied by Digital Equipment Corp. can operate with the 6100.

The MRI instructions either operate on the contents of a memory location or use the contents to operate on the AC or PC. Each MRI is broken into two parts: Bits 0 to 2 represent the operation code, the other nine bits the operand address.

Operate instructions are broken into three groups of microinstructions. Group 1 commands perform logic operations on the contents of the accumulator and link registers and are identified by a $\emptyset$ in the bit-3 position. Group 2 microinstructions primarily test the contents of the accumulator or link and then conditionally skip the next sequential instruction. They require a 1 in the bit-3 position and a $\emptyset$ in the bit-11 position. The Group 3 microinstructions perform logic operations on the contents of the AC and MQ registers and have a 1 in the bit-3 and bit-11 positions.

Operate microinstructions from a certain group can be microprogrammed with other microinstructions from that same group, thus reducing the number of lines of code. The actual code for a microprogrammed combination of two or more microinstructions is a logic OR of the octal codes for the individual commands.

IOT instructions initiate the operation of peripheral devices and transfer data between peripherals and the 6100. The instruction word is broken into three parts: Bits $\emptyset$ to 2 are set to 11$\emptyset$, bits 3 to 8 indicate the device selection code to control the desired peripheral (up to 64), and bits 9 through 11 contain the specific operation code that determines the actual I/O operation.

Direct memory accesses (DMAs), sometimes called data breaks, can also be implemented in the 6100 system. Data can be sent directly to a high speed peripheral, such as a magnetic disc or tape unit. Since the 6100 only sets up the transfer, tranfers occur on a "cycle stealing" basis with no μP intervention.

The 6100 has a direct addressing capability of 4 k words of memory. However, to permit combining operations and data, the memory is broken into 32 pages of 128 words each.

Only three addressing modes are possible:

■ *Direct addressing.* In this mode, bit 4 of the instruction word can be checked. If the bit is 1, the page address is interpreted as the current page; if $\emptyset$, the address is defined on page $\emptyset$. By this method 256 memory locations can be directly addressed (128 on page $\emptyset$ and 128 on the current page.

■ *Indirect addressing.* With this mode, all 4 k of memory can be addressed. When bit 3 is $\emptyset$ the operand address is obtained by first referencing a "pointer" address that is located either on the current page or page $\emptyset$ of the memory. The address of the data or instruction to be handled is in the location specified by the pointer.

■ *Auto-indexed addressing.* Within the 6100, provisions have been made for an external stack of eight registers (memory locations $\emptyset\emptyset1\emptyset$ to $\emptyset\emptyset17$, octal) that can be used for indexing applications. Whenever these locations are indexed indirectly, the contents are incremented by 1 and restored before they are used as an operand address.

Memory reference instructions

Mnemonic	Octal code	Operation
AND	0000	Logic AND
TAD	1000	Binary ADD
ISZ	2000	Increment, and skip if zero
DCA	3000	Deposit and clear AC
JMS	4000	Jump to subroutine
JMP	5000	Jump
IOT	6000	In/out transfer
OPR	7000	Operate

Operate instructions

Mnemonic	Octal code	Operation
NOP	7000	No operation
IAC	7001	Increment accum.
RAL	7004	Rotate accum. left
RTL	7006	Rotate two left
RAR	7010	Rotate accum. right
RTR	7012	Rotate two right
BSW	7002	Byte swap
CML	7020	Complement link
CMA	7040	Complement accum.
CIA	7041	Complement and increment accum.
CLL	7100	Clear link
CLL RAL	7104	Clear link - rotate accum. left
CLL RTL	7106	Clear link - rotate two left
CLL RAR	7110	Clear link - rotate accum. right
CLL RTR	7112	Clear link - rotate two right
STL	7120	Set the link
CLA	7200	Clear accum.
CLA IAC	7201	Clear accum. - Increment accum.
GLT	7204	Get the link
GLA CLL	7300	Clear accum. - clear link
STA	7240	Set the accum.
NOP	7400	No operation
HLT	7402	Halt
OSR	7404	OR with switch register
SKP	7410	Skip
SNL	7420	Skip on nonzero link
SZL	7430	Skip on zero link
SZA	7440	Skip on zero accum.
SNA	7450	Skip on nonzero accum.
SZA SNL	7460	Skip on zero accum. or skip on nonzero link or both
SNA SZL	7470	Skip on nonzero accum. and skip on zero link

SMA	7500	Skip on minus accum.
SPA	7510	Skip on positive accum.
SMA SNL	7520	Skip on minus accum. or skip on nonzero link or both
SPA SZL	7530	Skip on positive accum. and skip on zero link
SMA SZA	7540	Skip on minus accum. or skip on zero accum. or both
SPA SNA	7550	Skip on positive accum. and skip on nonzero accum.
SMA SZA SNL	7560	Skip on minus accum. or skip on zero accum. or skip on nonzero link or all
SPA SNA SZL	7570	Skip on positive accum. and skip on nonzero accum. skip on zero link
CLA	7600	Clear accum.
LAS	7604	Load accum. with switch register
SZA CLA	7640	Skip on zero accum. then clear accum.
SNA CLA	7650	Skip on nonzero accum. then clear accum.
SMA CLA	7700	Skip on minus accum. then clear accum.
SPA CLA	7710	Skip on positive accum. then clear accum.
NOP	7401	No operation
MQL	7421	MQ register load
MQA	7501	MQ register into accum.
SWP	7521	Swap accum. and MQ register
CLA	7601	Clear accum.
CAM	7621	Clear accum. and MQ register
ACL	7701	Clear accum. and load MQ register into accum.
CLA SWP	7721	Clear accum. and swap accum. and MQ register
SKON	6000	Skip if interruption on
ION	6001	Interrupt turn on
IOF	6002	Interrupt turn off
SRQ	6003	Skip if INT request
GTF	6004	Get flags
RTF	6005	Return flags
SGT	6006	Operation is determined by external devices, if any
CAF	6007	Clear all flags

Input/output instructions

Teletypewriter keyboard/reader		
KCF	6030	Clear keyboard/reader flag, do not start reader
KSF	6031	Skip if keyboard/reader flag = 1
KCC	6032	Clear AC and keyboard/reader flag, set reader run
KRS	6034	Read keyboard/reader buffer static
KIE	6035	AC 11 to keyboard/reader interrupt enable FF
KRB	6036	Clear AC, read keyboard buffer, clear keyboard flags

Teletypewriter teleprinter/punch		
SPF	6040	Set teleprinter/punch flag
TSF	6041	Skip if teleprinter/punch flag = 1
TCF	6042	Clear teleprinter/punch flag
TPC	6044	Load teleprinter/punch buffer select and print
SPI	6045	Skip if teletypewriter interrupt
TLS	6046	Load teleprinter/punch buffer, select and print and clear teleprinter/punch flag

Two available CMOS RAMs are the 6508 and 6518—1-k $\times$ 1-bit units. The 6508 comes in a 16-pin DIP, the 6518 in an 18-pin DIP. Both have maximum access times of 450 ns and their data retention is guaranteed for supply voltages as low as 2 V. Several 256 $\times$ 4 static RAMs in 16, 18 or 22-pin DIPs are also available. All these static RAMs have a maximum access time of 450 ns and, like the 6508 and 6518, are guaranteed to retain data with voltage supplies as low as 2 V.

Coming soon in a 16-pin DIP is a 256 $\times$ 4 fusible-link PROM built with CMOS devices. It consumes only 50 mW and will be pin compatible with the 16-pin RAMs (except for its $\overline{PE}$ input). The three-state output version, the 6611, and the open-drain version, the 6610, will both feature an access time of 450 ns.

System communication is easy

The 6402 and 6403 UARTs can interface the 6100 with an asynchronous-serial data channel (Fig. 4a). The receiver section converts serial start, data, parity and stop bits to parallel data and verifies proper code transmission, parity and stop bits. Conversely, the transmitter puts parallel data into serial form and automatically inserts start, parity and stop bits. The data word length can be 5, 6, 7 or 8 bits, and parity can be even or odd. Both the parity checking and generation can be inhibited and you can have 1.5 stop bits when transmitting a 5-bit code or 1 or 2 stop bits when handling 6, 7 or 8-bit codes.

Power requirements for either the 6402 or 6403 are a low 10 mW at clock frequencies up to 2 MHz (125 kbaud). Although there are some slight control differences between the 6402 and 6403, they function identically.

The 6101 PIE (Fig. 4b) provides addressing, interrupt and control for a variety of peripheral functions. Data transfers are controlled by the 6101's IOT instructions, control lines and 12-bit bus. The PIE consumes less than 5 μW in standby and about 5 mW when fully active. It is housed in a 40-pin DIP.

The basic timing of the 6100 is controlled either by the on-chip crystal oscillator or by an external frequency source. Several input lines control the μP's operation. The Reset input clears the AC, loads 7777_8 in the PC and halts the processor. The Run/Halt can start and stop the μP operation, while the Wait line can pause the unit in 250-ns steps so that slower memory circuits or peripherals can be connected to the μP.

The DMAREQ input signals the processor to transfer control of the busses to the external device on a cycle-steal basis with no processor intervention. The 6100 acknowledges that the request has been granted by generating a DMAGNT signal at the end of the current instruction. All fur-

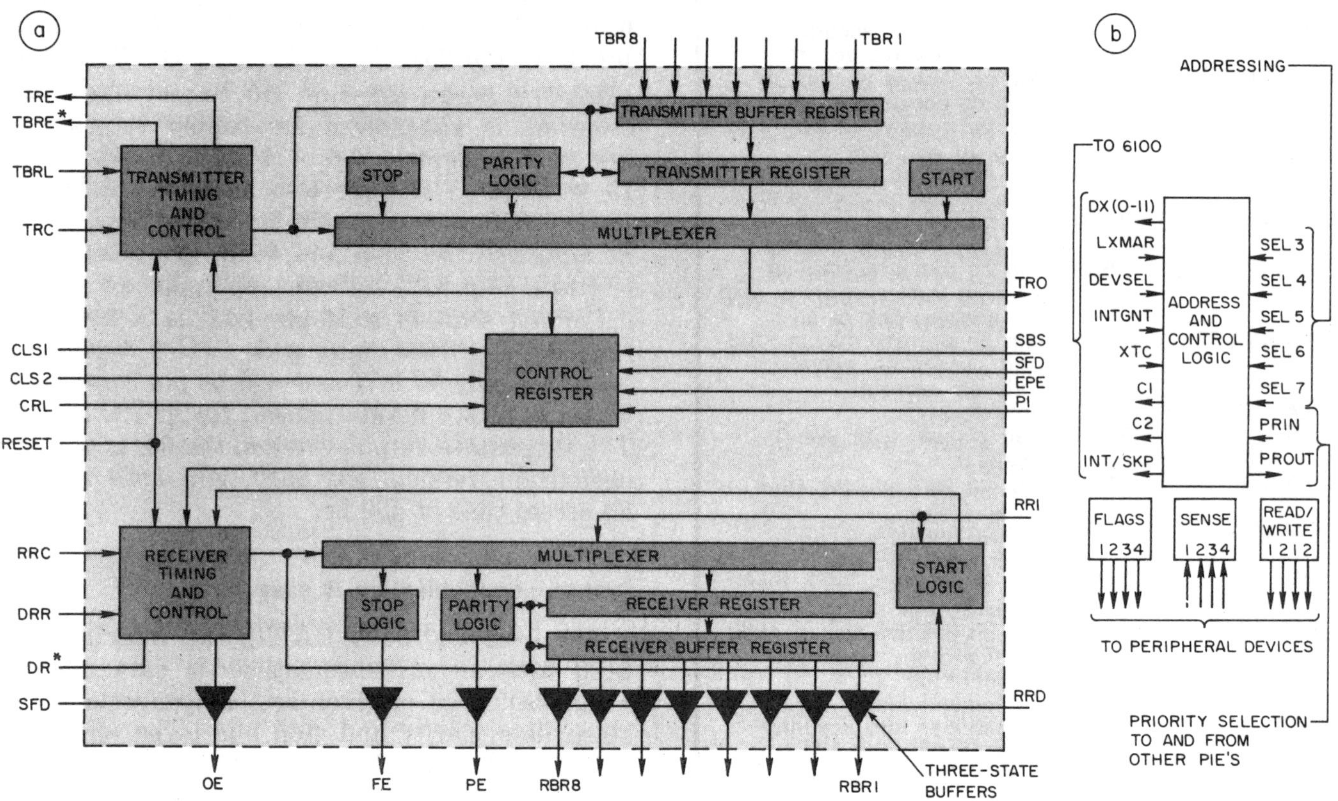

4. **Connecting the CMOS UART (a) or the PIE (b)** is very straightforward. The UART can operate at clock frequen- cies from dc to 2 MHz (up to 125-k baud) and the PIE can handle both vectored and nonvectored interrupts.

ther instruction fetches are suspended until the DMAREQ line is released.

An interrupt from an external device activates the 6100's INTREQ input, and the 6100 responds with a INTGNT signal at the end of the current instruction to acknowledge the interrupt. The current contents of the PC are dumped into location 0000_8, and the program fetches instructions, starting with location 0001_8. To return to the original program, the PC value must be retrieved from 0000_8. If nested interrupts are required, the addresses for the PC dumps must be stored in a software stack. Any IOT instruction will reset the INTGNT signal.

Peripherals are controlled and timed by the μP output (see the example of a teletypewriter interface in Fig. 5). The load-external-memory-address register (LXMAR) command latches the address appearing on the system bus. Four select lines distinguish which peripheral the μP has selected for a data transfer: one for memory (MEMSEL), one for the control panel (CPSEL), one for the switch register (SWSEL) and one for external devices used during IOT (DEVSEL).

Three other control lines designate data being transferred to the μP (XTA), data being transferred from the μP (XTB) and data ready for writing or reading (XTC). Other outputs signify the internal state of the μP.

After each instruction is completed, the μP internally scans its internal priority network to determine the next operation. The request lines, RESET, CPREQ, RW/HCT, DMAREQ and INTREQ, are sampled in the last cycle of an instruction execution. The worst response time to an external request can be calculated as the time required to execute the longest instruction, preceded by any six-state execution cycle (14 μs at 4 MHz).

If no external requests are pending, the next instruction in the normal program flow is executed. All indirect and auto-index, memory-reference instructions go through a common state sequence to generate the effective address of the operand. The subsequent sequence, known as the execute phase, is controlled by the functional class of the instruction. Internal and external IOT instructions have identical state sequences. Device addresses and the control bit are available in the external address register for internal IOT instructions.

Prototyping is simple, says Simon

The Simon prototyping microcomputer system is a 6100-based computer that has a buffered bus structure with three-state TTL-compatible I/O lines. It provides a simple way to evaluate 6100-family systems and components.

The basic system, described in Table 2, comes

```
           6341    WUART  = 6341
           6342    SKPDR  = 6342
           6340    RUART  = 6340
           6343    SKPTBR = 6343
           0105    *105
00105      7300    START,      CLA CLL
00106      1130                TAD BUFF
00107      3131                DCA BPTR
00110      6342    LISN,       SKPDR
00111      5110                JMP .-1
00112      7300                CLA CLL
00113      6340                RUART
00114      0133                AND K0377
00115      6341                WUART
00116      3531                DCA I BPTR
00117      1531                TAD I BPTR
00120      1132                TAD MDOLAR
00121      7450                SNA
00122      5125                JMP DONE
00123      2131                ISZ BPTR
00124      5110                JMP LISN
00125      7300    DONE,       CLA CLL
00126      3531                DCA I BPTR
00127      5134                JMP STARTW
00130      0155    BUFF,       0155
00131      0000    BPTR,       0000
00132      7534    MDOLAR,     7534
00133      0377    K0377,      0377
00134      7300    STARTW,     CLA CLL
00135      7000                NOP
00136      1130                TAD BUFF
00137      3131                DCA BPTR
00140      1531    CHRTY,      TAD I BPTR
00141      7450                SNA
00142      5134                JMP STARTW
00143      4146                JMS TYPE
00144      2131                ISZ BPTR
00145      5140                JMP CHRTY
00146      0000    TYPE,       0
00147      6343                SKPTBR
00150      5147                JMP .-1
00151      6341                WUART
00152      7300                CLA CLL
00153      5546                JMP I TYPE
```

5. **This short program** helps to interface the 6100 with a serial ASCII device such as a teletypewriter. When information is entered via the keyboard, the 6100 echos the characters back on the printer.

Table 2. Software support

Part number	Description	Price
0656-SW PDP-8/E	Extended software kit: Binary loader, PAL III assembler, Symbolic editor, DDT—dynamic debugger, ODT (low)—octal debugger, ODT (high)—octal debugger, RIM and binary punch, Octal memory dump, PDP-8 23-bit floating-point package.	$212.50
1656-SW FOCAL-8:	An interactive algebric language. It is similar to Basic & Fortran in many respects.	$152.50
2656-SW PDP-8/E	Diagnostic software: This software package consists of programs to perform extensive tests on the processor, memory and the teletypewriter.	$400.00
3656-SW FOPAL-III:	This is a cross assembler written in standard Fortran.	$125.00
6900-S SIMON:	Prototyping system used for software and hardware development. (Includes 0656-SW)	$3300.00
SIMON with dual floppy system.		In development

DECUS: Digitai Equipment Computer Users Society—This is a library of users programs. Listed are some of the categories available to any users:

Programming language, monitor, programming system

Text editing, text manipulation

Debugging, disassembly, simulation, trace, dump

Binary loading, binary punching

Duplication, verification

Numerical function, numerical input-output

Utility

Display

Data management, symbol manipulation, sorting

Probability, statics, curve-fitting

Scientific application, engineering application

Hardware control

Games, demonstration

Plotting

Desk calculator, business applications

Maintenance

with a control panel (similar to DEC's PDP-8/E), 4 k words of CMOS memory (with battery back-up for nonvolatility) and a PDP-8/E compatible teletypewriter interface designed for a 20-mA current loop.

All these functions fit on three boards. A fourth board slot inside the Simon cabinet can accommodate user-designed circuits. A built-in 5-V power supply can handle the three boards, the front panel and almost any built-in user circuit.

Simon executes the basic PDP-8/E paper-tape software supplied by DEC. However, to write a program using the Simon system, the symbolic editor can be used to generate the ASCII symbolic program by interactive entering and editing. Next, the symbolic program gets assembled by the PAL-III program—a two-pass assembler.

On the first pass of the assembler, all user symbols are defined and stored in an assembler symbol table. During the second pass, the binary equivalent of the input source language is generated and, if desired, punched.

Two service programs, ODT and DDT, can be used to run the user program and to use the teletypewriter keyboard to control program execution, examine registers, change register contents and make alterations to the user program. With DDT, you can debug the programs by using the symbolic language of the source program, whereas the ODT gives you the octal representation.

A cross-assembler, FOPAL-III, is identical to PAL-III but can run on any computer that supports Fortran.